IS ECONOMICS RELEVANT?
A Reader In Political Economics

ROBERT L. HEILBRONER
New School for Social Research

and

ARTHUR M. FORD
Southern Illinois University

GOODYEAR PUBLISHING COMPANY, INC.
Pacific Palisades, California

© Copyright 1971 by
GOODYEAR PUBLISHING COMPANY, INC.
Pacific Palisades, California

Library of Congress Catalog Card Number: 79-144840
ISBN: 0-87620-445-0 (P)
ISBN: 0-87620-446-9 (C)
Y4450-6 (P) Y4469-6 (C)

Current printing (last number):
10 9 8 7 6 5 4 3 2 1

C

Printed in the United States of America

Students and ternal Rea

IS ECONOMICS RELEVANT?
A Reader In Political Economics

For Joan and Ramona

CONTENTS

part **3**
Economic Philosophies   **209**

INTRODUCTION

ROBERT L. HEILBRONER

There is a word that makes professors of economics wince these days, as I can testify from personal experience. The word is, of course, *relevance*. There was a time, not so many years ago, when I could teach an introductory class the mysteries of diminishing marginal utility, explaining why the man in the Sahara desert would not be willing to pay as much for the third pint of water as for the second, confident that when the hands went up it would be because someone wasn't convinced that he shouldn't pay more, because his *total* utility was greater. Now when the hands go up, I know what the question is going to be: "That's clear enough, Professor Heilbroner, but we don't see how it's relevant."

Is it relevant? It is certainly easy enough to understand why it does not seem so. What has diminishing marginal utility to do with giant corporations, the military-industrial complex, imperialism, ghetto life? Isn't time spent on the study of marginal utility simply time diverted from the consideration of real issues, such as these? Worse, isn't the very act of taking seriously a figment like "diminishing marginal utility" apt to cultivate an ivory-tower frame of mind that will no longer wish to come to grips with the brute problems of the real world?

I think these are the kinds of misgivings that first come to the surface when economics students begin to ask questions about the discipline they are learning, rather than merely swallowing it down like so much medicine. Yet I do not think that these initial objections count for very much. As a rule, the aspect of economics that upsets those who begin to study it is its abstractness, its seeming removal from life, but any instructor worth his salt can reassure his students that this abstract quality is a strength and not a weakness if we are to study large-scale questions, and that the "unreality" of many economic conceptions conceals a sharp cutting edge.

Thus, for example, the rationale for progressive taxation hinges on nothing less than the belief that successive dollars of income, like successive pints of water in the Sahara, yield ever smaller increments of enjoyment to its recipients. In the same way, an ivory-tower idea such as pure competition, which every first-year student regards as utterly irrelevant, suddenly turns up as the indispensable starting point for an understanding of Marx's model of capitalism; or the rarified assumptions of Pareto Optimality (that imaginary condition in which no further efficiency or consumer satisfaction can be squeezed out of a given economic system by rearranging its inputs or outputs) take on an unexpected political and social relevance in discussing the problems of socialist planning.

Indeed, by the time an overly zealous instructor is through, the danger is that the shoe will be on the other foot, and that the class will have been persuaded that the charge of "irrelevance" is nothing but the ill-considered objections of those who have not yet mastered the subject. But if he proceeds this far, it is now the instructor who risks becoming irrelevant. For if the initial objections to the abstractions of economics tend to be wide of the mark, this is very far from saying that the feelings of unease aroused by the study of economics have no validity. What the freshman student wants from economics—and hopefully what he will continue to want when he has become an instructor—is a heightened ability to understand, and if possible to control, important aspects of the social system in which he lives. Long after he has accepted the need for the abstract character of economic thought, the student (and his instructor, too) may still feel that economics ignores the most pressing issues of society, or that it gives unsatisfactory answers to them. At that point, the charge of "irrelevance" is no longer an objection that can be easily overcome, but a serious challenge to the validity of the discipline itself.

Is economics a penetrative and reliable guide to the nature of society? The purpose of this book of readings is to demonstrate that it *can* be—that it can ask piercing questions, give cogent advice, and offer deep perspectives on history and on social evolution. To that extent, of course, economics is as relevant as any study of society can be. But in a sense, a book of readings that emphasizes the relevance of economics fails to explain the other side of the coin—the reasons why economics is often not relevant. It would hardly do to fill the pages of this book with examples of economics at its worst. Hence, in this initial essay I shall try to point out why and to what exent economics does not succeed in being useful; that is, why economics frequently does not ask the kinds of questions that would most clearly illumine society, or why it gets unsatisfactory answers to some of the questions it does ask, or why it often fails to offer us the historic or philosophic guidance we seek from it.

The Irrelevance of Economists

Let me begin this analysis of the failures of economics by taking up a touchy issue, but one that cannot be sidestepped. This is the fact that the "irrelevance" that most disturbs many students is the unwillingness of academic economists to ask disturbing or unpleasant questions with regard to the social order, and in particular to avoid social criticism that is radical in intent. Economics thus appears to many students not as a genuinely objective science that sheds its illumination on the good and bad aspects of society alike, but as a kind of high-level apologetics that tends to illumine only those issues for which economics has an "answer," and to overlook those for which it has none.

I think one should admit that, on the whole, this criticism is fairly taken. Most textbooks are bland in tone and pussyfoot around thorny questions. How many, for example, ever mention the issues of imperialism, or present the facts with regard to the concentration of wealth in the United States, or examine very deeply the behavior of the corporate sector? Moreover, students who have gone beyond the textbooks into the professional journals know that this blandness is by no means confined to the delicate atmosphere of the classroom, but extends into the dialogue that the profession holds with itself. With exceptions to which we will return, it is simply a fact that most of the things that economists write about are not matters of burning social importance, and that the prevailing tone in which they do write about social questions tends to be one of a sympathetic conservatism rather than of indignant radicalism.

Why are most economists so conservative in their outlook? Professor Stigler, one of the best-known exponents of the conservative economic philosophy, has contended that it is the result of the training that economists undergo, a training that disabuses them of heady notions with respect to the changes that socialism (or some other form of institutional rearrangement) could bring and that persuades them of the propriety of the market system.[1]

It is probably true that a study of economics does tend to make one

---

[1] Stigler's essay, "The Politics of Political Economists" first appeared in the *Quarterly Journal of Economics* (November 1959) and has been reprinted in his *Essays in the History of Economic Thought.* His actual words read: "It becomes impossible for the trained economist to believe that a small group of selfish capitalists dictates the main outlines of the allocation of resources. . . . He cannot unblushingly repeat such slogans as 'production for use rather than for profit.' He cannot believe that a change in the *form* of social organization will eliminate basic economic problems." (*Essays*, pp. 59–60.)

wary of sweeping statements and unconsidered jumps, as does the study of almost anything; but I am not wholly convinced by Stigler's argument that conservatism is somehow more *intelligent* than radicalism. I would rather raise another, less elegant, possibility as to why economists are predominantly conservative in their outlooks. This is because economists tend to be located in the upper echelons of the pyramid of incomes and thus tend to share, consciously or otherwise, the conserving attitude that is characteristic of top echelons in all societies. I do not mean that economists are the spineless servants of the very rich. But in 1967 the average income of associate professors of economics (the middle group of academic rankings) was $14,000 and the average income of a "superior" full professor was $21,000. That was sufficient to place associate professors in the top 10 percent of income receivers in the country, and superior full professors in the top 2 percent. I do not see why it should be doubted that economists, like all groups, take on the values and standards of the socioeconomic milieu in which they live.

Yet, what is generally true of the group as a whole is certainly not true of each and every member of it. If, as both Professor Stigler and I believe, the economics profession is marked by a general conservatism of views, there are still economists enough, including some very eminent ones, who do not share the prevailing attitude. What the essays in Part 1 of this reader will show is that economics can be a formidable vehicle of social criticism and a powerful agent of social change. Hence, it is not the discipline of economics, diminishing marginal utility and all, that can be held responsible for its lack of relevance, if we mean by this its frequently observed failure to direct its attention to important social issues. The fault lies rather with the reluctance of many of its practitioners to use their economic skills for purposes that may be intellectually uncomfortable, or politically risky, or simply out-of-step with their colleagues. To that extent, the irrelevance of which students complain lies not within the discipline of economics but within that of sociology, and the cure for the problem lies in the determination of these students to put their own skills to good use when they take the places of their former instructors.

The Limitations of Economics

But there is a second, and perhaps deeper, meaning to the charge that economics is "irrelevant." It is that the results produced by the application of conventional economics too often have no usefulness—that the answers that economics gives to the problems to which it does address itself are frequently untrustworthy as guides to social policy.

This is a charge that, as we shall shortly see, contains what I believe to be an important core of truth. Yet, before we examine the limits beyond which economic reasoning cannot be relied upon, it is important to establish the things that economics can do and the extent to which it can be put to practical use.

The dividing line, as I see it, that separates what economics can do from what it cannot, lies between the usefulness of economics in explaining the structural characteristics of a market economy, and its relative uselessness in predicting how a market economy will behave in a given instance. To put it differently, economics is extremely relevant when we want to know how the economy is constructed, so that we can trace the numerous possible connections between one part and another, but usually "irrelevant" (by which I mean unreliable) if we want to know exactly which of these connections will be triggered off by a particular economic stimulus.

We shall consider in a moment the reasons for this predictive failing of economics. But at this juncture, while we are still concerned with the positive, relevant aspects of conventional economic thought, it is important to emphasize the enormous contribution that the structural insights of economics offer us. Perhaps only someone who can remember the intellectual confusion of the Great Depression, or the sense of heretical shock that greeted President Kennedy's proposal to spur economic growth by deliberately incurring a federal budgetary deficit, can fully appreciate the gain that has been won by the gradual clarification of the macrostructure of the economy. For the first time in the history of industrial society, we have finally grasped the nature of the mechanism by which the critical aggregates of employment and income are determined. Even if we still cannot manipulate that mechanism very well, the gain in intellectual clarity in itself constitutes the strongest single claim that conventional economics has for its own relevance, and it is a powerful claim indeed.

Microeconomics is not far behind, moreover, in claiming for itself a similar relevance. As with macroeconomics, microeconomics is also a poor guide for prediction. But without its general structural concepts—its ideas of demand and supply, of short and long run, of elasticity and inelasticity, of marginal and average costs and revenues and products—the operations of a market system would be virtually impossible to conceive, much less to control. Since all economic systems, socialism included, depend to some extent on the operation of a market mechanism, the linkages revealed by microeconomic analysis are indispensable for the understanding of all modern industrial systems. Whether it is to determine the best way to alleviate poverty, or to curb pollution, or to distribute scarce resources, or to judge the incidence of a tax, or to gauge the effects of raising the price in a nationalized industry, it is to the apparatus of microeconomics with its criss-crossed lines and its bowl-shaped curves, that we must turn if we are to think clearly about the consequences of our actions.

The articles in the second section of this reader are selected to display the power of economic reasoning in action, and I doubt that anyone can read through these selections and not be impressed with the clarification that economic analysis can bring to tangled social problems. Yet I do not want to leave the impression that economics, in its conventional use, is therefore always relevant, in the sense of giving us clear answers and reliable solutions. Rather, as I have already stated, I believe that there are very important limits on the extent of the reasoning power of economics, and it is to these limits that I will now turn.

I have already indicated one of the limits—the poor capabilities of economics as a predictive science. One reason for this, with which we are all familiar, is the inability of the discipline to handle more than a limited number of variables at one time. Economics is forced to approach the complexity of real-life situations exactly as we do in the classroom, on a *ceteris paribus*—other things being equal—basis. But the one-thing-at-a-time approach often breaks down hopelessly when we try to apply it to the world. Economics calculates its predictions as if the disturbance it studies were the only stone dropped in a pond; whereas in fact, of course, the surface of the pond is covered with the expanding concentric waves of a hundred disturbances. It is hardly surprising that the patterns of the disturbance in which we are interested become confused with or indistinguishable from those of other disturbances, and that our predictions lose their sharpness accordingly.

There is, however, a deeper reason for the unreliability of economic prediction than this. It is that the entire predictive capability of macro- and micro-theory rests on a highly simplified set of assumptions with regard to economic activity itself. These assumptions tell us that human beings constantly try to maximize their receipts (or to minimize their expenditures) as the paramount "behavior directives" in the course of their daily lives. To the extent that firms or factors or consumers do not obey these assumptions—that is, to the extent that they do not constantly strive to move to the frontiers of their production possibilities or their indifference maps—economics loses virtually all of its ability to predict the effects of stimuli on the economic system. In that case, for example, we can no longer state with certainty that a rise in price will result in a fall in the quantity demanded and an increase in the quantity supplied, for both of these classical behavior patterns are nothing but maximization in action.

Do we actually maximize? The concept itself is full of ambiguities. Maximize what, over what period of time? If we define maximization to mean "psychic income" or "satisfactions," then the concept loses its predictive power because *any* course of action may be said to lead to maximum "well-being," since we have no objective measure of whether that well-being is really maximized or not. On the other hand, if we define maximization to mean something specific, such as cash income, then we encounter a problem with regard to predictions over any period of time but the shortest run. A giant corporation, consciously trying to maximize its income over a period of ten years, may rationally decide to undertake any number of actions—raising prices, lowering them, increasing or decreasing its current investment—depending on how it interprets the future. In this case, maximization may accurately enough describe the state of mind of the management, but it is of little use in foretelling exactly what management will do.

It is because of these difficulties that economics is much better at describing the *consequences* of various paths that corporations or consumers may follow, than in predicting exactly which they will in fact elect to take. But there is a still more troublesome limit to its power of prediction. For even if we could define maximization in such a clear-cut way that we knew precisely what course of action it would enjoin, economic theory still finds itself stymied before the awkward fact that maximization can lead to different—indeed, contradictory—behavior in different expectational settings.

Ordinarily, as we have just said, a factor or a firm will try to maximize its income by selling more of a commodity when its price goes up and less when its price goes down. But what if the rise in price leads us to believe that prices will continue to rise in the future? In that case, the road to maximization lies in a different direction, namely in holding back on our offerings today so that they can be sold at a better price tomorrow, or in buying more today before the price goes up further. In a word, when expectations tell us that an observed change in price will continue in the same direction, then the rational pursuit of maximum income bids us to behave in exactly the contrary fashion to that which we do "normally."

If this abnormal kind of economic behavior were limited to occasional periods of extreme crisis, we might relegate it to a footnote. But unfortunately, precisely this kind of behavior is all too normal, whenever the economy is moving from one prevailing psychology, whether boom or bust, to another. Then, typically, markets become unstable just because expectations change, and the predictive capabilities of economics diminish accordingly.[2] That is why even the most sophisticated econometric models of the economy do well only as long as the basic direction of economic movement remains the same, but fail badly in telling us the one thing we want to know; that is, when that basic direction itself will change.

[2] The most searching critique of the shortcomings of the conventional economics can be found in Adolph Lowe, *On Economic Knowledge* (Harper & Row, 1965, paperback, 1970).

Thus, one endemic shortcoming of economic reasoning is its inability to alert us to the timing of economic events. But there is a second quite different limitation to economic theory that interferes with its predictive capability from another angle. It is that economic reasoning is unable to connect changes in the economic variables with changes in the political and social spheres of social activity. As a result, economics makes its predictions as if the stimuli and constraints of the market were the only forces impinging on the activities of men, ignoring entirely the social and political and psychological consequences of economic action. To put the matter differently, conventional economics deals with the economy as if it were only a mechanism for allocating goods and services, and overlooks the fact that the economy is also a mechanism for allocating privilege and power.

As a result, economic predictions often fail because they do not anticipate the "feedbacks" of noneconomic activity. Typically, for instance, economic theory will project a growth path by calculating the effects of labor and capital inputs, capital-output ratios, and so forth, in this way arriving at a course of economic output in the future. But the trouble with these projections is that economic theory does not take into account the noneconomic changes that the growth process itself may initiate. Economics does not, for example, connect the trajectory of growth with social frictions to which the growth process may give rise, or with political resistances that may be encountered if growth brings a shift in income as between regions or social groups. Nor does it ask whether a growing level of income may alter our life-styles or our working habits in such a way as to change our labor inputs. In a word, economic theory gives us a picture of change from which the political or sociological elements have been rigorously excluded, although it is just these factors that are often all-important in determining the ultimate results of economic change itself.

This restricted scope of economic vision serves to limit the relevance of economic theorizing even more severely than its inability to handle the vagaries of economic behavior. Indeed, here is where the freshman's unease about the "abtractness" of economics comes home with a vengeance. But at this level of analysis the student's objections are not so easily brushed aside. No one denies that abstraction is an essential precondition for a social science if it is to reduce the complexity of the real world to manageable proportions. But we can now see that the sharper and clearer the abstract model we create, the less "interdisciplinary" that model tends to be. Thus we learn how to handle the idea of a "firm," but only by blotting out the political and sociological attributes of real corporations; or we invent the very convenient fiction of a "factor of production," but only at the cost of losing to sight the existence of individuals who are also voters and members of social classes.

The fault, however, is not just that of a failure of nerve on the part of economists. *The essential problem is that we do not know the nature of these subtle linkages between the economic mechanism and the political and social spheres of activity.* What we lack, in a word, is a unifying theory of social change in which the distinctions of "economics" and "sociology" and "political science" would yield to a new "holistic" science of society. As we shall see in our next section, there was a time when economics seemed to be close to such a holistic science. It is not today. Instead we stand impotent before the problem of understanding how to integrate our knowledge of the economic structure and of economic behavior (unpredictable though the latter often is), with a corresponding knowledge of political or sociological structures or of political or social behavior. The discovery of such a new integrating model or paradigm would be the greatest triumph of social science in our time, but at the moment no such paradigm exists. As a result, we must admit to a profound limitation to economic analysis for which no solution is now in sight.

The Relevance of Economic Philosophy

These considerations bring us to the last meaning that we can attach to the word *relevance*—the possibility of using economics as a guide for social philosophy, in the sense of helping us to understand the direction in which our social system is headed, or still more important, the direction in which it should head.

In the light of the severe limitations that we have put upon the predictive power of economics, can we really look to economics as a reliable guide for the future? The answer is necessarily disconcerting. We cannot. At best, an economist who postulates a rationale for the historic setting of our time or who projects the shape of society into the future is engaged in no more than a kind of controlled speculation. That these speculations can be both eloquent and plausible we shall leave for the reader to discover for himself in Part 3 of this book. But it would be wrong to pretend that even at their most convincing these speculations attain the status of genuine scientific effort, at least in the meaning that economics usually arrogates to that word.

This is an important matter to which we shall revert at the very conclusion of this essay. But meanwhile, for students who have read the works of Smith, Ricardo, Mill, or Marx, this must seem like a serious retreat for economics. For surely the great classical writers did not regard their large-scale economic philosophies as mere "controlled speculations." In their hands economics seemed capable of presenting a perspective on the present and the future in full accord with the scientific canons of their day. Why, then were they able to create economic philosophies of greater power than we can?

From the vantage point of contemporary history, we can discern two attributes of classical economic thought from which this extraordinary self-assurance emanates. One of these, which is frequently overlooked, is the strong feeling of social destination that infuses all the classical writers. Smith, Ricardo, Malthus, Mill, and above all Marx, firmly believed that they knew the direction in which society was heading, and moreover they strongly approved of that destination as being in the best interests of mankind. Thus, economics became for them not alone an objective explanation of the "laws of motion" of their respective economic societies, but also an instrument to assist the evolution of those societies in the various directions in which they wished them to hurry.

A second common attribute of their thought was their frank willingness to discuss their societies from the point of view of class composition and conflict. In place of the neutral "factors of production" with which modern theory deals, the classical writers spoke openly of a contest of landlords, workers, and capitalists, so that their theories of distribution (which were intimately intertwined with their theories of growth) were also guides to major political and social tensions within their societies. And whereas the outcome of the struggle among the classes was differently diagnosed by each writer, according to his differing assessments and assumptions regarding resources, demographic behavior, technology, and the psychology of the social classes, in every instance his pursuit of the logic of economic interaction led him directly to an associated drama of political and social change.

In our own day, both these underlying premises of classical reasoning have lost much of their erstwhile force. The blows of 20th-century history, devastating for the prospects of liberal capitalism and orthodox socialism alike, have largely obscured the vista of welcome historic destination that unified and fortified so much of classical thought. Today the great majority of social scientists, economists included, stand before the realities of 20th-century technology, bureaucracy, nationalism, and militarism with a sense of genuine perplexity, or even despair, that blurs the vision of even the boldest of them.

Then, too, the increased complexity and growing modest affluence of Western society have equally undermined the second of the premises of classical analysis—that the dynamics of social change could be directly predicted from the clash of social classes. In our day, the once decisive clash of classes has given way to the cohesion of a "mass society" in which the sources of social conflict take on wholly new forms, such as the conflict between generations. As a result, even the most fully worked-out philosophy of historic change and social evolution—the imposing structure of Marxism—finds itself in need of rethinking its traditional views in the light of present-day realities.[3]

Against these vast historic changes, it is hardly surprising that economics has lost the self-assurance of a former age. The problem of constructing a plausible model of social change is much more difficult in our day than in a simpler age, for all the reasons we have discussed in the previous section as well as in this one. Yet it is one thing to take cognizance of the difficulties of a task, and another to abandon it. Rarely has there been a period of history as much in need of illumination as our own, and however partial or uncertain, the controlled speculations of economic thought, meshed as best they can be with political and sociological analysis, still constitute the best response that we can make to our human situation.

Perhaps in the end, the answer to this impasse of the social sciences lies in a new appraisal of the relevance of *science* itself. When we said before that economics could offer no foresight that could be given the name "scientific," we may have inadvertently opened the direction in which to seek the new paradigm of social unity that we need. The word "scientific," as we commonly use it, refers today to a rigorous model of a mathematical kind from which all considerations of social values have been carefully excluded. In the great question of human destination, however, values must surely occupy a central place: the future is meaningful because it offers us choice. Perhaps, then, the very aim of economic philosophy as a "scientific" guide to the future must give way to economic philosophy as a consciously value-laden guide—a guide that uses the enormous powers of scientific analysis, not to predict the future, but to assist society in reaching the goals that it has elected to pursue. In such a basic reorientation of the discipline, economics would become the hand-maiden of politics, advising us of the institutional and behavioral and technical conditions necessary to achieve a destination that society has chosen through its political processes. Such a far-reaching suggestion takes us well beyond the confines of this essay, although not, I am glad to say, beyond the confines of what may ultimately be most relevant for economic thought.[4]

[3] The evolution of Marxist thought can be followed in such books as Ernest Mandel's *Marxian Economic Theory* (see the last essay in this collection), Ralph Milliband's *The State in Capitalist Society*, or in the various contributions to Erich Fromm's *Socialist Humanism*.

[4] See R. Heilbroner, "On the Possibility of a Political Economics," *Journal of Economic Issues*, December 1970, and "On the Limited Relevance of Economics," *The Public Interest*, Fall, 1970.

PART 1

Economic Critiques

What GNP Doesn't Tell Us

A. A. BERLE, JR.

A well-known expert on the corporation tells us that Gross National Product is a deceptive index, and suggests what we might do about it.

It is nice to know that at current estimate the Gross National Product of the United States in 1968 will be above 850 billions of dollars. It would be still nicer to know if the United States will be better or worse off as a result. If better, in what respects? If worse, could not some of this production and effort be steered into providing more useful "goods and services"?

Unfortunately, whether the work was sham or useful, the goods noxious, evanescent, or of permanent value will have no place in the record. Individuals, corporations, or government want, buy, and pay for stuff and work—so it is "product." The labor of the Boston Symphony Orchestra is "product" along with that of the band in a honky-tonk. The compensated services of a quack fortune teller are "product" just as much as the work of developing Salk vaccine. Restyling automobiles or ice chests by adding tail fins or pink handles adds to "product" just as much as money paid for slum clearance or medical care. They are all "goods" or "services"—the only test is whether someone wanted them badly enough to pay the shot.

This blanket tabulation raises specific complaints against economists and their uncritical aggregated figures and their acceptance of production as "progress." The economists bridle, "We," they reply, "are economists, not priests. Economics deals with satisfaction of human wants by things or services. The want is sufficiently evidenced by the fact that human beings, individually or collectively, paid for them. It is not for us to pass on what people ought to have wanted—that question is for St. Peter.

Reprinted from *Saturday Review* (August 31, 1968), pp. 10–12. Copyright 1968 Saturday Review, Inc. Reprinted by permission of the author and publisher.

A famous statistic in *America's Needs and Resources*—published by the Twentieth Century Fund in 1955—was that Americans in 1950 paid $8.1 billion for liquor and $10.5 billion for education. Maybe they ought to have cut out liquor and paid for more education instead—but they didn't, and value judgments are not our job. Get yourself a philosopher for that. We will go on recording what did happen."

What they are saying—and as far as it goes, they are quite right—is that nobody has given economics a mandate to set up a social-value system for the country. Fair enough—but one wonders. Closer thinking suggests that even on their own plane economists could perhaps contribute a little to the subject, although, as will presently appear, we must get ourselves some philosophy, too. One branch of social indicating may not be as far removed from cold economics as it would appear. Another branch is more difficult, though even it may yield to analysis.

Any audit of social result, any system of social indicators, requires solving two sets of problems. First, with all this Gross National Product reflecting payment to satisfy wants, did America get what it paid for? In getting it, did it not also bring into being a flock of unrecorded but offsetting frustrations it did not want? Essentially, this is economic critique. Second—and far more difficult—can a set of values be put forward, roughly expressing the essentials most Americans would agree their society ought to be, and be doing, against which the actual record of what it was and did can be checked? This second critique, as economists rightly contend, is basically philosophical.

As for the economic critique, let us take the existing economic record at face. Work was done, things were created, and both were paid for. The total price paid this year will be around $850 billion. But, unrecorded, not included, and rarely mentioned are some companion results. Undisposed-of junk piles, garbage, waste, air and water pollution come into being. God help us, we can see that all over the country. Unremedied decay of parts of the vast property we call "the United States" is evident in and around most American cities. No one paid for this rot and waste—they are not "product." Factually, these and other undesirable results are clear deductions from or offset items to the alleged Gross National Product we like so well.

The total of these may be called "disproduct." It will be a hard figure to calculate in dollar figures. Recorded as "product" is the amount Americans spent for television sets, stations, and broadcasts. Unrecorded is their companion disproductive effect in the form of violence, vandalism, and crime. Proudly reported as "product" are sums spent for medical care, public health, and disease prevention; unheralded is the counter-item, the "disproduct" of loss and misery as remediable malnutrition and preventable disease ravage poverty areas. Besides our annual calculation of "gross" national product, it is time we had some idea of Gross National Disprod-uct. Deducting it, we could know what the true, instead of the illusory, annual "net national product" might be. (Economists use "Net National Product" to mean Gross National Product less consumption of capital—but it is not a true picture.)

There is a difference, it will be noted, between "disproduct" and "cost." Everything made or manufactured, every service rendered by hu-man beings, involves using up materials, if only the food and living necessities of labor. These are "costs." They need not enter into this calcu-lation. Conventional statistics already set up a figure for "capital con-sumption," and we deduct this from "Gross National Product." That is not what we have in mind here. We are trying to discover whether creation of "Gross National Product" does not also involve frustration of wants as well as their satisfaction. Pollution of air and water are obvious illustra-tions but there are "disproducts" more difficult to discern, let alone measure.

Scientists are increasing our knowledge of these right along. For example, cigarettes (to which I am addicted) satisfy a widespread want. They also, we are learning, engender a great deal of cancer. Now it is true that at some later time the service rendered in attempting to care for cancer (generated by cigarettes manufactured five years ago) will show up as "product"; so the work of attempted cure or caretaking will later appear as a positive product item. But that item will not be known until later. What we do know without benefit of figures is that against this year's output of tobacco products whose cash value is recorded we have also brought more cancer into being—an unrecorded "disproduct." We know at the end of any year how many more automobiles have been manufactured. We also know that each new car on the road means added injury and accident overall. Carry this process through our whole product list, and the aggregate of "disproduct" items set against the aggregate of production will tell us an immense amount about our progress toward (or retrogression from) social welfare.

Once we learn to calculate disproduct along with product and dis-cover a true "net," as well as a "gross," we shall have our first great "social" indicator. We shall know what the country accomplished.

It could be surprising and disillusioning. It might disclose that while satisfying human wants as indicated by the "gross" figure, in the process we had also violated, blocked, or frustrated many of these same wants and, worse, had done a great deal we did not want to do. Carrying the calculation further, we would probably find (among other things) that while satisfying immediate wants from today's productivity, we had been generating future wants (not to say needs) to repair the damage, waste, and degeneration set up by current production.

Some of today's "gross" product carries with it a mortgage—it sets up brutal defensive requirements that must be met by tomorrow's work and things. Some forms of productivity may prove to generate more decay, damage, or waste annually than their total amount, while neglect of some production may annually place a usurious claim on future years. Failure to maintain cities at acceptable standards is a case in point: it sets up huge but unrecorded claims on the manpower and product of coming decades. It is entirely possible to score annual increases of Gross National Product as we presently figure it—and yet, after reckoning "disproduct," be little better off at the end of any year than at its beginning.

Calculation of "disproduct" is admittedly difficult. If seriously tackled, I think it at least partially possible. At first it would be far indeed from exact. All the same, "disproduct" is a plain fact of life—look out of your window and you can see some. Crude calculation of the probable amounts needed to offset many items of "disproduct" is not insoluble; technicians in some lines have fairly concrete ideas along these lines already. Actuaries compute the "disproduct" resulting from automobile accidents, and your car insurance bill is calculated accordingly. Carry the process through and a crude though probably incomplete item could be developed. Using it, one could judge whether, materially at least, the country had moved forward or backward.

In this first bracket of critique, economists are not required to make value judgments of what is "good or bad." They, with the advice of the technical men in the various sectors, could merely be asked to tackle calculation of "disproduct" as well as of "product."

The second branch of the problem is harder. It raises the question of whether a good deal of Gross National Product should not be steered by social or political action toward creating a more satisfactory civilization. That, of course, requires some elementary assumptions as to what a satisfactory civilization ought to be and do. Can any such assumptions be made?

Constructing enough of a value system to use as critique of a Gross National Product indeed does seem not beyond common-sense possibility. The job does, without question, require setting out some values on which there is sufficient agreement to engage social opinion and, one hopes, social action. Production steered toward realizing these values can be described as "good." Production frustrating or tearing them down can be stigmatized as "bad." Let us try drawing up a list, tentative in the extreme. I think there would probably be considerable agreement that it is "good"; but if not, make a dinner table game of drawing a better one:

1. People are better alive than dead.
2. People are better healthy than sick.
3. People are better off literate than illiterate.

4. People are better off adequately than inadequately housed.
5. People are better off in beautiful than in ugly cities and towns.
6. People are better off if they have opportunity for enjoyment—music, literature, drama, and the arts.
7. Education above the elementary level should be as nearly universal as possible through secondary schools, and higher education as widely diffused as practicable.
8. Development of science and the arts should continue or possibly be expanded.
9. Minimum resources for living should be available to all.
10. Leisure and access to green country should be a human experience available to everyone.

Anyone can add to or change this list if he likes, my point is that at least a minimum set of values can be agreed on. We have done more here than draw up a list of pleasant objectives. We have set up criteria. By applying our list to the actual and recorded output of our Gross National Product, we begin to discern that some of these values are perhaps adequately pursued, some inadequately, some not served at all. Even now, the Gross National Product figure is broken down into many lines. It would have to be split up further or differently for purposes of criticism. The elementary value-system we have projected (or some better edition of it) could provide the basis for critique. It could permit discovery of whether the recorded outturn of our vast hubbub of activity, after subtracting "disproduct" from "product," tended toward producing social results more or less in accord with the objectives implied by our values. If Governor Nelson Rockefeller is right in believing that in a decade the Gross National Product of the United States will be a trillion and a half dollars, it should be possible to steer increasing amounts of it toward realization of this or any similar list of values, and the objectives it suggests.

I am aware that no American value-system can be real except as it expresses a common divisor of the thinking of 200 million Americans. Only totalitarian police state dictatorships, denying their citizens choice of life and action, can lay down complete and all-inclusive value-systems, force their populations and their production into that mold, and audit the results in terms of their success in doing so. Free societies cannot. They must content themselves with common denomination of basic value judgments on which most of their people have substantial consensus—leaving them free to do as they please in other respects. When a free society attempts to impose value judgments going beyond consensus—as they did when the Prohibition Amendment was adopted in 1919—it fails. Yet because there is a wide measure of consensus on values, America does move along, does generate its enormous Gross National Product (and let us hope solid Net National Product) precisely because there is substantial agreement on what its people really want.

Also there is probably a high factor of agreement on priorities—that is, on what they want most. There are doubtful areas, of course. I will not risk a guess whether priority would be given to military preparedness over education were a Gallup Poll taken—more expenditures for defense and less for aid to education. But I am clear that both in values and in priorities a large enough measure of agreement does exist so that if we put our minds to it a critique of our outturn performance expressed in Gross National Product can be had.

And we ought not to be stopped or baffled or bogged down because philosophers cannot agree on the nature of the "good," or because scientists cannot predict with certainty the social effects of value judgments carried into action. Wrong guesses about values show up in experience, as happened in the Prohibition experiment. In light of experience, they can be corrected. With even rudimentary social indicators, the current cascade of emotional and sterile invective might be converted into rational dialogue. Constructive use of social-economic forces and even of currents of philosophical thinking might become possible.

I realize, of course, that up to now it has been assumed that social indicators, based on an expressed value-system, could not be achieved. Well, only a generation ago scholars assumed nothing could be done to alleviate the impact of assumedly blind economic forces, let alone guide them. We know better today; rudimentary capacity to control and steer these forces already exists; the so-called New Economics increasingly guides their use. Similar thinking and similar tools can provide material on which social policy can be based. Combined with the economic tools currently being forged, social objectives might be brought out of dreamland into range of practical achievement.

Discussion and debate would inevitably result from comparison of actual operations with desired results. More intense and perhaps more fruitful controversy would be engendered in areas where there were items not appearing in our tentative list of values for lack of sufficient consensus. Protagonists would insist they be included; opponents would object. This could be healthy. It would be ballasted by realization that, were consensus achieved, constructive action could be possible. Any caterwaul that American society is "sick" could be qualified by emerging factual knowledge showing that either the accusation was untrue or, if true, that measures for cure could be taken. The debate might disadvantage some people; for one thing, it might reduce the torrent of boring despair-literature presently drowning the reading public. Possibly even contrasting currents of new Puritanism might emerge perhaps providing a not unpleasant contrast, if not relief.

Knowing where American civilization is going is the first essential to saving it (if it is to be saved) or changing it (if it is to be altered).

How Useful Is Economic Growth?

E. J. MISHAN

Here is a deep and searching criticism by a distinguished British economist of the assumption that production always satisfies "wants."

The most commonly heard assumption to justify economic growth
is that any extension of the *effective* range of opportunities facing a person
(whether presented to him through the market or directly by the Government) contributes to an increase in his welfare. Similarly any reduction
in the effective range of opportunities contributes to a diminution of his
welfare.

However, even in a market economy in which government intervention is at a minimum, there is one important opportunity that is denied
to the customers; that of selecting the range of alternatives that will face
him on the market. He can choose only from what is presented to him
by the market—and a range of alternative physical environments is not
the only thing that the market fails to provide. For one thing, the so-called
extension of opportunities is not necessarily *effective*, in the sense defined.
When new kinds of goods or new models of goods appear on the market
the older goods or models are not always simultaneously available. They
are withdrawn from production at the discretion of industry.

The argument purporting to show how consumers' wants ultimately
control the output produced is facile enough: for it is, on the one hand,
admittedly profitable to be first to discover and cater to a new want, while,
on the other hand, it would seem unprofitable to withdraw from the market
any good for which the demand continues undiminished. It would not be
hard, therefore, to lay down conditions under which the wants of consumers tend quickly to influence the sorts of goods produced. But, unless

From Ezra J. Mishan, *The Cost of Economic Growth.* Copyright © 1967, pp. 109–112.
Reprinted by permission of Frederick A. Praeger, Inc.

9

the wants of consumers exist *independently* of the products created by industrial concerns it is not correct to speak of the market as acting to adapt the given resources of the economy to meet the material requirements of society. In fact, not only do producers determine the range of market goods from which consumers must take their choice, they also seek continuously to persuade consumers to choose that which is being produced today and to "unchoose" that which was being produced yesterday. Therefore to continue to regard the market, in an affluent and growing economy, as primarily a "want-satisfying" mechanism is to close one's eye to the more important fact, that it has become a want-*creating* mechanism.

This fact would be too obvious to mention, except that its implications are seldom faced. Over time, an unchanged pattern of wants would hardly suffice to absorb the rapid growth in the flow of consumer goods coming on to the markets of rich countries, the U.S. in particular, without the pressure afforded by sustained advertising. In its absence, leisure, one suspects, would be increasing faster than it is. National resources continue to be used to create new wants. These new wants may be deemed imaginary or they may be alleged to be as "real" as the original set of wants. What cannot be gainsaid, however, is that the foundation necessary to enable economists to infer and measure increases in individual or social welfare crumbles up in these circumstances. Only as given wants remain constant and productive activity serves to narrow the margin of discontent between appetites and their gratifications are we justified in talking of an increase of welfare. And one may reasonably conjecture that unremitting efforts directed towards stimulating aspirations and enlarging appetites may cause them to grow faster than the possibilities for their gratification, so increasing over time the margin of social discontent.

Be that as it may, in high consumption economies such as the United States, the trend is for more goods, including hardware, to become fashion goods. Manufacturers strive to create an atmosphere which simultaneously glorifies the "pace-setter" and derides the fashion laggards. As productivity increases without a commensurate increase in leisure the accent shifts ever more stridently to boost consumption—not least to boost automobile sales although cities and suburbs are near-strangled with traffic—in order, apparently, to maintain output and employment. The economic order is accommodating itself to an indigestible flow of consumer gadgetry by inverting the rationale of its existence: "scarce wants" have somehow to be created and brought into relation with rising industrial capacity.

Under such perverse conditions growthmen may continue, if they choose, to so juggle with words as to equate growth with "enrichment," or "civilization," or any other blessed word. But it is just not possible for the economist to establish a positive relationship between economic growth and social welfare.

TV Advertising at Work

DANIEL HENNINGER

The previous article questioned the validity of all consumer "wants."
Here is an excoriating critique of selling practices on TV.

For a decade Geritol's TV medicine man, Ted Mack, has been telling
drowsy viewers that Geritol would bring them back to life. And the Federal Trade Commssion has been telling Geritol, in formal complaints and
cease and desist orders, that its claims were deceptive and to discontinue
the misleading commercials. Geritol persisted. Last week [April 21, 1970]
the Justice Department filed a $1 million suit against Geritol ($500 thousand against manufacturer J. B. Williams and $500 thousand against the
Parkson Advertising Agency) for failing to comply with the Commission's
directives.

Geritol's pitch for its life-giving tonic is a direct descendant of the
frontier medicine show of a century ago. After a sword swallower, fire
eater, banjo player or singing girl had gathered the curious, a "slicker"
sold Jo–He Magnetic oil (a 75-cent, three-ounce bottle cured colds, piles,
ague, rheumatism, scald head, cancer and croup) or Indian Sagwa or
Wizard Oil. When he had most of the town on Wizard Oil, he moved on.
Other slickers dealt in fruit trees, sold with pretty-pictured catalogs but
which arrived from back East half dead, or lightning rods—installation
for $53 and an "inspector" to come by shortly with a $20 rebate.

A century later the salesman, now a corporation, partnered with
television to make available: extra dry deodorants, enzyme detergents
(12 brands), hair sprays, nose sprays, laxatives, sleeping pills, smoking
cures, anything. A 60-tablet bottle of Bufferin costs 88 cents, but enough

From "The One Eyed Slicker," by Daniel Henninger, *The New Republic* (May 1970),
pp. 17–19. Reprinted by permission of *The New Republic*, © 1970, Harrison-Blaine of
New Jersey, Inc.

of it is sold to make worthwhile the $9.25 million *Advertising Age* says Bristol–Myers spent on 882 Bufferin commercials in 1968. Television promotion does not come cheaply—60 seconds on network TV cost $40–60 thousand. Television commands that price because it guarantees a nightly audience of 125 million people. In a minute or less the advertiser tries to convince these millions that his product is *different* from the rest, faster working, longer lasting, better looking, etc. The medicine show lives.

Last year Dristan told allergy sufferers, "Do anything you darn well please without worryin' about hayfever miseries," and, "Now I can even chew on ragweed!" With considerably less verve Allerest said "... you can enjoy life the way regular people do if you take Allerest." The Federal Trade Commission filed complaints against Allerest and Dristan on the grounds that neither completely prevents or relieves allergy symptoms as their commercials implied. (The FTC holds that a commercial's deception turns not on its literalness but on the impression it gives viewers.) Both signed consent agreements and discontinued the ads. A commercial for Contac nasal spray squirted Contac and a competitor onto rice paper. Contac's bigger puddle proved it put "more decongestant where the sinus congestion is." The implication, the FTC said, was that Contac could better penetrate mucous membrane to relieve congestion, which it cannot do. Menley–James replied they were simply showing that Contac produces 40 percent more spray through the bottle's bigger hole. Vicks promoted Sinex nasal spray last year with a demonstration in which two men with congested noses lean over a breathing apparatus made of two vertical tubes in the middle of which is some cotton. One man squeezes Sinex into the bottom of his tube, looks up and says, "I can feel it." The other man, using the competition, says nothing got through the cotton in his tube. The voiceover comments that the vapors in Sinex are powerful enough to penetrate congestion. The Commission challenged the impression that Sinex passed through cotton and nasal mucous to effect instant free breathing. In its consent agreement Vicks denied any intention to demonstrate that Sinex penetrated the cotton.

When STP oil treatment made its television debut, its commercials featured Andy Granatelli, the racing buff, who told how well STP worked in his racers. The FTC compelled Granatelli to make clear in future ads that he is president of STP, Inc. Several years ago Colgate–Palmolive demonstrated Rapid Shave's beard-softening ability by spreading it on sandpaper, then shaving the sandpaper clean. An FTC investigation disclosed that that would have required soaking the sandpaper for over an hour, and in fact, the on-camera demonstration was performed with sand spread over glass. A recent Commission action against Colgate–Palmolive indicates how a technically honest commercial can mislead. A sandwich was wrapped in C–P's Baggie; another was wrapped in a competitor's plastic bag. They were submerged in water, bag X filled with water but Baggie did not: proof that Baggies keep food fresher. The FTC said the demonstration was valid but the conclusion was not—with normal use the competitor's bag keeps anything as fresh as does the amphibious Baggie. In another commercial, the remarkable clarity of Libbey–Owens–Ford auto glass was traced to the fact that the car's windows were rolled down. LOF said it was raining the day of filming.

One person who cares that TV commercials bilk consumers of millions annually is law professor John Banzhaf III. Banzhaf organized four George Washington University law students into a group called TUBE (Termination of Unfair Broadcasting Excesses). Watching TV the students compiled a small but representative list of televised deception. (TUBE's list would be longer had they been able to read the ad copy on file at the FTC, but the Commission says the copy for the televised commercials is confidential.)

TUBE found that children are easy marks for phonied-up commercials. During the Saturday morning cartoon and toy orgy a boy might see this ad for Johnny Lightning racing cars—Announcer: "Here come the 1970 Johnny Lightning *Challengers!* New triple threat three-engine dragster . . . the *speed* hungry spoiler . . . the *bug* bomb . . . the *powerful* smuggler . . . the *sand* stormer . . . the *explosive* TNT . . . they are beautiful and they are *fast!*" A small group of boys are staring at toy cars racing around a track. Backgrounds blur, the camera zooms in, cars fill the screen, leap into the air and are caught in slow motion and stop action. Little girls as well have been known to tire quickly of expensive dolls that don't dance and run like the ones on television. Like the running Barbie doll that suddenly becomes human—"Wow! She's real like me!" cries a thrilled little girl. Deception in these ads might be arguable because kids don't pay for toys and Dad knows he's been shilled when he buys them.

TUBE alleges many commercials for enzyme detergents are misleading (named were Ajax, Drive, Fab, Axion, Oxydol and Gain). A typical enzyme ad for Procter and Gamble's Gain says "We're at the San Pedro Wharf where the fish bloodstains put on this apron are a day old. Look! Set in, locked in bloodstains." Seconds later P & G's man produces a spotless apron. "Look! Set in, locked in bloodstains virtually Gone, Gone, Gone! . . . Everything is unbe*lieva*bly clean with the unbe*lieva*ble detergent—Gain!" What TUBE found hard to believe was the impression that one need only pop his clothes and some enzymes into a washer to work the miracle. In fact, says TUBE (and Consumers' Union), enzyme detergents require presoaking, often overnight, and are only effective on protein-base stains. Last winter Listerine mouthwash was touted as a weapon in the "cold" war: "This cold season, fight back with Listerine antiseptic." Whatever Listerine does, it doesn't prevent colds. Banzhaf believes that advertisers should have to indicate the damage their products may cause and cites as example some whitening toothpastes that contain abrasives harmful to tooth enamel. Arthur Godfrey moved in this direction when he told Colgate–Palmolive that he would no longer do commercials for Axion, a presoaker, unless allowed to say that phosphates in Axion were a water pollutant. C–P consented. Now Godfrey appears (less frequently) by a river in the Everglades and says that pollution is a serious problem, that Axion, like all detergents, pollutes water but until government and industry come up with a solution, stick with Axion.

One thing hyperbolic ad minds may do freely is "puff." Puffing is saying one's product is the best tasting, quietest, cleanest, smoothest, whitest, brightest and so on. The puffing principle evolved in the early days of television when it was thought that viewers would see, smell, listen, taste and feel for themselves. Over the years, though, some advertisers have puffed their products beyond this simple test: one detergent gets clothes "whiter than white"; another goes "all the way beyond white!" "The reason the laws allows this," says John Banzhaf "is that it can't think of any way around it. The courts can't get involved in tasting and things like that." A new ad genre is the spontaneous, man-on-the-street testimonial, a child of TV news interviews. In a Shell gasoline commercial, an actor posing as a gas station attendant berates a customer for using Shell, but the customer defends Shell gasoline like a Kuwaitian sheik. For this commercial, and others of its type, it may be necessary to film hundreds of people to capture the right offhand response.

All this soft-core fraud gets on television because no one can or wants to stop it. The three major networks have Standards and Practices departments which are supposed to screen out deceptive ads before they appear. The only requirement for the job is that one be able to see. Warren Braren, former head of the New York office of the National Association of Broadcasters' Advertising Code, says "the network editors have no legal or scientific training and they don't have any scientific authorities to turn to for opinions. For example you may have a case in which an editor's mother uses a particular laxative; it's fine for her, and on that basis he'll approve the claim. Or an editor may get substantiating reports on comparative claims for auto tires. The editor doesn't have the expertise to determine the validity of these tests, so he may discuss it with someone else in the department. The networks take these tests on face value and hope that nobody asks any questions." Another individual in the ad-regulation business says the editors are overworked and that pulling a deceptive ad isn't worth the grief: "NBC looks over maybe 2,000 ads a month handled by six or seven editors at a national level, not spot and local stuff. If it's in preproduction or script form and not blatant, they may let it go for lack of time. Or an ad may get by because it comes in as a final film already locked into a schedule. If the editor blows the whistle on a multimillion-dollar project, the agency's lawyers rush in saying if you don't take our schedule we'll switch to another network. It may go up to the vice president in charge of sales, pressure is put on and they accept the schedule. It's the facts of life."

Occasionally the networks pass on questionable ads to the Advertising Code at the NAB, the industry's self-regulatory agency. The Code has a Medical and Science Advisory Panel which serves on a limited, non-fee basis. When its opinion is sought, says Braren, "the outcome is often beneficial to the cause of truth in advertising." Last year the Code staff asked for some money to put several specialists on retainer. The NAB denied the money. Also denied was a request for a few thousand dollars to research problem areas like drugs, detergents and toothpastes. "Self-regulation," says Braren, "is thought of as a means of keeping the government off the broadcaster's back."

The government, the FTC, really doesn't cause the broadcasters much backache. About 75 percent of the complaints the FTC files against TV advertisers are settled by consent agreements in which the company answers a cease and desist order by promising not to continue the specific, offending commercial. There is no fine or sanction so consent agreements don't carry much punch. Despite Geritol's frequent contributions to the FTC consent file, it appears regularly on Huntley–Brinkley and Walter Cronkite. And consent agreements have no effect on similar claims by other manufacturers. Ignoring Geritol's run-ins with the FTC, Sterling Drug (Bayer aspirin) last year introduced Super Ionized Yeast for iron anemia deficiency ("Chances are you may have the Gray Sickness"). Sterling's consent agreement reads like a photocopy of the Geritol file. Most other FTC complaints are settled through lengthy litigation during which the commercial still may appear.

The Commission now is in a court fight with Bristol–Myers and the outcome may numb the entire analgesics industry which annually spends $125 million advertising aspirin and has yearly sales to retailers of over $400 million. About ten years ago, the FTC issued a complaint against Bristol–Myers' Bufferin and Excedrin. During the heyday of the hard-sell commercial, Bufferin's housewife burned clothes while ironing, her baby spilled milk and another child fell off his tricycle. "Tension! Tension! Tension!" echoed a voice with each disaster. The housewife took two Bufferin, which works "twice as fast as aspirin," and relieves "tension headache." An Excedrin ad in this vein claimed that Excedrin was 50 percent stronger than aspirin, reduced swelling tissue, relieved tension and was an antidepressant. (Since then Excedrin has somehow gotten stronger and slightly confusing. David Janssen, who as a doctor in the "Fugitive" was for three years the most believable man in America, says "Two Excedrin contains twice as much pain reliever as *four* of the best selling aspirin.") The FTC said their studies showed none of these claims to be true, and for similar reasons filed complaints against Anacin, Bayer and St. Joseph's aspirin. Shortly, the Commission dismissed the complaints, which would have produced endless litigation, in favor of rules to regulate the entire industry. The proposed rules would forbid the aspirin people from making any of the above claims unless they proved they had used nonprescriptive analgesics within legal limits to produce a more effective pain reliever (a difficult trick because the federal Food and Drug Administration has determined the types and amount of analgesic they may use). The rules also proscribe any efficacy or safety claim "which contradicts, or in any manner exceeds, the warnings, statements or directions" on the product's label, which specific were it applied to all TV commercials would do away with many of them.

The analgesics industry in the person of Bristol–Myers is challenging in court the Commission's authority to make such rules. The rules themselves will be contested at Commission hearings for which the manufacturers will produce house physicians to support their claims. Should the rules become final, the admen will work with the not very compelling fact that "aspirin is aspirin."

Troubling as these rules may be for the future of aspirin, they get at only part of the deception problem. For one thing it is never announced that last night's commercial demonstration was a hoax and will no longer be seen because the manufacturer signed a consent agreement. Few can forget the Colgate toothpaste commercials in which "Gardol's protective shield" saved the announcer from baseballs, golf balls and coconuts. Fewer still may recall the FTC proceeding that concluded that Colgate with Gardol didn't completely prevent cavities by creating a "protective shield" or anything else. And unlike the dissatisfied farmer of a century ago, you can't beat your money out of them. Senator Philip Hart has introduced a bill to give consumers more effective recourse than indignation. Hart's amendment to the FTC act would enable anyone to use a final cease and desist order as prima facie evidence of deception and would permit class actions, making it possible to sue a company over a product that sells for about a dollar, but that has sales of several hundred thousand dollars. Speaking before the American Advertising Federation earlier this year, President Nixon's national affairs counsellor Bryce Harlow characterized bills like Hart's as the work of "far-out consumer advocates." He urged the admen to support the President's Consumer Protection Act which permits fewer class actions. TUBE would dispense with the FTC altogether and has petitioned the FCC to suspend the license of any station airing deceptive commercials. For now reform of the advertisers, broadcasters and regulators isn't much more than a thought.

The Causes of Radical Black Militancy

REPORT OF THE TASK FORCE
ON LAW AND LAW ENFORCEMENT

An economic analysis of the position of the Negro in America today.

History teaches us that men's frustration over the material circumstances of their lives is a frequent cause of collective violence. The more intense and widespread the discontent is, the more intense and widespread the violence is likely to be. Of course, the occurrence, extent and form of economically motivated violence are strongly influenced by other factors: the degree of legitimacy which the discontented group accords to the existing social and political order; the effectiveness of agencies of direct social control such as the police; the extent to which political institutions afford peaceful alternatives to violence; and many other factors. But the economic motive, the frustrated desire for improved living con ditions, has undeniably been one important cause of violence in many periods of man's history.

Has this cause been operative in the rise of radical black militancy? The answer is clearly yes. A dominant theme of black protest in the United States has always been the improvement of the material circumstances of the Negro, and this goal has proved most frustratingly unobtainable precisely in the cradle of radical black militancy: the northern urban ghettoes.

The conditions of life in the racial ghetto have been exhaustively examined elsewhere, particularly by the Kerner Commission. It is unnecessary for our purposes to repeat these findings again in detail, since even

Reprinted from James S. Campbell, Joseph R. Sahid, and David P. Stang, *Law and Order Reconsidered: Report of the Task Force on Law and Law Enforcement to the National Commission on the Cause and Prevention of Violence.* (Washington, D.C.: U.S. Government Printing Office, 1969), pp. 99–105.

a few of the facts of life in the ghetto are enough to suggest the level of frustration that prevails there:

> Unemployment rates for Negroes are double those for whites. In the ghettoes in 1966 the unemployment rate was 9.3 percent overall and even higher for blacks. Moreover, in these urban poverty areas 2.5 times the number unemployed were *under*employed: part-time workers looking for full-time jobs, full-time workers earning less than $3,000 per year, or dropouts from the labor force. Among nonwhite teenagers—a group well represented both in riots and in radical black militant activities—the unemployment rate in 1967 in poverty neighborhoods was approximately 30 percent.

> Blacks own and operate less than 1 percent of the nearly five million private businesses in the country—typically small, marginal retail and service firms. Twenty-odd banks out of a national total of 14,000 are black-owned; seven automobile dealerships out of 30,000; fewer than 8,000 construction contractors out of a total of 500,000. In Washington, D.C., blacks comprise two-thirds of the population but own less than 7 percent of the business. Ninety-eight percent of all black income is spent outside the black community.

> In the metropolitan northeast, Negro students start school with slightly lower scores than whites on standard achievement tests; by sixth grade they are 1.6 grades behind the white students, and by twelfth grade, they are 3.3 grades behind. Many Negroes—between one-third and one-half among male students—fail to finish high school, the Negro drop-out rate being more than three times the white rate.

> In 1965 a black woman was four times as likely to die in childbirth as a white woman; the black child was three times as likely to die in infancy as the white child. White people on the average lived seven years longer than black people.

> In 1966 the national illegitimacy rate among non-white women was 26 percent; in many large city ghettos it is over 50 percent: in Harlem 80 percent of the first-born are illegitimate. In 1966 over 50 percent of the known narcotics addicts were Negroes. Rates of juvenile delinquency, violent crime, venereal disease, and dependency on public assistance are many times higher in disadvantaged Negro areas than in other parts of large cities.

In the face of undisputed evidence of the disadvantaged condition of blacks in the urban ghettoes, some persons tend to minimize the importance of deprivation as a cause of riots and of radical black militancy. Two observations are commonly offered in support of this point of view. First, it is pointed out that Negroes have long suffered from frustratingly inferior living conditions, yet they have never before resorted to collective violence of the magnitude that has occurred in the last 5 years. Second, it is urged that while the lot of the Negro may be an unsatisfactory one, nonetheless it has been continually improving, particularly during the precise period when the greatest violence has occurred. In support of this second point, the following facts can be offered:

> The nonwhite unemployment rate in 1966 and 1967 was the lowest since the Korean War, and in 1968 the black unemployment rate in poverty neighborhoods had dramatically declined by more than 50 percent in comparison with the 1966 figure.

> The seven black-owned automobile dealerships (out of a total of 30,000) are seven times as many as there were two years ago. New black-owned banks are in formation in seven cities, and one recent study showed that in certain areas of Harlem, black business ownership has risen to 58 percent. Between 1960 and 1967 there was a 47 percent increase in the number of blacks in white-collar positions, craftsmen and operatives—the better jobs—compared to a 16 percent increase in the number of whites in such jobs.

> The percentage of nonwhite persons enrolled in school is higher in each age group than it was in 1960. In central cities, the median years of school completed by Negroes 25 to 29 years of age has increased by about one year, and the proportion of this group completing high school has risen from 43 percent in 1960 to 61 percent in 1968.

> The nonwhite maternity mortality rate in 1965 was 20 percent less than what it was in 1960 and less than one-ninth of what it was in 1940. The proportion of nonwhite households situated in housing that either is dilapidated or lacks basic plumbing has decreased sharply since 1900 in all areas, especially in large cities. Although the *number* of nonwhite families living in poverty areas in large cities has been fairly constant between 1960 and 1966, of the total number of nonwhite families the *percentage* living in such areas has declined sharply since 1960.

One fatal difficulty, however, undermines most of this seemingly plausible case against the proposition that the disadvantaged condition of the Negro has been a significant cause of ghetto violence. That is the failure to pay adequate attention to the *comparative* economic condition of whites and Negroes, and to make this comparison over a longer period of time than the last few years. The lesson of history is not that poverty as such causes violence, but rather that frustrations arising out of poverty can cause violence. There may often be poverty but no frustration: the frustration is present only when the disadvantaged person expects, or feels entitled to, better material circumstances than those he is living under. Increasingly, the black man in America has come to expect living conditions on a par with those of the white man and has come to believe that he is entitled to such equality.

These expectations that the economic gap between black and white will be closed have stemmed in part from the Negro's experience of economic progress, and the frustration has occurred because in the late 1950s and early 1960s the gap between black and white stopped narrowing and in some respects began to widen.

One basic measure of the gap between black and white is median family income. Figure 1 plots median family income (total, white, and Negro) for the years 1950 to 1967. Examination of this Figure reveals that while median Negro family income has risen steadily since 1950, the dollar gap between white and Negro family income has also steadily increased in nearly every year.

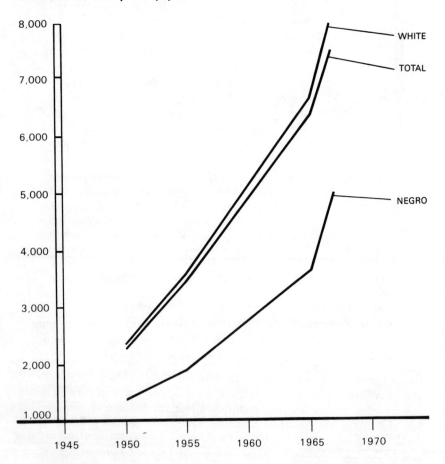

Figure 1. Median Family Income—Total, White and Negro.

Figure 2 expresses median Negro family income as a percentage of median white family income. It indicates no significant Negro progress in closing the gap between the years 1950 and 1965—but it does show a heartening upsurge between 1965 and 1967.

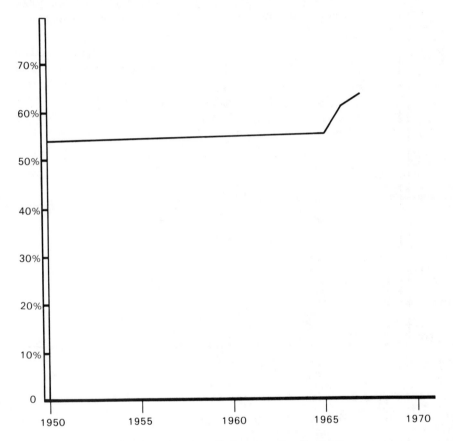

Figure 2. Median Negro Family Income as a Percentage of White Family Income, 1950 to 1967.

In Figure 3 a further refinement of this analysis is introduced. In that Figure the average family income for the total population and for the nonwhite population has been divided by the average years of schooling for each group, and the resulting figure for the nonwhite population has then been expressed as a percentage of the resulting figure for the total population. This percentage can be considered an "index of nonwhite economic satisfaction": if blacks and whites with the same amount of education were earning the same amount of income, the index would be 100 percent and blacks would be as satisfied economically as whites. Figure 3 shows that this is not the case, that the progress toward closing the gap between white and black stopped in the early 1950s, and that the relative economic position of the Negro worsened over the next ten years. Only in the last few years has the gap begun to close again, and still the index of nonwhite economic satisfaction is below its high point in the early 1950s.

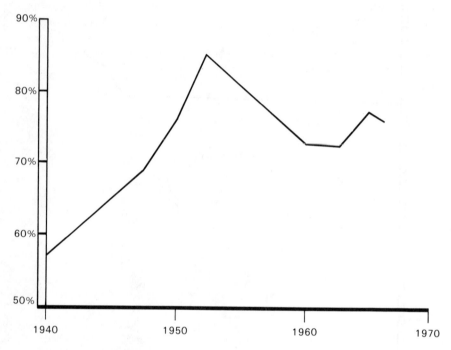

Figure 3. Index of Nonwhite Economic Satisfaction, 1940 to 1967.

The analysis in these three figures is confirmed by other economic and social indicators. Thus, for example, although the nonwhite unemployment rate in 1966 and 1967 was the lowest since the Korean War, the ratio of nonwhite to white unemployment remained roughly the same: two to one. Although the school enrollment gap has narrowed for kindergarteners and 16- and 17-year-olds, it has widened for persons in their late teens and early 20s, and proportionately more whites are going on to higher education. (Obviously, if proportionately higher percentages of nonwhite students do not continue on to college and graduate school, the relative gains of Negroes in professional and skilled jobs of the past decade may soon level off.) In 1940 the illegitimacy rate among nonwhite women was 17 percent; in 1966 it had risen to 26 percent. Between 1950 and 1966 the percentage of fatherless families among Negroes rose by one-third while the percentage of fatherless families among whites remained substantially constant.

What these facts all add up to is that after a period of black progress and rising expectations following the Second World War, a slackening of progress occurred and, by many indicators, the relative economic position of the Negro deteriorated over the next ten years. From defeated expectations of progress, and an unsatisfactory condition to start with, frustration arises. It was this frustration which has been one important cause both of the recent ghetto riots and of the rising violence of radical black militancy.

Economic Trends in Poverty

**ECONOMIC REPORT
OF THE PRESIDENT, 1969**

The following is a summary of recent trends in the "war against poverty."
What factors might inhibit recent trends from continuing?

...the policy of the United States [is] to eliminate the paradox of
poverty in the midst of plenty in this Nation by opening to everyone
the opportunity for education and training, the opportunity to work,
and the opportunity to live in decency and dignity.[1]

For over four years the United States has had an explicit national
commitment to eliminate poverty in our society, a commitment enunciated
by the President in the State of the Union Message of 1964 and confirmed
by the Congress in the above words later that year in the Economic Opportunity Act.

Americans are increasingly prosperous. Median family income in the
United States (in constant 1967 prices) rose from $6,210 in 1959 to $7,974
in 1967, a gain of 28 percent in eight years. Yet many families are still not
able to attain minimum living standards. A preliminary estimate indicates
that in 1968 about 22 million people lived in households with incomes
below the "poverty line." While this is far fewer than in the past—more
than 40 million were similarly situated in 1960—too many Americans
remain poor.

This chapter examines the recent progress in reducing poverty, the
nature of the task that remains, and the strategies available for eliminating
poverty.

From *The Economic Report of the President, 1969*. (Washington, D.C.: U.S. Government Printing Office, 1969), pp. 151–61.

[1] From Section 2, Economic Opportunity Act, 1964.

A family is "poor" if its income is insufficient to buy enough food, clothing, shelter, and health services to meet minimum requirements. Universally acceptable standards for determining these minimum needs are impossible to formulate since the line between physical necessities and amenities is imprecise.

The social and psychological aspects of poverty further complicate efforts to measure poverty. As average incomes rise, society amends its assessment of basic needs. Individuals who cannot afford more than a small fraction of the items enjoyed by the majority are likely to feel deprived. Consequently, an absolute standard that seems appropriate today will inevitably be rejected tomorrow, just as we now reject poverty definitions appropriate a century ago.

Even a rough measure of progress in reducing poverty requires an explicit definition, although the line drawn is unavoidably arbitrary. In its 1964 Annual Report, the Council used a poverty line of $3,000 annual family income. Since 1965, the Council has employed the more refined definition of poverty developed by the Social Security Administration (SSA).

The SSA poverty lines reflect the differing consumption requirements of families based on their size and composition, the age of members, and whether their residence is farm or nonfarm. The calculations center around the U.S. Department of Agriculture's Economy Food Plan, which in December 1967 added up to a per capita weekly food outlay of $4.90. For families of three or more, the SSA measure assumes all other family needs can be obtained for an amount equal to twice the family's food requirement. In 1967, the nonfarm poverty threshold for an average four-person family was $3,335 as compared to a median income, for families of that size, of $8,995. Poverty lines for different types of households are shown in Table 1.

The problems of low-income families neither begin nor end at any arbitrary poverty line. A sharp decline in poverty may be a misleading indicator of progress if a large number of families are raised just above the poverty line. Accordingly, the SSA has also developed a "near poor" standard averaging about one-third higher than the poverty line but still less than one-half of median income for many types of families. Near-poor income standards are shown in Table 1.

The SSA poverty definitions have some limitations. Since they are multiples of food costs, the poverty lines change only when food prices change, and these prices do not necessarily parallel the prices of other essentials. Regional differences in living costs are not reflected in the poverty line. The income data take no account of income in kind such as health care, subsidized housing, and foodstuffs (except for food grown on farms). No adjustment is made for either net assets or fluctuating in-

Table 1. Poverty and Near-Poverty Income
Lines, 1967

Household Characteristic[a]	Poverty Income Line	Near-Poverty Income Line
Nonfarm Households:		
1 member	$1,635	$1,985
65 years and over	1,565	1,890
Under 65 years	1,685	2,045
2 members	2,115	2,855
Head 65 years and over	1,970	2,655
Head under 65 years	2,185	2,945
3 members	2,600	3,425
4 members	3,335	4,345
5 members	3,930	5,080
6 members	4,410	5,700
7 members or more	5,430	6,945
Farm Households:		
1 member	1,145	1,390
65 years and over	1,095	1,330
Under 65 years	1,195	1,450
2 members	1,475	1,990
Head 65 years and over	1,380	1,870
Head under 65 years	1,535	2,075
3 members	1,815	2,400
4 members	2,345	3,060
5 members	2,755	3,565
6 members	3,090	3,995
7 members or more	3,790	4,850

[a]Households are defined here as the total of families and unrelated individuals.

Note: Poverty and near-poverty income standards are defined by the Social Security Administration; they take into account family size, composition, and place of residence. Income lines are adjusted to take account of price changes during the year.

Source: Department of Health, Education, and Welfare.

comes, and yet families with savings or temporary income interruptions have different problems than the chronically poor.

These problems are currently under study in an effort to refine the poverty concept. A different threshold could affect the distribution of measured poverty among various groups but would probably show much the same trend in total poverty over the long run.

With the general rise in family incomes in the postwar period, the incidence of poverty—the percentage of persons in poor households relative to the total population—has declined sharply from 30 to less than 12 percent (see Figure 1). The number of persons in poverty declined about 20 million over the past 20 years, including a drop of 12 million since 1963— an estimated 4 million in 1968 alone.

Figure 1. Number of Poor Persons and Incidence of Poverty.

MILLIONS OF PERSONS   PERCENT

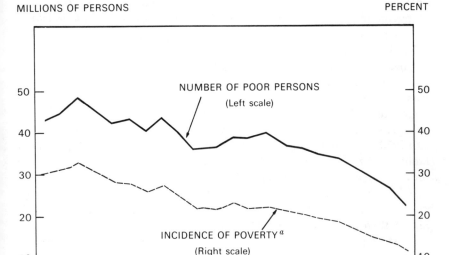

^aPoor persons as percentage of total noninstitutional population.

Note: Poverty is defined by the Social Security Administration poverty-income standard.

Sources: Department of Commerce, Department of Health, Education, and Welfare, Office of Economic Opportunity, and Council of Economic Advisers.

Along with the reduction in the number of poor households, the "poverty gap"—the difference between the actual incomes of the poor and the incomes necessary to place them above the poverty line—has been reduced. The poverty gap fell from $13.7 billion in 1959 to $9.7 billion in 1967, measured in current dollars.

The incidence of poverty is highest—23 percent—in those rural areas not in metropolitan counties, with the heaviest concentrations in the South and Appalachia. The incidence is also quite high—19 percent—in the smaller cities and towns outside of major metropolitan areas. In the central cities, the incidence is 16 percent and in their suburbs about 9 percent.

Most of the poor are white. In 1967 (the latest year for which detailed data on the poor are available), 71 percent of all poor families and 83 percent of all poor unrelated individuals were white. The incidence of poverty is far higher among nonwhites: about 1 household in 3 compared with about 1 in 7 among whites.

Of the 2.4 million nonwhite households in poverty, 2.3 million are Negroes; the remainder are mostly the original Americans—Indians and Eskimos. A 1964 survey revealed that 74 percent of the 55,000 families living on Indian and Eskimo reservations had incomes under $3,000.

Only recently has the reduction of poverty among nonwhites matched the reduction among whites. Between 1959 and 1962, the number of whites in poverty declined 2.8 million, but during the same period the number of poor nonwhites rose by 0.9 million. Between 1962 and 1967, white poverty was reduced another 7 million or about 28 percent, while poverty among nonwhites fell by 3.2 million—also about 28 percent.

The relative position of nonwhite families, after deteriorating in the late 1950s, has improved since 1961. Only since 1966 has nonwhite median family income as a fraction of white median family income surpassed its previous peak of 57 percent in 1952. Unemployment among nonwhite men age 25 to 54 has recently fallen below 1951 to 1953 levels, but unemployment rates for nonwhite women and nonwhite teenage males are much higher than during the early 1950s.

Most poor white families in the United States are not members of identifiable ethnic groups; however, two groups—Mexican-Americans, living largely in southwestern States, and Puerto Ricans, concentrated in New York City—exhibit disproportionately high incidences of poverty. In 1966, unemployment rates among Mexican-Americans in southwestern cities ranged between 8 percent and 13 percent, two to three times the national average. Subemployment—the sum of unemployment, employment producing earnings too low to provide an escape from poverty, and nonparticipation in the labor force by individuals who have given up hope of finding work—ranged from 42 to 47 percent in the Mexican-American sections of southwestern cities. And while Puerto Ricans constitute only about 8 percent of the New York City population, they have been estimated to represent over one-third of the recipients of welfare and about one-third of all occupants of substandard housing.

A program for reducing poverty has four principal economic dimensions.

First, sustained high employment and economic growth—key objectives of economic policy for a wide variety of reasons—are prime essentials.

Second, education, training, medical assistance, and access to well-paying jobs are needed by many of the poor to escape from chronic unemployment and low-paying, dead-end jobs.

Third, three-fifths of the heads of poor households cannot easily enter the labor force because of age or disability, or because they are mothers with sole responsibility for the care of young children. Some workers with large families are not likely—even with training and other types of employment assistance—to earn an income sufficient to pull their families out of poverty. Because increased employment opportunities will not eliminate poverty among these groups, some form of income maintenance is required.

Fourth, poverty is concentrated in "pockets"—city "ghettos" and certain rural areas. The numbers of poor in poverty pockets can be reduced by promoting public and private investment in these communities and by providing relocation assistance to those with employment opportunities elsewhere.

In addition to economic policies, social and psychological strategies have an important role to play. These include information about family planning for those who request it, legal assistance, and the encouragement of self-help organizations. Such programs lie outside the purview of this Report.

Virtually all the progress in reducing poverty over the past 20 years has occurred during periods of general prosperity. In three periods of sustained economic expansion—1949 to 1953, 1954 to 1956, and 1961 to the present—the annual decline in the number of individuals in poverty averaged 2 million or more a year. In contrast, during recessions the number of poor people has increased. The brief recession of 1954 wiped out half of the gains of the preceding four-year expansion, and several successive years of sluggish economic performance in the late 1950s increased the number of persons in poverty to about the level of seven years earlier (see Figure 1).

Poor families are affected unequally by economic growth and high employment, depending upon their ability to take advantage of expanded employment opportunities. Recent trends in poverty reduction for different groups are shown in Table 2.

Economic expansion has caused significant reductions in poverty among households headed by a working-age man. Tightening labor markets raise wages for the poor who are employed, and provide better employment opportunities for the unemployed and for those with very low-paying or part-time jobs. Furthermore, when prosperity pushes unemployment rates to low levels among skilled workers, business is more inclined to train poorly qualified workers for skilled jobs. From 1964 to 1966, the number of poor households headed by a working-age man with work experience fell 400,000 a year; in contrast, there had been no decline from 1959 to 1961.

The number of poor households headed by a working-age woman with job experience has not changed during the 1960s. The decline in the incidence of poverty among this group reflected a rise in the total number of households headed by working-age women.

Prosperity is less effective in reducing poverty among households headed by women for several reasons. Women are far less likely to be

Table 2. Number of Poor Households and Incidence of Poverty, Selected Years, 1959 to 1967

Characteristic of Head of Household	1959	1961	1964	1966[a] Originally Published	Revised	1967
				Millions		
Number of Poor Households:[b]						
Total	13.4	13.0	11.9	10.9	10.7	10.2
Head 65 years and over	3.9	3.9	3.8	3.9	4.0	3.8
Unrelated individuals	2.5	2.5	2.8	2.7	2.7	2.7
Families[c]	1.4	1.3	1.1	1.2	1.2	1.1
Head under 65 years	9.4	9.1	8.0	7.0	6.8	6.4
Unrelated individuals	2.6	2.4	2.3	2.1	2.1	2.2
White	1.9	1.8	1.8	1.6	1.6	1.6
Male	.6	.6	.6	.5	.6	.5
Female	1.3	1.2	1.2	1.1	1.0	1.1
Nonwhite	.7	.7	.5	.5	.5	.5
Male	.3	.3	.2	.2	.2	.2
Female	.4	.4	.3	.3	.3	.3
Families[d]	6.8	6.7	5.7	4.9	4.7	4.2
White	4.9	4.7	4.0	3.3	3.1	2.8
Male	3.8	3.7	3.0	2.3	2.2	2.0
Female	1.1	1.0	1.0	1.0	.9	.8
Nonwhite	1.9	2.0	1.7	1.6	1.5	1.4
Male	1.3	1.3	1.1	.9	.9	.7
Female	.6	.7	.6	.7	.7	.7
				Percent		
Incidence of Poverty:[e]						
Total households[b]	24.0	22.6	19.9	17.8	17.5	16.2
Head 65 years and over	48.6	43.8	40.0	38.5	38.9	36.3
Unrelated individuals	68.1	64.4	59.9	55.3	56.3	53.4
Families[c]	32.5	27.2	21.6	23.0	23.1	20.3
Head under 65 years	19.8	18.8	16.0	13.7	13.3	12.2
Unrelated individuals	36.8	33.9	31.0	28.3	28.7	27.0
White	32.9	29.7	28.3	25.8	25.5	24.4
Male	24.6	22.8	22.0	20.1	21.0	18.0
Female	39.1	35.2	33.0	30.0	28.8	29.0
Nonwhite	54.3	55.0	45.1	41.7	45.3	40.1
Male	47.1	45.5	34.6	29.1	35.5	29.4
Female	63.5	66.8	58.1	54.1	55.1	51.7
Families[d]	16.8	16.1	13.3	11.2	10.6	9.5
White	13.4	12.6	10.4	8.4	7.9	7.1
Male	11.4	10.7	8.5	6.5	6.1	5.4
Female	35.9	33.9	31.2	29.1	27.9	25.3
Nonwhite	48.6	47.8	27.8	34.3	33.4	29.9
Male	42.1	40.2	32.3	25.9	25.1	20.9
Female	71.3	72.3	62.4	61.2	60.3	54.9

employed than men; only about three-fifths of the women who head families have some job experience, compared to about 90 percent for male family heads. Many women who head families, being the adult solely responsible for young children, are unable to accept full-time employment unless day care is provided for their children. Furthermore, women are far less likely to escape poverty even if they do work, because their employment is less steady and they earn lower wages. Nonwhite families are more than twice as likely—and white families are more than 3 times as likely—to be poor if headed by a woman than if headed by a man.

During the 1960s, the number of poor elderly households fell slightly, while the incidence of poverty among this group decreased substantially. High employment has some immediate effect on poverty among the aged by providing more jobs for elderly individuals wishing to continue work. This opportunity is particularly important for those with retirement income below the poverty line.

Over the longer run, prosperity permits more workers to accumulate assets and to achieve higher pension rights prior to retirement. At present, an individual earning the minimum wage and working full-time in a job covered by social security is entitled to old-age benefits of approximately $120 a month upon retirement—only about $10 a month below the poverty line.

Reflecting both the higher lifetime earnings of the aged and statutory improvements, social security retirement benefits have increased greatly and have been the most important factor in reducing poverty among the elderly. Since 1961, legislation has increased social security retirement benefits 21 percent across the board—substantially greater than the increase in consumer prices. The minimum benefit increased 37 percent.

The ill and disabled have benefited least from recent prosperity and other efforts to alleviate poverty. Although the *incidence* of poverty among households whose heads are under 65 and not working for health reasons

---

[a]The revised estimates differ slightly from those originally published because of the use of a somewhat different estimating procedure. For an explanation of the two methods, see "Current Population Reports Series P-60, No. 54."

[b]Households are defined here as the total of families and unrelated individuals.

[c]Consists only of two-person families whose head is 65 years or over. All other families included in "head under 65 years."

[d]All families other than two-person families whose head is 65 years or over.

[e]Poor households as percentage of total households in the category.

Note: Poverty is defined by the Social Security Administration poverty-income standard; it takes into account family size, composition, and place of residence. Poverty-income lines are adjusted to take account of price changes during the period.

Detail will not necessarily add to totals because of rounding.

Sources: Department of Commerce and Department of Health, Education, and Welfare.

fell from 1959 to 1967, the *number* actually rose. Some disabled can be re-trained, and these individuals can obtain jobs more readily when unemployment is low. But many who are ill or disabled cannot take advantage of job opportunities.

Table 3 shows the number of households and the number of persons who were in the near-poor category in 1959 and 1967.

Table 3. Number of Near-Poor Households and Incidence of Near-Poverty by Age and Sex of Head of Household, 1959 and 1967

Age and Sex of Head of Household	Number (Millions)		Incidence of Near-Poverty (Percent)[a]	
	1959	1967	1959	1967
Near-Poor Households[b]	4.3	3.7	7.7	5.9
Families	3.8	2.9	8.3	5.8
Head 65 years and over[c]	.7	.8	15.2	14.0
Head under 65 years[d]	3.1	2.1	7.6	4.8
Male head	3.4	2.4	8.4	5.5
Female head	.4	.5	8.2	8.7
Unrelated individuals	.5	.8	5.1	6.0
Head 65 years and over	.2	.5	6.1	9.1
Head under 65 years	.3	.3	4.6	4.0
Male head	.2	.3	5.5	5.8
Female head	.3	.5	4.9	6.1
Addendum:				
Near-poor persons	15.8	12.0	9.0	6.1

[a]Near-poor households as percent of total number of households in the category; near-poor persons as percent of total persons.

[b]Households are defined here as the total of families and unrelated individuals.

[c]Consists only of two-person families whose head is 65 years or over. All other families included in "head under 65 years."

[d]All families other than two-person families whose head is 65 years or over.

Note: Near-poverty is defined by the Social Security Administration near-poverty-income standards; it takes into account family size, composition, and place of residence. Near-poverty-income lines are adjusted to take account of price changes during the period.

Detail will not necessarily add to totals because of rounding.

Sources: Department of Commerce and Department of Health, Education, and Welfare.

The compositions of the poor and the near-poor categories differ considerably. Most striking is the difference in the proportion of non-elderly households headed by a working-age woman. These households account for 46 percent of all nonelderly poor households; among the near-poor, they account for 22 percent. Except for the elderly, most near-poor families are headed by men who are employed, but at low wages.

The number of near-poor showed a considerable decline between 1959 and 1967. Many who rose from poverty were added to the near-poor, but at the same time an even larger number of the former near-poor moved to a higher income level.

As indicated above, prosperity has played a key role in reducing poverty and is essential to further progress. But sustained growth and high employment—in the absence of other more direct efforts to help the poor— cannot maintain the recent rate of decline in poverty.

If the 1961 to 1968 reductions in the number of poor persons could be continued, poverty would be eliminated entirely in about 10 years. If the record of 1968 could be continued, poverty would be eliminated in about 5.5 years. Maintenance of these rapid reductions will become increasingly difficult because, as poverty declines, an increasing fraction of the remaining poor are members of households whose economic status is least affected by prosperity. Households headed by women with children, disabled persons, or elderly persons accounted for 6.0 million or 59 percent of all poor households in 1967.

Much of the progress in the 1960s has been due to the lowering of the unemployment rate. As that rate fell, further declines were increasingly effective. The hard-core unemployed, the educationally disadvantaged, and the victims of discrimination are the last to be hired during a return to high employment and the first to be fired during a slowdown. Upgrading the unskilled and uneducated to fill shortages in skilled labor takes time. Consequently, if high employment is maintained, these adjustments will continue to reduce poverty, but their effects will gradually diminish. In the absence of increased direct assistance to the poor or further reductions in unemployment, present annual declines in poverty must be expected to become smaller.

The elimination of poverty will be long in coming if the incomes of the poor grow only at the same pace as the incomes of other households. If the real income (including transfer payments) of each poor household were to grow at 3 percent a year—approximately the average gain for all households during normal conditions of economic growth—eliminating only half of poverty would take 12 years for poor families and 17 years for unrelated individuals. To shorten substantially the period needed to reduce poverty, the incomes of the poor must grow faster than average income—some redistribution to the poor must be made from the benefits of growth.

Only a relatively small redistribution of the benefits of growth is needed to speed greatly the reduction in poverty. If the approximately 85 percent of households that are not poor and receive about 95 percent of total income are willing to make only a small sacrifice of the estimated 3 percent yearly growth in their real income per capita, the prospects for poverty reduction can be greatly transformed. If the increase in real income for the nonpoor is lowered merely from 3.0 percent to 2.5 percent a year and if that differential of about $2.8 billion annually is effectively transferred to those in poverty, then family incomes for those now poor can grow about 12 percent annually. This redistribution would eliminate the 1967 "poverty gap" of $9.7 billion in less than four years. Since any program of redistribution would be likely to reach some of the near-poor and might raise some poor families substantially above the poverty line before others are affected, perhaps a better projection of the time required would be six to eight years.

The rapid reductions in poverty during the 1960s paralleled a significant rise in the share of total family income going to the lowest income groups. In part, this shift in distribution has been accomplished by increased employment of poor adults at higher wages.

The combined effect of the tax and transfer payment systems at all levels of government also operates to redistribute income to the poor. The net gain or burden from the public sector for any group depends on the difference between all the benefits received from government expenditures and all the taxes paid. Many programs—like national defense—have benefits that are difficult to allocate by groups; however, the benefits of transfer payments—such as social security benefits, welfare payments, and unemployment compensation—can be allocated and compared with the tax burden. The impact of federal, state, and local taxes and of transfer payments on the distribution of income in 1965 is shown in Figure 2.

The tax system by itself redistributes income away from the poor. As a share of income, higher taxes are paid by households in the lower income classes than by those with incomes between $6,000 and $15,000. This reflects the heavy tax burden on low-income families from state and local taxes—primarily sales, excise, and property taxes. Federal taxes also contribute to this burden through the social security payroll tax.

The poor receive nearly as much from transfer payments as from all other sources. While these payments do not go exclusively to the poor, they do have a powerful redistributive impact. The ratio of receipts to household income (excluding transfers) is very high in the lowest income classes. As household incomes rise, the proportion of transfers to other income falls sharply.

When government transfer payments and taxes are combined, the concentration of transfer payments in the lower income groups much more than offsets their tax burden. But since average transfer payments fall rapidly as income rises, the excess of taxes over transfer payments as a fraction of income rises much more sharply from $0 to $4,000 than in higher income classes.

Figure 2. Taxes and Transfer Payments as Percentage of Income (Excluding Transfers), by Income Class, 1965.

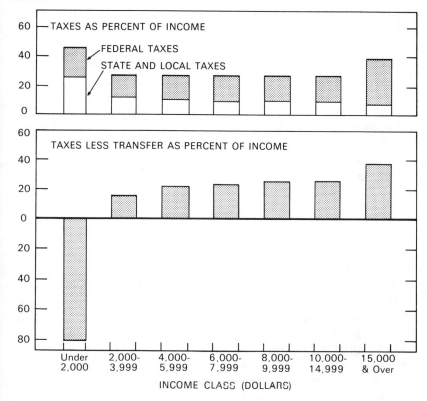

Source: Council of Economic Advisers, based on data from a variety of sources. Description available on request.

The Human Side of Poverty

MARY W. WRIGHT

Poverty tends to become a mere statistic. Here is a vivid portrayal of how it feels to be a poor Appalachian.

I know a man, I'll call him Buddy Banks. He lives in a ravine in a little one-room pole-and-cardboard house he built himself, with his wife, their 6 children, and baby granddaughter. Mr. Banks, 45 years old, is a sober man, a kindly man, and a passive man. He can read and write a little, has worked in the coal mines and on farms, but over the years he's been pretty badly battered up and today is "none too stout." Last fall, when he could no longer pay the rent where he was staying, his mother-in-law gave him a small piece of ground, and he hastened to put up this little shack in the woods before the snow came. If, as you ride by, you happened to glance down and see where he lives, and see his children playing among the stones, you would say, "White trash." You would say, "Welfare bums."

When the newspaper announced the new ADC program for unemployed fathers, I thought of Buddy Banks. There is not much farm work to be done in the wintertime, and Mr. Banks has been without a job since summer. Here in their ravine they can dig their coal from a hole in the hill, and dip their water from the creek, and each month he scratches together $2 for his food stamps by doing odd jobs for his neighbors, who are very nearly as poor as he is. Other than this there is nothing coming in. I thought, maybe here is some help for Buddy Banks.

Mr. Banks does not get a newspaper, nor does he have a radio, and so he had not heard about the new program. He said, yes, he would be

From "The Dusty Outskirts of Hope," by Mary W. Wright. Reprinted with permission from *Mountain Life & Work* (Spring, 1964), published by the Council of the Southern Mountains, Inc., and with permission of the author.

interested. I offered to take him to town right then, but he said no, he would have to clean up first, he couldn't go to town looking like this. So I agreed to come back Friday.

On Friday he told me he'd heard today was the last day for signing up. We were lucky, eh? It wasn't true, but it's what he had heard and I wondered, suppose he'd been told last Tuesday was the last day for signing up, and I hadn't been there to say, well, let's go find out anyway.

Buddy Banks was all fixed up and looked nice as he stepped out of his cabin. His jacket was clean, and he had big rubber boots on and a cap on his head. I felt proud walking along with him, and he walked proud. (Later, in town, I noticed how the hair curled over his collar, and the gray look about him, and the stoop of his shoulders. If you saw him you'd have said, "Country boy, come to get his check.")

When we reached the Welfare Office it was full of people, a crowd of slouchy, shuffly men, standing around and looking vaguely in different directions. I followed Buddy Banks and his brother-in-law, who had asked to come with us, into the lobby, and they too stood in the middle of the floor. Just stood. It was not the momentary hesitation that comes before decision. It was the paralysis of strangeness, of lostness, of not knowing what to do. A girl was sitting at a table, and after a number of minutes of nothing, I quietly suggested they ask her. No, they told me, that was the food stamp girl. But there was no other. So finally, when I suggested, well, ask her anyway, they nodded their heads, moved over, and asked her. I wondered how long they might have gone on standing there, if I'd kept my mouth shut. I wondered how long the others all around us had been standing there. I had an idea that if I hadn't been right in the way, Buddy Banks just might have turned around and gone out the door when he saw the crowd, the lines, and that smartly-dressed food stamp girl bending over her desk.

Yes, he was told, and after waiting a few minutes, he was shown behind the rail to a chair beside a desk, and a man with a necktie and a big typewriter began to talk with him. They talked a long long time, while the brother-in-law and I waited in the lobby. (They had asked the brother-in-law if he had brought the birth certificates. No, he hadn't, and so they said there wasn't anything they could do, to come back next Tuesday. He said nothing, stared at them a moment, then walked away. He stood around waiting for us all day long and never asked them another question. He said he would tend to it some other time. Fortunately, they got Mr. Banks sitting down before they inquired about the birth certificates.)

I knew what they were talking about: I have talked long times with Mr. Banks myself, and they were going over it again, and again, and I could imagine Mr. Banks nodding his head to the question he didn't quite understand, because he wanted to make a good impression, and it would be a little while before the worker realized that he hadn't understood, and so they would go back and try again, and then Mr. Banks would explain as best he could, but he would leave something out, and then the worker wouldn't understand, so that, in all, their heads were bent together for almost an hour and a half. It seemed a long time to take to discover Buddy Bank's need—a visit to his home would have revealed it in a very few minutes, but of course 12 miles out and 12 miles back takes time too, and there are all those eligibility rules to be checked out, lest somebody slip them a lie and the editorials start hollering "Fraud! Fraud!" Actually, I was impressed that the worker would give him that much time. It takes time to be sympathetic, to listen, to hear—to understand a human condition.

At last he came out, and with an apologetic grin he said he must return on Tuesday, he must go home and get the birth certificates. Then they would let him apply. (How will you come back, Mr. Banks? Where will you get the $3 for taxi fare by next Tuesday? Perhaps you could scrape it up by Monday week, but suppose you come on Monday week and your worker isn't here? Then perhaps you won't come back at all . . .)

While Mr. Banks was busy talking, I was chatting with one of the other workers. Because I am a social worker too, I can come and go through the little iron gate, and they smile at me and say, "Well, *hello* there!" We talked about all the work she has to do, and one of the things she told me was how, often, to save time, they send people down to the Health Department to get their own birth records. Then they can come back and apply the same day. I wondered why Mr. Bank's worker never suggested this. Maybe he never thought of it. (Maybe he doesn't live 12 miles out with no car, and the nearest bus eight miles from home. And no bus fare at that.) Or perhaps he *did* mention it, and Mr. Banks never heard him, because his head was already filled up with the words that went before: "I'm sorry, there's nothing we can do until you bring us the birth certificates," and he was trying to think in which box, under which bed, had the children been into them . . . ?

So I tried to suggest to him that we go now to the Health Department, but he didn't hear me either. He said, and he persisted, I'm going to the Court House, I'll be right back, will you wait for me? I tried to stop him: let's plan something, what we're going to do next, it's almost lunchtime and things will close up—until suddenly I realized that after the time and the tension of the morning, this was no doubt a call of nature that could not wait for reasonable planning, nor could a proud man come out and ask if there might not be a more accessible solution. And so, as he headed quickly away for the one sure place he knew, I stood mute and waited while he walked the three blocks there and the three blocks back.

I wonder if that's something anybody ever thinks about when they're interviewing clients.

Mr. Banks and I had talked earlier about the Manpower Redevelopment Vocational Training Programs, and he had seemed interested. "I'd sure rather work and look after my family than mess with all this stuff, but what can I do? I have no education." I told him about the courses and he said, yes, I'd like that. And so we planned to look into this too, while we were in town. But by now Mr. Banks was ready to go home. "I hate all this standing around. I'd work two days rather than stand around like this." It wasn't really the standing around he minded. It was the circumstances of the standing around. It took some persuading to get him back into the building, only to be told—at 11:30—to come back at ten to one. (Suppose his ride, I thought, had been with somebody busier than I. Suppose they couldn't wait till ten to one and kept badgering him, "Come on, Buddy, hurry up, will you? We ain't got all day!")

I tried to suggest some lunch while we waited, but they didn't want lunch. "We had breakfast late; I'm not hungry, really." So instead, I took him around to the Health Department and the Circuit Court and the County Court, and we verified everything, although he needed some help to figure which years the children were born in.

At ten to one he was again outside the Welfare Office, and he drew me aside and said that he'd been thinking: maybe he should go home and talk this whole thing over a little more. He felt that before jumping into something, he should know better what it was all about. This startled me, for I wondered what that hour and a half had been for, if now, after everything, he felt he must return to his cronies up the creek to find out what it all meant. So we stood aside, and I interpreted the program as best I could, whom it was for and what it required, and what it would do for him and his family, while he stood, nodding his head and staring at the sidewalk. Finally, cautiously, almost grimly, he once again pushed his way into that crowded, smoke-filled lobby.

"Those who are to report at one o'clock, stand in this line. Others in that line." Mr. Banks stood in the one o'clock line. At 1:15 he reached the counter. I don't know what he asked, but I saw the man behind the desk point over toward the other side of the building, the Public Assistance side, where Mr. Banks had already spent all morning. Mr. Banks nodded his head and turned away as he was told to do. At that point I butted in. "Assistance for the unemployed is over there," the man said and pointed again. So I mentioned training. "He wants training? Why didn't he say so? He's in the wrong line." I don't know what Mr. Banks had said, but what *does* a person say when he's anxious, and tired and confused, and a crowd of others, equally anxious, are pushing from behind and the man at the counter says, "Yes?" I butted in and Mr. Banks went to stand in the right line, but I wondered what the man behind us did, who didn't have any-body to butt in for him.

While Mr. Banks was waiting, to save time, I took the birth certifi-cates to his worker on the other side. I walked right in, because I was a social worker and could do that, and he talked to me right away and said, "Yes, yes, this is good. This will save time. No, he won't have to come back on Tuesday. Yes, he can apply today. Just have him come back over here when he is through over there. Very good."

At 1:30 Buddy Banks reached the counter again, was given a card and told to go sit on a chair until his name was called. I had business at 2:00 and returned at 3:00, and there he was, sitting on the same chair. But I learned as I sat beside him that things had been happening. He had talked with the training counsellor, returned to his welfare worker, and was sent back to the unemployment counsellor, after which he was to return once more to his welfare worker. I asked what he had learned about the training. "There's nothing right now, maybe later." Auto mechanics? Bench work? Need too much education. There may be something about washing cars, changing oil, things like that. Later on. Did you sign up for anything? No. Did they say they'd let you know? No. How will you know? I don't know.

At last his ADC (Unemployed) application was signed, his cards were registered, his name was in the file. Come back in two weeks and we'll see if you're eligible. (How will you get back, Buddy? I'll find a way.)

It was four o'clock. "Well, that's over." And he said, "I suppose a fellow's got to go through all that, but I'd sure rather be a-working than a-fooling around with all that mess." We went out to the car, and I took him home. "I sure do thank you, though," he said.

While I'd been waiting there in the lobby, I saw another man come up to the counter. He was small and middle-aged, with a wedding band on his finger, and his face was creased with lines of care. I saw him speak quietly to the man across the desk. I don't know what he said or what the problem was, but they talked a moment and the official told him, "Well, if you're disabled for work, then there's no use asking about training," and he put up his hands and turned away to the papers on his desk. The man waited there a moment, then slowly turned around and stood in the middle of the floor. He lifted his head to stare up at the wall, the blank wall, and his blue eyes were held wide open to keep the tears from coming. I couldn't help watching him, and when suddenly he looked at me, his eyes straight into mine, I couldn't help asking him—across the wide distance of the crowd that for just an instant vanished into the intimacy of human com-munion—I asked, "Trouble?" Almost as if he were reaching out his hands, he answered me and said, "I just got the news from Washington and come to sign up, and . . ." but then, embarrassed to be talking to a stranger, he mumbled something else I couldn't understand, turned his back to me, stood another long moment in the middle of the crowd, and then walked out the door.

Disabled or not disabled. Employed or not employed. In need or not in need. Yes or no. Black or white. Answer the question. Stand in line.

It is not the program's fault. You have to have questionnaires, and questionnaires require a yes or no. There is no space for a maybe, but . . .

Nor is it the people-who-work-there's fault, for who can see—or take time to see—the whole constellation of people and pressures, needs and perplexities, desires and dreads that walk into an office in the person of one shuffling, bedraggled man—especially when there are a hundred other bedraggled men waiting behind him? You ask the questions and await the answers. What else can you do?

Then perhaps it is the fault of the man himself, the man who asks—or doesn't quite know how to ask—for help. Indeed, he's called a lazy cheat if he does, and an unmotivated ignorant fool if he doesn't. It must be his own fault.

Or maybe it's nobody's fault. It's just the way things are . . .

The Merger Movement:
A Study in Power

PAUL M. SWEEZY AND HARRY MAGDOFF

How serious is the recent trend to "conglomerate" corporations? A radical analysis raises some interesting and surprising possibilities.

During the last year or so a tremendous amount of publicity has been devoted to the corporate merger movement, but to our knowledge there has not been much serious discussion of its significance. A review of some of the outstanding facts and what they mean and do not mean may therefore be useful.

To begin with, there can be no doubt about the impressive magnitude of the movement, measured by any relevant standard. The following table is constructed from Federal Trade Commission data as reported in *Business Week* of April 19, 1969:

	1966	1967	1968
Total number of acquisitions	1,746	2,384	4,003
Number of manufacturing and mining companies with more than $10 million assets acquired	101	169	192
Value of assets of acquired companies with more than $10 million assets (billion $)	4.1	8.2	12.6
Number of acquisitions made by 200 largest companies	33	67	74
Value of assets of companies acquired by 200 largest companies (billion $)	2.4	5.4	6.9

Complete data for early 1969 are not published in the article from which these figures are taken, but one statistic alone is enough to show that, far from coming to an end, the merger movement has actually

From *Monthly Review*, Vol. 21, No. 2 (June, 1969), pp. 1–19. Reprinted by permission of Monthly Review, Inc. Copyright © 1969 by Monthly Review, Inc.

accelerated in recent months. As against the $12.6 billion dollars of assets in companies with assets of $10 million or more which were gobbled up in 1968, the comparable rate of acquisition so far in 1969 has been running at about $18 billion.

As to the size of the present movement relative to earlier merger movements in U.S. history, *Fortune* magazine (February 1969, p. 80) states: "There have been merger movements in the U.S. before. One began in the 1890s and another in the 1920s; each lasted about a decade. But the current merger movement is lasting longer and is immensely bigger."

Radicals and anti-monopoly liberals frequently assume that the increasing dominance of the giants necessarily implies the decline and fall of small business. Nothing could be further from the truth. A recent story in the *Wall Street Journal* (April 10, 1969) begins as follows:

> Worried that conglomerates are gobbling up companies so fast that by the end of the century some 200 super-corporations will own all of American business?
>
> Take heart. Far more businesses are starting out than selling out these days.
>
> Most of the fledgling firms are small, of course, and many won't last a year, but they are being formed at the fastest clip since the years that immediately followed World War II.
>
> Analysts estimate that between 450,000 and 500,000 new businesses will be launched this year, about 25 percent more than a half-dozen years ago. By comparison, W. T. Grimm & Co., a Chicago financial consulting firm, predicts that some 5,400 companies will go out of existence through merger or acquisition in 1969.
>
> The government's new-business index, which measures the net growth in business formations (new businesses minus firms that discontinue operations), last December stood at the highest point since mid-1948.

The great majority of these new businesses of course are in either retailing or the service trades, but there are also many in various branches of manufacturing. And far from contradicting the interests of the giant corporations, this proliferation of small businesses serves their purposes in many ways. A detailed discussion of this problem would take us far afield, but it may be worthwhile to point out three specific ways in which the giants benefit from the existence of small businesses.

First, every big corporation buys thousands of items ranging all the way from huge machines to paper clips. Many of these are supplied by other big corporations, but many offer too little prospect of profit to interest the big ones and these become the domain of small business. This being the case, the giants naturally prefer that there should be an ample number of suppliers competing among themselves to ensure low prices and good quality.

Second, the markets for the products of the giants typically undergo seasonal and/or cyclical variations. This means that at any given time demand for a product can be divided into a large segment which can be looked upon as stable and reliable and a smaller segment which fluctuates and may even disappear with the vicissitudes of the market. The giants employ various strategies for dealing with this problem, depending on the nature of the product and the market; but in most cases at least one element in the strategy adopted is to allow a number of smaller companies to enter the industry and fill some part of the fluctuating demand. Benefiting from the giants' monopoly price umbrella, these small companies may do very well when demand is strong. The other side of the coin, of course, is that they may be hit hard or even wiped out when demand is weak. In any case, they act as a sort of stabilizer and balancer for the carefully calculating giants.

Finally, much of the innovating function under monopoly capitalism is carried out not by the giants but by small firms, often specifically organized to turn out a new product or try a new method of production or distribution. And this is done not against the will of the giants but with their hearty approval. Innovating is risky. Most small outfits that try it fail, but a few hit the jackpot and it is this glittering reward that motivates a host of new hopefuls to keep at it. From the point of view of the giants all this activity serves the extremely useful purpose of showing which lines of innovation are practical and profitable, with all the risk being borne by others. Later on, the giants can move in, either buying out the successful small firm or imitating its innovation with a version of their own.

There are other business and technical reasons for the existence and spread of small enterprises in the period of monopoly capitalism, but the three described above should be enough to dispose of the unfounded notion that there is any tendency for the concentration and centralization of capital to result in the disappearance of small business. The *relative* importance of the giants grows; but as long as the system as a whole expands (and capitalism cannot live without expanding), this not only does not preclude but actually requires an *absolute* proliferation of the dwarfs.

Our analysis to this point leads to the conclusion that the current merger movement, though undoubtedly massive by historical standards, is not likely to have any profound effects on either the functioning or structure of the U.S. economy. What it means is more of the same, not anything really new. And the same goes for the much-publicized fact that the most spectacular merging activity of the last few years has been by the so-called conglomerates, i.e., companies which operate not in one market or a few related markets but in dozens or even scores of often quite unrelated markets. Two of the top five companies on *Fortune*'s latest list of the 500 largest nonfinancial corporations (General Motors which is number one and General Electric which is number four) have long been conglomerates in this sense; and many, perhaps even a majority, of the others would qualify for the same designation. The real reason for the excitement about the "new" conglomerates lies elsewhere than in their newness.

For one thing, the latter-day conglomerates have been heavily promoted by all the devices of the Madison Avenue public relations industry and its Wall Street affiliates and confréres.

The purpose of all this fancy public-relations activity is of course to persuade Wall Street that the glamour stocks are worth a lot more than mundane balance sheets and profit-and-loss statements would seem to indicate. The desideratum is to attain, in the jargon of the stock market, the highest possible price/earnings (P/E) ratio. The stock of an old conservatively managed company which grows more or less in step with the economy as a whole (say at a rate of 4 to 5 percent a year) may sell at 10 to 15 times per-share earnings. The stock of a highly jazzed-up glamour company which has been able to show a record of rapid growth in the previous few years may, on the other hand, sell for 30 or 40 or even more times earnings. And therein lies the secret not only of the burgeoning of the latter-day conglomerates but also of the rise to wealth and prominence of a new stratum of the U.S. bourgeoisie. In order to be able to analyze this phenomenon properly, it will be useful to review some of the facts of corporate and financial life.

First, it is necessary to keep in mind as essential background the situation with respect to control of the typical giant corporation. Legally, of course, the stockholders are the owners of the corporation, and managements are simply their agents. In practice, however, the stock of most of the giants is widely dispersed among many thousands of holders, with no individual or group owning more than a small percentage of the shares. In these circumstances whatever management happens to be in power can normally remain in power and appoint its own successors.[1] In their famous work *The Modern Corporation and Private Property* (1932), Berle and Means found that 44 percent of the 200 largest nonfinancial corporations were management-controlled in this sense. An updating study by Robert J. Larner (published in the *American Economic Review* of Septem-

---

[1] In many companies, incumbent managements are the lineal descendants (often in the literal family sense) of managements which were installed in an earlier period by big stockholders owning all or most of the company's stock. In this way the families of these earlier big stockholders often continue to control big corporations long after their holdings have ceased to be a significant percentage of the total stock outstanding.

ber 1966) showed that by 1963 this proportion had risen to 84.5 percent. Reporting on Larner's work, *Business Week* put the following caption on a table comparing the situation in 1929 with that in 1963: "Professional managers have won ultimate control almost everywhere among the 200 largest nonfinancial corporations." Of course it is always possible for the management of such a company to be ousted by someone who succeeds in collecting proxies for a majority of the stock, and occasionally this does happen. But pulling off such a coup is very expensive and difficult: all the advantages are with the management, and under normal conditions it can go about its business without fear or attack from outsiders. Or at least that's the way it was until the new conglomerates came along. We shall return to this presently.

Next we need to know something of the way the conglomerates operate: how they grow by taking over previously independent companies and in the process generate the kind of increase in per-share earnings which is so important as a prop and booster to their P/E ratios.

We can distinguish two types of takeover: that which from the point of view of the acquired company is voluntary, and that which is involuntary. A company may want to be absorbed into another for many reasons. For example, a man may have a large part of his wealth in the form of stock in a company which he has built up in his own lifetime. If, as often happens, there is no ready market for this stock, his heirs will be in trouble when he dies. The obvious solution is for the man in question to sell out while he is still alive and to leave his heirs cash and/or securities for which there is a ready market. Another common reason why one company wants to be absorbed by another is that it needs capital for expansion and lacks the absorbing company's access to banks and the money market. Or the two merging companies may both want to be part of a larger enterprise with more prestige and less vulnerability to fluctuations in particular markets. In any case, regardless of the reasons a company may have for wanting to be absorbed, the fact that it acts voluntarily greatly simplifies the whole process. Voluntary mergers have figured prominently in the growth of all the conglomerates, old and new, and doubtless will continue to do so in the future.

Involuntary takeovers present different problems, and it is with them that we are mainly concerned in what follows. The acquired company here is usually (maybe always) one whose stock is widely dispersed among a large number of stockholders, in other words a company conforming to the type which, as we have already seen, predominates among the 200 largest nonfinancial corporations. The usual procedure is for the acquiring company to buy up secretly anything up to 10 percent of the target company's stock. (Ownership of 10 percent or more has to be disclosed to the Securities and Exchange Commission and immediately becomes public knowledge.) The next step may be for the aggressor (call it company A) to approach the victim (company B) with arguments and inducements designed to overcome the latter's resistance. If this fails, as it often does, A then plays its trump card, a tender offer to B's stockholders. This is an offer to buy shares in B—either all that are tendered or up to a certain percentage of the total outstanding—at a price which is invariably above the current market price and may be far above the market price. Payment may be made with cash or with A's own securities or some combination of the two. Once matters have reached this stage, B's management is all but defeated. Stockholders are an unsentimental lot, interested only in making money. If someone comes along and offers them more for their stock than they can get in the market, most of them will accept. There may be some hesitation when the payment is in A's securities rather than cash, and B's management will do its best to convince stockholders that they are better off with what they have than they would be with what they are being offered. But usually this doesn't work: stockholders who think poorly of A's prospects will simply turn around and sell the securities they receive in payment (at the time of the transaction always worth more than what they give up) and buy other securities which they like better.

How does it happen that acquiring companies can afford to make such generous offers to the stockholders of target companies? Here two factors come into play: first, the arithmetic of P/E ratios and stock prices; and second, the effects of the tax laws, especially in that they treat interest paid on debt securities as a cost which is deductible in calculating net income while dividends are paid out of net income. Two highly simplified examples will serve to illustrate the principles involved.

Call the acquiring company A, the target company B, and the merged company AB. Assume the following initial situation:

	Shares Outstanding	After-Tax Earnings	Earnings Per Share	P/E	Price Per Share
A	1,000,000	$1,000,000	$1	40	$40
B	1,000,000	$1,000,000	$1	15	$15

At this point A offers to exchange one share of its stock worth $40 on the market for two shares of B's stock worth $30, giving B's stockholders a gain of $5 a share or 33⅓ percent. But they are not the only winners. Assuming that the merged company continues to have a P/E ratio of 40, the combined result will be the following:

	Shares Outstanding	After-Tax Earnings	Earnings Per Share	P/E	Price Per Share
AB	1,500,000	$2,000,000	$1.33	40	

What has happened is that by reducing the total number of shares outstanding from two million to one and a half million, the same amount of earnings produce an increase in earnings per share, and the same P/E ratio yields a higher price for the stock (of which A's stockholders own the same number of shares as before). Everyone, it seems, gains—except B's management which is no longer its own boss and can be kicked out at the whim of A's management. This illustration shows the supreme importance of a high P/E ratio in the merger game and explains the lengths to which its adepts will go to present to the investing and speculating community an image of a super-streamlined perpetual-growth machine. And one of the ironies of the situation is that the more successful they are, the more they can create the appearance of growth (measured by the earnings-per-share yardstick) simply by acquiring more and more companies with lower P/E ratios.

The second example, showing the tax bonanzas that mergers can produce, is adapted from a report headlined "Conglomerate Maze" which appeared on the financial page of the *New York Times* of February 27, 1969. Company A has a million shares outstanding, annual after-tax earnings of $2 million ($2 per share), pays no dividends, sells at $40 a share. Company B has 10 million shares outstanding, earnings of $30 million after taxes ($3 a share), pays a dividend of $1.50, and sells at $39 a share. A offers for each share of B's stock one debenture (an unsecured bond) with a face value of $50 and paying interest at the rate of 7.5 percent ($3.75 a year). In order to make the offer more attractive, A also offers to throw in warrants good for the purchase of the merged company's shares in the future, but this does not affect the arithmetic of the immediate situation. B's stockholders thus stand to gain $11 a share in the value of their securities and $2.25 a share in their current income. It is assumed that the earnings *before* taxes of the combined company are the same as they were before, i.e., $64 million. But earnings *after* taxes are now quite different. From the before-tax earnings of $64 million the merged company deducts interest of $37.5 million before calculating taxable income of $26.5 million. After-tax income is therefore now $13.25 million. Since the only shares now outstanding are the one million of A stock, it follows that per share earnings of A's stock have risen from $2 to $13.25. The losers this time are the U.S. treasury, to the tune of $18.75 million, and of course B's management. A has in effect acquired B by making use of B's own earning power plus generous government financing, and in the process has added handsomely to the value of A's own stock.

By now it should be clear why any conservatively managed company to which the stock market does not assign a particularly high P/E ratio and which does not have a lot of debt in its capital structure is vulnerable to takeover by one of the high-riding conglomerates which does enjoy a fancy P/E ratio and which has no scruples about going in for debt financing in a big way. And what lends special importance to this situation is simply this: *the category of vulnerable corporations includes a very large proportion of the long-established giants which are at the top of the economic and political power structure of the United States.*

This process and its repercussions can be traced through three incidents: the takeovers of Wilson & Co. and Jones and Laughlin Steel Corporation by Ling–Temco–Vought, and the attempted takeover of Chemical Bank New York Trust Co. by Leasco Data Processing Equipment Corporation.

On the basis of its 1967 sales of $991 million, Wilson & Co., meat-packer and producer of sporting goods, was well within the charmed circle of the 100 largest nonfinancial corporations and bigger than James Ling's entire Ling–Temco–Vought conglomerate. And yet during that year Ling, through an intricate series of maneuvers and financial coups (including a multi-million dollar loan from a European banking syndicate), succeeded in taking over Wilson and in the process jumped from number 168 to number 38 in the 500-largest list. Other acquisitions in 1967 included Greatamerica Corporation, itself a diversified company owning, among other things, Braniff Airways. And then, just about a year after swallowing Wilson, Ling pulled off his greatest coup, the takeover of Jones and Laughlin Steel Corporation. J and L is the nation's sixth largest steel producer, a long-established member of what *Business Week* (May 18, 1968) called the "tight-knit steel fraternity," and closely allied to its Pittsburgh neighbors in the Mellon empire. This was a classic case of the tender-offer technique: J&L stock was selling at about $50 a share, and L–T–V offered the stockholders a package worth about $85 a share. The result was a foregone conclusion. L–T–V will probably rank among the 20 largest industrials when J&L is included among its subsidiaries.

This fast operator, but recently a parvenu even in Texas, had now marched into Pittsburgh. What was to prevent him and others like him from storming the ultimate bastions on Wall Street and Park Avenue? The answer was not long in coming and, as could have been predicted, it had two parts. On the one hand, the corporate establishment began to bring its enormous financial power into play; on the other hand, it called on its faithful servants in the seats of government to wake up and do their job.

Both parts of the answer were dramatically illustrated by the abortive attempt of Leasco Data Processing Equipment Corporation, a company built up by a 29-year-old financial "wizard" named Saul Steinberg, to take over the Chemical Bank of New York. Leasco operates in and around the computer industry and owns a big insurance company. Though growing rapidly, it was not large enough to be listed anywhere in *Fortune's*

1968 directory of largest corporations (issue dated May 1, 1968). Chemical Bank (formerly Chemical Bank New York Trust Company), on the other hand, was listed as the nation's sixth largest bank with assets of $8.4 billion. In February 1969, Leasco mounted an attack on Chemical and was obviously preparing the *coup de grâce* of a generous tender offer to Chemical's stockholders. Before the end of the month, however, Steinberg was forced to admit defeat. At the time, the reports in the business press were brief and largely bare of detail. But a couple of months later the real story came out. Here are excerpts from *Business Week's* article entitled "Why Leasco Failed to Net Chemical" in the issue of April 26th (the whole article is worth reading):

> "I always knew there was an Establishment," says Saul P. Steinberg, the chubby, 29-year-old multimillionaire chairman of Leasco Data Processing Equipment Corp. "I just used to think I was part of it."
>
> Leasco's abortive play last February for giant Chemical Bank of New York threw Steinberg against the real establishment of big, conservative money—a confrontation so jarring that Wall Street still clucks about it. In the end, says a Wall Street friend, "Saul found out there really is a back room where the big boys sit and smoke their long cigars."...
>
> Chemical Bank is old, rich (sixth-biggest commercial bank in the U.S. with $9 billion in assets), and very powerful. It is a money market bank—a lender to many of the bluest of blue-chip corporations and a big dealer in U.S. government securities. On its board sit top executives of such companies as AT&T, DuPont, IBM, Sears, U.S. Steel, Olin Mathieson, Uniroyal, New York Life, and Equitable Life.
>
> Never has so mighty a bank fallen to an outsider. To Chemical Bank, and to many of its best customers, Steinberg—young, sometimes brash, a Johnny-come-lately, and Jewish to boot—was very much an outsider. "Chemical" says a rival banker, "was afraid of losing a lot of its corporate and personal trust business if Leasco took over. Those people wouldn't sit still for a Steinberg."
>
> The bank was apparently threatened with the loss of some business, by customers who didn't want a nonbanker in a position to know so much about their financial affairs....
>
> Wall Street's choicest gossip for weeks has dealt with what happened during those 15 days [in February]—or what it thinks happened....
> One thing that did happen was that Leasco's stock plunged from 140 to 106 in two weeks—driven down, many on Wall Street believe, as bank trust departments sold what Leasco shares they held....
>
> At least one computer-leasing customer—and perhaps more—apparently threatened to take its business elsewhere if Leasco actually

made a bid for Chemical Bank. Leasco's prime investment banker, White, Weld & Co., told Steinberg on February 7 that he would have to try to take over Chemical Bank without that firm's help.

Investment banker Lehman Bros. admits that it was pressured by commercial banks to not help Leasco—a ticklish situation since Lehman is a heavy borrower of bank money.

The nation's big banks, rocked by the thought of one of their number being taken over, did cluster together to create what one banker calls "a massive groundswell of opposition that was felt in Washington and Albany. The whole industry was aghast."

In Washington, Chemical Bank found support high up in the Nixon administration, in Congress, and among the financial regulators. In Albany New York Governor Nelson Rockefeller asked for immediate legislation to shield banks in the state from takeover. A comparable bill, covering national banks, was introduced in Congress on February 28 by Senator John J. Sparkman (D-Ala.), chairman of the Senate Banking and Currency Committee.

It isn't clear how much of a hand Chemical Bank had in all this. In fact, as one man on Wall Street points out, "Chemical didn't have to do very much. It had so many friends, and every one wanted to help."

As it turned out, the corporate establishment's counter-attack in the Leasco–Chemical affair was only the opening salvo in a full-scale campaign to put the parvenus in their place. During the week of March 24th, the Justice Department, in what *Business Week* (March 29) called "Washington's first all-out assault on the merger-hungry giants," filed an anti-trust suit to separate Jones and Laughlin from Ling–Temco–Vought, and at the same time forced Ling to accept an agreement whereby, pending the outcome of the suit, J&L would be maintained as an organizationally independent entity, so that if the government wins J&L can be shifted to new ownership with a minimum of difficulty. Ling, it seems, is to be made to pay for approaching as near as Pittsburgh to the inner sanctum.

Finally, *Fortune*, in its "Report from Washington" column in the issue of May 1st, really pulled the curtain aside and showed what has been and is going on behind the scenes. Here are excerpts from another piece (captioned, appropriately enough, "It's open season on conglomerates, and established business couldn't be happier") which deserves to be read in full:

Washington in recent years has shown about as much interest in conglomerate mergers as in the prospects of the Washington Senators baseball team. The Justice Department under Lyndon Johnson did not view conglomerates as much of a threat to competition, and the Federal Trade Commission, after blocking Procter & Gamble's takeover of Clorox in 1967, became passive. . . .

Today, by contrast, antitrust and conglomerates would seem to rank only behind Vietnam, the ABM, and inflation in the capital's interest. A dozen federal investigations are under way into the antitrust aspects of conglomerate mergers. A slew of bills are before Congress to block airline and railroad mergers. Representative Wilbur Mills has introduced a bill to remove tax incentives to takeovers. Banking conglomerates . . . are the target of strict administration legislative proposals. For his part, the government's new trustbuster, Assistant Attorney General Richard McLaren, has launched this spring a broad legal attack against mergers. Of 12 recent large conglomerate mergers, five have been challenged by the government.

The result—not wholly unintended, perhaps—of these myriad federal moves was to knock more than $5 billion (21 percent) off the market values of 13 conglomerates' shares between January 27 and March 24 and, consequently, dampen their merger potential. . . .

This sudden free-form, uncoordinated attack on mergers has surprised even such dedicated antitrust Democrats as Representative Emmanuel Celler of New York and Senator Philip Hart of Michigan, who chair, respectively, the House and Senate judiciary subcommittees on antitrust. "I never thought that I would see the day when the business community would be pleading with the federal government for an investigation of business. But that is exactly what has resulted from the merger practices of some of our leading corporations." . . .

The events that triggered Washington into action are not hard to discern. It was not the number of mergers or the concentration ratios, but rather the threat to the established way of doing corporate business. "For years nobody paid a damn bit of attention to my antitrust hearings. But now such nice people are being swallowed up," says Senator Hart. . . .

Despite the near unanimity in the capital about the present dangers of mergers, there is in some quarters considerable support for James Ling's complaints about Washington's "conglomerate syndrome." . . . Even Senator Hart notes acidly that many of the proposals are not "referring to established conglomerates like General Electric, or R.C.A. or I.T.T. They are referring to the brand-new ones who are threatening the old-line companies." . . .

So much, then, for the attempts of the parvenu outsiders to crash the corporate establishment. They threw a scare into the big boys all right, but the latter now seem to be in the process of demonstrating that they still have what it takes to maintain a monopoly of real power in corporate America.

What lessons are the underprivileged multi-millionaires likely to derive from this experience? We don't know for sure as yet, of course. But it does seem likely that they will draw the obvious inference that economic and political power cannot be separated. If you want the one, you must aim also for the other. This consideration may lead them next time to try first of all to get control of the crucial legislative and bureaucratic agencies in Washington which could help rather than block future forays into the inner corporate circle. And for this they would need a political instrument to use against the corporate-establishment-controlled Republican and Democratic parties.

Upstart capital has always been an important source of financial support for fascist-type movements which seek to harness popular discontent and resentments to overturn existing political structures. The story recounted here of the rise and frustration of the new conglomerators may therefore have as a sequel a significant strengthening of the fascist tendencies which George Wallace's 1968 presidential campaign showed to be already well developed in certain regions of the country and strata of the population. The other side of the coin might well be that old wealth, fearful of the implications for its own power of a fascist victory, would cling more closely than ever to its tried-and-true political weapons.

But all we can say for certain at this stage is that the course of the great merger movement of the 1950s and 1960s seems certain to complicate what already promises to be a very confused and uncertain political situation in the period ahead.

Our Vietnamized Economy

MURRAY L. WEIDENBAUM

A careful report on the military-industrial complex seen at a distance. For a close-up view, see the next essay.

Although American troops have been stationed in South Vietnam since 1954, the major buildup occurred between the middle of 1965 and the middle of 1967. This substantial and rapid expansion in U.S. military spending—from $50 billion before the buildup to $80 billion now—has had many important effects. Fundamentally, it has altered the allocation of the nation's resources between the private and the public sectors. At the end of 1964, 20 percent of the Gross National Product was purchased by government agencies and the remaining 80 percent was available to the private economy. By early 1968, the government portion had risen to 27 percent and the private share had fallen to 73 percent.

The Johnson Administration consistently underestimated military expenditures, particularly during the crucial buildup period in late 1965 and much of 1966. Most economists and government administrators, moreover, failed to appreciate how quickly the military buildup was influencing the national economy—that the economic impact was occurring as soon as the defense orders were placed and, thus, substantially before the work was completed, paid for, and showing up in the federal budget. Furthermore, policy measures to offset inflationary pressures were not taken soon enough or in a substantial enough way. The January 1966 budget message of the President maintained that the United States could afford simultaneously to wage a two-front war without raising taxes: the domestic war against poverty and the war in Vietnam.

But the program choices made were not as simple as the classroom dichotomy of "guns vs. butter." In a sense, we chose both more guns (military spending) and more butter (more consumer purchases). However, we also chose—in part as tight money began to affect specific parts of the private economy—less housing and fewer automobiles. Simultaneously, the nation was voting for more social welfare programs—thus increasing both the military and the civilian portions of the public sector. As a result, 1966 witnessed what was then the most rapid period of price inflation since the Korean War.

Several major economic problems face the United States as a legacy of 1965–66. With the collapse of the stable price and cost situation prevailing prior to Vietnam, inflation is a major concern. Unusually high interest rates have been set in a thus far unsuccessful attempt to contain the inflation. Income taxes have been raised to reduce unprecedentedly large budget deficits ($25 billion in fiscal 1968). Despite forecasts to the contrary, a serious balance-of-payments situation continues. More basic than all this, the public's confidence in the ability to "fine tune" domestic economic stabilization policies has been undermined. The basic information and analysis released by the federal government to justify its policies has created more suspicion than trust.

There also have been, of course, positive impacts of governmental economic policy during the war. A fundamental imperative was successfully achieved; a large and rapid shift of resources from civilian uses or idleness to military programs was accomplished. At the same time—unlike either the World War II or Korean experiences—the nation managed to avoid direct controls over prices, wages, and materials generally (although relatively small amounts of copper and a few other metals were set aside for use by defense contractors).

Despite the increases in defense spending and the accompanying inflation, economic growth and real improvements in the living standard of the average American continued. Even after allowing for inflation, the average American has experienced a real growth in income, from $2,123 in 1964 to $2,473 in 1968. Also, expenditures for civilian government programs actually have increased by a larger amount than did the military budget—simultaneously with the $30-billion rise in defense spending due to the Vietnam war, civilian agencies of the Government have increased their expenditures by $35 billion since the war began.

The shift from cold to hot war not only has raised the size of the military budget, but also has changed its composition drastically. The fundamental change was the shift of emphasis from maintaining the potential capability to deal with world-wide or general war situations, in favor of moving toward a military establishment actually waging a difficult but limited war whose dimensions kept evolving.

Three specific shifts in military requirements took place. The amount of funds going for tanks, artillery, rifles, ammunition, and similar conventional battlefield hardware more than doubled from the prewar level. The relative—as well as absolute—importance of missiles was reduced drastically. Meanwhile, the military aircraft budget was reoriented from new long-range bombers to acquiring smaller "tactical" aircraft, particularly helicopters and supersonic fighters, such as the F-4 Phantom.

Once again, the traditional manufacturing industries—automobiles, mechanical equipment, textiles, clothing, tires—have become important suppliers of war material. The most dramatic increases have occurred in ammunition (orders have quadrupled since 1965), artillery and small arms (more than doubled), clothing and textiles (doubled), tanks and vehicles (up 68 percent), and food (up 66 percent).

Figure 1. U.S. Military Budgets (1964, 1969, 1974^a), in Billions of Dollars.

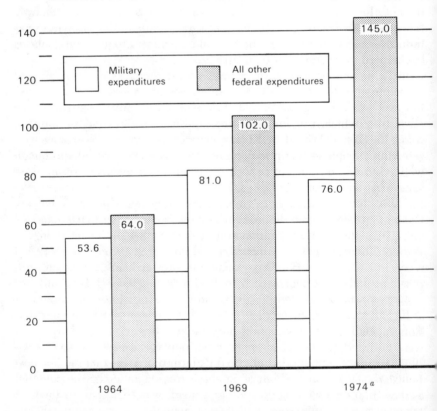

^{a}Projected, fiscal 1974, with no 10 percent surcharge, no wartime expenditures. Source: Research Institute of America.

The highly specialized, science-oriented aerospace and electronics firms, although still very significant defense contractors, have found their shares of defense business declining. The ten firms with the largest amount of defense contracts in fiscal 1968—General Dynamics, Lockheed, General Electric, United Aircraft, McDonnell–Douglas, AT&T, Boeing, Ling–Temco–Vought, North American Rockwell, and General Motors—received 29.9 percent of the total awards. This was down from their pre-Vietnam share of 32.2 percent. It is interesting to note that nine of these ten giants of the military market are aerospace and electronics firms.

Unlike the period of production of large weapon systems—such as ICBMs, which could be supplied only by a few of the industrial behemoths with especially sophisticated capabilities—the economic demands of Vietnam involve numerous smaller contracts with a variety of medium-sized firms. "Small" firms increased their share of defense contracts from 15.8 percent in fiscal 1963 to 18.4 percent in 1968. (Companies that made the Pentagon's list of the top 100 contractors in 1968, but were not in that roster earlier, include Atlas Chemical, Colt Industries, Lykes, McLean Industries, Automatic Sprinkler, Harris–Intertype, and National Presto Industries.) But many branches of the industrial economy—including leather, paint, plastic, paper, and furniture companies—have experienced virtually no increase in defense work in recent years.

Large proportions of the companies working on Vietnam orders are in the upper Midwest and in other relatively older industrial states in the East, all of which have long-standing positions in the industrial and consumer markets. The Far West, which since the Korean War had been receiving a dominant share of defense orders, has experienced absolute as well as relative declines as a military supplier. For example, Washington state firms (mainly Boeing) received $530 million worth of defense contracts in 1968, compared to twice that amount in 1964 ($1.1 billion). Colorado's $263 million of Pentagon orders in 1968 were down substantially from the $390-million level of 1964, reflecting a decline in missile work by the Denver Division of Martin–Marietta. Similarly, in 1964 Utah received $340 million in military contracts, down to $263 million in 1968, reflecting lower levels of work on the Minuteman ICBM.

Eight states received defense contracts in 1968 at rates at least twice as high as the pre-Vietnam levels. They are Tennessee, Texas, Connecticut, Illinois, Alabama, Mississippi, Minnesota, and Wisconsin. Six other states were awarded defense contracts at least 50 percent greater than in fiscal 1965, before the military buildup in Southeast Asia—Florida, Indiana, Louisiana, New York, Ohio, and Pennsylvania. Most of these states, such as those in the upper Midwest, are major producers of Army ordnance and other battlefield hardware. The most dramatic expansions have been among helicopter manufacturers, notably Bell Aircraft in the Dallas–Fort Worth area, Sikorsky Division of United Aircraft in the Hartford region, and Boeing–Vertol near Philadelphia. A special case of expanding effort is the TFX (F-111) supersonic aircraft being built by General Dynamics in Fort Worth.

Vietnam also has had important effects on the pattern of civilian employment. Overall, out of more than one million new jobs directly generated by the Vietnam war, the great majority has been in highly skilled and highly paid occupations—238,000 more professional and managerial employees vs. 30,000 more service workers (the latter being among the lowest-paid groups in the nation's labor force). While the war effort has resulted in 245,000 more skilled factory workers being hired, there have been only 65,000 more jobs for laborers, 178,000 more office jobs, and 29,000 more sales positions. Thus, indirectly, the war effort has intensified some of our domestic problems—by increasing jobs for the highly skilled and relatively highly paid, rather than for the lower-income, lower-skilled portions of the population. Only one out of every ten defense jobs bears a laborer's classification, while 22 percent of civilian jobs do.

Early optimistic appraisals of the economic environment following peace in Vietnam have glowed with visions of tax reduction, negative income taxes, federal tax sharing with the states, and massive increases in nondefense governmental activities. However, decisions already being made are strongly shaping the nature of economic adjustments to peace. A return to the prewar dollar "base" of military spending no longer seems feasible.

One reason for this is inflation. Prices on military procurements, and wages and salaries for the armed forces and civilian employees, have increased. Under existing law, the pay of both military and civilian employees of the Pentagon is scheduled to rise by about $2 billion in mid-1969. Several large weapon systems are in early production stages and the large expenditures will come in the next year or so. They include several nuclear carriers and destroyers (about $4 to 5 billion), the Poseidon and Minuteman III missiles (about $7 billion), and the Safeguard ABM system (estimated from $5 billion to several times that amount).

Moreover, because the non-Vietnam portions of the military budget have been squeezed in recent years, considerable "catching up" is needed especially in deferred maintenance, inventory replenishment, and advanced research and development. In 1968, for example, the Department of Defense spent less money than in 1965 on research and development in army ordnance and combat vehicles (tanks, artillery, etc.) and in military science.

This is all aside from future consequences of any new decisions to bolster the nation's long-term arsenal of weapon systems. Two portents of future Congressional action are recent reports by the influential House and

Senate Committees on Armed Services. After a year of detailed study and hearings on strategic forces—those designed for all-out nuclear warfare—the Senate Committee urged, "Prompt decisions should be forthcoming for the deployment of additional and more modern weapon systems and improvements to existing weapon systems." The Committee specifically recommended rapid development of a new long-range strategic bomber, and accelerated research and development on an advanced ICBM—each of which could cost $5 billion or more to develop and produce in quantity.

The House Armed Services Committee issued a similar report on sea-power, again recommending new hardware. The committee chairman described as "irrefutable" the conclusion that the Navy's most urgent requirement is new ships (nuclear escort ships currently cost about $125 million each, and nuclear carriers more than $500 million).

In addition, a large civilian space program is being recommended for the 1970s. Simultaneous development of a permanent space station plus continued exploration of the moon—after this year's scheduled manned landing—carries a price tag of $45 billion for the next decade. And development of a commercial supersonic transport, if carried out, will cost more than $1 billion. Over the whole economic structure, meanwhile, hangs the threat of inflationary pressures—which, as of this spring, were substantial.

Hence, because of these built-in momentums, the economic environment is not conducive to easy selection of new or expanded domestic social programs, regardless of urgency. Rather, economic factors tend to indicate the need for hard choices among the many pressures for government spending. A tough-minded sense of priorities and a careful weighing of benefits against cost are very much needed.

The Contract State

H. L. NIEBURG

Here is an analysis of the deeper implications of the military-industrial complex, suggesting that our entire system of capitalism is being subtly subverted by it.

Government has become the economy's largest buyer and consumer. The government contract, improvised, ad hoc, and largely unexamined, has become an increasingly important device for intervention in public affairs, not only to procure goods and services but to achieve a variety of explicit or inadvertent policy ends—allocating national resources, organizing human efforts, stimulating economic activity, and distributing status and power. The government contract has risen to its present prominence as a social management tool since World War II, achieving in two decades a scope and magnitude that now rival simple subsidies, tariffs, taxes, direct regulation, and positive action programs in their impact upon the nature and quality of American life. This evolution has occurred quietly and gradually through a series of improvised reactions to specific problems. Its central role has been achieved without public consideration of far-reaching social and political implications. Even today there is precious little consciousness of the trend; political leaders tend to see each contract as an isolated procurement action, overlooking the general pattern. Just as federal grants-in-aid to state and local governments have (since 1933) become principal means for national integration of divided local jurisdictions, so federal contracting with private corporations is creating a new kind of economic federalism.

The government contract has made it possible to perform new tasks

From *In the Name of Science*, by H. L. Nieburg, pp. 184–99. Reprinted by permission of Quadrangle Books from *In the Name of Science* by H. L. Nieburg, copyright © 1966, 1970 by H. L. Nieburg.

deemed essential without direct additions to the size of federal government, thus preserving the alleged rights of private property and profit. But these huzzahs ignore the real ambiguity of the system that is emerging—neither "free" nor "competitive," in which the market mechanism of supply/demand (the price seeking the level which best serves overall productivity and social needs) has been abolished for key sectors of the economy, its place taken by the process of government policy and political influence. Instead of a free enterprise system, we are moving toward a government-subsidized private-profit system.

Unlike older government-fostered industries, the new contractor empire operates without the yardsticks of adequate government in-house capability or a civilian market in areas where research and development has become *the* critical procurement and the crux of the system. As described in the 1962 Bell Report: The companies involved "have the strongest incentives to seek contracts for research and development work which will give them both the know-how and the preferred position to seek later follow-on production contracts." Favored corporations that win R&D work thereafter exploit a number of special advantages: They may achieve sole-source or prime contractor status, which eliminates competition and dilutes all cost and performance evaluation. The open-end, cost-plus nature of the contract instrument, the lack of product specifications, official tolerance of spending overruns, all of which increase the total contract and fee (in a sense rewarding wasteful practices and unnecessary technical complication), permit violation of all rules of responsible control and make possible multiple tiers of hidden profits. The systems-management or prime contractor role enables favored companies to become powerful industrial brokers using unlimited taxpayer funds and contract awards to strengthen their corporate position, cartelize the contract market, and exert political influence.

In less than a decade the area surrounding Washington, D.C., has become one of the nation's major R&D concentrations. Every large corporation has found it necessary to establish field offices in proximity to NASA, the Pentagon, and Capitol Hill. Most of these new installations emphasize public relations and sales rather than research and development. The Washington area now ranks first in the nation for scientific personnel (per 1,000 population), although the major product is company promotion and politics rather than science.

The gross figures provide an index of the economic impact; the 1966 federal budget called for $23.7 billion in new obligational authority for defense and space—$11.4 billion for Defense Department procurement of hardware and control systems, $6.7 billion for R&D; $5.26 billion for NASA (virtually all R&D), and an additional $272 million for space-related R&D conducted by the Weather Bureau, the National Science Foundation, and the Atomic Energy Commission. Over 90 percent of this flows to the highly concentrated aerospace industry. Another $3.3 billion was budgeted for other kinds of R&D, making a total of $27 billion. The 1967 budget allocated more than $30 billion to aerospace. Space, defense, and R&D together now comprise the single most substantial allocation of federal funds, towering over all other programs. In the mid-1960s government R&D (excluding related procurement) stabilized between 2 and 3 percent of the GNP. Cumulative missile space spending in the decade which began in 1955 amounted to over $100 billion (Defense Department, $84 billion; NASA, $18 billion), and the remainder of the sixties will add at least an additional $125 billion. Virtually every department and agency of the federal government is involved to some extent in R&D contracting, although the Defense Department and NASA account for more than 96 percent.

The first result of this staggering outpour has been the artificial inflation of R&D costs which has enabled contractors to raid the government's own in-house resources. Officials in the lower reaches of the government bureaucracy (both civilian and military), charged with administration of contracts, find themselves dealing with private corporate officials who often were their own former bosses and continue as companions of present bosses and congressional leaders who watchdog the agencies. A contract negotiator or supervisor must deal with men who can determine his career prospects; through contacts, these industrial contractors may cause him to be passed over or transferred to a minor position in some remote bureaucratic corner, sometimes with a ceremonial drumming before a congressional committee.

The military cutbacks that characterized the Eisenhower years were accompanied by expanding military budgets, a paradox explained by the systematic substitution of private contractors to carry out historically in-house activities. This trend was heralded as a move back to "free enterprise." Government installations and factories built in World War II were sold to industry, usually at a fraction of the taxpayers' investment. Others were leased at low fees to contractors who were then given government business to make the use of these facilities profitable. In some instances government built new facilities which it leased at nominal fees. Such facilities were permitted to be used, without cost, for commercial production as well.

The splurge of mobilizing private contractors for government work occurred as a part of the unprecedented growth of the Air Force. As an offspring of the Army, the new branch lacked the substantial in-house management, engineering, and R&D capability that the Army had built into its arsenal system. The Air Force sought to leapfrog this handicap in competing for jurisdiction over new weapons systems, turning to private contractors to correct the defect. In its rapid climb during the fifties, the Air Force fostered a growing band of private companies which took over a substantial part of regular miliary operations, including maintaining air-craft, firing rockets, building and maintaining launching sites, organizing and directing other contractors, and making major public decisions. In the area of missilery, junior officers and enlisted men were subordinated to the role of liaison agents or mere custodians.

This had several bonus effects, enabling the Air Force to keep its military personnel levels down in conformity with Defense Department and administration policies, while building an enormous industrial and congressional constituency with a stake in maintaining large-scale funding of new weapons systems. The Air Force's success over her sister services during the Eisenhower years established the magic formula that all federal agencies soon imitated. It set in motion a rush to contract out practically everything that was not nailed to the floor and, in the process, it decimated the government's in-house management, engineering, and R&D capability; inflated the costs of R&D through futile contests for supremacy among contractors financed by contract funds; and as a con-sequence reduced as well the scientific and engineering resources avail-able to the civilian economy and to the universities.

The Army learned an important lesson in its struggle with the Air Force during the Thor-Jupiter controversy—that its extensive in-house engineering-management capability was a positive *disadvantage* in mo-bilizing congressional and public influence to support military missions and budgets. Private industry had provided the Air Force with a potent weapon in Congress for outflanking the Army during all the years of stra-tegic debate over missile development and the role of infantry forces in a nuclear world. In part, the Air Force lobbying instrument of the 1950s contributed importantly to overdependence by the nation on nuclear weaponry and massive retaliation as the primary security doctrine, while the complete range of subnuclear military capabilities was allowed to wither. This lesson was inscribed on the Army-Navy skin by the budget-paring knife of the Eisenhower administration and led to gradual weaken-ing of the arsenal system. In the sixties all the military services and NASA sought to parade bankers, captains of industry, local business leaders, and politicians through the halls of Congress and the White House as lobbying cadres in every new engagement.

The old research triad—government, industry, university—has vir-tually disappeared. In its place is a whole spectrum of new arrangements, such as the so-called "systems-engineering and technical direction" firms operated on a profit or nonprofit basis (for example, General Electric is employed by NASA to integrate and test all launch facilities and space vehicles, while Bellcomm, a subsidiary of American Telephone and Telegraph, is employed for engineering and management of all NASA operations; Aerospace Corporation plays a similar role for the Air Force). In between are the major corporations, universities drawing a majority of their research budgets from government, nonprofit institutions conducting pad-and-pencil studies of strategic and policy matters for government agencies, and government laboratories operated by industry or by universities.

Knitting the complex together is an elite group of several thousand men, predominantly industrial managers and brokers, who play a variety of interlocking roles—sitting on boards of directors, consulting for government agencies, serving on advisory committees, acting as managers on behalf of government in distributing and supervising subcontracts, moving between private corporations and temporary tours-of-duty in government. Private corporations have contracts to act as systems engineers and technical directors for multi-billion-dollar R&D and production activities involving hundreds of other corporations. Instead of fighting "creeping socialism," private industry on an enormous scale has become the agent of a fundamentally new economic system which at once resembles traditional private enterprise and the corporate state of facism. A mere handful of giants (such as North American Aviation, Lockheed, General Dynamics, and Thompson–Ramo–Wooldridge) holds prime contracts over more than half the total R&D and production business. In dealing with their subcontractors and suppliers, these corporations act in the role of government itself: "These companies establish procurement organizations and methods which proximate those of the government. Thus, large prime contractors will invite design competition, establish source selection bids, send out industrial survey teams, make subcontract awards on a competitive or a negotiated basis, appoint small business administrators, designate plant resident representatives, develop reporting systems to spot bottlenecks, make cost analyses of subcontractor operations, and request monthly progress and cost reports from subcontractors."

They are in the position of deciding whether or not to conduct an activity themselves or contract it out, and they may use their power over a subcontractor to acquire his proprietary information, force him to sell his company to the prime, or make or break geographical areas and individual bankers, investors, and businessmen. They may themselves create "independent" subcontractors in order to conceal profits, to keep certain proprietary information from the government, or for other purposes. Generally, they can and do use their decision-making power to stabilize their own operations, expanding or contracting their subcontracts in accordance with the peaks and troughs of government business, thus protecting their economic strength at the expense of smaller and weaker companies, seeking to assure their own growth and standing among the other giant corporations by mergers, acquisitions, and investments in the flock of companies dependent upon them for government largess.

The same top 300 companies that perform 97 percent of all federal R&D also perform 91 percent of all private R&D. Most of the private R&D is a means of maintaining the inside track for new awards in anticipated areas of government need. Since these same companies do all or most of their business with government, the so-called "private" R&D is paid for by the government in the form of overhead on other contracts. For example, the U.S. is still paying for Douglas Aircraft's investment in developing the DC-3 30 years ago. A congressional committee noted the trend:

> At the moment a small number of giant firms in a few defense and space-related areas, with their facilities located principally in three states, and engaged almost exclusively in the application of existing engineering and physical knowledge to the creation of new products and processes, receive the overwhelming preponderance of the government's multi-billion dollar research awards. . . . Clearly, if the resulting technical discoveries are permitted to remain within these narrow confines rather than be disseminated widely through the society, a disproportionate amount of the benefits will be channeled into the hands of the few and further economic concentration will take place.

The dominant centers of corporate power have largely usurped the government's evaluation and technical direction responsibilities. Frank Gibney, one of the early consultants to the House Space Committee, observed that "the spectacle of a private profit-making company rendering national decisions makes the old Dixon–Yates concept look as harmless as a Ford Foundation Research Project."[1] The government's Bell Report of 1962 expressed concern at the erosion of its ability to manage its own affairs and to retain control over contracting, which ". . . raises important questions of public policy concerning the government's role and capability and potential conflicts of interest." The proliferation of quasi-public corporations, both profit and nonprofit, springing from the soil of R&D spending (such as Bellcomm, Aerospace Corporation, or Comsat Corporation), symbolizes the bewildering innovations of the Contract State. Congressmen throw up their hands trying to understand their relations to these new organizations under the traditional dichotomy between private and public enterprise.

[1]U.S. Congress House Select Committee on Government Research, Report, *Contract Policies and Procedures for Research and Development, Study VII,* House Report No. 1942, Union Columbus No. 835. Washington, U.S. Government Printing Office, 1964. p. 58.

There is no doubt that the flow of billions of federal dollars into narrow areas of the economy tends to create a self-perpetuating coalition of vested interests. With vast public funds at hand, industries, geographical regions, labor unions, and the multitude of supporting enterprises band together with enormous manpower, facilities, and Washington contacts to maintain and expand their stake. Pork-barrel politics and alignments with federal agencies and political leaders provide a powerful political machine to keep the contract flow coming.

The pattern is already in the process of filtering down to state and local governments. In the name of preserving and utilizing the "unique" systems-engineering and management capability that NASA publicists claim as one of the space program's major benefits to the civilian economy, underemployed aerospace industrial teams are now pushing for contracts in such areas as urban traffic management and water conservation.

Adherence of the R&D contract cult to the shibboleths of free enterprise may be a cloak to conceal the fact that the sharks are eating the little fishes and that a kind of backhanded government planning, in which they participate and from which they benefit, has come to replace free enterprise. In spite of such temporary stimulants as tax-cutting and the multiplier effect of missile-space spending, the civilian economy maintains a faltering pace of growth. The aerospace industries, on the other hand, ride high on unprecedented profits and diversify their holdings, biting deep into the most succulent portions of the civilian production machine in a new wave of economic concentration. In order that their "unique capability" not be wasted, defense firms are now moving into "systems management" of Job Corps camps and national conservation programs.

The politics of corporate finance have accelerated concentration not only in the government contract market but also in the civilian market, both of which are now thoroughly interpenetrated and interlocked. The aerospace giants have built huge conglomerate empires that span both markets, and the old respectable firms are playing major roles as public contractors. Among the top hundred prime aerospace contractors are such household names as General Electric, General Motors, AT&T, Westinghouse, Chrysler, Ford, Socony–Mobil, Firestone, Philco, Goodyear, and so on. Many of the aerospace companies are mere façades and legal fictions having no individual existence but representing entities of financial and/or political convenience. In a 1965 House Judiciary Committee report, the five largest aerospace firms were cited as flagrant examples of corporate interlock. Douglas has 15 directors interlocked with managements of 17 banks and financial institutions, one insurance company, and 28 industrial-commercial corporations (including Cohu Electronics, Giannini Controls, and Richfield and Tidewater Oil Companies). Not uncommon is the pattern by which each company holds stock in its nominal competitors (Mc-

Donnell Aircraft holds a large block in the Douglas Company "as an investment"). A study of 74 major industrial-commercial companies found that 1,480 officers and directors held a total of 4,428 positions. The antitrust subcommittee staff concluded that management interlocks today are as prevalent as they were in 1914 when the Clayton Act, prohibiting interlocking directorships, was passed.

During the second half of the nineteenth century the corporation proved a powerful vehicle for mobilizing and organizing productive resources to achieve rapid economic growth made possible by burgeoning technology. Its very success, the efficiencies of bigness, and the inevitable politics of corporate empire-building thrust into American skies the spires of monopoly power. Since that time sectional and economic interests have shifted and changed, the social and technological landscape has vastly altered, and government has emerged as guarantor of social interests against the claims of private power. Government contracting on its present scale has added another dimension. Business and industry have always been close to the centers of political power, but never before in peacetime have they enjoyed such a broad acceptance of their role as a virtual fourth branch of government—a consensus generated by the permanent crisis of international diplomacy. Sheltered by this consensus, government has accepted responsibility to maintain the financial status of its private contractors as essential to U.S. defense and economic health. Cost competitiveness, the traditional safeguard against corporate power and misallocation of national resources, has been suspended by R&D contract practices.

NASA and the Pentagon use their contracting authority to broaden the productive base in one area, maintain it in another, create more capability here or there for different kinds of R&D, create competition or limit it. Under existing laws they may make special provisions for small business and depressed areas and maintain contracts for services not immediately required in order to preserve industrial skills or reserve capacity for emergency needs. All of this represents national planning. But without recognition of planning as a legitimate government responsibility, planning authority is fragmented, scattered among federal agencies and Congress, and the makeshift planning that results serves the paramount interests of the most powerful political alignments. In place of forward planning responsible to the broad national community, the nation drifts sideways, denying the legitimacy of planning, yet backhandedly planning in behalf of narrow special interests whose corridors of power are closed to public control.

The result is severe distortion in the allocation of resources to national needs. For almost three decades the nation's resources have been commanded by military needs, consolidating political and economic power behind defense priorities. What was initially sustained by emergency comes to be sustained, normalized, and institutionalized (as emergency wanes) through a cabal of vested interests. The failure of nerve on the part of these interests to redirect this magnificent machine toward a broader range of values denies the nation what may be the ultimate basis of diplomatic strength and the only means to maintain the impetus of a mature economy, namely the fullest enjoyment by all of our people of the immense bounty of equity and well-being almost within our grasp.

The shibboleths of free enterprise perpetuate a system by which, one by one, the fruits of the civilian economy fall into the outstretched hands of the aerospace group. The so-called "Great Consensus" assembled by President Johnson is based on the paradox of support from great corporate giants as well as from labor and the Liberals. The civilian economy and home-town industry have been systematically neglected in the vicious circle of government contracts and economic concentration, leading the small businessman, vast numbers of middle-management, white-collar workers, and professional groups to embrace the simple formulas of Goldwater conservatism, directing the anxieties generated by incipient stagnation against the targets of autocratic organized labor and government spending for welfare and foreign aid. The exploitation of the myths of free enterprise have deflected attention from the feudal baronies of economic power and the tendency of the administration to attack the symptoms of growing inequality of wealth without disturbing the steepening slope itself.

The dynamics of the Contract State require close scrutiny lest, in the name of national security and the science-technology race, the use of the nation's resources does violence not only to civilian enterprise but also to the body politic. In place of sensational claims about the ability of the American system to meet the challenges of new tasks and rapid technological change, it is necessary to judge the appropriateness and adequacy of national policies that increasingly raise a question concerning the relation between government and private contractor: who is serving whom?

The R&D cult is becoming a sheltered inner society isolated from the mainstream of national needs. More and more it departs from the reality principles of social accounting, insulated against realism by the nature of its contract relations with government and its political influence. The elementary principle of economics applies: whatever is made cheaper tends to grow proportionately. Massive government subsidies to R&D facilitate its expansion beyond the point of rational response to international politics; it becomes a self-perpetuating pathology, intensifying the regressive structure of the economy and making further pump-priming exertions necessary.

As the arms race slows and is sublimated in space and science, as world politics break the ice of bi-polarity and return to the troublesome but more flexible patterns of pluralism, it becomes important that great nations achieve positive values. Military power, though essential, remains essentially a limited and negative tool. Economic and social equilibrium at maximum resource use may hold the key to ultimate international stability, prestige, and national power. Federal expenditures are a response to national needs and aspirations in all areas of public responsibility. The needs and aspirations are limitless, while the resources to satisfy them are relatively scarce. Many rich societies have withered because they allocated their resources in a manner that precipitated the circular pathology of inequity and instability. "Neither Rome's great engineering skills, its architectural grandeur, its great laws, nor, in the last analysis, its gross national product, could prevail against the barbarians."

The problem of bringing the Contract State under democratic control is but a new phase of a continuing challenge in Western industrial societies. The legal fiction that holds economic and political institutions to be separate and distinct becomes ever less applicable as economic pluralism is swallowed up by corporate giantism. The myths of economic freedom tend to insulate the giants from social control, protecting their private-government status and threatening the political freedom of the majority. The tension between private and public decision-making can be a self-correcting process when its causes are visible and understood, and when public authority is not wholly capitive to the pressures of narrow interest groups. The process is delicately balanced, and there are points of no return.

How Good Is Economic Prediction?

BUSINESS WEEK

Here are two predictions as to the course of economic events during 1970. By the time you read this, one of them will have proven wrong. Which is it? Why?

Prediction One

In the heated, and sometimes bitter, debate between the Keynesians and the Chicago School, Milton Friedman and his monetarist colleagues began with one distinct advantage: Unlike the "new economists," they gave only the sketchiest of forecasts and could not be pinned to the wall by their own predictions.

In the past year or so, however, that advantage has eroded. As the Chicago School has come into vogue, monetarists have had to put themselves on record about where they think the economy is headed. And they have had to spell out in much more detail just what is supposed to happen in the black box where, according to their theory, a kick in the money supply is converted to a jump in gross national product.

Last week, the Chicago School's neck was extended full length by the fullest disclosure yet of the box's logical circuitry. The Federal Reserve Bank of St. Louis, a stronghold of monetarist thinking, published the specifications and predictions of its own econometric model, the first to be built along strict lines of the quantity theory of money. The model is an expanded version of one unveiled by the St. Louis bank 18 months ago. But where the earlier model only forecast GNP, based on assumptions about growth in the money supply, this one takes a stab at predicting real output, prices, unemployment, and interest rates.

Prediction One from "Monetarists Enter Forecasting Sweepstakes," *Business Week* (May 2, 1970), pp. 100–102. Reprinted by permission of the publisher.

The model puts the St. Louis Fed into a race which, so far, has had no winners. No econometric model has done any better at forecasting business than "judgmental" analysts using rule-of-thumb techniques. And the only reason they have performed this well is that operators change the structures of their models to make the results conform with common sense.

For those used to large econometric models, such as the one at the University of Pennsylvania's Wharton School, even the expanded St. Louis model seems pretty skimpy. While Wharton employs nearly 150 equations to forecast GNP sector by sector, St. Louis uses only eight and limits itself to predicting broad aggregates.

The St. Louis model is abstract by design. It omits almost all of the human variables on which Keynesians can at least speculate to envision a rosier future amenable to the decisions of policymakers. For the monetarists, however, the cold figures spell out a kind of economic predestination. Once the values of a handful of variables have been determined, the mechanism inexorably grinds out the answers.

Actually, the St. Louis model does not try to forecast; it simulates the future. Rather than attempting to second-guess the Federal Reserve Board's monetary policy, the model presents three different paths the economy could travel in the next two years, assuming three different rates of growth in the money supply (narrowly defined as currency plus demand deposits).

What comes out, for the immediate future, is a picture of such unremitting pessimism that even the model's builders hope its predictions are off target. It sees no chance of avoiding some sort of recession this year, a conclusion that any monetarist would reach on the basis of last year's static money supply. But, more ominously, it sees no prospect over the next two years of either ending inflation or reducing interest rates by anything short of an economic downturn of classic proportions.

On the price side, the best the St. Louis model sees is a drop in the GNP deflator to 1.9 percent by the end of 1971, a rate of inflation close to the Nixon Administration's target. But this happens only if the economists assume zero growth in the money supply, a track that takes real output steadily downward and produces a 7.7 percent unemployment rate.

The best track for employment, produced by a constant 6 percent annual rate of growth in the money stock, still has the jobless rolls creeping upward to 5.7 percent by the end of 1971. Prices would be rising by 3.8 percent, and the triple-A corporate bond rate would be a high 7.2 percent.

The model's middle way, generated by a 3 percent annual increase in the money supply, has little except compromise to recommend it: a recession that bottoms out at the end of this year, followed by a sluggish recovery that keeps unemployment climbing to 6.7 percent and inflation declining only gradually.

These conclusions result from a combination of two elements. One is the quantity theory of money, which says that there is a mechanical relationship between changes in the money supply and changes in current dollar GNP. The other is an analysis of the way real output, prices, and interest rates respond to changes in money demand which leans heavily on the theories of such "classical" economists as David Ricardo and Irving Fisher.

By making these relationships explicit and trying to quantify them, the St. Louis model underscores some essential differences between the Chicago School and the Keynesians that tend to get blurred in the debate over whether it is the money supply or the federal budget that determines the direction in which the economy will go.

Conceptually, Keynesians start from the bottom and work up. They see GNP as the sum of various expenditures for personal consumption, investment, and government programs. Forecasting for the "new economists," even with econometric models, is essentially a sophisticated counting exercise that tries to predict the sum of individual spending decisions.

The economy looks distinctly different to the monetarists. They start from the top and work down. First of all, the amount of money the banking system makes available determines total spending, they say. Given this "money demand" (measured by GNP in current dollars), underlying economic forces decide how it is allocated between real output and inflation. This is where predestination comes in.

The monetarists argue that national economic managers can have little impact over the long run on actual output or employment. In the short run, the Federal Reserve System can play with aggregate money demand like a puppet on a string. Any speedup or slowdown in the growth rate of the money supply will have to be reflected by corresponding change in GNP, measured in current dollars. But whether this produces a change in real GNP will depend on price changes, which are independently determined.

For the Wharton and other Keynesian models, a forecast of current dollar GNP is the end product of dozens of interacting equations. For St. Louis, it is a simple calculation: An increase of $1 in money stock yields an increase of $5.57 in GNP over the next four quarters. The exact mechanism by which this happens remains obscure. The figure was derived from past data; in this sense, the St. Louis model offers no more than a glimpse into the black box.

The St. Louis bank does treat federal spending as one element in determining the direction of business. But, unlike the Keynesians, who see a change in government expenditures behind almost every turn of the business cycle, it thinks the net effect is minimal. The model's spending equation includes a measure of the federal budget as one of its two variables. A rise in federal outlays will have a positive effect in the first six months, with a dollar's increase in the full-employment budget yielding about a dollar's increase in GNP. This gain, however, is almost completely offset in the following three quarters as government expenditures "crowd out" private spending, unless monetary policy changes to allow both to expand. The St. Louis model can thus pretty well ignore the federal budget and simply predict what will happen under alternative courses of monetary policy.

With zero growth in the money stock for the rest of this year, GNP for 1970 would work out to $967.3 billion, about as low as the most pessimistic of current forecasts—which generally are more bearish the closer they get to Chicago. With a 3 percent growth rate, gross national product would be $972.7 billion. But, St. Louis says unless the Federal Reserve went wild with generosity—or panic—it could not produce the $985-billion GNP predicted by the Council of Economic Advisers.

This represents a consensus of monetarist thinking. At his University of Chicago office, Milton Friedman concedes that if the second quarter is a turning point, the money school will have some heavy explaining to do. "But," he says, "I don't see any sign that things are picking up."

Intramural disagreement comes in at the next stage of the model, where the St. Louis economists try to predict how nominal gains in GNP will be divided into real output and prices. All other econometric models have failed repeatedly at this point and other monetarists are generally skeptical about whether St. Louis has found the secret.

Here again, the monetary model is a mirror image of the Keynesian versions. The standard models estimate real and current dollar GNP more or less independently and subtract one from the other to get changes in the price level.

St. Louis' model predicts price change directly and treats real output at least in the short run, as a residual.

The bank uses only two variables to predict prices. First, it calculates "demand pressure"—a measure of changes in the preceding four quarters in the gap between real output and what the economy is capable of producing with its resources fully employed. Then, it feeds in "anticipated prices," measured by a weighted average of price increases over the preceding 16 quarters. In the short run, anticipated prices are by far the strongest force. And what gives the model its distinctly bleak outlook is that the period over which it calculates this factor corresponds precisely with the duration of the current inflation.

As the Chicago School sees it, the level of price increase that people have come to expect is an independent variable underlying all major economic decisions. With the economy at full employment, the monetarists argue, prices will not necessarily be stable but keep moving at the rate people have come to anticipate. Once inflationary psychology has taken hold, prices will stop rising only after an extended period of economic sluggishness.

The crucial point, then, is how rapidly people form—and reform—price expectations. St. Louis model builders admit that their anticipated price equation is on shaky empirical ground. "No one has any good notion about how expectations are formed," says staff economist Keith Carlson. The lag structure is derived from recent work on the behavior of long-term interest rates. These, according to classical theory, respond directly to price changes.

For this reason, the St. Louis model's interest rate projections show a pessimism that directly parallels its price predictions. They are different sides of the same coin. Almost every economist fervently hopes it will turn out to be counterfeit.

Prediction Two

Last November, the econometric forecasting model at the University of Pennsylvania's Wharton School announced that the U.S. had just moved into what it perceived to be a benign recession. It predicted that gross national product, after adjustment for price increases, would decline in 1969's fourth quarter. And, although it forecast further drops this quarter and next, the model did expect an upturn to get under way after midyear.

Now, with three more months of statistics under its belt, the computer confidently sticks to its guns and predicts no major recession for 1970. Moreover, thanks in part to some mathematical refinements, it predicts a lower rate of inflation than it did before.

Wharton's 1970 GNP forecast has been shaved to $974 billion in current-dollar terms, down from $980-billion three months ago. This is close to the low end of the range of predictions on record so far for this year. The model now sees the GNP price deflator rising at a modest 3 percent annual rate in the second half of 1970. (Last quarter, this price index rose at a 4.6 percent annual rate.)

After adjusting for higher prices, Wharton's computer still sees the economy starting off the year in reverse. Real GNP will fall another $1 billion or so this quarter, and then drop by around $800 million in the second. But the model foresees a sharp pickup after midyear—enough to lift real growth for the year as a whole up about one-half of 1 percent from 1969's level. As a result, the unemployment rate will rise to about 4.5 percent by midyear, then inch down. The 1970 average comes out to

Prediction Two from "Wharton's Model Says It Again," *Business Week* (February, 1970), p. 33. Reprinted by permission of the publisher.

4.2 percent—just about what Federal Reserve Chairman Arthur F. Burns and Council of Economic Advisers Chairman Paul W. McCracken have been predicting.

When it comes to profits, the model is still gloomy. On a quarter-to-quarter basis, corporate profits before taxes are expected to drop this quarter, and again in the second. And while a pickup is expected after midyear, comparisons with year-ago levels (the basis most businessmen use to assess their earnings performance) will not show pluses until a year from now.

The industries that will really feel pain as the economy moves deeper into the valley are those that specialize in durables. Auto expenditures will not really improve all this year, while housing will recover only sluggishly. And although capital goods outlays will grow this quarter, they are then slated to decline in each succeeding quarter as far ahead as the Wharton model can see.

Can Private Industry Abolish Slums?

MICHAEL HARRINGTON

The following article is a slightly revised version of testimony presented by the author of *The Other America* at a hearing of the National Commission on Urban Problems.

Many well-intentioned Americans are deceiving themselves and the public when they speak of abolishing the slums. The slums can be abolished, but not in the way they suggest.

A number of programs have been proposed to end the scandal of inhuman housing for the poor. I specifically want to address myself to the theory that some kind of partnership between government and the private sector will solve the problem, because I believe that this theory is an illusion. It will not work.

Although my analysis is radical, it can be documented in the official statements of the United States government.

The Council of the White House Conference on Civil Rights said that the United States must build 2 million housing units a year, with at least 500,000 especially designed for the poor, if it is going to live up to its responsibilities.

President Johnson this year proposed building 165,000 low-cost housing units, or 335,000 less than the White House Conference minimum. If past experience is any guide, the actual number constructed will come to a bit over 30,000, or a deficit of 470,000 units.

Moreover, none of the proposals now being discussed come near to the required number. For example, Senator Robert Kennedy's approach is clearly motivated by great compassion, yet it would only provide 400,000 units over seven years through a $1.5 billion tax subsidy to private enterprise.

From *Dissent*, 1 (Jan.-Feb., 1968), pp. 4–6. Reprinted by permission of the publisher.

There can be no creative federalist panacea, enlisting business in a social crusade, that will deal with this problem. The corporate sector, as Mr. David Rockefeller testified with great candor before the Ribicoff Subcommittee, is concerned with making money. Banks, and other business institutions, will only invest funds if they are going to get a return.

Yet the slums are, in business terms, a bad risk. Until August of 1967, the FHA excluded blighted areas from its mortgage insurance programs on the grounds that such undertakings were "economically unsound." I assume that the bloodshed in Detroit motivated the revision of this policy in August 1967. A governmental agency can thus decide, in the name of public social priorities, to make an "uneconomic" investment of money. A private enterprise will not and cannot.

Nor can this problem be dealt with by providing public subsidies to private builders. All such proposals now before the country—from Senators Percy and Robert Kennedy among others—are designed to operate on a publicly supported profit principle. Yet even with this federal support through tax incentives or artificial interest rates, every one of these suggestions ends up providing housing for families with incomes well over $4,000 a year.

There is certainly a need to give governmental support to the housing needs of people with incomes between $4,000 and $8,000. It is one of the great postwar scandals that lavish, but discrete, subsidies have been provided for the homes of the middle class and the rich in the form of cheap, federally guaranteed credit, income tax deductions, and other genteel doles which effectively exclude everyone with income of less than $8,000 from the benefits.

But the fact remains that the Kennedy and Percy proposals, if the published reports of their rent levels are correct, would not provide any housing for the poor and the almost-poor. The rents would be too high for, among others, the majority of Negroes in the United States.

And even if some way were found to bring the private sector into the slums, it could not and should not play the leading role. It is precisely the commercial calculus of land value that has exacerbated our crisis and can hardly solve it. As Mayor Lindsay's task force on urban design reported to him, beauty, charm, and history cannot compete with office buildings, and even a venerable structure like the Plaza Hotel will be torn down if present trends continue. Within the framework of such an "economic" approach, one builds most cheaply and profitably, while social and aesthetic considerations are secondary.

The issue raised here is simple: Who is going to design the "second America" President Johnson tells us we must build between now and the year 2000? We must construct more housing units than now exist. How? I submit that businessmen, whatever other qualifications they have, are not competent to design a new civilization and, in any case, have no democratic right to do so. The fundamental decisions on what America shall look like and what life in it will be like should be made by the people. And this is particularly important in the case of the slum poor, who have been excluded from the making of every important decision in the nation.

In arguing thus, I do not want to suggest that there is no role for the private sector. It is just that the social and aesthetic choices—those "uneconomic" options—must be democratically planned and, because of the logic of money-making, publicly financed. Then, and only then, can the companies and corporations contract to carry out the public will; but they should not determine it.

The necessity of such innovation cannot be evaded by magic schemes for "rehabilitation." The worst of our urban slums are criminally overcrowded. To rehabilitate them successfully would mean removing half to three-quarters of the people now living there to new housing. Moreover, the rehabilitation formulas often take the reality of segregation as a given.

I believe that our present crisis allows this country a marvelous opportunity to promote racial integration.

In fact if not in theory, our postwar housing has financed segregated, white suburbs. Now that the government has officially recognized that we must more than double the present supply of housing in the next third of a century, there is the possibility of reversing this ugly policy. There should not be one federal cent for "new towns," either outside of the present metropolitan areas or within them, that are not designed to promote racial integration.

And this points up the need for new public institutions of democratic planning. Our post-war housing deficit is not measured in simple terms of our scandalous discrimination in favor of the rich and against the poor; it is a matter of the failure of the democratic imagination as well. Without thought of social or aesthetic consequences, we have proliferated superhighways and suburbs and made slums more miserable, employment more distant for the poor, old age more lonely for those left behind in the central city, and so on.

There is obviously no simple solution to such a complex crisis. But we should start immediately by adopting Senator Ribicoff's proposal of last January and spend approximately a billion dollars on finding out what we want to do. This would be a wiser investment, as the Senator suggested, than the present Model Cities program. (The monies which Ribicoff spoke of were the $287 million budgeted for three years of the Demonstration City program.) We cannot go on forever "demonstrating" techniques and leaving the main problem areas untouched.

And in the process of such a massive planning expenditure, every level of American society should be involved in the debate. I do not say this simply out of democratic conviction or populist sentimentality. For I am convinced that where decisions on public subsidy are made at high levels of expertise, there the priorities of money, rather than those of society, prevail. There is only one way of establishing the social and aesthetic values which will guide the "uneconomic" expenditure of money. That is through democracy.

In summary, we know that we have to build 500,000 units of housing for the poor every year. We are not doing so.

In market terms, business cannot be expected to go into the job of slum eradication because it is a bad risk.

Even if the market terms are modified by federal subsidy, as in various proposals now before the nation, all the poor and the majority of Negroes would be effectively excluded from the benefits.

There must, therefore, be an "uneconomic" investment of public funds motivated by considerations of social and aesthetic values rather than by a calculus of private profit.

In this process, the private sector must play a subordinate role as the contractor for the popular will. For the basic decisions involved are not susceptible to business priorities and even hostile to them. These are issues in the public sector of American life.

Moreover, the urban crisis *allows* the country a chance to use federal funds to promote, rather than, as has been the case until now, to thwart racial integration.

Finally, the enormous undertaking I outline here clearly requires new public institutions for democratic planning. There is no other way to design a new civilization.

Economics and Ecosystems

JON BRESLAW

The problem of ecology has emerged as one of the main challenges of our time. Here is an economic analysis of how its challenges can be met.

The American economy can be best represented by the concept of a competitive market. If one regards the market as a black box, then there are two processes which do not come within the market's sphere of influence—inputs and outputs. The inputs are raw materials, or resources, used in the economy—air, water, metals, minerals, and wood. The outputs are the residuals—sewage, trash, carbon dioxide and other gases released to the atmosphere, radioactive waste and so on. We shall consider the residuals first.

The environment has a certain limited capability to absorb wastes without harmful effects. Once the ambient residuals rise above a certain level, however, they become unwanted inputs to other production processes or to final consumers. The size of this residual in fact is massive. In an economy which is closed, the weight of residuals ejected into the environment is about equal to the weight of input materials, plus oxygen taken from the atmosphere. This result, while obvious upon reflection, leads to the surprising and even shocking corollary that the disposal of residuals is as large an operation, in sheer tonnage, as basic materials production. This incredible volume has to be disposed of. It is at this stage that the market process breaks down.

If the functioning of the economy gave rise to incentives, such as prices, which fully reflected the costs of disposing of residuals, such incentives would be very much in point. This would be especially true if the

80

incentives fully reflected costs to the overall society associated with the discharge of the residuals to the environment. But it is clear that, whatever other normative properties the functioning of a market economy may have, it does not reflect these costs adequately.

Market economies are effective instruments for organizing production and allocating resources, insofar as the utility functions are associated with two-party transactions. But in connection with waste disposal, the utility functions involve third parties, and the automatic market exchange process fails.

Thus the need to see man's activities as part of an ecosystem becomes clear. The outputs from the black box go through other black boxes and become inputs again. If our black box is putting out too much and overloading the system, one can only expect trouble—and that is what one gets.

If we look at a particular production process, we find that there is a flow of goods or services that consumers or businesses get whether they want it or not. An upstream river may be polluted by an industry, and the downstream user cannot usually control the quality of the water that he gets. If the polluted water wipes out a fishing industry, then there is some cost (the profit that used to be made by the fishing industry) that does not appear on the balance sheet of the upstream user. Similarly, there may be benefits involved—the upstream user may use the stream for cooling, and the hot water may support an oyster farm downstream.

The activities of an economic unit thus generate real effects that are external to it. These are called externalities. A society that relies completely on a decentralized decision-making system in which significant externalities occur, as they do in any society which contains significant concentrations of population and industrial activities, will find that certain resources are not used optimally.

The tool used by economists, and others, in determining a course of action in making social decisions is the technique of cost-benefit analysis. The basis is to list all the consequences arising from a course of action, such as building a new freeway, and to make estimates of the benefits or costs to the community of all these consequences. This is done in terms of money values and a balance is drawn up, which is compared with similar estimates of the consequences of alternative decisions, such as building a rapid transit network or doing nothing. The sensible decision is to go ahead with those projects where the benefits come out best, relative to the costs. The art of cost-benefit analysis lies in using the scanty information available to assign money values to these costs and benefits. Differences in house prices are a way of getting at noise valuation. Time is obviously worth money: how much can be estimated by looking at what people do when they have a choice between a faster and more expensive way of going from A to B and a slower but cheaper way?

Going back to our slaughtered fish, if the cost of reducing pollution by 50 percent were less than the profit that could be realized from fishing at this level of pollution, then it makes sense to spend that amount. In fact, the level of pollution should be reduced until the marginal cost of reducing pollution (the cost of reducing pollution by a very small amount) is just equal to the marginal revenue from fishing (the extra revenue that is received as a result of that amount less pollution). The question is, where there is no market, how does one get to this state of affairs?

Method One is to internalize the problem so that a single economic unit will take account of all of the costs and benefits associated with the external effects. To do this, the size of the economic unit has to be increased. A good example of this is where one has several fisheries for one limited species of fish, e.g., whales. If the fisheries operate separately, each concern takes as many as it can, regardless of the effect on the total catch. If the fisheries were to act in unison, then the maximum catch compatible with a stable population of whales would be taken, and no more—the externalities would have been internalized. Unfortunately, waste products are often so widely propagated in nature and affect so many diverse interests that the merger route is not feasible.

Method Two is the one mostly used at the moment: the use of regulations set up by the government and enforceable by law. There are many examples of these: minimum net hole size in fishing, parking regulations on busy streets, limited number of flights at airports during the night, zoning regulations as applied to land use, and certain water quality laws for industrial and municipal river users. Ideally, these regulations would take into account the different nature of the environmental difficulty, varying both over place and time, e.g., high and low flows in streams, windy days for smoke control, etc. There are two main objections to such regulations. In the first place, they are often difficult to enforce, especially if there are high monetary returns involved and the likelihood of being caught is small—flushing oil tanks in the English Channel. The other objection is more sophisticated: in a competitive market the imposition of regulations does not normally lead to the best use of resources. It is better to do this by means of pricing, since this method makes it possible to balance incremental costs and gains in a relatively precise manner. Also, regulations do not provide the funds for the construction and operation measures of regional scope, should these prove economical.

Method Three involves the legal system and the law of nuisance. Thus when there is an oil spill on your shore and you and your property get covered in goo, then in such an obvious and easy case one would expect prompt damages—but ask the residents of Santa Barbara what they think of courts and oil companies. Thus, though in theory the courts provide a solution, in practice, they are slow and inefficient.

Method Four involves the paying of some monetary rent in order to get the practice of pollution stopped. One way is to pay a producer to stop polluting. Although such payments would be received favorably by the industries involved, the sheer size of the total payments necessary as a means of preventing pollution would put an impossible strain on any budget, and such a solution is only feasible for "special case" industrial operations. Moreover, if a steel mill is discharging its waste into a river, without charge, it is producing steel that is artificially cheap. Paying the mill to stop pollution does nothing to get the steel price back to its rightful value (i.e., when all costs are met) in the short run. In the long run, this remains true only if the assumption of a competitive market is weakened.

Another way to implement Method Four would be to charge a polluter for the pollution that he causes. Examples of such charges or taxes would be a tax on sewage effluents which is related to the quality and quantity of the discharge; or a surcharge on the price of fuels with a high sulfur content which is meant to take account of the broader cost to society external to the fuel-using enterprise. This procedure is one usually favored by economists, since it uses economic incentives to allocate the resources (the waste assimilative capacity of the environment) similar to those generated where market mechanisms can balance costs and returns. The revenue from these charges can be used to finance other antipollution facilities.

The use of charges for the wasted assimilative capacity of the environment implies that you have to pay in order to put things out of the black box. Before the environment's waste assimilative capacity was overloaded, it was not used to its full capacity. A resource which is not fully utilized has a zero price; once it is utilized it receives a positive price—which is why charges now have to be imposed. From an ecological point of view this is very good, since now that one has to pay to get rid of a product, it means that this product has a value attached to it, albeit negative. The effect is to restructure industrial processes to take this into account. A society that allows waste dischargers to neglect the offsite costs of waste disposal will not only devote too few resources to the treatment of waste, but will also produce too much waste in view of the damage it causes. Or more simply, if you charge for waste disposal, industries will produce less waste, and the wastes produced will often find use in some other process—recycling. A paper-producing company using the sulphite method will find it advantageous to change to the sulphate method through increased effluent charges. In England, many firms have found profitable uses for waste products when forced to stop polluting. In a few instances, mostly in already depressed areas, plants may be capable of continuing operation only because they are able to shift all or most of that portion of production costs associated with waste disposal to other economic units. When this situation is coupled with one in which the plant is a major part of the employment base of a community, society may have an interest in assisting the plant to stay in business, while at the same time controlling the external costs it is imposing. However, these would be special cases which are used to help the adjustment to the new position of equilibrium rather than change the position of the new equilibrium.

Just such an operation has been used in the Ruhr Valley in Germany, starting in 1913. The political power of the Ruhrverband lies in the governing board made up of owners of business and other facilities in the Ruhrverband area, communities in the area, and representatives of the waterworks and other water facilities. It has built over 100 waste-treatment plants, oxidation lakes, and waterworks facilities. Capital came from the bond market, and operating expenses from a series of charges contingent on the amount and quality of the effluent discharged by the industries and municipalities in the region. This scheme is so successful that, though the Ruhr River flows through one of the most heavily industrialized regions of Germany, one can find ducks living on it. Shed tears for the Potomac.

The inputs to our black box consist of renewable resources, such as food and water, and nonrenewable ones such as minerals and land. In considering free resources, it was stated that in a decentralized competitive market economy such resources are not used optimally. In fact, they are overutilized—rivers are overutilized as disposal units, hence pollution; roads are utilized above their intended capacity with resultant traffic snarl-ups. The same holds true for nonrenewable resources: they are not used optimally.

Given a fixed technology, at any time in the past we would have run into a critical condition with respect to our supplies of minerals and metals. It is only changing technology, which makes for the profitable extraction of pretechnical-change unprofitable deposits, that has enabled us to manage without really bad shortages. Hence, the present rate of extraction is only justifiable in the belief of future technical progress. Yet this is just the assumption that is now undergoing examination. In the past, man's technical progress was a function of man's incentive and ingenuity; now, however, he has to take into account another factor—the ability of the environment to accept his ravages.

As any child will comment, on observing the empty beer cans and discarded packets lying on the roadside and around "beauty spots," this is wrong. It is wrong because we do not put sufficient value on the natural resource—the countryside—to keep it clean. It is wrong for the same reason a second time: we do not put sufficient value on the natural resources—aluminum, plastic, paper or whatever—so that when we have used them for their original purposes, they are disposed of, as rapidly as possible.

The conclusion is clear: both our renewable and nonrenewable resources are not being used optimally.

Take a specific example—oil. What are the factors that determine its price? As usual, demand is a decreasing function of price, and supply an increasing function. The point of intersection dictates the price and quantity sold. When the optimal use of oil is considered, there are two points of view that have to be taken into account. One is the value of the oil to future generations, and the other is the social cost of the use of the oil.

In considering future generations, optimal behavior will take place in a competitive economy (with private ownership) if the private rate of return is the same as the social rate of return. In noneconomic terms, all this means is that the rate at which the future is discounted by individuals is the same as the rate at which it is discounted by society. There is dispute on this point—that is, whether the two rates are equal or not. However, even if they are, because the individual companies seek to maximize their private benefit, like in the fisheries example, the total exploration of the resources is likely to not be optimal.

At this stage, government comes into the picture. On the conservation side, a scientifically determined MER—maximum efficient rate (of oil flow)—is determined for a particular site. The main effect of this is to stop large fluctuations in the price of oil. Since half the total revenue of oil companies goes into the discovery and development of new deposits, this produces a high overhead cost. In the U.S., the aim is to produce as large a growth in the GNP as possible, subject to constraints (inflation, full employment, balance of payments, etc.). Hence the tradition of allowing industries to write off the cost of capital equipment against tax, since new capital stimulates the economy (investment) and makes for more efficient production. The oil industry felt that the same principal should apply to its capital costs—the rent it pays on oil deposits. Hence the oil depletion allowance, which allows the costs of rents to be partially offset against profits. The effect of this is to move the supply curve to the right—which results in more oil being sold at a lower price. Thus it encourages oil companies to extract more oil and find new deposits. This is great from a military point of view, but disastrous when the effect of such exploitation of the environment is considered: oil spills at sea, the probably permanent scarring of the tundra in Alaska, and smog in our cities. Yet this is exactly what is meant by social costs, the externalities which do not get considered in the market price.

If the oil depletion allowances were removed or sharply reduced, the oil producing industry could not continue to function at its accustomed level of operation and maintain its accustomed price structure. Similar considerations apply to minerals (mineral depletion allowance). Yet this is only the first step. Another method that would produce the same desired results would be to make the extractor pay for the quantity of mineral or metal that he mines, just as he should pay for the right to discard his waste. This solves a whole lot of problems—by making the original substance more expensive, the demand is reduced, be it for power-using dishwashers, oil-eating automobiles, or resource-demanding economies. Moreover, these products, being more expensive, will not be discarded, but recycled, thus solving in part a pollution problem, as well as a litter problem (if they can be separated). By recycling, there will be less demand for the minerals or metals from the mining companies, since there is this new source of these materials.

To a certain extent, this view of things is recognized. In England, one of the proposals considered for solving the problem of scrapped cars around the countryside was to charge an extra twenty-five pounds on the price of each new car. This would be refundable when the vehicle was brought in for scrapping—a bit like returnable bottles. In the U.S., the use of natural gas as boiler fuel was recognized as an inferior use of an exhaustible resource. "One apparent method of preventing waste of gas is to limit the uses to which it may be put, uses for which another more abundant fuel may serve equally well" (Supreme Court, 1961). This same result could have been achieved by charging the gas producer for the quantity of gas that he took (as well as rent to the owner of the gas deposit for the right to extract gas from his property). The prices that should be charged, like the prices charged for sewage disposal, vary from location to location and depend upon the characteristics of the environment. The price should be high enough to make recycling, if physically possible, both a feasible and desirable process. If the use of the resources causes some social cost—like air pollution—then this should be reflected in the price. So too should the relative scarcity of the resource, compared to substitutable alternatives, be a consideration.

If the socioeconomic system fails to change quickly enough to meet changing conditions, then it is incumbent on the people to facilitate such change.

A prerequisite to any lasting solution to environmental pollution is a zero growth rate—the birth rate equaling the death rate. However, a stable population produces a difficult economic problem in an economy like that of the United States. To remain healthy (to stay the same size or grow), the economy needs a growing market, since only in a growing market can the capital goods sector remain efficient, given present technology. At first sight, then, the achievement of a stable population is linked to a recession. One might make the assumption that a growing market could still be achieved by allowing per capita consumption to increase at the same rate as the growth of the GNP. However, with restrictions on extraction industries, this will probably not provide a total solution. The slack is more likely to be made up by producing a different type of service—education at regular periods throughout one's life, the move from cities to smaller communities and the investment involved in such a move, the rebuilding (or destruction) of old cities compatible with their new uses. Put another way, the economic slack that will have to be taken up to avoid a depression gives us the opportunity to plan for the future, without worrying about providing for an expanding population.

The essential cause of environmental pollution is overpopulation, combined with an excessive population growth rate; other antipollution measures can be used temporarily, but so long as the central problem is not solved, one can expect no lasting success.

A New Left Critique of Economics

MICHAEL ZWEIG

Here is a critique, not directed against specific economic problems, but against economics itself. It is interesting to compare Zweig's strictures with those in the introductory essay to this book.

A new left critique of economics begins with a critique of contemporary American society. We see that the United States is, and has been for a long time, fundamentally racist and imperialist. Racism has sometimes changed in style and imperialism has sometimes fastened upon new objects to dominate, but their fundamental presence in America shapes our view of the world and our expectations and demands of economics.

Many of us began our studies of the economy after sensing that there is much wrong with America. Others had been economists in various capacities before realizing and rejecting some of the fundamental premises of the American social order. We come together in our attempts to understand America, the more effectively to change it radically. We find that standard economic analysis is not helpful in understanding the United States and how it might be changed.

Our charge against economics is precisely that it is at best not helpful to the construction of a decent society, and at worst supportive of the present order. There are a number of specific characteristics of economic procedure and substance which we find pernicious.

Our dissatisfaction with marginalism goes beyond the practical issues raised in, say, the Lester–Machlup debates in the *American Economic Review* after World War II, or the issues so caustically raised by Veblen. Marginalism is appropriate as a technique under two fundamental conditions: (1) scarcity; (2) a desire for maximization (or minimization). Mar-

From Michael Zweig, "A New Left Critique of Economics." Reprinted with permission of the author and the Union for Radical Political Economics, Inc.

ginal analysis is legitimate only as long as the fundamental character of the thing being analyzed is legitimate. We recognize that marginal calculus is a powerful tool for formal analysis of the traditional class of microeconomic problems, but we belive that a dedication to marginal analysis has kept economists from dealing systematically with important questions of American economic institutions and relations, not the least of which concerns their legitimacy.

Without denying that many resources are in fact scarce and that marginalist techniques might be useful to technical solutions of some particular problems faced by poor and oppressed peoples, it is important to answer Galbraith, Theobald and others who ask if this scarcity is not itself manufactured by industry and advertising in the quest for consumerism. Who will be the economists helping to undo the artificial rat-race? Who will be the operations-analysts in the hippie communities? Who will analyze a world in which more stuff is *not* better? In the absence of effective scarcity marginalism loses its relevance.

Marginalist analysis can be pernicious as well as irrelevant. The spirit of marginalism is one of small adjustments on the periphery of some large aggregate whose fundamental and overall character is not an issue. (This spirit is particularly well suited to the bureaucratic mind.) But the larger questions are almost never asked. The spirit of marginalism is ill suited to radical questioning of the precepts of economic and social arrangements, and it is equally ill suited to deep, revolutionary change. Its political analog is reformism and lesser-of-two-evils politics. Reform may be good. A marginal adjustment may be good. But it may be best to construct a whole new order based on wholly new institutional arrangements. Those committed to marginalist thinking are intellectually (and even emotionally) incapable of handling these larger questions. This is why we think that marginalism is fundamentally counter-revolutionary.

Maximization subject to constraint is central to much of economic analysis. Aside from the marginalist procedure discussed above, the very concept of economic man's response to constraint is counter-revolutionary. Economic man will do the most he can within limits imposed upon him. More likely, we think, in many social circumstances one recognizes constraints imposed externally, and one sets out to remove the constraint before doing anything else. Decision making may always have to be done subject to constraint, but orthodox economics supports a social order based upon a population whose rationality (sanity?) is measured by the extent to which it is willing to accept those particular existing constraints and values and to play by other people's rules. This is consistent with an elitist, manipulated society, such as contemporary America—the kind of society we seek to change.

The one branch of economics which purports to deal with how

"good" a situation is also belongs to microeconomics theory. There are a number of theorems in welfare economics designed to prove that competitive equilibria are best from a welfare standpoint. These theorems have been challenged in a number of ways, largely on the grounds that the perfectly competitive markets on which the theorems depend do not exist. The theory of second best, in its several variants, tries to extend welfare analysis to more real world situations in which imperfections are included, but the results become indeterminate, so far as is known.

The central problem with welfare theory lies not in these practical difficulties. With clever work a solution to the technical problem may be found. But then what will we have? Will we know how to make a good world? No. But we might if the premises on which the analysis proceeds were reflective of human decency. One of the postulates of welfare economics is that utilities are independent. What I want and like cannot be influenced at all by knowledge of what anyone else, friend or foe, likes or wants. Economists have acknowledged that this postulate is unsatisfactory. Samuelson notes that people do not behave this way, but reassures us that "many of the conclusions of welfare economics will remain valid." Which will be spared and which not has never been systemically analyzed.

That this postulate is not a very good reflection of a lot of people is not so important, since some degree of abstraction and generalization is necessary. It is an unacceptable basis for analysis of "welfare" because it posits a world of wholly selfish and isolated people, a world in which it does seem that satisfaction can be at most marginal. Given such a postulate it is foolish and inconsistent to construct theorems concerning equity and other matters of fundamentally interpersonal concern. Economists have postulated a rotten world and have set about to see under what circumstances it might be good, subject to the unchallenged constraining postulate which makes it rotten to begin with. Welfare economists are living contradictions, all by themselves.

Welfare economics is effectively silent on the questions which we think are crucial to human welfare. What are the economic principles and institutions which would provide the continuance of life to everyone as a matter of right, not privilege based on income? How long can economists calmly note that the distributions of income and wealth are, alas, irrelevant, to the characteristics of economic welfare optima? What is "welfare" if it has nothing to do with equity, and what have economists to say about equity? What are the theoretical and policy implications of Proudhon's correct observation, at least as applied to much of contemporary America, that property is theft?

The U.S. economy is deeply rooted in a set of institutions and values peculiar to our own culture. The bulk of literature in the development field, and virtually all of the practical work in various countries by U.S.

economists, follows from the proposition that to develop, a country must adopt American standards and sensitivities. Much of the work reflects or tries to create economic and social institutions specific to the U.S. experience. Development plans seem always to tie the developing country economically and politically to the United States through trade schemes as well as by fostering Western ideology in the third world.

We reject this ethnocentric view of development for both technical and political reasons. Insistent imposition of U.S. standards and institutions fails to recognize the potential for amassing energy for development present in indigenous institutions or in models of the socialist or other heterodox variety. Western technology is generally inappropriate to third world countries, given the character of specialized labor and the extent of the market in such economies. But the presence of western institutions and technology is consistent with and part of U.S. imperialism, the effort to control the economic and social order of countries around the world. Development economists might do more for development and for freedom if they stopped trying to devise more sophisticated ways of imposing American intitutions and values onto other countries and spent their time instead understanding and expunging imperialism.

The government has only recently been recognized as a major economic actor along with consumers and investors. Although economists have theories about the effects each of these actors has on the others, and itself, we have no well defined theory of the state to explain its economic motivation and character. Economists say little explicitly about the nature of government decision making, deferring to political scientists. It is increasingly clear that the U.S. government acts in the economy to stabilize the social order, ostensibly in the "national interest." This 20th-century liberal view of government is challenged among economists principally by Milton Friedman and others of the "Chicago school." We too challenge this concept of government, although sometimes for reasons different from those offered by the Chicago school.

There is no such thing as the "national interest." Only people have interests, and within the nation there are conflicting interests. Any particular economic policy of the government serves some economic interest group and our understanding of the policy is incomplete until we know whose interests it serves. "The national interest" is used to camouflage the particular effects of many kinds of programs. It should be integral to the function of economists whose interests lie in policy areas to see through the camouflage and report on the political economy of the country as well as on the technical economic mechanics of various programs and policies. For example, part of knowing the economics of reserve currency status should be knowing whose particular interests such a policy serves in the United States and abroad, and whose interests would be served by going to, say, freely fluctuating rates after abandoning the reserve status of the dollar.

The notion of stability has entered into the center of economic analysis only in recent decades, particularly in macroeconomics. Economists talk about Stabilization Policy, the effect of which is to leave undisturbed the central features of American society. This development parallels the drift from entrepreneurial to managerial dominance in the economy and reflects the increasing conservatism of the American mentality. The spirit of stabilization goes well with the spirit of marginalism, each contributing to an intellectual and emotional baggage unsuited to understand and support large scale social disequilibrium and change. Stabilization is a means. Why should something corrupt, dangerous or oppressive be stabilized?

Economists pay insufficient attention to the distribution of economic power, and especially to its relation to the distribution of political power. From Keynes' *General Theory* we have constructed an elaborate set of analyses and policies while neglecting Keynes' own concluding remarks on the critical importance of income redistribution. Welfare economists claim to have little to say about income distribution since it is neutral with respect to economic efficiency, although equity considerations are usually briefly noted. But economists have at least been aware of the importance of personal income distribution (and changes in it) for some time, even though very little substantive work has been devoted to the issues thus raised.

There remains a whole class of questions about the distribution of economic gain which are crucial to understanding the economy, but which hardly have been raised. Because of the riots and the talk about poverty, we are learning something about the average distribution of employment and unemployment among various groups in the country, with a much less clear view of the marginal response of employment among different groups traceable to particular types of government policies. What about different distributions of profits and sales among different sized (or otherwise classified) establishments resulting from different types of government programs? How do different patterns of government expenditures influence various regions or types of establishments? How can this information lead to an understanding of the construction and implementation of government economic policy? Whose interests are served by those policies?

Economists disaggregate the economy along the lines of the national accounts or discuss functional share distribution of income. There are other ways of disaggregating (e.g., *Fortune's* 500, all other enterprises with sales exceeding $1 million annually, all other enterprises; or firms with at least 40 percent million annually, all other enterprises; or firms with at least 40 percent of sales in international transactions, firms with at least some direct foreign trade, all other enterprises) which would be useful in understanding the political economy of the United States. Disputes over the control of resources and the distribution of power dominate domestic and international developments, but economists are unprepared and usually unwilling to address these crucial issues.

Economists have long argued whether or not government policies of various sorts are neutral with respect to the market, but it is generally held that economic analysis itself is neutral with respect to political ideology; the economic efficiency is the same in any society faced with scarce resources; that capital accumulation is required for growth, no matter what the mechanism of accumulation might be.

Standard economics equates efficiency with profit maximization. But efficiency is at most a property of a means to some end, which may easily be different from financial profit. The "conflict" between efficiency and equity is a confusion. Equity is an end. Efficiency is not even a means, and cannot be in conflict with anything. Equity conflicts with other ends, like profit or growth or the preservation of private property. An economics geared to profit maximization is not neutral, but loaded with a particular end and a set of institutions which serve that end. It is also incorrect to claim that the notion and operation of economic efficiency are neutral, since that efficiency is based in part on market prices, which reflect a particular income distribution, which is certainly not socially, politically or ethically neutral. The notion that standard economics is somehow neutral, presumably because it is a "science" which can be used equally for good or evil, is fundamentally incorrect. The preceding discussion indicates some other ways in which the standard economics violates neutrality by militating against asking and answering certain radical questions. Economics is not, and cannot reasonably be expected to be, neutral.

Some economists are sympathetic to radical questions, but find the search for answers (if not the questions themselves) unprofessional, outside the realm of economics. This is felt either because the principles of standard economics are called into question, or because the search leads to other social and behavioral sciences. This narrow division of labor among disciplines results in diminished capabilities for asking and answering nonmarginal questions about the foundations of our society. Fragmentation of knowledge may be effective for certain purposes, but it militates against effective, intelligent radical change.

We study economics because of a curiosity and concern about people and the way people interact. Our reference point is human activity and interests, not the latest journal article. We are committed to change in the United States, deep change to turn away from poverty, racism and imperialism. Some of us tend towards an anarchist vision of a just society.

Others tend to socialist principles. We are all committed to a scholarship which aids our understanding of society and of ways to change it. In these matters the margin is unimportant. There can be no accommodation with the constraints of "national interest," nor with the artificial bureaucratic boundaries among the social sciences and within economics itself.

The temperament as well as the substance of these concerns are outside the bounds of standard economic thinking. In trying to come to grips with American economic activity we have felt a tension with the profession. We see an America which has to change, and we see a body of knowledge and social outlook among economists unsuited to that change. We are trying to resolve that tension by searching for a new economics which will be consistent with and relevant to a society ordered differently from our own.

People all over the world are fighting for freedom—from oppression by racists, from domination by imperialists, from want generated by scarcity and consumerism alike, from "the national interest." Oppression is the problem. Liberation is the solution. We are trying to construct an economics and an economy which will be part of the solution, not part of the problem.

Join us.

PART 2

Economic Reasoning at Work

The Economics of the 1960s —
A Backward Look

OTTO ECKSTEIN

A former member of the Council of Economic Advisors evaluates the pluses and minuses of the New Economics.

The 1960s are behind us. What have we learned? And what should we forget? Regretfully, there still is little study of the history of economic policy. Historians record the minutiae of foreign affairs and domestic politics, but the successes and failures of economic policy, which affect the lives of the people more directly than the struggles of personalities for power, are still not the subject of serious study. The books by Arthur Schlessinger and Eric Goldman on the Kennedy and Johnson administrations give short shrift to economic management.

This essay cannot fill that void. It presents only the reflections of a brief participant in the economic policies of the 1900s, and a partial assessment of that decade in the area of domestic policy.

In 1959 the Joint Economic Committee studies on *Employment, Growth, and Price Levels* expressed concern about the slow growth of the economy in the 1950s, the rising unemployment, and the increasing frequency of recessions. All these were blamed on the restrictive policies in the management of aggregate demand, a low rate of increase in the money supply of only 1.9 percent for 1953 to 1959, and a destabilizing fiscal policy because of the gyrations of the defense budget. The Committee issued reports about the dimensions of poverty and the inadequacy of health care, but it implicitly argued that if the economic growth rate was increased, poverty would be reduced and the resources would be created

From Otto Eckstein, "The Economics of the 1960's—A Backward Look," *Public Interest* (Spring, 1970), pp. 86–97. Copyright 1970 National Affairs, Inc. Reprinted by permission of the author and publisher.

to help solve all our problems. Economic growth, then, was the major issue as we entered the 1960s.

The critics of the 1950s maintained that the "natural" growth of the American economy was substantially higher than the performance. By "natural" growth they meant the performance that is possible, given advancing technology, the institutional arrangements (e.g., sector distributions) of the economy, and full utilization of this potential. Leon Keyserling, who made economic growth a major issue, argued that the economy was capable of growing at a full 5 percent a year. James Knowles, in his pioneer aggregate production function study for *Employment, Growth, and Price Levels*, produced a medium estimate 3.9 percent, with a half percent on either side for low or high growth policies. In reply to these voices, Edward F. Denison, in his famous study *Sources of Economic Growth*, concluded that the natural rate of growth was only 3 percent, implying that the policy of the 1950s was not in error, and that even major changes in investment in physical and human capital would accelerate the rate of growth by only a few small decimals. If 1 percent sounds like a quibble, we should realize that an additional 1 percent of economic growth during the decade is $85 billion of extra output by 1969.

Actually, the economy grew at an annual average of 4.6 percent during the decade 1959 to 1969. To obtain the natural rate of growth one must correct for the gap of 4 percent between actual and potential GNP in 1959 and for an overfull employment of 2 percent of potential in 1969. Thus, the apparent growth of potential GNP was 4 percent for the decade; James Knowles was right.

Where did Denison go wrong? The depression of the 1930s did more harm to the economy than the Denison analysis indicated. The loss in capital formation, and perhaps the lost technology and innovations as well, were not fully made up when World War II brought full employment. High employment has raised potential growth above prewar standards.

How was the high growth rate achieved in the 1960s? Economic measures enacted in 1962 stimulated the rate of growth of the economy's potential through the investment credit and more liberal depreciation allowances. The neoclassical school of investment analysts, led by Dale Jorgenson, assigns great weight to this stimulus, though other equations can probably explain the historical record as well. Without doubt, these measures helped accelerate capital goods spending by mid-1963. They led to certain abuses, including an excessive growth of leasing. But the investment credit idea has not obtained a firm place in our institutional structure and is about to disappear.

The central feature of economics in the 1960s was the triumph of modern fiscal policy. It was a victory slow in coming. Six years passed from the time in 1958 when many economists, Arthur Burns as well as the

Keynesians, saw the need for a tax cut until the needed policy prevailed. Why did it take so long to take the commonsense step of reducing an excessive burden of taxation, so obviously in the interest of politicians and their constituencies? It is a dramatic example of the power of established prejudices over self-interest, even of ideas that were quite wrong.

First, even Keynesian economists forgot the lesson of their master, that an economy could remain at underemployment equilibrium. Public and scientific opinion had come to accept the necessity of government deficits when the economy was sliding into recession. But the classical view of the natural tendency to return to full employment remained deeply ingrained. At the bottom of the 1958 recession, the leading indicators established that the lower turning point had been reached and tax reduction was ruled out. The Samuelson task force to president-elect Kennedy concluded that the economy was in an upswing, and therefore did not endorse immediate tax reduction. Even this sophisticated group fell into the classical trap. (Or was it political realism?) Recovery proceeded, and by 1962 unemployment had fallen to 5.5 percent. But then the economy stalled. Months dragged by as a good set of figures would raise hopes of renewed advance and the next month would dash them. Only gradually was it recognized that the tax burden was excessive and that the economy was going nowhere. In this respect, the Council of Economic Advisers understood the issue long before its academic allies.

Second, the concept of the annually balanced budget and the fear of debt still held many persons in its grip. Few outside the government believed that a tax cut would pay for itself—as it did—and so it appeared that the initial impact of tax reduction would be an enlargement of the budget deficit.

Third, the structuralists, with a following both in the Federal Reserve Board and the Department of Labor, argued that the high unemployment was the outcome of an imbalance between the new, technologically advanced jobs and the supply of unskilled, disadvantaged workers. The structuralists had a legitimate point in advocating an upgrading of a portion of the labor force. But in overstating their case they were obstructionists to modern fiscal policy. When the economy finally approached full employment after 1964, the job gains of the unskilled and of the disadvantaged greatly exceeded the gains of the more skilled; we discovered the social power of a tight labor market.

Fourth, Professor Galbraith's voice, carrying from Delhi to Washington, argued that tax reduction would permanently lower the government's ability to command resources. He favored the traditional Keynesian route of stimulating the economy through expenditures. Whatever the merits of greater public spending, the simple fact was that the Congress of the early 1960s would not go that route.

Fifth, advocates of tax reform felt that tax reduction offered them the only opportunity to put together a political package which would make the Congress accept the closing of loopholes. The theory was that Congress would give the President some tax reform in exchange for the privilege of cutting taxes. Actually it was the President and his advisors who wanted tax reduction, while tax reform was a millstone around fiscal policy.

Sixth, the monetary school of economists argued that tax reduction was a minor element in economic policy, and that what was really needed to stimulate the economy was a more suitable increase in the money supply. At the time of the great fiscal debate, however, the monetary school had little influence and cannot be said to have been a significant factor in the delay.

After six years the taxes were cut. By July 1965, before defense contracts began to rise, unemployment was down to 4.5 percent and falling rapidly, the economy was growing at over 5 percent a year, and wholesale prices were still stable and no higher than five years earlier. The economy had shown, at least for 18 happy months, that it could prosper without war with sensible, modern economic management; doubts about fiscal policy were wiped out, and for a year or two economists rode high indeed.

Then came the Vietnam war and the end, for a period at least, of modern fiscal policy. The budget underestimated defense spending by $10 billion for fiscal 1967 and $5 billion for fiscal 1968. The impact on the economy was underestimated by larger amounts because of the greater jumps in defense contracts. If the economic impact of the war had been known, the excise taxes would not have been cut in the summer of 1965. In early 1966 there should have been a broad across-the-board tax increase. But taxes were not increased because the President could not get the American people to pay for the war. In the end, the war paralyzed the political process, producing the surrealistic debate over the tax surcharge from mid-1967 to mid-1968. International financial crises followed one on another. Demand became excessive. The tax surcharge of mid-1968, which Congress voted, finally restored some fiscal order.

The impact of the federal budget on the economy in the 1960s can be measured crudely by the high employment budget surplus—an estimate of the surplus that the budget would produce if the economy were at full employment and producing revenues accordingly. The excessively restrictive policies of the 1950s had raised the full employment budget surplus to about $13 billion in 1960. Increased expenditures to fight recession, the military buildup over the Berlin crisis, and the investment credit and depreciation reform lowered the surplus to about $6.5 billion in 1962. Delay in tax reduction and a slowdown in expenditure increases raised the surplus once more, reaching an $11 billion peak at the end of 1963.

The tax cuts, and the increases in spending, caused an enormous swing in the federal budget. By the beginning of 1967, the full employment budget showed a deficit of $12 billion—a welcome stimulus during the slowdown; but its deepening to $15 billion by mid-1968 was a disaster. Once the tax surcharge was passed and expenditure restraint became effective, the swing in the opposite direction was equally massive. By the second quarter of 1969 the high employment surplus approached $10 billion again. No wonder that the economy got rather out of hand, and now faces a period of slow growth.

What judgment can be passed about discretionary policy in the light of this record?

First, while the necessary alternative model simulations have not been done, and so answers must remain qualitative at best, the record of the 1960s seems to repeat the verdict of the 1950s. Discretionary policy did harm as well as good. The policy proposed by the Committee for Economic Development in 1947, if it had been followed, would have done better. The CED recommended that the government maintain a small full employment surplus in its budget, and normally eschew the attempt to pursue a more ambitious, discretionary stabilization policy. The CED policy would have avoided the excessive full employment surpluses in the late 1950s and the early 1960s, the swings which led to the reemergence of a very large surplus in 1963, and it would have forced the financing of the Vietnam war by current taxes. The Great Society programs still could have been financed out of the increase in full employment revenues during a period of rapid growth.

Second, it is evident that the major movements in the full employment surplus were not the result of deliberate stabilization policy. The big swings were due to exogenous events; i.e., the Vietnam war and the inability of the political process to make revenues respond to swings in expenditures. Even if the government had abandoned discretionary policy altogether, and sought to maintain a steady full employment balance of small surplus, the same political difficulties would have gotten in the way. Taxes would have had to be raised. It is likely that the political process would have failed to execute the CED policy, just as it failed to carry out a rational discretionary policy.

In the 1960s, expenditures by government rose at a substantially higher rate than the gross national product. The total outlays (on national income account) of all levels of government were 27.1 percent on the GNP in 1960; by 1969, the figure rose to 31.4 percent. The outlays of states and localities rose from 9.9 percent to 13.1 percent of GNP; federal outlays rose from 18.5 to 20.5 percent.

This increase in part represents the Vietnam war, which absorbed about 3 percent of GNP, some of it at the expense of other defense outlays.

Most of the remainder was due to the growth of public activities in response to a rising population and to slow productivity growth of government service activities. But a major reason for the rise of government
spending was the Great Society programs enacted from 1964 to 1966.

It is important to understand how this change in the public-private
mix came about. So long as the issue was posed in Galbraithian terms—
public versus private spending—the Congress did not respond. The Great
Society programs were made possible by the large spurt in the growth rate
from 1964 to 1966. Public spending came out of economic growth, not out
of private spending.

These are the summary figures: in 1964, before the Great Society
programs, the federal government collected $113 billion and spent $119
billion, producing a $6 billion deficit. By 1968, following the substantial
tax reductions, revenues were up to $154 billion, a rise of $41 billion, expenditures were up to $179 billion, a rise of $60 billion. As a result, the
$6 billion budget deficit rose to $25 billion. What happened is clear
enough: military spending, mainly for Vietnam, rose by $27 billion. Spend-
ing on education at the federal level rose from $2 to $7 billion; on health,
from $2 to $10 billion; and the total of all other fields, including Social
Security, agriculture, urban affairs, and the old-line programs, went up
from $61 to $81 billion.

Thus, during the period of the Great Society legislation, there was
plenty of spending for old and new programs, civilian and military. Economic growth produced the revenues, though in the end we did stumble
into an enormous deficit.

Because human beings are fallible and policy-makers all over Washington are subject to common tides of opinion and politics, the record of
monetary policy has similarities to fiscal policy. Until 1965, monetary
policy accommodated the gradual recovery to full employment, while
interest rates remained fairly stable. One might argue that interest rates
should have risen as the economy moved toward full employment, but
one should also remember that interest rates were already high at the
beginning of the decade because of the excessively restrictive monetary
policies of 1959.

The monetary school of economists, led by Milton Friedman, claims
that the recovery to full employment was really due to a good expansion
of the money supply, perhaps prompted by the need to finance the budget
deficits. The theoretical debate about the relative importance of fiscal and
monetary policy is not likely to be settled here; but one can observe a
striking contrast for the period under review. The rhythm of the economy
seemed to respond to changes in fiscal policy. Unemployment stayed high
so long as the budget aimed for large high employment surpluses. It fell
after the tax cut of 1964. The increase in the broad money supply was

fairly steady, both in the period of high level stagnation and during full recovery. If easy money alone sufficed, full employment should have come more quickly.[1]

From 1965 on, the Federal Reserve Board no longer fully accommodated the economic growth, and interest rates began to rise. With the benefit of hindsight about the war, the federal deficit, the capital goods boom, and the inflation, it is now evident that monetary policy should have become tougher earlier. Further monetary policy was too aggressive during the 1967 slowdown, and if ever there was a case of overkill, the antirecession fiscal and monetary policies of 1967 were an example. In the summer of 1968, monetary policy eased too quickly after the passage of the tax surcharge, and the authorities have been struggling ever since to bring the banking system and inflation under control.

The monetary theorists sing a siren song which says that if money supply is expanded at a constant rate, we would free ourselves of the fallibility of human judgment about the timing of restricting or loosening the amount of money in response to the economic cycle. There is little doubt that we have overmanaged money, perhaps never more so than during the extreme restraint of 1969-70. But there are hurdles on the way to a more stable policy: if it really is the money supply that is to be regulated, there had better be agreement on the figures. The record of the money supply for the first half of 1969 has been rewritten, as it was for several other crucial periods. Who would rest a policy on so weak a statistical reed? Further, it is difficult to define a "neutral" policy. Structural changes in the financial system give different growth trends to the various monetary magnitudes.

There has been little study of the quantitative relationships between the various monetary measures, explaining the differences in the growth of such variables as unborrowed reserves, the narrow money supply, the broad money supply, the monetary base, total bank credit, bank loans, total credit in the economy, etc. Until this work is done, adoption of any rule applicable to one concept will simply convert the present disputes into a quarrel about the selection and care of statistics.

The level of interest rates is also an indicator of monetary policy, and to me still the most unambiguous. But it is evident from experience that a stable interest rate is not a neutral policy. Interest rates should rise and fall with the business cycle. Indeed, a stable interest rate policy is prob-

---

[1]For the statistically inclined reader, let me add a few regression results on this point. For the period 1961 to 1965, correlations of quarterly data, utilizing poly-nomial distributed lags of third degree, four quarters, constrained to zero at the remote end show the following: the unemployment rate on the Full Employment Surplus: .82; on the rate of increase of the money supply: .64. The results are not as clear cut for other periods; but the first half of the 1960's does seem to have been fiscal policy's day.

ably significantly destabilizing for the economy. Thus, while interest movements are a useful gauge, they do not provide a simple rule which policy can follow.

By the end of the 1950s the need to reconcile full employment and price stability was widely recognized. The new administration, building on earlier *Economic Reports,* established "Guideposts for Wage-Price Stability." At first the guideposts only asserted some rather bland principles about price and wage behavior which a competitive economy would achieve on its own. It reminded labor that wage increases beyond productivity served mainly to raise prices; it reminded business that price increases beyond trend costs raised profits only temporarily. But until January 1966, when the guideposts were breached by the New York subway settlement, the administration had pursued an active policy of seeking to hold settlements close to the productivity rate.

The guidepost policies must be understood in the context of their day. The economy was moving toward full employment; industrial operating rates were rising. Productivity was advancing rapidly and wage demands were predicated on stable consumer prices. The longer the stable costs and prices could be preserved, the closer the economy could come to full employment without stumbling into the inflationary difficulties which had haunted us in the mid-1950s.

In their heyday, in 1964 to 1966, the guideposts were a major element of government policy. Government spending programs, fair labor standards proposals, minerals stockpile policy, civil service pay, agricultural policy, and protective measures for specific industries both internal and at the frontier, were examined, at the president's direction, for their effect on cost-price stability. This probably was the first time in history that an administration examined its policy proposals fully from the objective of price stability.

In addition, the guideposts partially reoriented the usual government interventions in collective bargaining. Settlement of industrial conflicts was not an objective by itself but was coordinate with cost stability. For some time, at least, a Democratic government modified its traditional role of urging management to settle for large increases in order to restore industrial harmony. On the price side, presidential intervention slowed down the increases of some highly visible basic materials and a few final products.

Did these policies have any effect? Wage equations which explain other years of the postwar period fail during the guidepost years. To be sure, other explanations have been found for the extraordinarily low wage increases of 1963 to 1966, but they are not totally convincing. Without claiming statistical proof, I would evaluate the episode as prolonging the virtuous circle of high productivity growth, stable costs, and stable price expectations by some months, and slowing the pickup of the price-wage spiral.

The guidepost policies were politically very difficult. Every time the president reduced a government program, intervened in a labor dispute, rolled back a price, let goods in from abroad, or made a release from the stockpile, he trod on sensitive toes. In due time, the affected industries sought retribution through the political process. Only a president elected by an enormous majority and commanding firm control over the Congress could withstand the politicking of industries, which President Johnson did.

As the Vietnam war escalated and the president's popularity began to fade, the authority of the guidepost policies shrank. When the president lost his command over the Congress in the 1966 elections, the most active phase of guidepost policies drew to a close, though there were some successful interventions as late as the summer of 1968.

There has been criticism of the guideposts as violating the principles of a free market economy. These criticisms are misplaced. The markets in our economy are relatively free compared to other economies; but many industries benefit from government programs, from government purchases, government-enforced production controls, import restrictions and tariff, artificial reductions of supply through stockpile policies, and so on. Similarly, the strength of labor unions is immensely aided not only by the basic laws which redress the balance between employer and worker, but also by the Davis–Bacon Act which strengthens the grip of the construction unions, Walsh–Healey, and so on. We saw in the opening months of 1969 that the government cannot shelve all its powers to influence wage and price decisions. The absence of guidepost policies does not make the government neutral.

The guidepost episode and the recent inflationary explosion leave a nagging question: is the inflationary bias of the economy excessive at a 4 percent unemployment rate, and does the rate of inflation inevitably worsen at full employment? The United States has never had uninterrupted prosperity before. Now that we have unlocked the secret, are we unable to use it because we do not know how to live with full employment?

What should we have learned? What mistakes have we no right to repeat? And where is the new ground that should be broken? A review of the predictions made at the beginning of this decade indicates that one cannot anticipate what will be the dominant problems. In 1960 no one thought about the Vietnam war or appreciated that the inequality of economic opportunity and disparities between black and white would become the central social problem. The impact of an advancing economy on the physical environment was not totally a surprise, but was far down the agenda of the decade. Even such traditional items as the deterioration of the cities, the improvement of health and education, housing, and rural opportunity had little specificity ten years ago. So don't expect much help here in pinpointing the major problems of the 1970s even within the area of economic performance.

Nonetheless we owe it to ourselves to attempt to distill a few points from the review of the past period.

1. The natural rate of growth of the economy for the 1970s exceeds 4 percent and we should judge economic performance accordingly. The growth of the labor force accelerated in the mid-1960s and will remain at a high rate. The advance of technology gives every sign of remaining very rapid. The current high rate of growth of the capital stock indicates the prospect of a natural rate of growth at least as great as in the 1960s.

   We will begin the decade with a very slow growth year. The overfull employment of recent months will be converted into a small gap between actual and potential output in 1970. If we focus economic policy exclusively on fighting inflation, and if the fight on inflation is confined to the strictly classical medicine, we condemn ourselves to several years of slow growth and the development of a considerable gap between actual and potential output.

2. The economy still seems unable to reconcile full employment with price stability. The need for structural changes to improve the competitiveness and flexibility of markets and to minimize the harm of government protectionist policies remains as strong as ever. Government machinery could be strengthened for these pursuits.

3. The trend cycle in the private economy will be in an upswing phase at the beginning of the decade. While government policy may temporarily slow the conversion of fundamental strength into economic activity, rapid family formation with the resultant need for housing and durables will keep the underlying tone of the private economy strong. This is in sharp contrast to the beginnings of the 1960s.

4. Fiscal and monetary policies should avoid the extreme swings which have characterized them in the last 20 years. Very full employment surpluses and deficits have been mistakes without exception. Periods of extreme advance or no advance in the money supply have been mistakes without exception.

5. The informed public finally understands the question of priorities of resource use. The searching examination of our military budget and the attempt to determine the economic costs of our foreign policy commitments contain the promise of a more rational approach to resource allocation in the public sector.

6. Economic performance is increasingly judged by its ability to meet the social and environmental goals of the society. The 1960s have shown that good macro-performance is a necessary but not a sufficient condition for adequate social progress. The realization that the resources are available may well have heightened the impatience of the black and the young with our halting efforts. The systematic changes in the private and public sector necessary to assure adequate social progress and halt deterioration of the environment appear to be the main challenges to economic policy for the 1970s. But then again, the main tasks may prove to be something else; by 1980 we will know.

Macroeconomics
of Unbalanced Growth:
The Anatomy of Urban Crisis

WILLIAM J. BAUMOL

In this now-classic article, Professor Baumol gives an analysis of the persistent inflation and urban decay of recent years.

There are some economic forces so powerful that they constantly break through all barriers erected for their suppression. Such, for example, are the forces of supply and demand which have resisted alike medieval efforts to abolish usury and contemporary attempts to control prices. In this paper I discuss what I believe to be another such mechanism which has colored the past and seems likely to stamp its character on the future. It helps us to understand the prospective roles of a wide variety of economic services: municipal government, education, the performing arts, restaurants, and leisure time activity. I will argue that inherent in the technological structure of each of these activities are forces working almost unavoidably for progressive and cumulative increases in the real costs incurred in supplying them. As a consequence, efforts to offset these cost increases, while they may succeed temporarily, in the long run are merely palliatives which can have no significant effect on the underlying trends.

The justification of a macroeconomic model should reside primarily in its ability to provide insights into the workings of observed phenomena. Its aggregation of diverse variables usually deny it the elegance and the rigor that are provided by microeconomic analysis at its best. Yet macro models have succeeded in explaining the structure of practical problems and in offering guidance for policy to a degree that has so far eluded the more painstaking modes of economic analysis. This article hopes to follow in the tradition—the structure of its basic model is rudimentary.

William J. Baumol, "Macroeconomics of Unbalanced Growth: The Anatomy of Urban Crisis," *American Economic Review* (June, 1967), pp. 415–26. Reprinted by permission of the author and publisher.

Yet it can perhaps shed some light on a variety of economic problems of our generation.

Our model will proceed on several assumptions, only one of which is really essential. This basic premise asserts that economic activities can, not entirely arbitrarily, be grouped into two types: technologically progressive activities in which innovations, capital accumulation, and economics of large scale all make for a cumulative rise in output per man-hour and activities which, by their very nature, permit only sporadic increases in productivity.

Of course, one would expect that productivity would not grow at a uniform rate throughout the economy so it is hardly surprising that, given any arbitrarily chosen dividing line, one can fit all goods and services into one or the other of two such categories in whatever way the dividing line is drawn. I am, however, making a much stronger assertion: that the place of any particular activity in this classification is not primarily a fortuitous matter determined by the particulars of its history, but rather that it is a manifestation of the activity's technological structure, which determines quite definitely whether the productivity of its labor inputs will grow slowly or rapidly.

The basic source of differentiation resides in the role played by labor in the activity. In some cases labor is primarily an instrument—an incidental requisite for the attainment of the final product, while in other fields of endeavor, for all practical purposes the labor is itself the end product. Manufacturing encompasses the most obvious examples of the former type of activity. When someone purchases an air conditioner he neither knows nor cares how much labor went into it. He is not concerned one way or the other with an innovation that reduces the manpower requirements for the production of his purchase by 10 percent if the price and the quality of the product are unaffected. Thus it has been possible, as it were, behind the scenes, to effect successive and cumulative decreases in the labor input coefficient for most manufactured goods, often along with some degree of improvement in the quality of the product.

On the other hand there are a number of services in which the labor is an end in itself, in which quality is judged directly in terms of amount of labor. Teaching is a clear-cut example, where class size (number of teaching hours expended per student) is often taken as a critical index of quality. Here, despite the invention of teaching machines and the use of closed circuit television and a variety of other innovations, there still seem to be fairly firm limits to class size. We are deeply concerned when elementary school classes grow to 50 pupils and are disquieted by the idea of college lectures attended by 2,000 underclassmen. Without a complete revolution in our approach to teaching there is no prospect that we can ever go beyond these levels (or even up to them) with any degree of equanimity. An even more extreme example is one I have offered in another context: live performance. A half-hour horn quintet calls for the expenditure of 2.5 man-hours in its performance, and any attempt to increase productivity here is likely to be viewed with concern by critics and audience alike.

The difference between the two types of activity in the flexibility of their productivity levels should not be exaggerated. It is a matter of degree rather than an absolute dichotomy. The jet airplane has increased the productivity per man-hour of a faculty member who is going from New York to California to give a lecture. Certainly the mass media have created what may be considered a new set of products that are close substitutes for live performance and by which productivity was increased spectacularly. In addition, there are, as the reader will recognize, all sorts of intermediate activities which fall between the two more extreme varieties. Yet, the distinction between the relatively constant productivity industries and those in which productivity can and does rise is a very real one, and one which, we shall see, is of considerable practical importance.

In addition to the separability of activities into our two basic categories I shall utilize three other assumptions, two of them primarily for ease of exposition. The reader will recognize, as we proceed, that neither is essential to the argument. The first of the incidental premises consists simply in the assertion that all outlays other than labor costs can be ignored. This assertion is patently unrealistic but it simplifies greatly our mathematical model. A second, far more important, and more realistic assumption is that wages in the two sectors of the economy go up and down together. In the long run there is some degree of mobility in all labor markets and consequently, while wages in one activity can lag behind those in another, unless the former is in process of disappearing altogether we cannot expect the disparity to continue indefinitely. For simplicity I will in the next section take hourly wages to be precisely the same in both sectors, but the model is easily complicated to allow for some diversity in wage levels and their movements.

A final inessential assumption which is, however, not altogether unrealistic, asserts that money wages will rise as rapidly as output per man-hour in the sector where productivity is increasing. Since organized labor is not slow to learn of increases in its productivity it is likely to adjust its wage demands accordingly. This assumption affects only the magnitude of the absolute price level in our model, and does not influence the relative costs and prices that are the critical elements in the analysis. The entire analysis can be stated rather simply in intuitive terms. If productivity per man-hour rises cumulatively in one sector relative to its rate of growth elsewhere in the economy, while wages rise commensurately in all areas, then relative costs in the nonprogressive sectors must inevitably rise, *and these costs will rise cumulatively and without limit.* For while in the progressive sector productivity increases will serve as an offset to rising wages, this offset must be smaller in the nonprogressive sectors. For example (ignoring nonwage costs), if wages and productivity in the progressive sector both go up 2 percent per year, costs there will not rise at all. On the other hand, if in the nonprogressive sector productivity is constant, every rise in wages must yield a corresponding addition to costs—a 2 percent cumulative rise in wages means that, year in year out, costs must be 2 percent above those of the preceding year. Thus, the very progress of the technologically progressive sectors inevitably adds to the costs of the technologically unchanging sectors of the economy, unless somehow the labor markets in these areas can be sealed off and wages held absolutely constant, a most unlikely possibility.

We see then that costs in many sectors of the economy will rise relentlessly, and will do so for reasons that are for all practical purposes beyond the control of those involved. The consequence is that the outputs of these sectors may in some cases tend to be driven from the market. If their relative outputs are maintained, an ever-increasing proportion of the labor force must be channeled into these activities and the rate of growth of the economy must be slowed correspondingly.

These observations can be used at once to explain a number of observed phenomena. For example, there is evidence that an ever-increasing portion of the nation's labor force has been going into retailing and that a rising portion of the cost of commodities is accounted for by outlays on marketing. Now there have been several pronounced changes in the technology of marketing in recent decades: self-service, the supermarket, and prewrapping have all increased the productivity per manhour of the retailing personnel. But ultimately, the activity involved is in the nature of a service and it does not allow for constant and cumulative increases in productivity through capital accumulation, innovation, or economies of large-scale operation. Hence it is neither mismanagement nor lack of ingenuity that accounts for the relatively constant productivity of this sector. Since some sort of marketing effort is an inescapable element in economic activity, demand for this service is quite income elastic. Our model tells us what to expect in this case—cumulatively increasing costs relative to those of other economic activities, and the absorption of an ever-growing proportion of society's resources by this sector—precisely what seems to have been observed.

Higher education is another activity the demand for whose product seems to be relatively income elastic and price inelastic. Higher tuition charges undoubtedly impose serious hardships on lower-income students. But, because a college degree seems increasingly to be a necessary condition for employment in a variety of attractive occupations, most families have apparently been prepared to pay the ever larger fees instituted in recent years. As a result higher education has been absorbing a constantly increasing proportion of per capita income. And the relatively constant productivity of college teaching leads our model to predict that rising educational costs are no temporary phenomenon—that they are not a resultant of wartime inflation which will vanish once faculty salaries are restored to their prewar levels. Rather, it suggests that, as productivity in the remainder of the economy continues to increase, costs of running the educational organizations will mount correspondingly, so that whatever the magnitude of the funds they need today, we can be reasonably certain that they will require more tomorrow, and even more on the day after that.

But not all services in the relatively constant productivity sector of the economy face inelastic demands. Many of them are more readily dispensable than retailing and education as far as individual consumers are concerned. As their costs increase, their utilization tends therefore to decrease and they retreat into the category of luxury goods with very limited markets or disappear almost completely. Fine pottery and glassware produced by the careful labor of skilled craftsmen sell at astronomical prices, though I am told the firms that produce them earn relatively little profit from these product lines which they turn out primarily for prestige and publicity, obtaining the bulk of their earnings from their mass production activities. Fine restaurants and theaters are forced to keep raising their prices, and at least in the case of the latter we know that volume is dwindling while it becomes ever more difficult for suppliers (the producers) to make ends meet.

An extreme example of an activity that has virtually disappeared is the construction (and, indeed, the utilization) of the large and stately houses whose operation even more than their construction allows for little in the way of enhanced productivity, and whose rising costs of operation have apparently decreased their salability even to the wealthy.

These observations suggest something about the likely shape of our economy in the future. Our model tells us that manufactures are likely to continue to decline in relative cost and, unless the income elasticity of demand for manufactured goods is very large, they may absorb an ever smaller proportion of the labor force, which, if it transpires, may make it more difficult for our economy to maintain its overall rate of output growth.

The analysis also suggests that real cost in the "nonprogressive" sectors of the economy may be expected to go on increasing. Some of the services involved—those whose demands are inelastic—may continue viable on the free market. Some, like the theater, may be forced to leave this market and may have to depend on voluntary public support for their survival. Our hospitals, our institutions of private education and a variety of other nonprofit organizations have already long survived on this basis, and can continue to do so if the magnitude of contributions keeps up with costs. Some activities will either disappear or retreat to a small scale of operation catering primarily to a luxury trade. This fate may be in store for restaurants offering true *haute cuisine* and it is already the case for fine hand-worked furniture and for clothes made to measure. Some activities, perhaps many of the preceding among them, will fall increasingly into the hands of the amateurs who already play a considerable role in theatrical and orchestral performances, in gastronomy, in crafts such as woodworking and pottery. Finally, there is a considerable segment of nonprogressive activity that is dependent on tax support. Some of the problems that go with this position will be considered in the remainder of this paper.

In all the observations of this section there is one implicit underlying danger that should not escape the reader: the inherent threat to quality. Amateur activity has its virtues, as an educational device, as a good use for leisure time and so forth. But in a variety of fields it offers a highly imperfect substitute for the highly polished product that can be supplied by the professional. Unbalanced productivity growth, then, threatens to destroy many of the activities that do so much to enrich our existence, and to give others over into the hands of the amateurs. These are dangers which many of us may feel should not be ignored or taken lightly.

One of the major economic problems of our times is the crisis of the larger cities. Together with their suburban periphery the cities are attracting ever greater segments of our population. Yet at least the core of the metropolis is plagued by a variety of ills including spreading blight as entire neighborhoods deteriorate, increasing pollution of its atmosphere, worsening traffic, critical educational problems, and, above all, mounting fiscal pressures. The financial troubles are perhaps central to the entire issue because without adequate funds one cannot hope to mount an effective attack on the other difficulties. More than one reform mayor has taken office determined to undertake a radical program to deal with the city's difficulties and found himself baffled and stymied by the monstrous deficit which he discovered to be hanging over him, a deficit whose source appeared to have no reasonable explanation. There seems in these cases to be no way to account for the growth in the city's financial needs—for the fact that a municipal budget far above that which was roughly adequate a decade earlier threatens to disrupt seriously the city's most vital services today. Where the political process is involved it is easy to blame growing costs on inefficiency and corruption but when they take office, reform administrations seem consistently puzzled by their inability to wring out the funds they require through the elimination of these abuses.

A critical element in the explanation becomes clear when we recognize how large a proportion of the services provided by the city are activities falling in the relatively nonprogressive sector of the economy. The bulk of our municipal expenditures is devoted to education which, as we have already seen, offers very limited scope for cumulative increases in productivity. The same is true of police, of hospitals, of social services, and of a variety of inspection services. Despite the use of the computer in medicine and in traffic planning, despite the use of closed-circuit television and a variety of other devices, there is no substitute for the personal attention of a physician or the presence of a police patrol in a crime-ridden neighborhood. The bulk of municipal services is, in fact, of this general stamp and our model tells us clearly what can be expected as a result. Since there is no reason to anticipate a cessation of capital accumulation or innovation in the progressive sectors of the economy, the upward trend in the real costs of municipal services cannot be expected to halt; inexorably and cumulatively, whether or not there is inflation, administrative mismanagement or malfeasance, municipal budgets will almost certainly continue to mount in the future, just as they have been doing in the past. This is a trend for which no man and no group should be blamed, for there is nothing that can be done to stop it.

Though these may be troubles enough for the municipal administrator, there are other compelling forces that plague him simultaneously. Among them are the general class of externality problems which have so long been the welfare economist's stock in trade.

Since the appearance of Marshall's and Pigou's basic writing in the area a most significant development has been the growing impact of external costs on urban living. No longer are road crowding and smoke nuisance only quaint cases serving primarily as textbook illustrations. Rather, they have become pressing issues of public concern—matters discussed heatedly in the daily press and accorded serious attention by practical politicians. Newspapers devote headlines to an engineer's prediction that the human race is more likely to succumb to its own pollutants than through a nuclear holocaust, and report with glee the quip that Los Angeles is the city in which one is wakened by the sound of birds coughing.

Now there are undoubtedly many reasons for the explosion in external costs but there is a pertinent observation about the relationship between population size in a given area and the cost of externalities that seems not to be obvious. It is easy to assume that these costs will rise roughly in proportion with population but I shall argue now that a much more natural premise is that they will rise more rapidly—perhaps roughly as the square of the number of inhabitants. For example, consider the amount of dirt that falls into the house of a typical urban resident as a result of air pollution, and suppose that this is equal to kn where n is the number of residents in the area. Since the number of homes in the area, an, is also roughly proportionate to population size, total domestic soot-fall will be equal to soot per home times number of homes $= kn \cdot an = akn^2$. Similarly, if delays on a crowded road are roughly proportionate to n, the number of vehicles traversing it, the total number of man-hours lost thereby will increase roughly as n^2, since the number of passengers also grows roughly as the number of cars. The logic of the argument is simple and perhaps rather general: if each inhabitant in an area imposes external costs on every other, and if the magnitude of the costs borne by each individual is roughly proportionate to population size (density) then since these costs are borne by each of the n persons involved, the total external costs will vary not in proportion with n but with n^2. Of course I do not maintain that such a relationship is universal or even that it is ever satisfied more than approximately. Rather I am suggesting that, typically, increases in population size may plausibly be expected to produce disproportionate increases in external costs—thus pressures on the municipality to do something about these costs may then grow correspondingly.

Economic theory indicates yet another source of mounting urban problems. These are the processes of cumulative urban decay which once set in motion induce matters to go from bad to worse. Since I have discussed these elsewhere I can illustrate the central proposition rather briefly. Public transportation is an important example. In many urban areas with declining utilization, frequency of service has been sharply reduced and fares have been increased. But these price rises have only served to produce a further decline in traffic, leading in turn to yet another deterioration in schedules and another fare increase and so on, apparently ad infinitum. More important, perhaps, is the logic of the continued flight to the suburbs in which many persons who apparently would otherwise wish to remain in the city are driven out by growing urban deterioration—rising crime rates, a growing number of blighted neighborhoods, etc. Once again, the individuals' remedy intensifies the community's problems and each feeds upon the other. Those who leave the city are usually the very persons who care and can afford to care—the ones who maintain their houses, who do not commit crimes, and who are most capable of providing the taxes needed to arrest the process of urban decay. Their exodus therefore leads to further deterioration in urban conditions and so induces yet another wave of emigration, and so on.

It is clear that these cumulative processes can greatly increase the financial pressures besetting a municipality and can do so in a variety of ways: they can increase directly municipal costs by adding to the real quantities of inputs required for the upkeep of buildings, to maintain levels of urban sanitation, to preserve the level of education attained by an average resident, etc.; they can reduce the tax base—the exodus of more affluent urban inhabitants cause a decline in the financial resources available to the city; and with the passage of time the magnitude of the resources necessary to arrest and reverse the cumulative processes itself is likely to grow so that the city may find it increasingly difficult to go beyond programs that slow the processes slightly.

The story is perhaps completed if we add to the preceding observations the fact that each city is in competition with others and with its own surrounding areas for industry and for people with the wherewithal to pay taxes. No city government acting alone can afford to raise its tax rates indefinitely. Even if they were politically feasible, mounting tax rates must eventually produce diminishing and perhaps even negative returns as they depress the tax base further.

We can now quickly pull the pieces of our story together. We have just seen that our municipalities are perhaps unavoidably subject to a variety of growing financial pressures: the limited sources of tax funds, the pressures imposed by several processes of cumulative decay, the costs of externalities which seem to have a built-in tendency to rise more rapidly than the population. These phenomena imply that the activities of the municipality will have to be expanded if standards of city life are to be maintained. But the funds available for the purpose are extremely limited. And over all this hangs the shadow cast by our model of unbalanced growth which has shown that the costs of even a constant level of activity on the part of a municipal government can be expected to grow constantly higher.

The picture that has been painted is bleak. It suggests strongly that self-help offers no way out for our cities. All of this would then appear to offer stronger theoretical support for the Heller–Pechman proposal that the federal government can provide the resources necessary to prevent the serious crisis that threatens our larger urban communities and whose effects on the quality of life in our society may become one of the nation's most serious economic problems.

Should the Government
Share Its Tax Take?

WALTER W. HELLER

The problem of state and local finance has long been a serious cause of social disrepair. Walter Heller, chairman of the Council of Economic Advisors under President Kennedy, proposes a solution.

Washington *must* find a way to put a generous share of the huge federal fiscal dividend (the automatic increase in tax revenue associated with income growth) at the disposal of the states and cities. If it fails to do so, federalism will suffer, services will suffer, and the state-local taxpayer will suffer.

Economic growth creates a glaring fiscal gap; it bestows its revenue bounties on the federal government, whose progressive income tax is particularly responsive to growth, and imposes the major part of its burdens on state and local governments. Closing that gap must take priority over any federal tax cuts other than the removal of the 10 percent surcharge. And even this exception may not be valid. For, as New York Governor Nelson A. Rockefeller has proposed, the revenue generated by the surcharge can easily be segregated from other federal revenue and earmarked for sharing with the states. So perhaps even the taxpayer's "divine right" to get rid of the surcharge may have to give way to the human rights of the poor, the ignorant, the ill, and the black.

For when the state-local taxpayer is beset with—and, indeed, rebelling against a rising tide of regressive and repressive property, sales, and excise taxes, what sense would it make to weaken or dismantle the progressive and growth-responsive federal income tax? Whether our concern is for justice and efficiency in taxation, or for better balance in our fed-

"Should the Government Share Its Tax Take," by Walter W. Heller, Regents' Professor of Economics of the University of Minnesota, *Saturday Review* (March 22, 1969). Copyright 1969 Saturday Review, Inc.

eralism or, most important, for a more rational system of financing our aching social needs, there is no escape from the logic of putting the power of the federal income tax at the disposal of beleaguered state and local governments.

Calling for redress of the fiscal grievances of our federalism is, of course, far from saying that state-local government has reached the end of its fiscal rope. The taxpayer's will to pay taxes may be exhausted, but his capacity is not:

> Our overall tax burden—roughly 28 percent of the GNP—falls far short of the 35 to 40 percent levels in Germany, France, the Netherlands, and Scandinavia. Small solace, perhaps, but a strong suggestion that the U.S. taxpayer has not been squeezed dry.
>
> Untapped and underutilized tax sources still abound in state and local finance. For example, 15 states still have no income tax, and six still have no sales tax. If all 50 states had levied income taxes as high as those of the top ten, state income tax collections in 1966 would have been $11 billion instead of $5 billion. The same type of computation for state and local sales taxes shows a $5-billion add-on. As for that sick giant of our tax system the property tax, the aforementioned top-ten standard adds $9.3 billion to the existing collection of $24.5 billion.

It is only fair to point out, however, that states and localities have not been exactly reticent about tapping these revenue sources. In spite of taxpayer resistance and the frequent political penalties that go with it, the 50 states have been doing a land-office business in new and used taxes. In the past ten years, the six major state taxes (sales, personal and corporate income, gasoline, cigarette, and liquor) were the subject of 309 rate increases and 26 new adoptions. Instead of slowing down, the pace has speeded up; in 1967 to 1968, the states raised major taxes on 80 occasions and enacted seven new levies. Meanwhile, property tax burdens have risen faster than anyone thought possible ten years ago.

Yet, this effort has all the earmarks of a losing battle. Economic growth generates demands for new and better services while leaving a massive problem of water, air, land, and sound pollution in its wake. Population growth, especially the rapid rise of taxeaters relative to taxpayers (the number of Americans in the school-age and over-65 groups is increasing more than twice as rapidly as those in-between), is straining state-local budgets. And inflation—which increases the prices of goods and services bought by state-local governments about twice as fast as the average rate of price increase in the economy—also works against state-local budgets.

Figure 1. Federal, State, and Local Tax Receipts[a] (Selected Fiscal Years 1927–1968) in Billions of Dollars

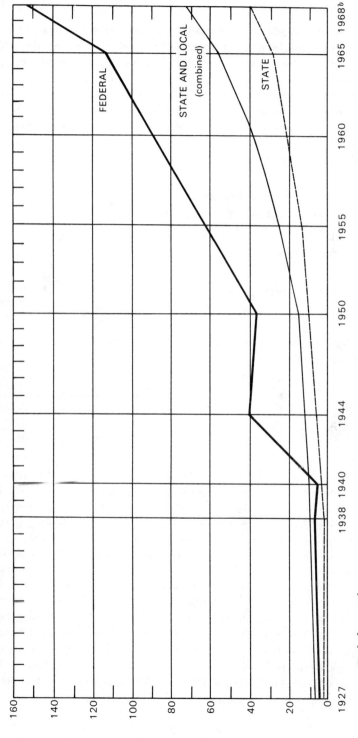

[a]Includes social insurance taxes
[b]Data for 1968 estimated
Source: Department of Commerce, Bureau of the Census.

119

In trying to meet these spending pressures, state and local governments are inhibited by fears of interstate competition, by limited jurisdiction, by reliance on taxes that respond sluggishly to economic growth, and by fears of taxpayer reprisals at the polls. But it would be a mistake to assume that the case for federal support rests wholly, or even mainly, on these relentless fiscal pressures and handicaps. Far from being just a fiscal problem—a question of meeting fiscal demands from a limited taxable capacity—the issue touches on the very essence of federalism, both in a political and in a socioeconomic sense.

Table 1. Federal Aid to State and Local Governments
(Selected Fiscal Years of 1949–1969)
in Millions of Dollars

	1949	1959	1967	1968[a]	1969[a]
Agriculture	86.6	322.5	448.0	599.4	644.0
Commerce and transportation	433.6	100.6	226.3	431.7	618.6
Education	36.9	291.3	2,298.7	2,461.9	2,398.2
Health, labor, welfare	1,231.5	2,789.7	6,438.0	8,207.1	9,135.0
Housing, community development	8.6	188.4	768.3	1,185.2	1,812.5
Highway and unemployment trust funds	—	2,801.2	4,501.7	4,773.1	4,796.7
Other	5.5	319.7	1,120.2	1,239.9	1,418.0
Total	1,802.7	6,813.4	15,801.2	18,898.3	20,823.0

[a]Data estimated
Source: Bureau of the Budget

Indeed, it is from the realm of political philosophy—the renewed interest in making state-local government a vital, effective, and reasonably equal partner in a workable federalism—that much of the impetus for more generous levels and new forms of federal assistance has come. The financial plight of state-local government cannot alone explain the introduction of some 100 bills in Congress for various forms of revenue sharing or unconditional block grants since 1954, when my proposal for apportioning taxes was first made public and converted into a detailed plan by the presidential task force headed by Joseph A. Pechman.

In this connection, I have been amused by how often the following sentences from my *New Dimensions of Political Economy*, published in 1966, have been quoted, especially by surprised conservatives: "The good life will not come, ready made, from some federal assembly line. It has to be custom-built, engaging the effort and imagination and resourcefulness of the community. Whatever fiscal plan is adopted must recognize this need." In expressing similar thoughts publicly for a quarter-century, I have not been alone among liberals. Yet, the statement is now greeted as if the power and the glory of decentralization has just been revealed to us for the first time. May I add that when we are embraced by those "who stand on their states' rights so they can sit on them," we may be forgiven for wincing.

Moving from the political to the economic, one finds strong additional rationale for new and expanded federal support in the economic—or socioeconomic—theory of public expenditures. It is in this theory that our vast programs of federal aid to state and local governments—projected to run at $25 billion in fiscal 1970 (triple the amount in 1960)—are firmly anchored. All too often, they are thought of simply as a piece of political pragmatism growing out of two central fiscal facts: that Washington collects more than two-thirds of the total federal, state, and local tax take; and that nearly two-thirds of government public services (leaving aside defense and social security programs) are provided by state-local government. Throw in the objective of stimulating state-local efforts through matching provisions, and, for many people, the theory of federal grants is complete.

In fact, it is only the beginning. Consider the compelling problems of poverty and race and the related problems of ignorance, disease, squalor, and hard-core unemployment. The roots of these problems are nationwide. And the efforts to overcome them by better education, training, health, welfare, and housing have nationwide effects. Yet, it is precisely these services that we entrust primarily to our circumscribed state and local units.

Clearly, then, many of the problems that the states and localities tackle are not of their own making. And their success or failure in coping with such problems will have huge spillover effects far transcending state and local lines in our mobile and interdependent society. The increasing controversy over the alleged migration of the poor from state to state in search of higher welfare benefits is only one aspect of this. So, quite apart from any fiscal need to run hat in hand to the national government, states and cities have a dignified and reasonable claim on federal funds with which to carry out national responsibilities. Only the federal government can represent the totality of benefits and strike an efficient balance between benefits and costs. Therein lies the compelling economic case for the existing system of earmarked, conditional grants-in-aid. Such grants will, indeed must, continue to be our major mechanism for transferring funds to the states and localities.

But the interests of a healthy and balanced federalism call for support of the general state-local enterprise as well as specific services. It is hard to argue that the benefits of sanitation, green space, recreation, police

122 Economic Reasoning at Work

and fire protection, street maintenance and lighting in one community have large spillover effects on other communities. Yet, in more or less humdrum services such as these lies much of the difference between a decent environment and a squalid one, between the snug suburb and the grinding ghetto.

Given the limits and inhibitions of state-local taxation and the sharp inequalities in revenue-raising capacity—compounded by the matching requirement in most categorical grants, which pulls funds away from nongrant activities—too many of the states and the cities are forced to strike their fiscal balances at levels of services well below the needs and desires of their citizens. The absence of a system of federal transfers to serve the broad purpose of upgrading the general level of public services, especially in the poorer states, is a serious gap—both economic and political—in the fiscal structure of our federalism. Tax sharing could fill it.

The core of a tax-sharing plan is the earmarking of a specified share of the federal individual income tax take for distribution to states and localities, on the basis of population, with next to no strings attached. The so-called Heller–Pechman plan has the following main elements:

> The federal government would regularly route into a special trust fund 2 percent of the federal individual income tax base (the amount reported as net taxable income by all individuals). In 1969, for example, this would come to about $7 billion, roughly 10 percent of federal individual income tax revenues. This amount would be channeled to the states at fixed intervals, free from the uncertainties of the annual federal appropriation process.
>
> The basic distribution would be on a straight population formula, so much per capita. Perhaps 10 percent of the proceeds should be set aside each year as an equalization measure—to boost the share of the 17 poorer states (which have 20 percent of the nation's population).
>
> To insure that the fiscal claims of the localities are met, a minimum pass-through—perhaps 50 percent—to local units would be required. In this intrastate allocation, the financial plight of urban areas should be given special emphasis.
>
> The widest possible discretion should be left to the state and local governments in the use of the funds, subject only to the usual accounting and auditing requirements, compliance with the Civil Rights Act, and perhaps a ban on the use of such funds for highways (for which there already is a special federal trust fund).

How well does the tax-sharing plan (also called revenue sharing, unconditional grants, and general assistance grants) measure up to the economic and sociopolitical criteria implicit in the foregoing discussion? Let me rate it briefly, and sympathetically, on six counts.

First, it would significantly relieve the immediate pressures on state-local treasuries and, more important, would make state-local revenues grow more rapidly, in response to economic growth. For example, a 2-percentage-point distribution on a straight per capita basis would provide, in 1969, $650 million each for California and New York, $420 million for Pennsylvania, $375 million for Illinois, $140 million each for Mississippi and Wisconsin, $125 million each for Louisiana and Minnesota, and about $65 million each for Arkansas and Colorado.

The striking growth potential of this source of revenue is evident in two facts: (1) had the plan been in effect in 1955, the distribution of 2 percent of the $125-billion income-tax base in that year would have yielded a state-local tax share of about $2.5 billion; and (2) by 1972, the base should be about $450 billion, yielding a $9-billion annual share.

Second, tax sharing would serve our federalist interest in state-local vitality and independence by providing new financial elbow room, free of political penalty, for creative state and local officials. Unlike the present grants-in-aid, the tax-shared revenue would yield a dependable flow of federal funds in a form that would enlarge, not restrict, their options.

Third, tax sharing would reverse the present regressive trend in our federal-state-local tax system. It seems politically realistic to assume that the slice of federal income tax revenue put aside for the states and cities would absorb funds otherwise destined to go mainly into federal tax cuts and only partly into spending increases. Given the enormous pressures on state-local budgets, on the other hand, tax shares would go primarily into higher state-local expenditures and only in small part into a slowdown of state-local tax increases. Thus, the combination would produce a more progressive overall fiscal system.

Fourth, tax sharing—especially with the 10 percent equalization feature—would enable the economically weaker states to upgrade the scope and quality of their services without putting crushingly heavier burdens on their citizens. Per capita sharing itself would have a considerable equalizing effect, distributing $35 per person to all of the states, having drawn $47 per person from the ten richest and $24 per person from the ten poorest states. Setting aside an extra 10 percent for equalization would boost the allotments of the 17 poorest states by one-third to one-half. Thus, the national interest in reducing interstate disparities in the level of services would be well served.

Fifth, the plan could readily incorporate a direct stimulus to state and local tax efforts. Indeed, the Douglas Commission (the National Commission on Urban Problems), like many other advocates of tax-sharing plans, would adjust the allotments to take account of relative state-local tax efforts. In addition, they propose a bonus for heavy reliance on individual income taxation.

A more direct stimulant to state and local efforts in the income tax field would be to enact credits against the federal income tax for state income taxes paid. For example, if the taxpayer could credit one-third or two-fifths of his state and local income tax payments directly against his federal tax liability (rather than just treat such taxes as a deduction from taxable income, as at present), it would lead to a far greater use of this fairest and most growth-oriented of all tax sources.

Ideally, income tax credits should be coupled with income tax sharing and federal aid in a balanced program of federal support. But if relentless fiscal facts require a choice, the nod must go to tax sharing because (1) credits provide no interstate income-level equalization; (2) at the outset, at least, much of the federal revenue loss becomes a taxpayer gain rather than state-local gain; and (3) since one-third of the states still lack broad-based income taxes, the credit would touch off cries of "coercion." Nevertheless, it is a splendid device that ought to have clearcut priority over further tax cuts.

Sixth, and finally, per capita revenue sharing would miss its mark if it did not relieve some of the intense fiscal pressures on local, and particularly urban, governments. The principle is easy to state. The formula to carry it out is more difficult to devise. But it can be done. The Douglas Commission has already developed an attractive formula that it describes as "deliberately 'loaded' to favor general purpose governments that are sufficiently large in population to give some prospect of viability as urban units." I would agree with the Commission that it is important not to let "no-strings" federal aid sustain and entrench thousands of small governmental units that ought to wither away—though I still prefer to see the tax-sharing funds routed through the 50 state capitals, rather than short-circuiting them by direct distribution to urban units.

Supported by the foregoing logic, espoused by both Democratic and Republican platforms and candidates in 1968, and incorporated into bills by dozens of prestigious Senators and Congressmen, one would think that tax sharing will have clear sailing as soon as our fiscal dividends permit. Not so. The way is strewn with obstacles and objections.

For example, tax sharing poses threats, or seeming threats, to special interest groups including all the way from top federal bureaucrats who see tax sharing's gain as their agencies' and programs' loss; through the powerful lobbyists for special programs such as housing, medical care, and pollution control programs, who recoil from the prospect of going back from the federal gusher to 50 state spigots; to the Senators and Congressmen who see more political mileage in tax cuts or program boosts than in getting governors and mayors out of their fiscal jam.

But, of course, opposition goes far beyond crass self-interest. It also grows out of philosophic differences and concern over the alleged shortcomings of tax sharing. There is the obvious issue of federalism versus centralism. A strong contingent in this country feels that the federal government knows best, and that state and local governments cannot be trusted. Others fear that revenue sharing or unrestricted grants will make state-local government more dependent on the federal government—a fear for which I see little or no justification.

On the issues, some would argue that it is better to relieve state-local budgets by taking over certain burdens through income-maintenance programs like the negative income tax; while others feel that too much of the revenue-sharing proceeds would go down the drain in waste and corruption. Here, one must answer in terms of a willingness to take the risks that go with an investment in the renaissance of the states and the cities. Some costs in wasted and diverted funds will undoubtedly be incurred. My assumption is that these costs will be far outweighed by the benefits of greater social stability and a more viable federalism that will flow from the higher and better levels of government services and the stimulus to state-local initiative and responsibility.

In sum, I view tax sharing as an instrument that (1) will fill a major gap in our fiscal federalism; (2) will strengthen the fabric of federalism by infusing funds *and* strength into the state-local enterprise; and (3) will increase our total governmental capacity to cope with the social crisis that confronts us. The sooner Congress gets on with the job of enacting a system of tax sharing, even if it means postponing the end of the 10 percent surcharge, the better off we shall be.

The Rich, the Poor, and the Taxes They Pay

JOSEPH PECHMAN

Redistribution of income as well as revenue is, or should be, a goal of tax policy. Here is an analysis of the distributive impact of modern taxes. What do you think the impact has been?

The distribution of income has always been a hotly debated subject. Whatever has happened or is happening to the distribution of income, some people will always assert that the rich are getting a bigger share of the pie than is "fair," while others will seek to show that this is not the case. Few people, however, bother to find out the facts and fewer still understand what they mean.

The same applies to the tax system. Everybody knows that there are loopholes in the federal tax laws, but few realize that there are loopholes for persons at all income levels. Even fewer have a clear idea about the effects on the distribution of income of closing the more controversial loopholes. And only the experts know the state-local tax structure is in more urgent need of reform than the federal structure.

This article is intended to put these matters in perspective by summarizing the available information. What has happened to the distribution of income before taxes in recent years, and how has the tax system modified it? What's wrong with the national tax system? What reforms are needed to make it a fairer system? What are the chances of getting these reforms? And, beyond such reforms, what would be the shape of a tax distribution that most Americans today might agree to be "fair"?

Despite the proliferation of sophisticated economic data in this country, the United States government does *not* publish official estimates

Reprinted from *Public Interest* (Fall, 1969), pp. 21–43. Copyright 1969 National Affairs, Inc. Used with permission of the author and publisher.

of the distribution of income. Such estimates were prepared by the Office of Business Economics for a period of years in the 1950s and early 1960s, but were discontinued because the sources on which they were based were acknowledged to be inadequate. We have data from annual field surveys of some 30,000 households conducted by the Bureau of the Census, as well as from the annual *Statistics of Income* prepared by the Internal Revenue Service from federal individual income tax returns. But both sources have their weaknesses: the Census Bureau surveys systematically understate income, particularly in the top brackets; tax returns, on the other hand, understate the share received by low income recipients who are not required to file. Nevertheless, if used with care, the two sources provide some interesting insights.

Before turning to the most recent period, it should be pointed out that a significant change in the distribution of pre-tax income occurred during the Great Depression and World War II. All experts who have examined the data agree that the distribution became more equal as a result of (a) the tremendous reductions in business and property incomes during the depression and (b) the narrowing of earnings differentials between low-paid workers and higher-paid skilled workers and salaried employees when full employment was reestablished during the war. The most authoritative estimates, prepared by the late Selma Goldsmith and her associates, suggest that the share of personal income received by the top 5 percent of the nation's consumer units (including families and un-related individuals) declined from 30 percent in 1929 to 26.5 percent in 1935 to 1936; the share of the top 20 percent declined from 54.4 percent to 51.7 percent in the same period. The movement toward greater equality appears to have continued during the war up to about 1944. By that year, the share of the top 5 percent had dropped another notch to 20.7 percent, and of the top 20 percent to 45.8 percent.

The income concept used by these researchers did not include undistributed corporate profits, which are a source of future dividends or of capital gains for shareholders; if they had been included, the movement of the income distribution toward equality from 1929 to 1944 would have been substantially moderated, but by no means eliminated.

The movement toward equality seems to have ended during World War II, at least on the basis of the available statistics. In 1952, for example, the share of the top 5 percent was 20.5 percent and of the top 20 percent, 44.7 percent. (The differences from the 1944 figures are well within the margin of error of these data, and can hardly be called significant.)

To trace what happened since 1952, we shift to the census data that provide the longest continuous and comparable income distribution series available to us. The best way to appreciate the trend is to look at the figures for income shares at five-year intervals:

Table 1. Before-Tax Income Shares, Census Data
(Percentage)

Year	Top 5 Percent of Families	Top 20 Percent of Families
1952	18	42
1957	16	40
1962	16	42
1967	15	41

Source: Bureau of the Census. Income includes transfer payments (e.g., social security benefits, unemployment compensation, welfare payments, etc.), but excludes capital gains.

The figures indicate that the share of the top 5 percent declined slightly between 1952 and 1957, and has remained virtually unchanged since 1957; the share of the top 20 percent changed very little. Correspondingly, the shares of the groups at the bottom of the income scale (not shown in the table) also changed very little throughout the period.

Tax data are needed to push the analysis further. These data are better than the census data for our purposes, because they show the amount realized capital gains and also permit us to calculate income shares *after* the federal income tax. But the great disadvantage of the tax data is that the bottom part of the income distribution is underrepresented because of an unknown number of nonfilers. Furthermore, the taxpayer unit is not exactly a family unit, because children and other members of the family file their own income tax returns if they have income, and a few married couples continue to file separate returns despite the privilege of income splitting, which removed the advantage of separate returns with rare exceptions.

There is really no way to get around these problems, but the tax data are too interesting to be abandoned because of these technicalities. So, we make an assumption that permits us to use at least the upper tail of the income distribution. The assumption is that the top 10 or 15 percent of the nation's tax units are for the most part similar to the census family units and the cases that differ represent roughly the same percentage of the total number of units each year. Because we have official Department of Commerce estimates of income (as defined in the tax code) for the country as a whole, the assumption enables us to compute income shares before and after tax for the top 1, 2, 5, 10, and 15 percent of units annually for the entire postwar period.

The tax series confirms much of what we learned from the census series, and adds a few additional bits of information besides. Here are the data for selected years chosen to represent the three sets of federal income tax rates levied, beginning with the Korean War:

Table 2. Before-Tax Income Shares, Tax Data
(Percentage)

Year	Top 1 Percent of Tax Units	Top 2 Percent of Tax Units	Top 5 Percent of Tax Units	Top 10 Percent of Tax Units	Top 15 Percent of Tax Units
1952	9	12	19	27	33
1963	8	12	19	28	35
1967	9	13	20	29	36

Source: *Statistics of Income*. Income excludes transfer payments, but includes realized capital gains in full.

According to tax returns, the share of total income, including all realized capital gains, going to the top 1 percent of the tax units was about the same for the entire period from 1952 through 1967. But the shares of the top 2, 5, 10, and 15 percent—which, of course, include the top 1 percent—all rose somewhat. These trends differ from the census figures which show that the entire income distribution was stable. By contrast, the tax data show that the 14 percent of income recipients just below the top 1 percent—this group reported incomes between $12,000 and $43,000 in 1967—*increased* their share of total income from 24 percent to 27 percent.

If the figures are anywhere near being right, they suggest two significant conclusions:

First, in recent years the very rich in our society have not enjoyed larger increases in incomes, as defined in the tax code, than the average income recipient. Although realized capital gains are included in our figures, they do not include nonreported sources, such as tax-exempt interest and excess depletion; correction for these omissions would probably not alter the results very much, because the amounts involved are small relative to the total of reported incomes. Even a correction for the undistributed profits of corporations wouldn't change the result very much because undistributed gross corporation profits have remained between 10 and 13 percent of total reported income since 1950.

Second, a change in the income distribution may have occurred in what are sometimes called the "middle income" classes. These classes consist of most of the professional people in this country (doctors, lawyers, engineers, accountants, college professors, etc.) as well as the highest paid members of the skilled labor force and white-collar workers. The increase in their share of total income from 24 percent to 27 percent, if it actually occurred, represents a not insignificant improvement in their relative income status.

Clearly, this improvement in the income shares of the middle classes could come only at the expense of the lower 85 percent of the income distribution. But this is not the whole story. These figures contain only incomes that are generated in the private economy; they do not include transfer payments (e.g., social security benefits, unemployment compensation, welfare payments, etc.) which are, of course, concentrated in the lower income classes. Correction of the figures for transfer payments might be just enough to offset the increased share of the middle income classes. If this is the case, the constancy of the shares of pre-tax income shown by the census data is fully consistent with the growth in shares of the middle incomes shown by the tax data. And, if this is the explanation of the constancy of the income shares in the census distribution, it means that the lower classes have not been able to hold their own in the private economy; large increases in government transfer payments were needed to prevent a gradual erosion of their income shares.

Since one of the major objectives of taxation is to moderate income inequality, it is appropriate to ask how the tax system actually affects the distribution of income and whether it has become more or less equalizing. We examine first the impact of the federal individual income tax, which is the most progressive element in the nation's tax system and for which data by income classes are readily available, and then we speculate about the effect of the other taxes in the system.

While everybody grumbles about the federal income tax, few people realize that tax rates have been *going down* for about two decades. Even with the 10 percent surtax, the rates are lower today than they were from 1951 through 1963. Briefly, the history of the tax is as follows: tax rates reached their peak, and exemptions their low point, during World War II. They were reduced in 1946 and again in 1948, when income splitting and the $600 per capita exemption were also enacted. Rates were pushed up close to World War II levels during the Korean War, but were reduced in 1954 and again in 1964. The surtax that became effective for individuals on April 1, 1968 moved the rates only halfway back to the 1954-to-1963 levels.

The structure of the tax has been remarkably stable during this entire period, despite all the talk about closing loopholes. The preferential rate on long-term capital gains was enacted in 1942; income splitting became effective in 1948; interest on state and local government bonds has never been taxed by the federal government; percentage depletion dates back to the 1920s; and the deductions allowed for interest charges, taxes, charitable contributions, medical expenses, and casualty losses date back to 1942 or earlier. The 1954 law introduced a 4 percent dividend credit, but this was repealed in 1964. (As a compromise, the $50 exclusion for dividends, which was enacted along with the credit, was raised to $100.) A few abuses have been eliminated from time to time, but the revenues involved have not been significant.

The single major victory for tax reform occurred in 1964, when the dividend credit and the deductions for state and local taxes other than income, sales, property, and gasoline taxes were eliminated. All told, these revenue-raising reforms amounted to about $750 million, and they were accompanied by revenue-losing reforms of $400 million (mainly the minimum standard deduction which benefitted only those with very low incomes).

Given this history, it follows that the effective tax rates at specific absolute income levels have been going down since World War II. For example, from 1947 to 1967, the effective rate of tax paid by taxpayers with adjusted gross income of $5,000–10,000 declined from 13.8 percent to 9.5 percent; for those in the $15,000–20,000 class, the decline was from 24.6 percent to 14.0 percent; and above $100,000, the decline was from 57.4 percent to 39.5 percent. (These figures understate actual declines because adjusted gross income excludes half of long-term capital gains that were much larger relative to total income in 1967 than in 1947.)

Although such figures are of considerable interest, they are not directly useful for an analysis of the effect of the tax on the income distribution. For it must be remembered that most people moved up the income scale almost continuously throughout this period; under a progressive tax, they would be taxed more heavily as a result of this upward movement. There is a case for the argument that, as incomes rise, it is only "fair" that progressive tax rates—established on the basis of an earlier income distribution that was considered "fair"—ought to go down somewhat. The key question is: how much? Specifically, has the progressive taxation of increased incomes been offset by the reduction in tax rates, or has there been a "surplus" on the side of either income or taxation?

To answer this question, the effective tax rates were computed for the top 1, 2, 5, 10, and 15 percent of the income tax units, but in this case the full amount of realized long-term capital gains, and also other exclusions, were included to arrive at a total income concept. The data show that, on this basis, average effective tax rates were substantially lower in

Table 3. Effective Federal Tax Rates on Total
Income (Percentage)

Year	Top 1 Percent of Tax Units	Next 1 Percent of Tax Units	Next 3 Percent of Tax Units	Next 5 Percent of Tax Units	Next 5 Percent of Tax Units
1952	33	20	16	14	12
1963	27	20	16	14	13
1967	26	18	15	13	12

Source: *Statistics of Income.* Total income is the sum of adjusted gross income and excluded capital gains, dividends, and sick pay.

1967 than in 1952 for the top 1 percent, slightly lower for the next 1 percent, and roughly constant for the next 13 percent. Note also that the effective rate of tax paid in 1967 by the top 1 percent, whose before-tax income was $43,000 and over, was only 26 percent of their total reported income, including all their realized capital gains.

It is a fairly simple matter to deduct the tax paid by each of these groups from their total income to obtain their disposable income. The results modify the conclusions we drew on the basis of the before-tax incomes in only minor respects. The shares of disposable income of the top 1 percent remain stable, and the shares of the top 2, 5, 10, and 15 percent go up from 1952 to 1967. Furthermore, the shares of the "middle income classes"—the 14 percent between the top 1 and top 15 percent—rise from 23 to 27 percent on a disposable income basis, or about as much as on a before-tax basis (see Table 4).

Table 4. Shares of Total Disposable (After-Tax) Income (Percentage)

Year	Top 1 Percent of Tax Units	Top 2 Percent of Tax Units	Top 5 Percent of Tax Units	Top 10 Percent of Tax Units	Top 15 Percent of Tax Units
1952	7	10	16	24	30
1963	7	10	17	26	33
1967	7	11	17	26	34

Source: *Statistics of Income.* Disposable income is total income less federal income tax paid.

We may conclude that the federal individual income tax has moderated the before-tax income distribution by roughly the same proportions since 1952. Thus, while tax rates at any given absolute income level have declined, the effect of progression has just about offset the decline, leaving the relative tax bite about the same in the top 15 percent of the income distribution. Furthermore, similar calculations suggest that the post-World War II income tax is just about as equalizing as it was in 1941. The tremendous movement upward in the income distribution pushed much more taxable income into higher rate brackets, but this has been offset by the adoption of income splitting and the increase in itemized deductions.

It should be emphasized that the foregoing data omit large chunks of income that are received primarily by high-paid employees of large business firms. Tax-exempt interest and percentage depletion have already been mentioned. In addition, beginning with the imposition of the very high individual income tax rates and the excess profits tax during World War II, methods of compensation were devised to funnel income to business executives in nontaxable forms. The devices used are well known: deferred compensation and pension plans, stock option arrangements, and direct payment of personal consumption expenditures through expense accounts. There is no question that these devices are used widely throughout the corporate sector. But little is known about the amounts involved, and even less is known about the impact on the distribution of income.

A recent study by Wilbur G. Lewellen for the National Bureau of Economic Research concluded that, even after allowance is made for the new compensation methods, the after-tax compensation (in dollars of constant purchasing power) of top executives in industrial corporations was no higher in the early 1960s than in 1940. The more important finding from the income distribution standpoint is that stock options, pensions, deferred compensation, and profit-sharing benefits rose rapidly as a percentage of the executives' compensation package from 1940 to 1955, and then stabilized. The study did not attempt to measure the value of expense accounts, and omitted firms in industries other than manufacturing. Nevertheless, the results of the study suggest that extreme statements about the possible effects of these devices on the distribution of income in recent years are not warranted.

The corporation income tax was enacted four years before the individual income tax and it has been a mainstay of the federal tax system ever since. It produced more revenue than the individual income tax in 17 out of 28 years prior to 1941; today, it is the second largest source of federal revenue. The general corporation tax was reduced to 38 percent after World War II. It was raised to 52 percent during the Korean War and remained there until 1964, when it was reduced to 48 percent.

Public finance experts have argued the merits and demerits of a corporation tax for a long time, but the issues have not been resolved Its major purpose in our tax system is to safeguard the individual income tax. If corporate incomes were not subject to tax, individuals could avoid the individual income tax by arranging to have their income accumulate in corporations, and later on selling their stock at the low capital gains rate, or holding on until death at which time the capital gains pass to their heirs completely tax-free. Short of taxing shareholders on their share of corporation incomes (a method which is attractive to economists, but is anathema to businessmen and most tax lawyers) and taxing capital gains in full, the most practical way to protect the individual income tax is to impose a separate tax on corporation incomes.

Some people have argued that a large part or all of the corporation income tax is shifted forward to the consumer in the form of higher prices. On this assumption, the corporation income tax is a sales tax—a very peculiar one, to be sure—and is therefore regressive. But the majority view among tax experts is that the corporation income tax comes out of corporate profits, as was intended, so that the tax is borne by shareholders. Despite the large post-World War II increases in the number of shareholders, stock ownership is still concentrated in the highest income classes. This means that the corporation income tax is, to some extent at least, a progressive tax.

The major change in the corporation tax in the last two decades has been the enactment of more generous depreciation deductions in 1954 and 1962 and of the investment credit in 1962. As a result, despite relatively constant rates, the corporation tax has declined as a ratio to gross corporate profits (i.e., profits before deduction of depreciation) from 33 percent in 1954 to about 27 percent in 1967. It rose in 1968 to 30 percent as a result of the imposition of the 10 percent surtax. The impending expiration of the surtax and repeal of the investment tax credit will just about offset one another, so that the post-surtax ratio will continue at 30 percent until the continuously growing depreciation allowances will tilt it downward once again. Thus, although the contribution of the corporation tax to the progressivity of the national tax system has declined somewhat (for economic reasons that most economists regard as persuasive), the contribution continues to be on the progressive side.

In theory, estate and gift taxes are excellent taxes because they have little effect on incentives to earn income and, if effective, would reduce the inequality of the distribution of wealth that in turn accounts for much of the inequity in the distribution of income. In practice, the yield of these taxes is disappointing. Tax rates are high, but there are numerous ways to escape them. The result is that the federal government receives little of its revenue from these tax sources—about 1.7 percent in the current fiscal year. The effective rate of estate taxes on wealth passed each year from one generation to the next must be less than 10 percent; and the gift tax is even less effective. While these taxes are progressive, they have little effect on the distribution of wealth.

We now turn to the features of the national tax system that, in combination, more than offset the progressivity of the federal income and estate and gift taxes. The social security payroll tax, which is levied at a flat rate on earnings up to a maximum of $7,800 under present law, was enacted in 1935 as the basic method of financing social security on the principle that the workers were buying their own insurance. This idea is doubtless responsible for the widespread acceptance of social security as a permanent government institution in this country; but the insurance analogy is no longer applicable to the system as it has developed. Present beneficiaries receive far larger benefits than the taxes they paid would entitle them to—a situation that will continue indefinitely as long as Congress raises benefits as prices and wages continue to rise. The trust funds have not grown significantly since the mid-1950s; the payroll taxes paid by the workers have not been stored up or invested, but have been paid out currently as benefits. When benefits promised to people now working come due, the funds for their payment will be provided out of tax revenues as of that future date.

Nevertheless, the insurance analogy has a strong hold on the thinking of the administrators of social security and the Congressional tax-writing committees. Every time a benefit increase is enacted, the payroll tax rates (or the maximum earnings subject to the tax) are raised, in order to balance out the revenues and expenditures for the next 75 years on an actuarial basis. In a relatively short time, the trust funds begin running large surpluses, which then become the justification for another round of benefit increases by Congress. This requires a further increase in rates for actuarial reasons, payroll taxes are again raised, and so on.

As a result of this process, payroll taxes have been raised seven times since the beginning of 1960. The combined employer-employee tax was 6 percent on earnings up to $4,800 on January 1, 1960; this year the tax is 9.6 percent on earnings up to $7,800. Most economists believe that the burden of the employer tax, as well as the employee tax, falls eventually on the workers (either by substituting for larger wage increases or inflating prices). Thus, the federal government has been placing more and more weight on this regressive element of the federal system.

Although the federal tax system is progressive on balance, the state and local tax system is highly regressive. The states rely heavily on sales taxes, while the local governments rely on property taxes. Personal and corporation income taxes account for only about 11 percent of state-local revenues from their own sources. This situation is disturbing because the state-local tax system is the growing element of the national system. Whereas the federal government has been able to reduce income tax rates several times beginning in 1954, and has eliminated virtually all of its excise taxes, state governments continue to enact new taxes and to raise the rates of old taxes to keep up with their increasing and urgent revenue needs; meanwhile, local governments keep raising the already excessively burdened property tax.

Federal tax receipts have moved within the narrow range of 19 to 21 percent of the Gross National Product since 1951. By contrast, state-local receipts rose from 7.1 percent of the GNP in 1951 to 11.9 percent in 1968. Assuming that state-local taxes respond more or less proportionately to the rise in the national product (a reasonable assumption), the states and local governments must have increased rates by 68 percent in these 17 years to push up their tax yields to current levels. The net result is, of course, that a greater degree of regression is being built into the national tax system by the states and local governments as they continue to seek for more revenues.

Parenthetically, it might be observed that the "tax revolt" which has been so much in the news of late must have been a reflection of the increasing burden of state and local taxes. The revolt is allegedly concentrated in the "middle income" classes living in the suburbs. In this, there is a paradox: this group probably pays a smaller proportion of its income in taxes than the poor and near poor (see below), but the taxes they have been paying, or recently began to pay, are highly visible. Their incomes have risen sharply in recent years, so that their federal income taxes are higher in dollar amounts despite the 1964 rate reduction. Six states have enacted new income taxes in the past eight years and ten states have enacted new sales taxes; many others have raised the rates of both taxes substantially. Most of the new suburbanites are now paying property taxes directly as home owners, rather than indirectly as tenants, and property taxes have also been rising everywhere. Tax morale was, therefore, generally at a low ebb when the federal government requested more taxes to finance a budget containing $30 billion to fight an unpopular war. Since the request was in the form of a surcharge on those already paying taxes, and did nothing about those who escaped, the existing inequities in the federal income tax at last became evident to large masses of taxpayers who have no difficulty in communicating their unhappiness to their Congressmen.

It is not easy to arrive at an accurate estimate of the impact of the whole tax system at various income levels. Taxes are reported to different federal, state, and local government agencies. No single agency has the responsibility to compel reporting of taxes on a meaningful and consistent basis. A number of isolated attempts have been made by students of public finance to piece together from the inadequate data estimates of the distribution of all taxes by income classes. These studies were for different years, make different assumptions for the incidence of the various taxes, and use different statistical sources and methodologies to correct for the inconsistencies in the data. Nevertheless, they all arrive at similar conclusions regarding the relative tax loads at different income levels.

The most recent estimates were prepared by the Council of Economic Advisers for the year 1965. They show the distribution of taxes by the income classes of families and unattached individuals, income being defined exclusive of transfer payments. The estimates for taxes and transfers separately, and in combination, are summarized in Table 5.

The following are the major conclusions that can be drawn from these and previously published estimates:

1. Since at least the mid-1930s, the federal tax system has been roughly proportional in the lower and middle income classes, and clearly progressive for the highest classes. Federal income tax

Table 5. Taxes and Transfers as Percentage of
Income, 1965

| Income Classes | Taxes | | | Transfer Payments | Taxes Less Transfers |
	Federal	State and Local	Total		
Under $2,000	19	25	44	126	−83[a]
$ 2,000– 4,000	16	11	27	11	16
4,000– 6,000	17	10	27	5	21
6,000– 8,000	17	9	26	3	23
8,000–10,000	18	9	27	2	25
10,000–15,000	19	9	27	2	25
15,000 and over	32	7	38	1	37
Total	22	9	31	14	24

[a]The minus sign indicates that the families and individuals in this class received more from federal, state, and local governments than they, as a group, paid to these governments in taxes.

Source: *Economic Report of the President*, 1969. Income excludes transfer payments, but includes realized capital gains in full and undistributed corporate profits.

data suggest that the preferential rate on capital gains, and the exclusion of interest on state and local bonds and other items from the tax base, have produced some regressivity for the very small group at the top of the income pyramid, say, beginning with incomes of $100,000 or more.

2. State and local taxes are regressive throughout the income scale.
3. The combined federal, state, and local tax burden is heaviest in the very bottom and top brackets, and lowest in the middle brackets. This statement is, of course, based on averages for each group and there are wide variations around these averages for specific individuals, depending on the sources of their incomes, the kind of property they own, and where they live.
4. The poor receive numerous transfer payments (e.g., social security unemployment compensation, public assistance, etc.) that are financed by this tax system. The net effect of transfers as against taxes is distinctly progressive, because transfer payments make up such a large proportion of total income at the bottom of the income distribution—56 percent for those with incomes of less than $2,000 in 1965. (To some extent, this progressively is overstated because the transfers do not always go to the same people who pay taxes, the best example being social security retirement benefits that are received only by retirees—many of whom are not poor—while $1.5 billion of the payroll tax levied to pay for these benefits are paid by the poor.) There is no reason in the abstract, why a nation should not levy taxes on and pay

transfers to the same groups; but while the nation wages a war on poverty, it is surely appropriate to consider the possibility of providing additional financial assistance to the poor by *tax reduction* as well as through transfer payments.

The preceding discussion indicates that the agenda for reforming this country's tax system to correct its regressive features is lengthy and complicated. It involves reconstruction of the tax systems at all levels of government, and the development of new forms of intergovernmental fiscal relations. State and local governments need to rely more heavily on income taxes, relieve the poor of paying sales taxes, and deemphasize the property tax. At the federal level, the most important items on the agenda are to alleviate the payroll tax on the poor, to deliver—at last—on promises made by both political parties to close loopholes in the income taxes, and make the estate and gift taxes more effective.

There are no easy solutions to the state-local problems, given the political constraints under which our federal system operates. At the state level, the trend is for moderate income and sales taxes—34 states already have both, and the number increases every year. Six states have adopted simple per capita credits against income taxes for sales taxes paid (with refunds for those who do not pay income taxes) to alleviate the sales tax burden on the poor. This device eliminates the regressive feature of the sales tax and makes it more acceptable on grounds of equity. Progress on the adoption of state income taxes has been slow, but there has been a new surge of adoptions by the states in the past couple of years as governors and legislators have realized that they cannot get along without the growth-responsive revenues from an income tax.

The states are also beginning to take a more responsible attitude toward their local governments, although the situation is admittedly bad in many parts of the country. More of the states' own revenues should be allocated to local governments through grants-in-aid to prevent the development of city income and sales taxes that tend to drive wealthy taxpayers and businesses to the suburbs. An ideal arrangement, that is already in operation in Maryland for income tax purposes, would be to have state-wide income and sales taxes along with modest "piggyback" local taxes—all collected by the state government and subject to state control so that individual communities will not get too far out of line with their neighbors. (As a long-run goal, the federal government should collect state-local, as well as federal, income taxes on the basis of a single return.)

The local governments need to improve local property tax administration to remove the haphazard way in which the tax applies to properties of equal values. The states can help by providing technical assistance and also by forcing the communities to meet minimum standards of administration. Consideration should also be given to the development of new local revenue sources to take some of the pressure off the general property tax. The best alternatives are the "piggyback" income and sales taxes already mentioned, always with the credit or refund for sales taxes paid by the poor.

In addition, it is time to tap the high and rising land values for some of the urgently needed local revenues. The National Commission on Urban Problems, which was chaired by former Senator Paul Douglas, has estimated that land values rose from $269 billion in 1956 to $523 billion in 1966, or about $25 billion a year. This tremendous increase in wealth was not created by the landowners but by society as a whole. This is, of course, the basis of the old "single tax" idea that was oversold by the zealots as a complete and final solution to the nation's tax problems, although correct in principle. The revenue potential of special taxes on land values or on increases in land values is modest, but the approach has merit even if it will not solve the financial problems of our cities and suburbs by itself. It would also discourage the hoarding of land for speculative purposes and thereby encourage more efficient use of land in and around the nation's cities.

But there is no hope for the states and local governments, whatever they do on their own initiative, unless the federal government cuts them in on its superior tax resources. It is true that federal grants to states and local governments have increased rapidly in recent years—from $5 billion in fiscal year 1958 to an estimated $25 billion this year—but the need is even greater than that. To satisfy this need, more money will have to be allocated to the categorical grants already authorized for such programs as education, health, welfare, and housing. Also, a federal-state-local income tax revenue-sharing system should be established to moderate the huge disparities in fiscal capacities of the 50 states and to give governors and local officials unrestricted funds that can be used to help solve their own particular problems. The Nixon administration's proposal, based on a plan devised by a Johnson task force, is a good—though modest—beginning.

Mayors and county managers are suspicious of revenue sharing because they have little faith that the states will distribute the funds fairly. To answer this criticism, various formulas have been devised to require the states to "pass through" at least a minimum percentage of the revenue-sharing grants. Disagreement over the details of the "pass-through" should not be allowed to delay the adoption of an idea that will relieve some of the fiscal pressure at the state and local levels and, at the same time, provide revenues from a progressive tax that otherwise would be raised mainly on a regressive basis. Ultimately, the federal government should allocate 2 percent of the federal individual income tax base to revenue sharing, which would amount to $8 billion at current income levels and as much as $12 billion in 1975.

Much has been said about the need for removing the poor from the income tax rolls, and Congress seems to be prepared to remedy this anachronism. But the more urgent problem is to remove the much heavier payroll tax burden of the poor. The federal income tax bill of the families and individuals who are officially classified as poor is only $200 million a year, as compared with the $1.5 billion they pay in payroll taxes. In addition, the regressive feature of the payroll tax at the higher income levels should be moderated immediately and ultimately eliminated entirely.

Several different approaches might be taken to achieve these objectives.

First, part or all of the payroll tax could be converted into a withholding tax for income tax purposes. No formal change in the payroll tax need be involved; at the end of the year, individuals would receive credit against their income taxes (or a refund if they are not income tax payers) for the amount of payroll taxes paid.

Second, contributions from general revenues might be made, on the basis of a fixed formula, to the social security and other trust funds. Such a possibility was foreseen in the earlier days of social security.

Third, the social security system might be combined with a liberalized and modernized public assistance system or some variant of a negative income tax. The negative income tax payments to the aged in such a system would be financed out of general revenues.

But whatever is ultimately done about the payroll tax as the basic revenue source for social security financing, the poor should be relieved of paying this tax as soon as possible. The principle of a minimum taxable level under the income tax—soon to be raised to the poverty levels—should be carried over into the payroll tax. The Internal Revenue Service is already proficient at handling tens of millions of refunds per year under the income tax; the additional payroll tax refunds would not be an excessive burden.

As this was being written, Congress was working hard to complete a tax reform bill. The details of the final legislation are still unclear, but it might be useful to list the most important issues that must be settled, now or later.

1. Revision of the treatment of capital gains is the highest priority item. Profits from sale of assets held more than six months are taxed at only half the regular rates up to a maximum of 25 percent, but even this tax may be avoided indefinitely if the assets are transferred from one generation to another through bequests. In the case of gifts, capital gains are taxed only if the assets are later sold by the recipient. As a result, billions of dollars of capital gains are subject to low rates or are never taxed.

Capital gains receive favored treatment for two reasons: first, full taxation in a single year of a large realized gain accumulated over many years would be unfair, unless the impact of the graduated income tax rates were moderated; second, too high a rate on capital gains might "lock" most security holders into their present portfolios. The first of these problems could be solved by averaging capital gains over the period they were held. The "lock-in" effect would be moderated by such an averaging provision, and also by taxing capital gains when assets are transferred, either by gift or at death. Both changes would reduce the advantages of holding on to assets whose values had risen.

A complete reform of the capital gains tax would raise perhaps $8 billion in additional revenues annually, mainly from the top 15 percent of the income population. But the more likely package—including a lengthening of the holding period from six months to a year and elimination of the maximum 25 percent tax rate (but not the exclusion of half of long-term capital gains)—would yield only about $700 million a year.

2. The toughest issue involves percentage depletion for oil, gas, and other minerals industries. These allowances are similar in many respects to ordinary depreciation. The difference is that the amounts written off as depreciation are limited to the cost of the asset, but percentage depletion can—and does—substantially exceed the amount invested. In addition, an immediate write-off is permitted for certain capital costs incurred in exploration and development, thus providing a double deduction for capital invested in these industries. Most economists who have studied the matter have concluded that present allowances are much too generous.

If the preferential treatment for all the minerals industries were entirely eliminated, revenues would be increased by $1.6 billion a year. If the oil depletion allowance is reduced from 27 percent to 20 percent and the other allowances are scaled down proportionately, as seems possible at this moment, additional revenues would amount to about $400 million a year.

3. The tax exemption of interest on state and local government securities is unfair because it benefits only the wealthy. It is also inefficient because the wealthy benefit from the full amount of the interest differential for the tax exemption, which is set by the market at the point where the marginal (and lower income) investor is encouraged to buy tax-exempts. According to one study, the federal government loses $2 of revenue for every $1 of interest subsidy received by the states and local governments. If state-local bond interest were taxed, the revenue could be used directly to help the states and local governments. The estimated revenue gain would be small initially because any legislation that might be enacted would apply only to future issues and a considerable part of the new revenue would be returned to the states in the form of a "sweetener" over and above what the present tax exemption is worth to them.

4. The most irrational and expensive provisions are the deductions for charitable contributions, interest payments, medical expenses, state

and local taxes, and other personal expenditures that cut out billions of dollars from the tax base. These deductions are designed to improve the definition of income on which taxes are to be based; in fact, many of the deductions are merely subsidies for particular types of personal expenditures that hardly merit government encouragement.

Deductions for state income taxes do not protect taxpayers against excessive rates. There is also some justification for continuing the deduction for sales and income taxes as a device to encourage further state use of these taxes to raise the revenues they desperately need. But the same rationale does not apply to property taxes; and there is certainly no excuse for deducting gasoline taxes, which are levied to pay for benefits received by highway users. The present method of computing the deduction for charitable contributions is also questionable. Limiting the deduction to contributions in excess of, say, 3 percent of income would encourage larger-than-average gifts to charity and save $1.5 billion of revenue each year. In addition, Congress should repeal the unlimited charitable deduction for those whose taxes and contributions together exceed 80 percent of their income for eight out of ten consecutive years. This provision has permitted many wealthy people to escape tax entirely by donating appreciated assets on which capital gains tax has not been paid but which are deductible at their full value (including the gain) against other income.

A series of reforms along these lines might bring in revenues in the neighborhood of $5 billion a year. But Congress will probably do very little in this area—except perhaps to eliminate the unlimited charitable deduction which will bring in $50 million annually and to raise the standard deduction (which will add to the erosion of the tax base—at a cost of $1.4 billion—and do nothing to refine the taxable income concept in a manner that would improve interpersonal equity).

5. The federal income tax has been particularly solicitous of the aged. Taxpayers over 65 years of age have an additional exemption of $600, pay no tax on their social security or railroad retirement pensions, and receive a tax credit on other retirement income if their earnings are below $1,524. These benefits are worth more than $3 billion a year. There is every reason to help the aged through public programs, but the tax system is a bad way to do this because it gives the largest amount of relief to those who need it least. It would be better to eliminate these deductions and use the revenue to increase social security benefits for all aged persons. The Kennedy and Johnson administrations recommended a more modest approach that would limit the income tax relief to low-income aged, but not raise any additional revenue.

6. Income splitting was enacted in 1948 to equalize the tax burdens of married persons living in community and noncommunity property states. (The former had already been able to split their incomes for tax

purposes.) But the provision introduced an unfair discrimination against single people, and reduced taxes by an estimated $10 billion a year. There are ways to eliminate this discrimination without introducing the old community property problems, but the large revenue loss—which goes almost entirely to married couples with incomes above $10,000—is probably irretrievable. This year, Congress seems to be in a mood to extend half the advantages of income splitting to single people aged 35 years or older and this will cost $650 million a year.

7. A few years ago, the Senate refused to accept a relatively simple House plan to withhold income tax on interest and dividends. Instead, they required information returns by corporations and financial institutions, a copy of which would go to the taxpayer. There was some improvement in the reporting of interest, but not nearly enough (dividends were underreported very much). The introduction of withholding is the only practical method of recovering the estimated $1 billion of tax that is now lost annually through the carelessness, inadvertence, and dishonesty of taxpayers (mainly in the lower and middle income classes).

8. Although some income tax avoidance will be eliminated by the new legislation, the final bill will not close all the loopholes. As a safeguard to prevent a few wealthy people from taking advantage of the special provisions that would remain, two reforms are now being seriously considered by the Congress. The first would require the allocation of personal deductions allowed to individuals between taxable and nontaxable income sources. Thus, if only half of a taxpayer's income is subject to tax, he would be entitled to only half his deductions. The second would introduce a minimum income tax at half the ordinary rates on an individual's total income (including all nontaxable sources) or require an individual to pay tax at the full rates on at least half his total income. These revisions would add $800 million of tax revenue a year if the income definition included all sources of income. But they are not a substitute for comprehensive reform, but they will be needed until all the income tax loopholes have been plugged—and that is not likely to happen very soon.

9. The corporation income tax would not be in bad shape if the depletion allowances were modified, but a few technical reforms are also needed. Corporations should not be allowed to reduce their taxes by splitting up into a large number of smaller corporations. (Each corporation has a $25,000 exemption against the corporation normal tax, which is worth $6,500 for each corporation.) Banks and other financial institutions have overly generous allowances for additions to reserves for losses on their loans; these should be made more realistic. Real estate operators should not be allowed to deduct depreciation at accelerated rates and then, when the property is sold, taxed at the capital gains rates on their profits (which is partly the result of the excessive depreciations). These

revisions, which are incorporated in this year's reform bill (except that the real estate loophole was kept open for residential construction), would add close to $2 billion a year to the corporation income tax yield. In addition, the $100 deduction for dividends under the individual income tax—worth about $200 million a year in lost revenue—is silly and should be repealed.

10. Taxes on property transferred from one generation to the next are avoided in two ways. First, wealthy people put money in trust funds for their wives, children, and grandchildren that are taxed when they are set up but not when the income passes between generations or when the trusts terminate. It is possible to escape estate taxes for two or three generations in this way. Second, since gift tax rates are much lower than estate tax rates, wealthy individuals can reduce the taxes on their wealth or eliminate them entirely by systematically distributing the assets over a period of years through gifts.

Avoidance through gifts can be reduced by combining the estate and gift taxes into one tax. (An integrated tax would reduce the avoidance through gifts, but not eliminate it entirely, because an individual could earn interest on any tax he postponed.) The trust loophole is more difficult to close, but methods have been devised to tax trust assets once every generation. Another improvement in the estate and gift taxes that would lower rather than raise revenues, would be to permit husbands and wives to transfer wealth freely between them without tax; under present law, half of these transfers are taxable.

The long list of needed revisions in our federal, state, and local tax system should convince anyone that the reforms now being contemplated will not make a significant change in the progressivity of the system. Congress could, if it wishes, increase the yield of the present tax system by $25 billion a year, an amount that would be sufficient substantially to relieve the tax burdens of the poor and low-income nonpoor and to lower tax rates clear across the board. Instead, the revenue to be gained from this year's tax reform bill—a Herculean effort by past standards—may be in the neighborhood of $3 billion a year and much of this will be used to reduce the taxes of the "middle" income classes by what amounts to little more than a pittance, while the poor continue to bear much heavier tax burdens.

According to the Council of Economic Advisers, total taxes of those with incomes below $2,000 amounted to $7.3 billion in 1965, of which $4.2 billion were state and local taxes and $3.1 billion were federal. Those with incomes between $2,000 and $4,000 paid another $11.5 billion consisting of $6.8 billion federal and $4.7 billion state-local taxes. The total tax bill of $18.8 billion of those with incomes below $4,000 suggests what regressivity really means in a country collecting taxes amounting to about 31 percent of its GNP.

The classic objection against an attack on tax regressivity has been that there is simply not enough income in the higher classes to do the job. Would a substantial reduction in regressivity require confiscatory rates? To appreciate one of the significant magnitudes involved, suppose the federal government decided to refund all general sales, payroll, and property taxes on housing paid by those who are officially classified as poor. (The remaining taxes are selective excise taxes levied for sumptuary purposes or in lieu of user charges, which could not be refunded in any practical way. After this year, the poor will not pay any federal income taxes.) These refunds would amount to about $4 billion—perhaps three-quarters of the total tax burden of the poor and one-sixth of the burden of those with incomes below $4,000—less than what this year's tax reform bill may give away in higher standard deductions and rate reductions.

It might be thought that such a proposal—to lift three-quarters of the tax burden of the poor—is too timid. Why not go further? That indeed could be done, but only as part of a larger redistribution of the tax burden. After all, it is both inequitable and politically impossible to create a noticeable "tax divide" between the poor (a fluid concept, in any case) and the rest of society. To make the tax system progressive, it would not be enough drastically to reduce the tax burden of the poor; the burdens of the near poor and others at the lower end of the income scale would have to be cut simultaneously. Indeed—again on principles of equity and political feasibility—the relief should be diffused upwards until it benefits, say, the lower half of the income distribution (or, more technically, those receiving less than the median income, which is now in excess of $9,000).

There are a number of ways of modifying the tax system to redistribute the tax burden in this way. The most straightforward—and perhaps even the most practical, given the federal system of government in this country—would be to give taxpayers credits against the federal income tax for a declining percentage of the major taxes they now pay to federal, state, and local governments, except for income taxes. Suppose we make refunds to the poor for the general sales, payroll, and property taxes they pay and permit others to claim credits against their federal income taxes for 75 percent of these same taxes if they are in the $2,000–4,000 class, 50 percent in the $4,000–6,000 class, and 25 percent in the $6,000–8,000 class. (Obviously, refunds would be paid to those with credits larger than their federal income taxes.)

Let us further assume that the taxes paid by those with incomes between $8,000 and $10,000 remain the same, and that the revenues needed to pay for the relief below $8,000 would come from those with incomes above $10,000 in proportion to the taxes they now pay. Again, we need not be concerned with the details of how this can be done. It would certainly be more equitable to close the major federal income tax loopholes first and then raise whatever additional revenue is needed by an increase in the rates above $10,000. Either way, the ratio of total taxes to income for any specific income class could be set at the same figure, although the burden *within* each class would be distributed much more equitably if the loopholes were closed first.

It turns out that, in 1965, the credits (and refunds) would have reduced taxes for those with incomes of less than $8,000 by $19 billion, and this would have required an increase in the taxes paid by those in the $10,000–15,000 class from an average of 27 percent to 32 percent and by those above $15,000 from 38 percent to 46 percent, or an average tax increase of about a fifth. The resulting effective rates of tax in this system compare with the rates as they were in 1965 as follows:

Table 6. Taxes as Percentage of Income, 1965

Income Classes	Present Tax System	Alternative Tax System
Under $2,000	44	13
$ 2,000– 4,000	27	14
4,000– 6,000	27	19
6,000– 8,000	26	23
8,000–10,000	27	27
10,000–15,000	27	32
15,000 and over	38	46
Total	31	31

Note: Income includes capital gains, but excludes transfer payments.

A glance should convince anyone that this tax system would by no means eradicate taxes at the lower end of the income scale. Most people would regard tax burdens of as much as 13 to 14 percent for those with incomes below $4,000 and 23 percent for those between $6,000 and $8,000 as much too high. Yet, the idea of relieving tax burdens for the lower half of the income distribution even in this relatively modest way is clearly impractical; Congress would face a revolt if it tried to raise taxes on incomes above $10,000 by an average of 20 percent.

Perhaps we exaggerate the difficulties by using 1965 figures? Incomes have risen substantially so that there is much more income to be taxed above $15,000. But state and local taxes have also risen and the degree of regressivity in the tax system has been aggravated. On balance, the rise in incomes has probably been more powerful, but not enough to alter very much the general conclusions that we have reached from the 1965 data.

The prospects for making the tax system progressive are more discouraging when one notes the way Congress usually behaves when it reduces taxes. On the basis of past performance, one can predict with certainty that Congress will not limit income tax reduction to the lowest income classes. In 1964, when federal income taxes were reduced by an average of 20 percent, incomes above $15,000 were given a tax cut of 14 percent. This year, much more than the revenue to be gained from closing the loopholes and repealing the investment credit may be given away in tax rate reductions. Of course, these actions reflect the pressures on the Congressmen. The influence of the groups arrayed against a significant redistribution of the tax burden is enormous, and there is no effective lobby for the poor and the near poor.

It may be that, at some distant future date, the well-to-do and the rich will have enough income to satisfy not only their own needs, but also to help relieve the tax burdens of those who are less fortunate. In the meantime, the tax system will continue to disgrace the most affluent nation in the world.

The Case for an Income Guarantee

JAMES TOBIN

Not whether to, but how to, eliminate poverty has become a top priority economic question. Here is the rationale of a former member of the Council of Economic Advisers.

In the national campaign to conquer poverty there are two basic strategies, which may be labeled concisely, if somewhat inaccurately, "structural" and "distributive." The structural stategy is to build up the capacities of the poorest fifth of the population to earn decent incomes. The distributive strategy is to assure every family a decent standard of living regardless of its earning capacity. In my opinion both strategies are essential; correctly designed, they are more complementary than competitive. To date the main emphasis of the federal "war on poverty" has been the structural approach. I shall argue that the war will not be won without a new and imaginative distributive strategy as well.

General economic progress raises the earning capacities of the populations at large—even of the less educated, less skilled, less experienced, less motivated, and less healthy. Even without federal programs (other than overall fiscal and monetary policies to keep the labor force fully employed and the economy growing), the incidence of poverty gradually declines. Measuring poverty by the government's official income standard ($3,130 a year for four-person nonfarm families, and amounts estimated to yield comparable standards of living for households of other sizes and circumstances), its incidence has fallen from 22 percent to 17 percent since 1959.

From James Tobin, "The Case for an Income Guarantee," *Public Interest* (Summer, 1966), pp. 31–41. Copyright 1966 National Affairs, Inc. Reprinted by permission of the author and publisher.

148

The "war on poverty" testifies that the decline has not been fast enough for the American conscience. But accelerating it by structural measures is bound to be a slow and expensive process. Adults must be trained or retrained; they must acquire work experience, good work habits, self-confidence, and motivation; they must be made medically fit for regular employment; they must be placed in jobs and often moved to new locations. What is required is almost a case-by-case approach. Leaving the aged aside, there are about 8 million poor households including 9.5 million persons aged 22 to 54 and 3 million aged 16 to 21. The task of upgrading the earning capacities of the present generation of adults is staggering, a fact which in no way diminishes the importance of the effort or the value of each individual success.

The earning capacities of the next generation may be successfully raised by general structural measures—radical improvements in the education, health, and residential environment of the 14 million children of the poor. Again, the urgent importance of these efforts is in no way dimmed by recognizing the great difficulties they confront.

But the structural strategy will take many years, probably more than a generation. Even then its success will be incomplete; there will remain a hard core of families with inadequate earning capacity because of ineradicable physical, psychological, or circumstantial disabilities. And in the interim many more families, with disabilities remediable but not remedied, will fail to earn a decent living.

A distributive strategy is necessary, too, and the sooner the better. Families must have a minimally decent standard of living, whether or not they now have the ability to earn it in the job market. This can be provided by public assistance, and to withhold it from poor families is neither just (since their disabilities are, if not irremediable, the consequences of past discriminations and deficiences in public services) nor necessary (since the upper four-fifths of the nation can surely afford the 2 percent of Gross National Product which would bring the lowest fifth across the poverty line).

Sometimes income assistance is scorned as treating the symptoms of poverty, in contrast to the structural strategy, which treats the causes. This reproach is not justified. For one thing, there is nothing intrinsically wrong with treating symptoms, and sometimes it is the best the doctors can do. More seriously, the symptoms of today's poverty may be the causes of tomorrow's. The conditions of life in which many children now grow up may predestine them to low earning capacity as adults.

However, many of those who distrust the distributive strategy have a more sophisticated point in mind. They are afraid that more generous income assistance to the poor will actually retard improvements in their earning capacities. If a decent standard of living is guaranteed, why should anyone work to get it or to acquire the ability to earn it on his own? For centuries this cynicism about human nature has been the excuse by which the affluent have relieved their individual and collective consciences and pocketbooks of the burden of their less fortunate brethren.

We cannot dismiss the question just because it has a shabby history. "Human nature" is not a reason to withhold public subsidies from people with low-earning capacity. But it definitely is a reason to give the subsidies in a way that does not destroy but indeed reinforces the incentives of the recipients to work and to increase the economic value of their work. The war on poverty needs a distributive strategy, but one that is carefully designed to support and strengthen its structural strategy.

Unfortunately our present congeries of public assistance programs—federal, state, and local—has just the opposite effect. The incentives built in to our present subsidy programs are perverse. Unless public assistance is reformed and rationalized, it will seriously handicap the structural weapons deployed in the campaign against poverty. An improved public assistance program will not be cheap. If it is designed to aid rather than retard the conquest of poverty, its cost will for some years be more than our present programs. But it offers the hope that the conditions giving rise to the need for public subsidies will gradually be remedied.

What are the defects of public assistance today? First is its inadequacy. Our governments administer a bewildering variety of welfare and social insurance programs, from Federal Old Age, Survivors, and Disability Insurance (OASDI) to township relief. *Yet half of the poor benefit from none of these; and most of the public money spent to supplement personal incomes goes to families above the poverty line.*

These facts are shocking but not as surprising as they may at first appear. Eligibility to benefit from most government income supplements depends on circumstances quite remote from current economic need. For social insurance—OASDI and unemployment compensation—eligibility and size of benefits depend on past contributions by the individual or his employer. Many programs assist particular groups—veterans, farmers, retired railroad workers, the blind, etc.

Even in the main noncontributory general assistance programs, economic need is a necessary condition for benefits but not a sufficient one. The most important of these is Aid for Dependent Children (AFDC), administered under federal supervision by the states and localities, and financed almost wholly by federal funds. AFDC payments are based on need, but the several states define need with widely varying degrees of realism and seldom attempt to meet fully even their own calculations of need. A 1961 study showed that the Middle Atlantic states met all the income requirements they estimated. The East South Central States—

Kentucky, Tennessee, Mississippi, and Alabama—estimated need at 20 percent less, met on average only 61 percent (Mississippi 38 percent) of the
need so estimated, and met full need in only 3 percent of their cases.
Federal law permits payments only to families with children, and of these
only to families without an employed male adult—where, in effect, the
father has died or deserted, or is disabled or unemployed. Most states
restrict eligibility more than the federal law requires.

There are also federally financed programs of assistance to the aged
and disabled, which fill some of the gaps Social Security still leaves both
in eligibility and in adequacy of benefits. For the indigent who qualify for
nothing else there is old-fashioned local relief, but here the applicant may
run afoul of local residence requirements and other defensive stratagems.

Second, public assistance is geared to need in a manner that provides
perverse incentives to those dependent upon it. One major destructive
incentive is the one which AFDC gives for the break-up or nonformation
of families. *Too often a father can provide for his children only by leaving
both them and their mother.* It is hard to imagine a social contrivance
more surely designed to perpetuate dependence on "welfare" in one generation after the other. We know that the major problems of poor people
of all colors are related, as both cause and effect, to unstable and chaotic
family structures. We know that, for historical reasons, Negro families
tend to be matriarchal. We know the crucial importance of home environment in education, and we know the dangers of depriving boys of male
adult models. To accentuate all these difficulties by deliberate public
policy is a piece of collective insanity which it would be hard to match.

The "means test" provides other disincentives—disincentives to work,
to save, to gain skills. The "means test" seems innocent enough in appearance and intent. It says that the welfare payments shall be made only if,
and only to the extent that, the family cannot meet its needs (as officially
calculated) from its own resources. Thus if, in a given locality, the effective standard of need (which may be only a fraction of an estimated minimal budget) for a mother and four children is $2,500 a year, the family
will receive $2,500 from the state if its members earn nothing on their own,
$1,500 if they earn $1,000, $500 if they earn $2,000, and so on. This arrangement, under which your total take-home pay is the same no matter how
much you earn, is obviously not designed to encourage work or training
for future work. One way to describe it is to say that the marginal tax rate
on earnings is (so long as earnings do not exceed $2,500 in the example)
100 percent. The accuracy of this description, so far as incentive effects are
concerned, is not impaired by the fact that the "tax" on additional earnings
is not a literal payment to the government but a reduction in the government payment to the family.

The means test also discourages thrift. Consider two self-supporting families, one of whom saves while the other incurs debts. When and if misfortunes occur, the welfare authorities will give full help to the second but will generally force the thrifty family to use up its savings. Similarly, a man who has over a lifetime of work acquired his own home may be required to surrender title to it if he can't get by without public assistance in his old age.

It is true that there remains the incentive to escape public assistance entirely, and, since the welfare standard of life is a meager one at best, this incentive may seem substantial. But to many welfare households, especially the broken homes, it is too big a jump to be a realistic aspiration. Unattainable goals may be demoralizing rather than motivating. Most welfare dependents cannot set their sights higher than part-time, low-paid employment. Yet this may be extremely important, both to acquire work experience and rudimentary skill and to build up the family's morale and sense of achievement. The system is rigged against it; there is nothing in it for them.

The welfare system of the United States contains plenty of ironies. A nation which regards the integrity of the nuclear family as the very backbone of its social structure provides incentives for its dissolution. A society which views high marginal income tax rates as fatal to the incentives for effort and thrift essential to its economy imposes 100 percent rates on a large fraction of its population. The explanation of such bizarre behavior is probably that present welfare policies represent an uneasy compromise among several principles. Since the thirties our society has acknowledged its responsibility to assure through government a minimal standard of living for all citizens. But the corollary charge on the public purse has been accepted grudgingly, and the fear that the "privilege" of welfare might be abused has dominated policy.

A by-product of this dominant fear is that much of the considerable administrative effort in public welfare reduces to detective work, to make sure there are no "cheaters" on the rolls, and to close surveillance of the clients' sources and uses of funds, to make sure that tax money is not wasted in riotous living. Everything confirms welfare families in the demoralizing belief that they cannot manage their own affairs. This tendency is reenforced by the propensity of legislators to give assistance in kind—surplus foods, subsidized housing, medical care for the indigent or "medically indigent." Eligibility for these specific benefits is usually defined by a maximum income limit, awkward to administer and perverse in incentive effects.

An alternative approach, which commands the support of many economists of all political and ideological shades (Milton Friedman, Goldwater's chief economic advisor in 1964, was one of the first to suggest it) is a national system of income supplements graduated to income and to family size. For more fortunate citizens, personal income taxes likewise depend on income and family size; therefore the proposed income supplements can be called, not very felicitously, negative income taxes. They may also be regarded as federally guaranteed incomes, since they involve, among other things, federal payment of a specified amount to every family with zero income.

Various proposals embodying one or more of these features have been set forth; and, as with all reform causes, the proponents differ widely in their reasons. Some—like Robert Theobald and W. H. Ferry of Robert Maynard Hutchins' Center for the Study of Democratic Institutions—are interested mainly in the income guarantee. They believe that automation is rendering work for pay obsolete, and that government handouts are the only way to give the public the means to buy the immense bounty produced by the automatons. They do not share, therefore, the concern of economists to provide incentives for work and for building up earning capacity. I disagree strongly with their diagnosis, but for other reasons I also advocate what amounts to an income guarantee.

The personal income tax would become a two-way street. At present, calculations of the tax form lead to two alternative outcomes: either the citizen owes something or he owes nothing. Under the proposal there would be a third possibility: the government owes him something. This would not carry the stigma of charity or relief; it would be a right of national citizenship symmetrical to the obligation to pay taxes. It would be uniform across the nation. A poor family would not suffer because of residence in a poor or unresponsive state or county, or because of migration. The government payment would not depend on the supposed causes of need (absence or disability of the husband, etc.) but simply on the fact of need as scaled to family income and size. Finally, the graduation of the "negative tax" to the family's income would, like that of the existing positive tax, give the family an incentive to earn more on its own.

For illustration, consider the following scheme: The Internal Revenue Service pays the "taxpayer" $400 per member of his family if the family has no income. This allowance is reduced by 33⅓ cents for every dollar the family earns; the incentive is that the family improves its situation by two-thirds of every dollar it earns. At an income of $1,200 per person the allowance becomes zero. Above that income, the family pays taxes, still at the rate of one-third on each additional dollar. At some higher income its tax liability so computed becomes the same as it is now, and beyond that point the present tax schedule applies.

The impact of the proposal is exemplified for a married couple with three children in Table 1. The first two columns show how the present tax schedule treats the family. They assume that the family qualifies only for the standard deduction. The last two columns show how the proposed

Table 1. Illustration of Impact of Proposed Income Allowances: Married Couple with Three Children

Family Income before Federal Tax or Allowance	Present Tax Schedule		Present Tax Schedule with Public Assistance		Proposed Schedule	
	Tax (−)	Income After Tax	Tax (−) or Assistance (+)	Income After Tax or Assistance	Tax (−) or Allowance (+)	Income After Tax or Allowance
$ 0	$ 0	$ 0	$+2,500	$2,500	$+2,000	$2,000
1,000	0	1,000	+1500	2,500	+1,667	2,667
2,000	0	2,000	+ 500	2,500	+1,333	3,333
2,500	0	2,500	0	2,500	+1,167	3,667
3,000	0	3,000	0	3,000	+1,000	4,000
3,700	0	3,700	0	3,700	+767	4,467
4,000	−42	3,958	−42	3,958	+667	4,667
5,000	−185	4,815	−185	4,815	+333	5,333
6,000	−338	5,662	−338	5,662	0	6,000
7,000	−501	6,499	−501	6,499	−333	6,667
7,963[a]	−654	7,309	−654	7,309	−654	7,309
8,000	−658	7,342	−658	7,342	−658	7,342

[a]Income level at which the present and proposed methods of calculating tax coincide; above this income the present tax schedule applies.

integrated schedule of allowances and taxes would treat the same family. The middle columns superimpose on the present tax law hypothetical public assistance, designed to see that the family has $2,500 and administered by a strict means test. The proposed improvement in the incentive to the family to earn income on its own (to move down in the table) is clear from comparing columns 5 and 7.

Similar tables would apply to families of other sizes. It may not be desirable, however, to apply the basic formula of $400 per capita across the board. Instead, a financial incentive to limit family size could be built in by diminishing and perhaps eliminating the extra amount allowed for an additional child when the size of the family is already large. This would make sense if, and only if, the government simultaneously were making sure that birth control information and technique are widely disseminated.

In the design of an integrated allowance and tax schedule a compromise must be struck among three objectives: (1) providing a high basic allowance for families with little or no earnings, (2) building in a strong incentive to earn more, and (3) limiting the budgetary cost of the scheme, and in particular minimizing the payment of benefits to those who do not need them. For example, in Table 1 the initial allowance might be raised to $3,000. But if the 33⅓ percent "tax rate" were retained for incentive reasons, all the entries in columns 6 and 7 would be increased algebraically by $1,000 (the last one only approximately so), and the table would have to be considerably lengthened to cover all the beneficiaries of the proposal. Obviously the government would be paying sizable benefits to families who do not need them. This implication of a $3,000 initial allowance could be escaped by raising the new "tax rate" to 50 percent, the break-even income level, at which there is no tax positive or negative, would remain $6,000. But the right to retain half of one's own earnings is a less powerful incentive than retention of two-thirds.

I do not contend that the particular compromise struck in my illustrative proposal is optimal. But in discussing alternatives it is essential to keep in mind that some compromise is necessary, that there are inexorable conflicts among the three listed objectives.

The illustrative proposal sketched above would reduce the net take of the federal income tax by roughly $12–15 billion a year. Against this cost must be set the eventual savings of a large part of the $55 billion a year now spent by federal, state, and local governments for categorical public assistance. How would the cost be met?

From an overall economic point of view, there is no cost to the nation. This is a redistribution of income and consumption, not a governmental draft on productive resources such as is involved in building missiles or schools. But a burden nonetheless falls on those whose taxes are higher than they would be otherwise. It will doubtless be easier for them to accept the plan if the cost to them is a tax rate reduction foregone rather than an actual boost in rates.

An income allowance plan of this design in no way conflicts with the structural measures of the war on poverty. Indeed, people on welfare would have more, not less, incentive to enroll in training and apprenticeship programs. They will keep more of what they are paid while training, and more of what they subsequently earn. After financial detective work is turned over to the experts of the Internal Revenue Service, social workers can concentrate on their proper professional specialties, family guidance and rehabilitation. The crucial substantive needs in the public sector—for Headstart classes, community schools, clinics, hospitals, day care centers, etc.—must be attacked by other means. But a new distributive strategy can make its beneficiaries better able and better motivated to take advantage of improved public services.

Automation in a Market Economy

Do machines displace labor? The controversy is an old, and still un-
settled one. Here is an analysis that raises some disturbing issues.

Traditionally, there have been two kinds of antitechnological thinking: the Neo-Luddite, which emphasizes the displacement of workers'
jobs, and the Tory Romantic, which emphasized the shattering of traditional social patterns. The latter position has recently been developed in
its extreme form by Jacques Ellul, who argues that the dominance of technique totally undermines the traditional moral concerns of Western culture. Both contain important elements of truth, but the first fails to
recognize the potential for new industries and even a whole new matrix
of social interdependence, in which nearly everyone's living standard is
higher; the second denies the possibility of technology leading to a new
form of social structure where technique would become a means for man
to dominate his environment.

Nevertheless, to people who experience none or few of the benefits
of technological change, or experience them only by accident or fate,
technology will appear destructive, arbitrary, constraining, pervasive, and
independent of human concerns. To the dispossessed, for example, technological progress means a better equipped, more efficient, quietly inhuman police, a more elaborate bureaucracy, and a more complicated
environment. To them, and to many others, it means urban sprawl, air
pollution, smog, traffic, noise, and unpredictable changes in the job market.
Nor does technological change present this face only to the weak and
downtrodden. The employee whose job is suddenly altered or abolished

From Pamphlet No. 2. Published by Movement for a Democratic Society, the off-
campus, non-student wing of Students for a Democratic Society.

through a decision in which he had no part, the city official whose problems appear to multiply, exponentially and autonomously, the citizen suddenly aware of his perilous existence in the shadow of nuclear weapons, the housewife confronted by a bewildering array of prepackaged foods, and everyone confronted by the mass media—all find themselves powerless to control and unlikely to benefit from humanly created power to shape—and destroy—our natural and social environment.

Both the distribution of the benefits of technical progress and the disposition of the power to control it depend on the social structure; in particular, on economic and legal or property relations. The primary benefits of new technical methods go quite literally to those who profit from their introduction; and the power to control technical progress rests largely with those who control the large corporations capable of underwriting research. For the most part civilian technical advances are introduced in response to market criteria—will the improvement increase profits, will it improve sales or secure the firm's competitive position or improve its public image? (This applies even to civilian government agencies which, with some notable exceptions, are obliged to operate with "economic efficiency.") Technical advances in military and space activities certainly involve market criteria where process efficiency is involved; but though decisions, say, as to whether or not to produce new types of weapons will depend, not on the market, but on military judgment, whatever that is. The market, in turn, can be influenced through the media of communication and by the use of appropriate sales and marketing techniques, and military judgment and Congressional appropriations can be influenced through lobbying. This is not to suggest that a small, unified group holds the technological destiny of America in its hands and directs it according to its own ends. On the contrary; a small, disunited number of men in key positions—primarily business leaders, but including political and military decision-makers—with divergent and conflicting interests, determine the technological future, and hence, to a considerable extent, the pace and nature of social change, as an incidental by-product of competitive decision-making on quite different matters. Technological change, and all the attendant social development and dislocation, emerge as unintended, often unforeseen, consequences of competition for market shares, profit and political influence. Technological change is determinate, but no one consciously and responsibly determines it.

The importance of understanding this can hardly be overstressed today, particularly since we may be on the verge of really major technological advances, which the market system, at least as presently constituted, may be increasingly unable to absorb. The claims of Theobald, Seligman and others that a Technological Revolution is actually underway may seem exaggerated, but there can be no doubt that qualitatively a different kind of technological change has appeared on the horizon. The statistical picture is varied. The average rate of technical progress (rate of increase in output per man-hour) from 1909 to 1947 was 2 percent; during the years 1957 to 1963 this rose to slightly over 3 percent (3.6 percent in 1964, 2.8 percent in 1965). One striking feature of the postwar period has been the remarkable performance of agriculture. In spite of relatively slight investment, productivity per man-hour increased an average 5.7 percent per annum from 1947 to 1963 (7.3 percent in 1965). In the nonagricultural sector productivity has tended to rise since 1957 at an average rate exceeding 2.5 percent, but while above the previous half-century average, this is not above the average for the boom decade 1919 to 1929. Productivity among production workers in the manufacturing sectors (where automation might be expected to proceed fastest) has increased most rapidly (3.5 percent per year, on average) but apparently less rapidly than during the period 1919 to 1929 (5.6 percent). These figures hardly support a claim for a "revolution." But matters are different when we look at specific technological proposals. Major break-throughs have occurred in metallurgy, metal processing, machine tools, warehousing, printing and communications, transport and materials handling, design of industrial manipulators, and, of course, agriculture. Pilot projects indicate substantial and overdue progress in prefabricated construction of high-rise dwelling units. These developments are significantly linked; just as, historically, improvements in various industries all clustered around the substitution of mechanical (steam) power for human power, and later around both the assembly line principle and electrical light and power, so new improvements in industrial technique tend to cluster around the introduction of self-correcting automatic control systems—the principle of negative feedback. The substitution of mechanical for human guidance of tools in shaping materials marked the transition from a craft to an industrial economy. Mechanical control is nothing new. But automatic self-correction in such control is. This feature becomes even more significant when combined with the ability to calculate and solve problems, since then a flexible sequence of complicated operations can be programmed, allowing the computer to decide the appropriate order in which to perform them on different occasions. In this way mechanical decision-making and mechanical calculation can be substituted for human. The social implication of this is that machines can now, for the first time, be expected to replace men in the services sector and at lower management levels. Previously these areas had absorbed labor displaced from manufacturing and agriculture. Now no sector can be relied upon to absorb displaced labor.

Nor is the new automation prohibitively expensive. Leontief has estimated its cost as 6 percent of total plant cost. He contends that while to date no great change in employment has taken place, the same could have been said for horses in 1909. Like labor today, their working conditions were better, pay higher and hours shorter than ever before. Projected, the trend showed a steady rising curve of affluence, and the automobile counted for no more than a fleck on the horizon. The analogy is disquieting—the more so when we consider that almost 75 percent of current research and development effort is channeled into war-related industries. If this were shifted to projects in the civilian economy we could expect an enormous increase in productivity of those industries whose goods appear on the market.

By contrast, military hardware is not marketed in the economist's sense of the term; there is no autonomous demand for it, nor can it be "consumed" in any reasonable sense. It is paid for out of taxes and the amount bought depends partly on military estimates of need (which are strongly influenced by the politics of interservice rivalry) and partly on the effectiveness of defense-industry lobbies. Technical progress in military goods can be absorbed without displacing workers so long as Congress can be persuaded to foot a given size of the bill. This progress simply means more bang for a buck, and Congress seems willing to buy virtually any amount of bang.

But in the civilian market economy people are not always so agreeably willing to spend. If technological progress speeds up, their regrettable parsimony may lead to an impasse. With given wage contracts, technical progress (during a year) shifts distributive shares in favor of profits, and, except in times of acute labor shortage, the wage increases subsequently granted seldom restore the original distribution. But the recipients of profits normally spend additional income at a lower rate than wage-earners. Even if the additional income resulting from technical progress were evenly divided, higher investment (in absolute terms) would be required to absorb the higher savings resulting, but if a higher proportion of the extra income goes to profits, a higher ratio of investment to income would be needed to maintain full utilization of capacity. Investment, however, will be undertaken only if there is a reasonable prospect that the products of new plant and equipment can be sold. If consumer demand as a fraction of national income is falling, as extremely rapid technical progress would entail, the incentive to invest will be appreciably weakened, no matter how high productivity has become. The result will be a lower level of utilization of capacity, which usually means laying off workers. This, in turn, means a further fall in consumption expenditure, and, at least in non-union industries, pressure on wage rates, as employers can threaten to replace employed workers with unemployed ones at lower wages. Lower wage rates, if they come about, also mean a fall in consumption spending, and a still further weakening of the incentive to invest.

In short, if a high rate of technical progress leads to a rise in profit's share of national income, and if spending out of additional profit income is less than spending out of additional wage income—both very plausible assumptions—then rapid technical progress will tend to lead to a slump. To avoid this, government intervention will be necessary. But there are significant limits to what government can do in a free enterprise system in which political activity must be financed by those who possess substantial income-bearing property. He who pays the piper calls the tune. Government spending will not normally be allowed to compete with private enterprise, either in the provision of marketable goods and services, or in the market for scarce factors of production. One suggestion, of course, is that the government could spend funds to eliminate poverty and improve conditions in the cities.

But a successful and widespread poverty program might well put a rather high floor under wages, particularly the wages of nonunion workers, with adverse effects on marginal and small businesses. This suggests limiting the poverty program, e.g., to training and retraining workers for areas in which there is a demand. Perhaps more important, any poverty program that involves organizing the poor is bound to upset the balance of political power in the cities. A program that does not involve organizing the poor is unlikely to have much impact. The most acceptable way for the government to spend is to contract with private firms operating on a profit-making basis for goods which the government in turn will consume itself, and so will never put on the market in competition with privately produced commodities. The areas of government activity which most obviously meet these conditions are military and aero-space enterprises, and these accounted for nearly 70 percent of the 1966 $144 billion appropriations budget (current military: 53.6 percent; national debt: 8.9 percent; veterans: 4.8 percent; space: 3.4 percent, to which some part of foreign relations: 2.2 percent should probably be added)

This suggests that the market system, as presently constituted, cannot easily handle the impact of rapid technological improvement in a way that would permit any widespread sharing of the benefits. In addition, the market system fails in two important ways to provide adequate incentives to introduce technical progress. First, in advanced economies many of the most important innovations involve "public goods," goods that must be used or consumed collectively, and many of which must be produced by "natural monopolies," e.g., media of communication, systems of transportation, education, etc. But, as our experience shows, the market system is not well adapted to make optimal use of these; regulation and subsidies are required even for suboptimal operation, but such regulation is usually easily influenced by industry's portion of fixed costs. In the face of a drop in sales a fully automated firm has little "flexibility"—it cannot lay off workers. It can shut down, but short of that it cannot easily adapt its current costs to its rate of sales. There may well be ways of avoiding this im-passe (e.g., by installing a series of small plants rather than one large one), but to adopt them is to adapt technology to financial considerations—it is likely to mean choosing a technologically inferior system to provide finan-cial safety, of capitalism, but even in the absence of such ownership rights net income—the value of the surplus of current output over production and replacement needs—could be distributed through the market, e.g., by paying each member of the labor or supervisory force a fraction of the surplus proportional to the market, the course of prudence, but hardly a recommendation for the capitalist system.

Faced on the one hand with the inability of the market to respond to rapid technological change in a way that will spread its benefits and on the other with the market's inability in certain spheres to provide incen-tives to innovate, the liberal's solution is to try to reform the market system. Each difficulty is treated as a specific failure of the system to "work," for which specific remedies must be found. Liberals have had considerable success in this and their ingenuity must not be underrated, but it is on this issue that liberals and the New Left divide. The objection to the liberal program is not that reform is impossible, but that it is irrelevant; it is not merely the working of the society that is deficient, it is what it is working at. To the New Left the organization of the social production and distribu-tion of goods and services around the profit motive is inherently objection-able, and the fact that it is working badly suggests that the time is ripe to consider an alternative mode of organization.

Production, Consumption,
and Externalities

ROBERT U. AYRES AND ALLEN V. KNEESE

Here the relationship between externalities and environmental pollution
is explored along with a proposal for coping with them.

For all that, welfare economics can no more reach conclusions applicable to the real world without some knowledge of the real world
than can positive economics . . .[1]

Despite tremendous public and governmental concern with problems such as environmental pollution, there has been a tendency in the
economics literature to view externalities as exceptional cases.

We believe that at least one class of externalities—those associated
with the disposal of residuals resulting from the consumption and production process—must be viewed quite differently. They are a normal, indeed,
inevitable part of these processes. Their economic significance tends to
increase as economic development proceeds, and the ability of the ambient
environment to receive and assimilate them is an important natural resource of increasing value. We will argue below that the common failure
to recognize these facts may result from viewing the production and consumption processes in a manner that is somewhat at variance with the
fundamental law of conservation of mass.

Nature does not permit the destruction of matter except by annihilation with anti-matter, and the means of disposal of unwanted residuals
which maximizes the internal return of decentralized decision units is by

From Robert U. Ayres and Allen V. Kneese, "Production, Consumption, and Externalities," *American Economic Review* (June, 1969), pp. 282–8. Reprinted by permission
of the American Economic Association and the authors.
[1]E. J. Mishan, "Reflections on Recent Developments in the Concept of External Effects,"
Canadian Journal of Economic Political Science, (Feb. 1965), pp. 1–34.

discharge to the environment, principally, watercourses and the atmosphere. Water and air are traditionally examples of free goods in economics. But in reality, in developed economies they are common property resources of great and increasing value presenting society with important and difficult allocation problems which exchange in private markets cannot resolve. These problems loom larger as increased population and industrial production put more pressure on the environment's ability to dilute and chemically degrade waste products. Only the crudest estimates of present external costs associated with residuals discharge exist but it would not be surprising if these costs were in the tens of billions of dollars annually. Moreover, as we shall emphasize again, technological means for processing or purifying one or another type of waste discharge do not destroy the residuals but only alter their form. Thus, given the level, patterns, and technology of production and consumption, recycle of materials into productive uses or discharge into an alternative medium are the only general options for protecting a particular environmental medium such as water. Residual problems must be seen in a broad regional or economy-wide context rather than as separate and isolated problems of disposal of gas, liquid, and solid wastes.

Frank Knight perhaps provides a key to why these elementary facts have played so small a role in economic theorizing and empirical research.

> The next heading to be mentioned ties up with the question of dimensions from another angle, and relates to the second main error mentioned earlier as connected with taking food and eating as the type of economic activity. The basic economic magnitude (value or utility) is service, not goods. It is inherently a stream or flow in time. . . .

Almost all of standard economic theory is in reality concerned with services. Material objects are merely the vehicles which carry some of these services, and they are exchanged because of consumer preferences for the services associated with their use or because they can help to add value in the manufacturing process. Yet we persist in referring to the "final consumption" of goods as though material objects such as fuels, materials, and finished goods somehow disappeared into the void—a practice which was comparatively harmless so long as air and water were almost literally free goods. Of course, residuals from both the production and consumption processes remain and they usually render disservices (like killing fish, increasing the difficulty of water treatment, reducing public health, soiling and deteriorating buildings, etc.) rather than services. Control efforts are aimed at eliminating or reducing those disservices which flow to consumers and producers whether they want them or not and which, except in unusual cases, they cannot control by engaging in individual exchanges.

To elaborate on these points, we find it useful initially to view environmental pollution and its control as a materials balance problem for the entire economy. The inputs to the system are fuels, foods, and raw materials which are partly converted into final goods and partly become waste residuals. Except for increases in inventory, final goods also ultimately enter the waste stream. Thus goods which are "consumed" really only render certain services. Their material substance remains in existence and must either be reused or discharged to the ambient environment.

In an economy which is closed (no imports or exports) and where there is no net accumulation of stocks (plant, equipment, inventories, consumer durables, or residential buildings), the amount of residuals inserted into the natural environment must be approximately equal to the weight of basic fuels, food, and raw materials entering the processing and production system, plus oxygen taken from the atmosphere. This result, while obvious upon reflection, leads to the, at first rather surprising, corollary that residuals disposal involves a greater tonnage of materials than basic materials processing, although many of the residuals, being gaseous, require no physical "handling."

Figure 1 shows a materials flow of the type we have in mind in greater detail and relates it to a broad classification of economic sectors for convenience in our later discussion, and for general consistency with the Standard Industrial Classification. In an open (regional or national) economy, it would be necessary to add flows representing imports and exports. In an economy undergoing stock or capital accumulation, the production of residuals in any given year would be less by that amount than the basic inputs. In the entire U.S. economy, accumulation accounts for about 10 to 15 percent of basic annual inputs, mostly in the form of construction materials, and there is some net importation of raw and partially processed materials amounting to 4 or 5 percent of domestic production. Table 1 shows estimates of the weight of raw materials produced in the United States in several recent years, plus net imports of raw and partially processed materials.

Of the active inputs, perhaps three-quarters of the overall weight is eventually discharged to the atmosphere as carbon (combined with atmospheric oxygen in the form of CO or CO_2) and hydrogen (combined with atmospheric oxygen as H_2O) under current conditions. This results from combustion of fossil fuels and from animal respiration. Discharge of carbon dioxide can be considered harmless in the short run. There are large "sinks" (in the form of vegetation and large water bodies, mainly the oceans) which reabsorb this gas, although there is evidence of net accumulation of CO_2 in the atmosphere. Some experts believe that the latter is likely to show a large relative increase, as much as 50 percent by the end of the century, possibly giving rise to significant—and probably, on bal-

166

Figure 1. Materials Flow.

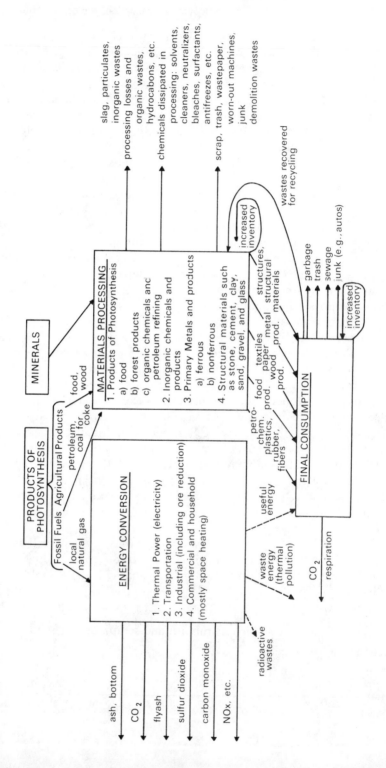

Table 1. Weight of Basic Materials Production in the
United States Plus Net Imports, 1963 (10⁶ tons)

	1963	1964	1965
Agricultural (including fishery and wildlife and forest) products			
Food { Crops (excluding livestock feed)	125	128	130
Food { Livestock	100	103	102
Other products	5	6	6
Fishery	3	3	3
Forestry products (85 percent dry weight basis)			
Sawlogs	53	55	56
Pulpwood	107	116	120
Other	41	41	42
Total	434	452	459
Mineral fuels	1,337	1,399	1,448
Other minerals			
Iron ore	204	237	245
Other metal ores	161	171	191
Other nonmetals	125	133	149
Total	490	541	585
Grand total[a]	2,261	2,392	2,492

[a]Excluding construction materials, stone, sand, gravel, and other minerals used for structural purposes, ballast, fillers, insulation, etc. Gangue and mine tailings are also excluded from this total. These materials account for enormous tonnages but undergo essentially no chemical change. Hence, their use is more or less tantamount to physically moving them from one location to another. If this were to be included, there is no logical reason to exclude material shifted in highway cut and till operations, harbor dredging, land-fill, plowing, and even silt moved by rivers. Since a line must be drawn somewhere, we chose to draw it as indicated above.

Source: R. U. Ayres and A. V. Kneese, "Environmental Pollution," in U.S. Congress, Joint Economic Committee, *Federal Programs for the Development of Human Resources,* Vol. 2, p. 360. Washington, 1968.

ance, adverse—weather changes. Thus, continued combustion of fossil fuels at a high rate could produce externalities affecting the entire world. The effects associated with most residuals will normally be more confined, however, usually limited to regional air and water sheds.

The remaining residuals are either gases (such as carbon monoxide, nitrogen dioxide, and sulfur dioxide—all potentially harmful even in the short run), dry solids (such as rubbish and scrap), or wet solids (such as garbage, sewage, and industrial wastes suspended or dissolved in water). In a sense, the dry solids are an irreducible, limiting form of waste. By the application of appropriate equipment and energy, most undesirable substances can, in principle, be removed from water and air streams, but what is left must be disposed of in solid form, transformed, or reused. Looking at the matter in this way clearly reveals a primary interdependence between the various waste streams which casts into doubt the traditional classification of air, water, and land pollution as individual categories for purposes of planning and control policy.

Residuals do not necessarily have to be discharged to the environment. In many instances, it is possible to recycle them back into the productive system. The materials balance view underlines the fact that the throughput of new materials necessary to maintain a given level of production and consumption decreases as the technical efficiency of energy conversion and materials utilization increases. Similarly, other things being equal, the longer that cars, buildings, machinery, and other durables remain in service, the fewer new materials are required to compensate for loss, wear, and obsolescence—although the use of old or worn machinery (e.g., automobiles) tends to increase other residuals problems. Technically efficient combustion of (desulfurized) fossil fuels would leave only water, ash, and carbon dioxide as residuals, while nuclear energy conversion need leave only negligible quantities of material residuals (although thermal pollution and radiation hazards cannot be dismissed by any means).

Given the population, industrial production, and transport service in an economy (a regional rather than a national economy would normally be the relevant unit), it is possible to visualize combinations of social policy which could lead to quite different relative burdens placed on the various residuals-receiving environmental media; or, given the possibilities for recycle and less residual-generating production processes, the overall burden to be placed upon the environment as a whole. To take one extreme, a region which went in heavily for electric space heating and wet scrubbing of stack gases (from steam plants and industries), which ground up its garbage and delivered it to the sewers and then discharged the raw sewage to watercourses, would protect its air resources to an exceptional degree. But this would come at the sacrifice of placing a heavy residuals load upon water resources. On the other hand, a region which treated municipal and industrial waste water streams to a high level and relied heavily on the incineration of sludges and solid wastes would protect its water and land resources at the expense of discharging waste residuals predominantly to the air. Finally, a region which practiced high level recovery and recycle of waste materials and fostered low residual production processes to a far-reaching extent in each of the economic sectors might discharge very little residual waste to any of the environmental media.

Further complexities are added by the fact that sometimes it is possible to modify an environmental medium through investment in control facilities so as to improve its assimilative capacity. The clearest, but far from only, example is with respect to watercourses where reservoir storage can be used to augment low river flows that ordinarily are associated with critical pollution (high external cost situations). Thus internalization of external costs associated with particular discharges, by means of taxes or other restrictions, even if done perfectly, cannot guarantee Pareto optimality. Investments involving public good aspects must enter into an optimal solution.

To recapitulate our main points briefly: (1) Technological external diseconomies are not freakish anomalies in the processes of production and consumption but an inherent and normal part of them. (2) These external diseconomies are quantitatively negligible in a low-population or economically undeveloped setting, but they become progressively (nonlinearly) more important as the population rises and the level of output increases (i.e., as the natural reservoirs of dilution and assimilative capacity become exhausted). (3) They cannot be properly dealt with by considering environmental media such as air and water in isolation. (4) Isolated and ad hoc taxes and other restrictions are not sufficient for their optimum control, although they are essential elements in a more systematic and coherent program of environmental quality management. (5) Public investment programs, particularly including transportation systems, sewage disposal, and river flow regulation, are intimately related to the amounts and effects of residuals and must be planned in light of them.

It is important to develop not only improved measures of the external costs resulting from differing concentrations and duration of residuals in the environment but more systematic methods for forecasting emissions of external-cost-producing residuals, technical and economic trade-offs between them, and the effects of recycle on environmental quality.

Economics, Economic Development, and Economic Anthropology

GEORGE DALTON

An economist asks the question that is the title of this book.

Little else is requisite to carry a state to the highest degree of opulence from the lowest barbarism, but peace, easy taxes and a tolerable administration of justice.

Adam Smith

There is a deep-seated yearning in social science to discover one general approach, one general law valid for all time and all climes. But these primitive attitudes must be outgrown.

Alexander Gerschenkron

I should like to address the question, "Is economic theory culture-bound?" in two contexts: as the question relates to the economist's field, economic development, and as it relates to the anthropologist's field, economic anthropology.

In the last ten years several prominent economists have questioned the relevance of conventional economics (for example, price, aggregate income, and growth theory) for dealing with the processes and problems of economic development. This is an old theme stated in a new context. Similar examples are the German *methodenstreit* debate; von Mises and von Hayek versus Taylor, Lange, and Lerner on planning without market prices under socialism; and the marginalist controversy after World War II. In all of these, the same question was debated: the extent of realism, relevance, and adequacy of formal economics in dealing with real-world processes and problems of importance.

From *Journal of Economic Issues* (June, 1968), pp. 172–86. Reprinted by permission of the publisher.

In order to answer the question as it relates to economic development, one must first answer two other questions: What are those special characteristics of the structure and performance of underdeveloped countries which lead some economists to question the relevance of economics? What are those special characteristics of conventional economics which seem to these economists to be misleading or irrelevant in the context of underdevelopment? We turn first to the special characteristics of underdeveloped countries.

1. The basic fact of the underdeveloped world is the existence of some one hundred underdeveloped nation-states, principally in Africa, Asia, Latin America, and the Middle East. The economic, political, and social differences among them are much greater than are the differences among the few developed capitalist nations of Western Europe and North America for which economic theory was invented. The fact of extreme diversity within the underdeveloped world—that it includes Liberia as well as India and Mexico—means that nothing like a single analytical model of underdevelopment is feasible: the structures, processes, and problems are too different.

2. Half or more of these countries are developing their polities and societies as well as their economies. They are in the process of structural transformation politically and culturally as well as economically and technologically. They are combining their Industrial Revolutions with their French Revolutions and their nation-building Mercantilist periods. They are creating nationwide political and social institutions as well as national systems of banking, taxation, and transportation.

One reflection of this simultaneity of structural change is that all the other social sciences now have interests in Asia, Africa, and Latin America which are counterparts to the interests of economists. What economists call development, political scientists call "modernization," sociologists, "role differentiation," and anthropologists, "culture change." These accompanying political and social changes make economic-development processes even more complicated. Indeed, from a Western economist's viewpoint, a sort of non-Euclidean universe is sometimes created: If building roads and radio transmitters, in order to connect hitherto isolated regions in African countries, is thought to provide valuable integrating devices for increasing the political interaction among ethnically different citizens of what is now one nation and for spreading the usage of English or French, then cost-benefit analysts must guess at the worth of these amorphous political and linguistic benefits of roads and radios.

3. These countries are not only underdeveloped, they are also over-exposed. By this I mean two things: They are pursuing development deliberately, consciously, and quickly; and they are following policies which, except for Japan and Soviet Russia, are outside the experience of the already developed nations. The United States and Britain developed less

consciously, less as a matter of deliberate national effort, less as an urgent responsibility of governmental initiative. One consequence of current development as an effort of conscious purpose is that the economic policy of governments is pressing. Whatever one means by the economics of development, it is not a field or pure theory but an applied field. Neither Marshall nor Keynes invented economic theory with civil servants waiting in the next room to put it into practice. A second consequence of this over-exposure—this pressing public need to formulate development policy in the quick pursuit of higher income—is the creation of impossible expectations and therefore inevitable disappointments. Satisfaction or disappointment with development progress is a fraction, the numerator being realized results, the denominator, expectations. Rarely in the underdeveloped world does the fraction approach one.

There are other reasons, moreover, for built-in disappointment with realized results. Not only is development policy conscious, deliberate, and pressing; too often, as Wolfgang Stolper reminds us, it is made on the basis of fragmentary data. In primary producing countries, it should be remembered, economic policy is very much less autonomous than it is in developed economies. Underdeveloped countries are dependent upon external prices and financial aid to an unusual extent.

4. Finally, the least-developed one-third or more of the underdeveloped countries have what I shall call micro-development problems of a sort which are unfamiliar to Western economists but which in part are familiar to Western agricultural economists and rural sociologists: problems of how to transform subsistence agriculture and how to create more persons of entrepreneurial initiative.

To sum up: The reality of underdevelopment—the set of real-world circumstances to which economists address their theory—entails the following: wide diversity because of the large number of countries included; social, cultural, political, and economic complexity because of the simultaneous changes toward modernization being experienced; and the pressing need to make policy decisions within constraints set by inadequate information and exaggerated expectations.

We turn now to the second set of components which bear on our problem, those characteristics of economics which make some economists argue that conventional economics is irrelevant or downright misleading for the analysis of the processes and problems of development. Here I need only summarize what has been so clearly spelled out by Myrdal, Seers, Hagen, and others. It is useful, I think, to put these characteristics of economics into three sets that are by no means mutually exclusive.

1. Many economic concepts, such as the multiplier, and much economic analysis, such as the Keynesian theory of aggregate income determination, were contrived in response to the special problems (for example,

chronic unemployment) of already industrialized, already developed, nationally integrated, large-scale market economies; underdeveloped countries have other problems for which neither the concepts nor the analysis is relevant.

2. Many economic concepts, such as the accelerator, and much economic analysis, such as growth theory, are interesting, useful, applicable—indeed, even operational—because of the special structure of already industrialized, already developed, nationally integrated, large-scale market economies; underdeveloped economies have different structures, and neither the concepts nor the analysis is relevant.

3. The leading ideas of economics, such as equilibrium analysis, and the inherited policy preferences of economists, such as laissez faire, reflect the special ethic of Anglo-America—a sort of Marshallian mentality—and the special political, social, and even religious institutions and traditions of Anglo-America. Africans, Asians, and Latin Americans have markedly different histories, social structures, and political experiences and therefore find the leading ideas and policy preferences of conventional economics uncongenial.

Among the development economists, two utterly different things are meant by "applying economic theory." It means a general method of approach used to identify problems, to measure sectoral relationships, and to put important questions to an economy. Here, the economist as diagnostician of structure and measurer of performance is useful in all underdeveloped countries. The second meaning is quite narrow: it is that the micro- and macro-market processes which economists analyze in developed economies somehow have functional equivalents in underdeveloped economies, and so the analyses and the policy conclusions drawn from them somehow can be directly "applied" in underdeveloped economies. This second meaning of "applying economic theory" is the one that rightly has been criticized.

One of the sad ironies of underdevelopment is that the less developed economically a country is, the less able it is to apply economic analysis and policy because of its social and political structures. Those countries needing economic improvement the most are the least capable of making effective use of both economic analysis and economic aid.

The interesting question is not: "Is economics relevant or irrelevant for underdeveloped countries?" This is not a good question because there is so much economics and so many underdeveloped countries. A better question is: "For which underdeveloped countries is what portion of economics directly relevant; and how must economics, where it is not relevant, be supplemented with socioeconomic analysis, and of what sort?"

The work of Irma Adelman and Cynthia Taft Morris serves as a point of departure. They have shown that the large set of underdeveloped countries can be divided into three groups, low, intermediate, and high, and that such a separation into subsets is analytically useful because the socioeconomic structures and the socioeconomic problems of development for each subset are markedly different.

At the lowest level of development are countries which are principally but not exclusively in sub-Saharan Africa and are overwhelmingly agricultural, having large subsistence sectors, a few primary commodities for export, little social capital, and few market institutions. In economic terms, these are not yet national economies, but rather congeries of primitive and peasant villages hardly linked at all to the national society, polity, or economy. Direct taxation and banking do not reach the bulk of the village communities, and markets transact considerably less than half of what is produced. There is no national integration culturally or politically; rather, there is ethnic and linguistic diversity. (The small West African country, Liberia, is in the middle of this lowest group. It is a "dual" economy and an "enclave" economy. Foreign firms producing iron ore and rubber for export account for most of the commodities produced for sale.)

To this least developed subset of countries, whose economies, polities, and societies are least like those of developed nations, we can put the question: "How relevant is conventional economics to analyze their processes and problems?" The answer, I think, is that economics is necessary but not sufficient and that only a relatively small portion of that large set of concepts, theories, and measurements which we call economics is applicable.

The most directly applicable economics in such countries is statistical measurement to establish quantitatively the nature of each one's structure and performance. The first job of the economist in such countries is to create or improve national income accounts and other hard-data series—to establish the factual base necessary to avoid costly mistakes.

The second job of the economist is that which former Secretary of Defense McNamara is reputed to have accomplished so successfully in the underdeveloped Pentagon: to establish cost-benefit criteria for making policy decisions. Here the economist is very much at home, whether he is at the Pentagon or in agricultural Nigeria. Economics is a gigantic machine to compare costs with benefits.

In the subset of least developed countries, there are other important jobs of analysis for economists to do, but these jobs are socioeconomic analyses, which require the economist (alone, or in collaboration with other social scientists) to analyze and make policy within the special institutional constraints of each country: how to transform subsistence agriculture, how to increase agricultural productivity, what kind of educational system to establish and with what priority of budgetary outlay.

If someone should tell me that conventional economics was not designed to answer such questions, I would agree; but I would also reply that neither does conventional sociology, anthropology, political science, or psychology answer such questions. And I would argue further that economists—from Marx and Veblen to Lewis and Hagen—have been notably more successful in doing socioeconomic analysis than the other social scientists have been in crossing over into socioeconomic analysis from their special subjects.

To sum up: For that subset of underdeveloped economies which is least developed, only a narrow range of economics is directly applicable, and the most formidable problems encountered are socioeconomic and purely political and social problems entailed in creating modern nationwide institutions.

Economic theory is culture-bound in the sense that its main lines of analysis relate to the special structures and problems of large-scale, industrialized, developed capitalist economies. Economic development, as done by economists, and economic anthropology, as done by anthropologists, are recent fields of specialization whose subject matter is a hundred or more national economies, on the one hand, and hundreds (if not thousands) of small-scale village economies, on the other, in Africa, Asia, Latin America, Oceania, and the Middle East. A large proportion of both sets of economies have economic and sociopolitical structures and problems markedly different from those of the already-developed economies. Except for the most advanced subset of the underdeveloped national economies, institutional processes and problems of a sort unfamiliar to economic analysis are pervasive, and they make necessary socioeconomic analyses of a novel sort. A number of economists—Myrdal, Lewis, Hagen, Adelman and Morris, and Polanyi—have already made important contributions to the socioeconomic analysis of underdeveloped national and village economies.

There is a methodological lesson to be learned from these literatures of contention in economic development and economic anthropology. The fact that intelligent men can disagree—and disagree rather heatedly—over long periods of time almost certainly means there are ingrained semantic difficulties underlying their disagreement. They are attaching different meanings to the same words. In both disciplines, the crucial words are "applying economic theory." The anthropologists think they are applying economic theory when they use the vocabulary of price theory to describe whatever transactions they observe in primitive economies. Instead of saying that a Trobriand Islander gives yams to his sister's husband partly to fulfill an obligation to his closest female relative and partly in recognition of her rights to land he is using, they say the Trobriander is "maximizing prestige." This is to use the terminology of economics as a fig-leaf to cover their theoretical nakedness.

The development economists who are critical of conventional economics are really saying that many underdeveloped countries have social and political processes and problems which impede economic development and have economic structures of a sort for which aggregative concepts like "gross investment" are not operational. They are right. However, the conclusion should be not to discard economics, but to learn about social and political processes, and to disaggregate.

Is Scarcity Dead?

KENNETH E. BOULDING

In asking rhetorically if scarcity is dead, Professor Boulding finds a renewed basis for the relevance of economic analysis.

Economics is first and foremost the science of scarcity. This is why it is a dismal science. Its problems arise only if there is not enough to go around. One of its greatest principles, though not necessarily the truest, I have sometimes called the "Duchess's Law," enunciated by the Duchess in *Alice in Wonderland:* "The more there is of yours, the less there is of mine." A variant is Goering's law: "We cannot have both guns and butter." What he actually seems to have said, incidentally, according to the invaluable Bartlett, is that, "Guns will make us powerful; butter will only make us fat."

There is a fundamental conflict which has gone on through almost all of recorded history between the heroic and the economic, between greatness and prudence, between extravagance and sobriety, and between glory and common sense. Economics is the good, gray, rational science. After the charge of the Light Brigade, economics asks the reason why. Byronic frenzy may inspire us to say, "Let joy be unconfined"; the economist says: "You will have to pay for this tomorrow." Even when St. Francis urges us to give and not to count the cost, the economist says that somebody has to count the cost; and when somebody wants a Great Society, the economist says: "Who is going to pay for it?" It is no wonder that the economist is not very popular.

At this point someone is sure to come up and say, "But we have changed all that. Science and technology have produced the age of

Chapter 9 of *A Great Society?* edited by Bertram M. Gross, pp. 209–26. © 1966, 1967, 1968 by Basic Books, Inc., Publishers, New York.

affluence. Scarcity has been abolished. Let us eat, drink, and be merry; there is plenty for all." Among biology, automation, and systems engineering, we can produce all we need with a fraction of the labor force, and today not even the sky is the limit. There are a good many voices today urging that we can have both guns and butter, "more for everybody and more for me too," and that economics can be put in the ash can.

This view seems to me to involve delusions of grandeur and a totally unwarranted euphoria derived from the careless and poorly sampled observation of a few special cases. It is true, of course, that the Duchess's Law is only a half-truth. Where there is economic development, where the total to be distributed is increasing, then it is possible that the more there is of yours, the more there is of mine too. We can all indulge in the delightful positive-sum game of getting richer together. It is true also that the process of economic development in a very real sense diminishes scarcity, and diminishes the urgency of rational choice. This is the essential point that Galbraith is making in *The Affluent Society*, and qualitatively it is perfectly valid. One of the principal delights of being rich is that we do not have to economize so much—that is, we do not have to devote so much time and attention to the careful balancing of gain against loss at the margin, and what Wordsworth decries as "the lore of nicely calculated less or more."

There is a familiar proposition in economics that the richer we are, the less is the marginal utility of money, and the less significance for our welfare is the expenditure of an extra dollar in any particular line. Using money as a symbol of resources in general, we can expand this proposition to say that the richer we are, the less is the marginal utility of a unit of general resources, and the less it matters, in effect, whether we make mistakes in allocation. For a poor man in a poor society, a mistake in allocation may be fatal; a rich society can afford to be careless and extravagant. Another billion dollars is only two thousandths of the GNP, so why not spend it? Furthermore, even though unemployment is now down below 4 percent, we should be able to get it down to 3 percent. There is still a good deal of slack in the economy, and by absorbing it we could easily raise the GNP by 5 or 10 billion and in these circumstances practically anything we want to do is virtually costless, it simply comes out of unemployed resources. In a sense World War II was virtually costless to the American consumer. Come on in, everybody, the water's fine! By this time, any economist who defends scarcity looks like a Prohibitionist on a bathing beach. Truth, however, requires me to adopt the garment of gloom, and to start an anti-euphoria society. In the face of "Scarcity Is Dead" theology which is celebrated with such enthusiasm in certain segments of our society, the economist needs to bring to the attention of the celebrants a few skeletons at their feast.

In the first place, there is no evidence that we are undergoing anything very unusual in the way of technological change and economic developments. If we take, for instance, the indices of output per man-hour calculated by the Department of Labor, we find, for example, that in the last 18 years the average rate of increase of output per man-hour has been 3.4 percent per annum for the total private sector, 5.9 percent in agriculture, and 2.8 percent in the non-agricultural industries. The only thing that approaches the spectacular is the remarkable increase in agriculture, though even this is only a speeding up of what has been going on for more than a hundred years. In spite of automation, the rate of increase in output per man-hour in nonagricultural industries is not spectacular, and since agriculture is a constantly declining proportion of the total economy, its impact on the total gets smaller all the time. It is, indeed, one of the paradoxes of economic development that the more successful any segment of the economy is in achieving rapid technological progress, the more it is likely to decline as a segment of the total. Hence there is a constant tendency for the more stagnant sectors of the economy, such as government, education, the service trades, and so on, to increase in the proportion which they bear to the total, and, inversely, rapid technological change in one sector of the economy has in it, as it were, the seeds of declining influence.

Furthermore, the American economy is by no means the most rapidly developing in the world. It is indeed quite a long way down the list. Direct productivity measures are not easy to come by for comparative purposes, but in cases where the proportion of total resources employed is approximately constant, the rise in the gross national product per head is a good first approximation measure of the rate of technical change. On this score, the record of the United States in the last 20 years is by no means impressive. In the 1950s there were 45 countries that had a higher rate of economic development than the United States. This figure is a little unfair, because the 1950s were to some extent a period of stagnation for the United States and of unusually rapid development in other countries, and the record of the 1960s will unquestionably look rather different. Nevertheless, in the last 20 years, some countries, notably Japan, West Germany, and some other European countries on both sides of the Iron Curtain, have achieved rates of development which are unprecedented in human history. A sustained rate of development of 8 percent per annum per capita, as in the case of Japan, for instance, represents a new phenomenon in human history. It is almost a quantum jump from anything which has happened before. In the period before World War II, no country sustained a rate of increase in per capita GNP of more than about 2.3 percent. The difference between 2.3 percent and 8 percent may be dramatically illustrated by pointing out that under conditions of what might be called successful prewar development, the children are twice as rich as the parents; per capita income approximately doubles every generation. At 8 percent per annum, the children are six times as rich as the parents. Whether this can be kept up for more than a generation is of course a question. It is true also that both Japanese and West German rates of development reflect the recovery of defeated and destroyed societies which, however, preserved their essential knowledge structure. They represent also an abnormal proportion of the GNP devoted to investment; hence, cannot wholly be attributed to a high rate of technological change.

Even when we have made all these downward adjustments, however, the fact remains that we seem to be in the presence of a new phenomenon which is associated in my mind with what might be called the second impact of the scientific revolution on economic life.

The first phase was the period from, shall we say, 1860, to World War II, in which we began to get the science-based industries such as electrical engineering, chemical engineering, the nuclear industry, and so on. Before 1860 the impact of science on the economy was very small. The so-called Industrial Revolution of the 18th century was in fact the tag-end of the long process of developing folk technology of the Middle Ages.

Now I think we can identify a second phase of the impact of science on economic life which is reflected in very widespread scientific technologies in a great many sectors: in agriculture, in virtually all forms of industry, in organization and information processing, and so on. It is this second phase of the impact of science on economic life that produces these 8 percent per annum rates of growth, whereas 2 to 3 percent per annum was characteristic of the first phase.

By this criterion, the United States is still in the first phase, and is in a very real sense a backward country; or should we say more politely, a developing country of the second rank, in spite of the fact that we are by reason of our past growth and history still, by far, the richest country in the world. If present trends continue, however, we will not remain in this relatively advanced position for very long. I have calculated what I call the "overtake dates," based on the countries' performance in the 1950s; that is, at what dates would various countries overtake the United States in real GNP per capita, if the growth of all countries continued to be what it was in the 1950s. In the 1960s, of course, the picture looks rather different. Rates of economic growth in the United States have increased, mainly, however, because we have been absorbing unemployed resources, and not because our rate of technological progress has increased. Rates of growth in many other countries, especially in the socialist camp, have declined, perhaps because of certain horizons which socialist organizations tend to impose, especially in agriculture. The table of overtake dates, therefore, was obsolete as soon as it was calculated. Nevertheless, it represents a certain possibility which cannot be ignored, and certainly any blithe and unthinking optimism about the future of economic development in the United States would be quite unjustified.

What are the reasons behind what I have sometimes called the mononucleosis of the American economy, a condition in which we are not sick enough to go to bed but in which nobody can pretend that we are operating in perfect health? Part of it unquestionably is the result of fiscal and financial timidity, and our unwillingness or ineptitude in pursuing a full-employment policy. Certainly no European country would have tolerated the levels of unemployment which the United States has tolerated in the last 20 years. Part of this arises from an almost paranoid fear of inflation on the part of the Federal Reserve and financial institutions. Another part arises from an equally paranoid fear of government deficits on the part of Congress. Thanks to the extraordinary success of the tax cut in 1964, we may now have learned a little better and be entering a somewhat new era. It is still early, however, to be wholly optimistic, and the fact that so many Americans seem to attribute the long prosperity to the war in Vietnam is a bad sign. We have certainly done better than we did in the 1930s. The Council of Economic Advisers and the Joint Economic Committee have exerted fairly persistent pressure toward economic policies for high levels of employment, and they must be credited with at least a modest success. Nevertheless, the best that can be said about economic policy in the last 20 years is that we could have done worse. The level of unemployment which we have tolerated has probably prevented a more rapid spread of technical improvements. The fact that it has been concentrated so heavily in two segments of the population, the Negroes on the one hand and young people on the other, is enough to offset much that has been done in these 20 years toward the integration of both youth and the Negro into the larger society. In 1965, for instance, when unemployment rates for all workers were only 4.6 percent, the rate was 13.6 percent for young people between 14 and 19, 8.3 percent for nonwhites, and only 2.4 percent for married men. The fact that unemployment is so unevenly distributed, therefore, makes it a much more serious problem than it seems from the overall figures.

One should not, of course, overlook the genuine accomplishments of the American economy in this period. In the last generation we have approximately doubled per capita real income, and this increase has been quite widely distributed. The real wages of the employed have almost doubled; the proportion of national income going to labor has actually shown some increase; and the record of the 20 years after World War II is unquestionably much superior to the record of the 20 years after World War I, which was a total failure. However, the fact that we could have done worse, perhaps much worse, should not blind us to the fact that we also could have done better. The record should inspire neither despair and self-hatred nor smugness and self-congratulation. We should at the same time be glad that we have done as well as we did and ashamed that we didn't do better.

At least of equal importance with fiscal conservatism in explaining the sluggish performance of the American economy is the absorption of the whole American society in international political and military competition, its neurotic determination to be the only great power, and the consequent absorption of a large proportion of our total effort by the war industry, or what might be called the space-military complex. The rise of the war industry has been far and away the greatest internal change in American society in the last generation. In the 1930s it was barely 1 percent of the gross national product. Today it is between 9 and 10 percent, and if the Vietnam war continues to escalate, it will almost certainly go beyond 10 percent. This change exceeds by whole orders of magnitude any other change in the system. The only other proportional change in the last generation which anywhere approaches it is the decline in agriculture. Furthermore, from the point of view of growth and development, the 10 percent of the GNP which is absorbed by the war industry greatly understates its impact. Seymour Melman has estimated that some 60 percent of the total research and development effort is channeled into the space-military operation. Melman's claim that the technological development of the civilian sector of the economy has been severely and adversely affected by this absorption of what might be called the growth resource by the space-military complex is to be taken very seriously. It is one of the astonishing facts of our times that there has been no comprehensive economic study of the distribution and impact of technological change in detail over the economy as a whole. The many instances which Melman cites of depletion and of relative technological stagnation in our society (for example, in railroad, shipbuilding, machine tools, civilian electronics, and in education and health—the list is frighteningly large) are of course selective, and can be offset to some extent by reports of spectacular technical change in other selected cases, e.g., due to automation. Nevertheless, the evidence for widespread technological malaise in the American economy is not to be dismissed. The most obvious explanation is the absorption of such an enormous proportion of our intellectual, research, engineering, and growth resources by the relatively sterile activities of the space-military complex.

It may be argued, of course, that those activities are not as sterile as I have accused them of being, and that there are in fact considerable spillovers from the space-military industry into the civilian economy. In the early days this may have had some truth to it. Certainly, for instance, we would not have had the jets as early as we did if it had not been for the enormous research resources devoted to the military industry. It is becoming increasingly apparent, however, that those spillovers are declining, mainly because the space-military complex is now at least a whole technological generation ahead of the civilian economy as a result of the enormous resources that have been put into it. There are very great difficulties involved in the transfer of technology between two societies, or even between two parts of the same society, where one is more than a technological generation ahead of the other. We see this problem in its extreme form in the difficulty of translating Western agricultural techniques into forms which have any use for the poor countries of Asia and Africa. The two technologies speak such totally different languages that they cannot communicate at all. There may be a few side transfers from one to the other, as, for instance, in the use of pesticides, but often these attempts to transfer from a high technology to a low technology are more disruptive of the low technology than they are helpful. We have seen many examples of this in different parts of the world.

The same phenomenon is now becoming apparent between the space-military complex within the United States and the civilian economy. While there may be long-run technological payoffs on earth for all this elaborateness of space and rocketry, miniaturization, and so on, the payoffs do not seem to be for this generation. A recent study of the Denver Research Institute, for instance, suggested that the spillover effects from the space-military operation in Colorado into the civilian economy were very small. Melman, again, has given a number of instances in which there has been complete failure to make this transfer.

The end result of all this enormous resource devoted to the space-military complex may be the self-subsistent household or grounded space capsule, resting comfortably on earth, but getting all its power from solar batteries, all its food from algae on the roof, and all its information from predigested tapes. This seems a long way off and I am not sure I want it even if we can get it.

In considering the impact of "greatness" on the American economy, we must take into account not merely the direct alternative costs for economic development and human welfare of the space-military complex, high as these are; we must also take into account the possible discounted costs of deterrence as an international system, particularly when deterrence itself is threatened by greatness in the sense of a Napoleonic desire to impose our will and our way of life on all the peoples of the world. Even if we suppose that the international system operates by pure deterrence, or balance of terror, it can be shown that this has a fairly high negative present value. A system of deterrence is a system of mutual threat and counter-threat, summed up by the mutual posture: "If you do something to me, I will do something nasty to you." In the case of the United States and the Soviet Union, and eventually other potential nuclear powers, the "something nasty" is very large indeed. It could involve the loss of more than half of the total population, and perhaps considerably more than half of the total capital. We do not really know much about the full consequences of a large-scale nuclear exchange. It is certain, however, that it would alter the whole ecological system of the earth very adversely from the point of view of man's welfare, and the probability that the disaster might prove to be irretrievable in view of its ecological consequences is at least an uncomfortably high number. In a system of deterrence, however, the probability that the threats will be carried out *must* be above some "noticeable" minimum. Otherwise the credibility of the threats falls to zero, and since the stability of the system depends on the credibility of the threats being above a certain threshold, it is clear that if the probability of the threats being carried out falls below a certain point, the whole system collapses. Either it simply ceases to organize human behavior—that is, the bluff is called—or in an attempt to restore credibility, the threats are actually carried out. There is, of course, no empirical method of estimating the probability of nuclear disaster in any one year. In the light of the previous history of the international system, however, in which systems of deterrence have rarely lasted more than 25 years, it would seem not unreasonable to put this probability at something between 1 and 5 percent per annum. Even if we take the lower of these figures, this cumulates rather alarmingly in a hundred years. Thus the probability of its not coming off in a hundred years is $(99/100)^{100}$, which is 0.36. So that the probability of disaster in any hundred years' period under this system is 0.64—two in three! If the chance is 5 percent per annum, of course, the chance of disaster even in 20 years is 0.64, and in one hundred years is 0.994! In making any estimate of the cost of the Great Society, therefore, assuming that the Great Society implied a rather grand Napoleonic military posture, we should calculate the present value of the possible loss from nuclear warfare and subtract this from the gross national product. In spite of the fact that there is no empirical method of estimating these probabilities and any figures can be only illustrative, it is clear that this deduction from the real value of the GNP could easily be very large, even on the order of magnitude of the GNP itself. If the disaster is really irretrievable, then even the smallest chance of it reduces the real value of the GNP to zero, or, rather, reduces the capital value in terms of human welfare of the United States itself as an organization to zero. Consequently, in any decent world the United States would be bankrupted and dissolved. It is quite possible, therefore, that the real cost of the Great Society is so high as to make its net value zero or even negative.

Economists are notoriously interested in the long run. They have a habit, indeed, of regarding themselves as the trustees for posterity. I may be excused, therefore, as an economist, for looking beyond the immediate political and economic exigencies of the present day and asking, what does the Great Society mean in the longer perspective of human history? I have elsewhere expanded on the idea that the present period in human history represents an extraordinary transition, what I have sometimes called the Third Great Transition, from the age of civilization which began with the urban revolution of 3000 B.C. to something which is qualitatively different and which I now call the Developed Society. The Developed Society, of course, is the kind of world that will result from the process of development as we see it going on today. It is very important, therefore, to ask of any particular political program what is its contribution toward this great transition. Is it going to make it more dangerous or less dangerous? Will it speed it up or slow it down? Or will it even prevent it altogether? I am not arguing, of course, that the Developed Society will be a stagnant perfection. I do argue, however, that the evolutionary process throughout its whole vast span of time has been characterized by short periods of very rapid change followed by rather long periods of slow change, and one sees this also in human history. We have already gone through two transition periods of very rapid change. One from the paleolithic to the neolithic, the other from the neolithic to civilization. The present period is entirely comparable to these and of even greater magnitude. If we are interested in development, therefore, it is quite legitimate to ask what the developed society looks like, even though we are not going to be able to spell it out in detail, and even though the developed society itself will undergo a continuous change and transformation, albeit, one suspects, at a somewhat slower rate than we are having now.

The present transition is characterized by, and indeed largely caused by, a mutation in the process of growth of human knowledge which we call science. We are still very much in the middle of this process. In fact, it is doubtful whether we have yet reached the middle, and it seems probable that the next 50 years will see a rate of change at least equal to what we have seen in the last century, perhaps even greater. Certainly, the impact of the biological sciences on the condition of man and the nature of his social system is going to be as spectacular as the impact of physics and chemistry, and we have hardly seen the beginning of this. Some people tend to view the transition as a prospect of absolutely unlimited expansion. This tends to be the communist view, with the deification of man and what seems to me a naïve faith in his absolutely unlimited powers.

I take a somewhat more restricted and pessimistic view myself: that the real significance of this transition is that it represents a change from an open society characterized by a through-put of material (with ores and fossil fuels as inputs and pollutable reservoirs as recipients of outputs), to a closed society in the material sense, in which there are no longer any mines or pollutable reservoirs, and in which therefore all material has to be recycled. This is what I have called the "spaceship earth," since a spaceship, especially if it has to go on long voyages, will have to be a miniature of a closed system of this kind. In a spaceship, clearly there are no mines and no sewers. Everything has to be recycled; man has to find a place in the middle of this cycle. The spaceship earth simply repeats this on a larger scale. Up until the present transition, man has always lived from the point of view of his own inner image of himself and his environment, on a great plane. There has always been somewhere to go, mountains or oceans to cross, new sources of supply to exploit, and new geographical worlds to conquer. Today the great plane has become a sphere, and the spherical closed nature of man's physical environment is becoming increasingly a part of his image. When we look at the earth from space, we realize very closely what a small, closed, crowded spaceship it is. National boundaries are virtually invisible even from a jet, and nobody has the nerve to claim national sovereignty beyond the atmosphere.

The consequences of this transition from the great plane to the closed sphere are profound in all spheres of life. In economics, this represents a transition from what I have called the "cowboy economy" of exploitation and pollution to the "space man economy" which is characterized by extreme conservation. Whether the desperate necessity of conservation will produce conservatism is an interesting problem. It is certainly not beyond the bounds of possibility that one of the things we will need to conserve is change itself, and the ability to change. In the spaceship economy, consumption is no longer a virtue but a vice; and a mounting GNP will be regarded with horror. Human welfare will clearly be seen to depend not on the through-put of the society—that is, not on the amount it can produce and consume—but on the richness and variety of its capital stock, including, of course, the human capital. Consequently, anything which will conserve consumption and enable us to maintain a larger and more elaborate capital stock with smaller production would be regarded as desirable. Great stress would have to be placed on durability, both of things and of people. We may find, indeed, that the spaceship economy is not feasible without a substantial extension of human life, as George Bernard Shaw suggested in *Back to Methuselah*. I have discussed elsewhere the appalling short-run consequences of cracking the aging barrier and extending human life beyond the Biblical allotted span. Nevertheless, if the spaceship earth is to be tolerable at all, it may well be that the consumption of human knowledge which takes place by the frightful toll of aging and death at the average age of 70 will be more than the resources of a depleted planet can cope with. We may end up, indeed, with a society not unlike the extraordinary vision of Godwin:

> The whole will be a people of men, and not of children. Generation will not succeed generation or truth have, in a certain degree, to recommence her career every 30 years. . . . There will no war, no crimes, no administration of justice, as it is called, and no government. Besides this, there will be neither disease, anguish, melancholy, nor resentment. Every man will seek, with ineffable ardour, the good of all.

What seemed absurd utopianism in 1793 may not seem absurd at all by 2500, for this may be the only way of life left open to the depleted earth.

A spaceship society does not preclude, I think, a certain affluence, in the sense that man will be able to maintain a physical state and environment which will involve good health, creative activity, beautiful surroundings, love and joy, art, the pursuit of the life of the spirit, and so on. This affluence, however, will have to be combined with a curious parsimony. Far from scarcity's disappearing, it will be the most dominant aspect of the society. Every grain of sand will have to be treasured, and the waste and profligacy of our own day will seem so horrible that our descendants will hardly be able to bear to think about us, for we will appear as monsters in their eyes.

How far, then, does the Great Society assist in making this transition? It is hard to avoid giving it some rather bad marks. Greatness is a totally inappropriate moral attitude for a spaceship society, which has to be, above all things, modest. Greatness is all right on the great plains or on the great plane. It is wholly inappropriate to a tiny, fragile sphere. A spaceship cannot afford cowboys. It probably cannot even afford horses, and it certainly cannot afford men on horseback. It looks like a tea ceremony, not a parade ground. The slightest touch of grandiosity could ruin it. It involves conservation, coexistence, extreme care in conflict resolution, and, above all, no rocking of the boat. The careless expansionism which is characteristic of the idea of greatness is not merely inappropriate, it is a deep threat to the system.

It may be that I am being profoundly unfair, that I am confusing rhetoric with reality, and that my attack on the concept of greatness, which I fear and despise, is an attack only on political rhetoric, a rhetoric which is not to be taken seriously. Certainly the present administration should not be damned merely for its rhetoric, it should be judged also by its acts. My own rhetoric is that of the modest society, as I put it in speeches these days: "a little society where little people can have a little fun." Still, you may say, are not many of the acts of the present administration consistent with this? Is there not the antipoverty program, the Peace Corps, Medicare, the new interest in the reform of cities, pollution control, civil rights, and so on? I am prepared to give credit here and without grudging. The antipoverty program is a token, but it also represents a real social invention which may have large consequences for the future in the whole idea that the poor should organize themselves. The Peace Corps is likewise a token, but it is perhaps a symbol of better things to come, and returned Peace Corps members will unquestionably be a force for the enlivening and purification of American life. Medicare is a last act of a long drama of social security, and is at least designed to meet a real need. Possibly the new Department of Housing and Urban Development can act as a long-run force to undo some of the damage that has been done by public housing and urban renewal, which has been a ruthless destroyer of communities and, by and large, an instrument to inconvenience the poor with the object of restoring the central city to the middle classes.

I try to be fair, I even feel a desire to be helpful, yet I find myself seized with an uncontrollable revulsion which reduces me to a state of complete political incapacitation. At this point I cannot help being personal, and what follows has no pretensions to science, nor even to philosophy. Something about the senseless cruelty of the war in Vietnam and the attitude of self-righteous grandiosity which is implied has produced in me a political revulsion so deep that I have called into question the whole political movement of the last 40 years, and I now perceive it as a gigantic piece of overlearning and mislearning. I belong to a generation which was traumatized by three great episodes: World War I, the Great Depression, and World War II. If graded, the world social system to which I belong clearly deserves a failing mark. On the other hand, my dissatisfaction with western liberalism does not drive me into the socialist camp, for what I see over there I like even less. I see there revolutionary sentimentality, oblivious of the fact that most revolutions have cost two generations of growth. I see miserable corruption of the arts; an appalling centralization of power; enormous and costly mistakes in social planning, such as the First Collectivization in the Soviet Union and the Great Leap Forward in China. I see sentimental imperialism, in the case of both the Soviet Union and China—there is no reason why Lithuania, Uzbekistan, Tibet, and so on should not be at least as independent as Poland or Rumania—and I see also an obsolete ideology corrupting the sciences as well as the arts and oppressing the free spirit of man. Where, then, do we go? To what standard do we repair? There seems to be nothing but sleazy national flags and obsolete slogans.

In this vast political and spiritual desert one looks for cases, where the springs of alienation can perhaps water new political mutations. One looks, perhaps for an uneasy alliance of right and left, producing hybrid vigor. The trouble with the center is that it is enormously powerful, for it can move either way, just as the present administration holds down the Right with its foreign policy and the Left with its domestic policy. The dissidents of both Right and Left are helpless and powerless, unless they can join to form a new center. A very critical question today, therefore, is whether the political spectrum is a line or a circle, and whether a new constellation is conceivable in which the learning process, of which the center is almost incapable because of its very success, can go on at the edges and unite to form a new center. This sounds almost absurd. Nevertheless, the political crisis of the world is so deep, the present system so untenable and outrageous, that the time may be ripening for a profound dialectical shift. Ordinarily I am not much impressed by dialectics, having much more faith in the long, slow, continuous changes which produce growth and knowledge and development. Yet, there are times when certain regroupings occur and are fruitful. This may be one of them.

It is far too early to try to spell out a program for the Right-Left, especially since if this comes off at all, there will have to be some hard bargaining. Each side will have to sacrifice something, and it is not altogether clear what will be sacrificed. Nevertheless, one might outline some tentative principles upon which such a bargain might be made:

1. A rediscovery of individualism, or what might, to get the best of all possible worlds, be called social individualism, as a political and social objective. This means stress on variety, peculiarity, even eccentricity; on the freedom to develop innumerable small subcultures; on the richness and variety of human potentiality. The enemies of this are conformity, consensus, compulsory chapel, the draft, monopolistic public education, the corporate image, and everything that tries to force people into too few molds. Granted that there must be molds, let's have a lot of them.
2. If social individualism is the objective, we must have a fairly sophisticated view as to how to get it. Freedom does not just happen, it has to be organized. Freedom is not anarchy, but neither does government necessarily produce it. The problem of how to organize social life in order to maximize freedom is a good operations-research type of problem, the solution to which, however, is by no means easy. In searching for the solution, some things must be borne in mind.
   (a) The market and the price system are enormously useful devices for the reconciliation of personal freedom with social control. I have illustrated this in my "green stamp plan" for population control, whereby every person receives by right

of being an individual a license to have the socially desirable average number of children. Then a market is established in these licenses or fractions thereof, so that the philoprogenitive can buy them from those who do not wish to have children. Wide individual freedom is assured in a highly sensitive area, and yet overall social control can be established, which is absolutely necessary in the spaceship earth. Political democracy and the legal system must be looked at as essentially generating and distributing processes for information and knowledge, and they must eventually be integrated with the broadening knowledge and methodology of the social sciences. There must be room here for social inventions yet to come, at the same time that traditional values are cherished. One speculates about limited world government, an antitrust law for nations, the breakup of the larger nations into smaller states to give something like perfect competition, the political legitimation of international business, and all sorts of problems which cannot be dealt with here.

(b) There must be some doctrine about the dynamics of the transition from the great to the "modest" society. Revolution is out, since this just creates and reinforces greatness, pomposity, corruption of taste, and is likely to establish tyrannies. If revolution is out, however, we need to have an image of a dynamic by which legitimacy is gradually withdrawn from the old system and is acquired by the new, to the point where eventually the old system becomes merely a show and cannot cause any trouble. I am convinced that the dynamics of legitimacy is the key to this whole problem. The trouble is that I don't know anything about the dynamics of legitimacy.

Are there any signs in the above of the alliance of Right and Left to which I have referred? There are strong signs of social individualism on the Left. The New Left in the United States is far more individualistic than the old, much more concerned with freedom, with personality, really more anarchist than socialist, and it has at least a different set of illusions from its fathers. Even in the socialist countries, especially in Yugoslavia and Poland, one can see a movement toward social individualism. One sees this, for instance, in the revolt of the artists, one sees it in the extraordinary reawakening of interest in the market. Yugoslav economists come through all the time preaching Adam Smith and the virtues of the market, though none will go so far as to recommend a stock exchange. It may be that the collapse of empires and the doubling of the number of nations in the last 20 years is again a symptom of something very important—the realization that national greatness is too expensive and that the people of a modest nation have a much better time, or at least a better chance in the long run of a better time.

In social policy one even finds curious alliances, for instance, on the principle of a guaranteed annual income or a negative income tax as a substitute for welfare, social security, and the whole impertinent apparatus of parental government. Furthermore, the rise of the peace movement, feeble as it is, in both the socialist and the liberal nationalistic world, is again a symptom of a deep longing, of a profound dissatisfaction with the world as it is, even if at the moment it seems pitifully weak.

I am prepared therefore to detect an oasis, fed perhaps by two different springs. If their flow can be increased, the desert may yet turn into a garden.

Scientific and Ideological Elements in the Economic Theory of Government Policy

JAMES O'CONNOR

How do values enter into economic analysis? Is economics—or should it be—value free? Here is an analysis of the values implicit in conventional economic theory and the implication of these values for government policy based on this economic theory.

In our time . . . faith in the manipulative omnipotence of the State has all but displaced analysis of its social structure and understanding of its political and economic functions.
Paul A. Baran, "On the Political Economy of Backwardness," A. N. Agarwala and S. P. Singh, Editors, *The Economics of Underdevelopment.*
In no other field [than public finance] has the intrusion of metaphysics done so much harm as here.
Gunnar Myrdal, *The Political Economy in the Development of Economic Theory.*

There is a large and growing body of economic doctrine on the subject of state expenditures and taxation which attempts to lay down guidelines for state fiscal policy. "Such studies," in *The Growth of Public Expenditure in the United Kingdom,* Peacock and Wiseman have written, "attempt to set up criteria for the size and nature of government expenditures and income by utilizing techniques usual in the study of market economics. Starting from some concept of economic welfare, defined in terms of individual choice, they attempt to specify the taxing and spending activities of government that would conduce to the ideal condition of such welfare."

The general questions which are raised are: how large should the state budget be, and how should budget expenditures be allocated between

From *Science and Society,* Vol. 33, No. 4 (1969), pp. 385–414. Reprinted by permission of the publisher.

alternative ends? What should be the burden of taxes on various groups? Put another way, what elements should make up a normative theory of "public finance"? Immediately we can see that the conventional phrase "public finance" reveals the ideological content of bourgeois economic thought by prejudging the question of the *real* purpose of state expenditures. In other words, it remains to be shown just how "public" are the real and financial transactions that take place in the state economic sector.

Our first task is to develop as clearly as possible a statement of the two main lines of orthodox theory, one based upon neoclassical microeconomic theory, the second based on Keynesian macroeconomic theory. It should be said at the outset that although many bourgeois economists consider the analysis of public finance to be concrete, practical "precepts for action," others are aware that the theory is devoid of any significant social and political content, and hence represents little more than a "counsel of perfection."

The second purpose of this paper is briefly to review the critique of orthodox microeconomic theory, or welfare economics, developed by orthodox economists themselves. This critique is based solely on the lack of internal consistency or logical clarity of the theory, and in no way challenges its underlying assumptions. These underlying assumptions, as we shall see, are based on the criteria of competitive markets and welfare maximizing. In turn, these criteria take for granted the system of private ownership of the means of production and the economic, social, and political institutions that go with private ownership. We believe that these criteria are based on a one-dimensional view of man and his real potentialities, and, moreover, on a historically specific and short-lived system of political economy.

Thus our third purpose is to develop our own critique of orthodox public finance, one which challenges the assumptions of both micro and macro theory and goes beyond an attempt to reveal certain logical inconsistencies or contradictions implied by it. We do not, however, attempt to answer the question: What should the state do? We do not attempt to reconstruct the normative theory of state finance, because that would take us into a different subject altogether, the political economy of socialism. What state revenues and budgetary expenditures should be in a non-capitalism society would depend on the specific type of socialism to emerge from United States capitalism, the circumstances surrounding the struggle for socialism, the coalition of forces which lead the struggle, and so on. These questions would obviously take us well beyond the scope of our subject matter.

In its approach to the role of the state under capitalism, welfare economics, based on microeconomic analysis, adopts the principle of "neutrality." It is contended that the state (including state tax policy) should refrain from disturbing the pattern of resources allocation determined by private market relationships except in the event that the existing allocations are at odds with the competitive norm—the types of allocations which prevail in a regime of perfect competition—with "welfare maximizing."

The concept of ideal output is central to the normative theory of public finance. We have no intention of doing anything like full justice to the range and complexity of problems arising from and variations on the idea of ideal output, but rather make a simple and somewhat old-fashioned statement of it. Pigou in his *Economics of Welfare* defines ideal output as that composition of production such that "no alternative output which could be obtained by means of reallocation among the various industries of the economy's resources would leave the community better off than before." To put it differently, "... any reallocation of the resources employed in producing the ideal output will so affect the various members of the economy that those who are better off as a result of the change will be unable to compensate those who are worse off as a result of the change and at the same time make a net gain for themselves. . . ."

The question next arises, when will private market relationships depart from ideal output, or, to put it differently, when will the private market misallocate economic resources, thus providing the "justification" for state intervention?

First, markets organized along monopolistic rather than competitive lines may lead to a misallocation of resources. Monopoly tends to keep prices higher and outputs lower than those prevailing under competition. Thus a tax to force the monopolist to lower the price, or a policy to restructure the market in order to bring the price down, is justified. In the event that the marginal social cost exceeds marginal private cost, however (the case of heroin production, for example), monopoly restrictions may improve the allocation of resources, and an attack on the monopoly by the state would not be "justified."

Second, there is the more general case of the existence of externalities in production. The full-blown name for the concept is "technological economies or diseconomies of scale," which arise in many industries where the costs facing the firm depend not only on the size and efficiency of the firm itself, but also on the size and efficiency of the industry in which the firm operates. Marshall was the first to formalize this concept, and limit it to "technological" (compared with pecuniary) economies and diseconomies.

For example, in the fishing industry, the more operators are engaged in fishing, the higher will be the costs facing any individual operator. In this case, there are said to be external diseconomies of production. In this event, marginal social costs (MSC) will exceed marginal private costs (MPC). Thus the price of the commodity will be lower than it would be if the divergence between MSC and MPC were to be eliminated. In this event, orthodox theory argues that a tax is in order, to discourage private production, and thus reduce social costs to the point where there is no disparity between social and private costs.

A good example of an industry in which there are considered to be external economies of scale is education. It is argued that social costs fall well below private costs because the educated individual contributes more than the uneducated to capitalist society's growth and political stability. The same kind of argument is made regarding transportation facilities. In these cases state subsidies are in order, or even public ownership.

A third departure from ideal output is the presence of increasing returns to scale in the production of a commodity. If a commodity is produced under conditions of increasing returns (air transport, for example), then just as in any industry, marginal revenue should be set equal to marginal costs to maximize profits and hence welfare. But marginal costs will be below average costs because average costs by definition are declining. Thus in order to have an efficient resource allocation, the industry must be subsidized. Otherwise, the firm must restrict output to cover average costs and thus command a higher price. On the other hand, taxes should be imposed on decreasing return industries; in these sectors, a policy of pricing to cover costs will mean that marginal costs are higher than average costs, signifying a misallocation of resources.

The extreme example of decreasing costs or increasing returns is the case of the "public good." The public good is defined as an activity where the additional cost of extra use is zero, or to put it another way, where my consumption does not reduce what is available to you. Standard examples are radio and television programs, lighthouses, and the Defense Department. Welfare economics teaches that for public goods price should be zero or near zero. With a price in excess of zero, ideal output exceeds actual output because more people could be better off and no one made worse off by an expansion of output.

It should be noted that the concept of a public good has little or nothing to do with whether the facility is owned by private capital or the state. Theoretically, private capital could own and manage lighthouses and the state could subsidize private capital so that prices could be set at zero and profits still made. To put it another way, lighthouses and television can be priced on the basis of private market principles; for example, radar could be placed on lighthouses to prevent free-riders by means of electronic scrambling of signals. And there is, of course, pay television. There is a category of public goods, however (military goods are given as the main example), in which the problem of "revealed preferences" arises. One could choose whether or not to pay to see a television program. But in the case of a military establishment, it is thought that there would be a general tendency to underpay via voluntary contributions because once "defense" is provided, everyone is "protected" whether or not he wants the protection. It is not possible to bomb North Vietnam in the name of some Americans and not others. In these cases, private ownership of the means of production, in our example, the means of destruction, is not warranted because there is no entrepreneurial function provided. Thus public goods, no matter what their special character, should be either heavily subsidized or owned publicly.

There is a fourth category of market imperfections which "justify" state interference in the private economy. This is a catch-all category which includes the following special cases: first, the case of neighborhood effects or spillovers. To take one or two examples: my unwillingness to conform to quarantine laws or mosquito control will affect everyone in the community, and thus it is justified for the state to coerce me to conform. Or, the existence of a public highway may raise property values locally. Thus the state is justified in paying transit deficits with property taxes. Or, situations where one firm affects the efficiency in the employment of resources by other firms. Suppose, for instance, that a farmer on a mountainside cuts down trees to cultivate his land, affecting adversely the ecological cycle by flooding the valley. These are not true technological externalities because the scale of the industry per se has nothing to do with the increase or decrease in the costs of the specific firm. Other examples come to mind in the capitalist labor market. For example, capitalists may have short-time horizons and hire workers with life-time horizons, such that work time is optimum in the short run but shortens a man's working life in the long run. Historically, hours laws can be traced to the irrationality of individual capitalists in the labor market, and the need for the state to preserve the labor power for all capitalists from the depredations of individual capitalists.

A final case is a situation where external economies or positive spillovers are so vast, and hence costs and prices under competition are so high, that the commodity does not even get produced. In this event, few people are even aware of the possible "advantage" to society. Good examples are import-substitute activities in underdeveloped capitalist countries which may benefit the economy greatly in the long run but which are not begun in the absence of protective state policy.

We offer so many examples of cases which do not fit neatly into the standard orthodox categories only to emphasize the fact that faced with real concrete situations it is often possible to "justify" any particular government interference after the fact—justify it in terms of orthodox criteria. Thus the idea of consumer sovereignty and welfare maximization (or ideal output) implies state intervention but offers few clear criteria. Because these criteria are so abstract, the dictum that taxes should be "neutral" except in the event that they are consciously designed to improve resource allocation is somewhat empty. More important, there is nothing in normative theory to tell us whether or not the dictums are realistic in a political sense—or to suggest precisely what externalities the state can be expected to capture and which cannot be.

The traditional perspective on welfare maximizing and state policy has come under increasing fire from contemporary orthodox economists, not because there are so many cases which do not fit neatly into the increasing cost or externality categories where the "correct" state policy is relatively straightforward and unambiguous, but rather because of the internal logic of the traditional view itself. Modern welfare economics rejects any partial analysis (an analysis restricted to one industry or branch of the economy) which purports to show that any given sector of the economy should be expanded to seize externalities in production. The arguments of contemporary welfare economists are highly mathematical and we will not reproduce them here. The gist of the main argument is that given external economies and necessary equilibrium conditions for the economy as a whole, it can be shown under certain assumptions no more or less arbitrary than those used by the traditional school that expanding sectors of the economy where there are no externalities may increase output even more than expanding sectors where there are. Further, there is the argument that there is no way to know whether a tax to correct an external diseconomy is better than some alternative measure, including the alternative of doing nothing.

One of the latest words on the subject has been said by Professor Baumol, who wrote that if "external economies are . . . strong . . . and persist, it will indeed pay society to increase all activity levels indefinitely." Moreover, in the past decade there has been a sustained critique, again from an orthodox standpoint, of the theory of consumer behavior on which welfare economies is based.

Three major points have been made. First, consumers may not be consistent in their choices; thus, it is not possible to say that they are better off in one situation rather than another. Second, externalities in consumption, or collective aspirations and well-being, have no place in traditional theory. Third, the argument is made that if the community is made up of one set of persons at one time, and another at another time, how can it be said when and if the community is better off?

We can safely conclude from this brief review of the critics of traditional theory that welfare economics, even one based on the assumption that capitalism as a system is eternal, offers no firm criteria for state policy.

The reason is that the critics of traditional welfare economics, as well as its few remaining defenders, accept criteria based on values which are in turn derived from a system based on the domination of private capital.

To put it another way, any notion of economic rationality which is independent of the "rationality" of the competitive private market is still taboo.

For this reason, claims by some economic theorists that value judgments have no place in their analysis are without any real foundation. Many traditional and modern welfare economists may claim that they attempt merely to determine the circumstances in which people with given economic interests may pursue these interests more "efficiently" by broadening the role of the state in the economy. But, at the same time, the theorist accepts these interests as valid—as worth defending and realizing. In the event that he rejected the given private interests, he would hardly waste time deducing from them implications for state action under varying sets of circumstances. It follows that the welfare economist ideologically supports the dominant private interests at the expense of the politically weakest private interests.

Another technical school of economics is the positive school. The positive economist views himself as a *technician* who rules out explicit normative theorizing, and finally, accepts the preferences of the "authorities" as given. The customary role of the positive economist is either an adviser to the state or some private group, or a technician faced with a "maximization" problem chosen by himself.

In the first case, the economist claims a certain neutrality with respect to the wisdom or lack of wisdom of some change proposed by the state, and confines himself to formulating alternative means to a given end. Needless to say, the positive economist accepts without question the desired end and, moreover, ordinarily fails to consider *all* possible alternative means to this end. There are no economists, for example, currently employed to work out the economic implications of nationalizing the drug industry or the oil interests, even though on pure efficiency criteria alone many economists would be compelled to give these industries very low marks. Thus the economic technician is to one degree or another merely a normative economist in disguise.

This is not a surprising conclusion; what is surprising is the economists' claim that they are merely "objective" analysts. If anything, the positive economist-technician adviser is less objective today than in the past. It can no longer be written as confidently that "economists treating government influences on the economy have largely neglected the essential institutional and procedural aspects of government action. That is why their analyses and recommendations are often characterized as utopian and unrealistic by the specialist in public finance." Today the "objective" economist is more willing to dispense with independent critical judgments than in the past, and, conversely, accept more constraints ("institutional and procedural aspects of government action") in his analysis.

In the second case, the economist analyzes an economic maximization problem chosen by himself; for example, the "optimum" investment in some new water resource. If all existing constraints—physical, legal, administrative-budgetary, and so on—are incorporated in the analysis, then the economist is bound "to exclude the interesting solution," to quote Otto Eckstein. What is meant by this is that a given market situation determines a certain set of prices, level of investment, and so on, and thus in order to put his apparatus to work, the economic technician must ignore at least one given political, property, financial, or other given relationship. The choice of which constraint to "assume away" is, of course, a normative judgment. Even here, the economist's values are in the center of his work.

The only important issues of state economic policy which the traditionalist does not refer to the welfare norm are the distribution of income, economic stabilization (including international stabilization), and economic growth. So far as the distribution of income is concerned, after many decades of debate, contemporary orthodox economists by and large reject the neoclassical fiction of "tax justice." The economist *qua* economist is powerless to make comparisons of "interpersonal utility" and thus cannot justify a progressive tax structure, or any other tax structure, without reference to given legal norms, precedent, "public opinion," and so on. Among orthodox economists the general consensus appears to be that the market distributes income more or less "fairly" in advanced capitalist countries— even though there is some recognition that everyone does not have equal access to the capital market (e.g., higher education)—although the more sophisticated writers are fully aware that this is not a necessary attribute of the market. For example, Samuelson rebuts those who accept the marginal productivity doctrine as a normative theory of income distribution between economic classes in the following way: "Under appropriate conditions of demand and technology, a marginal productivity theory might impute 99 percent of the national income away from labor, which would be exploitation enough in the eyes of radical agitators."

Thus it would appear that contemporary economics has traveled a long way to go (admittedly) a very short distance, yet on one crucial question the subject remains in the Dark Ages. We refer to the tendency to separate the ("ethical") question of income distribution from the ("scientific" or "objective") question of resource allocation and market efficiency. From the standpoint of formal *logic*, this separation is unobjectionable. However, an analysis of the political economy which ignores the actual connections between distribution and allocation is unreal. Clearly, economic efficiency depends on the distribution of output and income, and thus it is impossible to develop any fully satisfactory norms for resource allocation independent of the given distribution of income. Furthermore, it is not at all certain that a more equal income distribution would not automatically be accompanied by an increase in social consumption at the expense of private consumption as status symbols and material emulation in general would figure much less prominently in the social economy.

In a world of conspicuous consumption, for example, leveling income may greatly increase welfare. For another thing, if the satisfaction that one individual gets from his consumption depends in part on another individual's consumption, then changing the income distribution will change ideal output and hence welfare.

Lastly, in order to promote what *some* economic classes and groups consider to be an equitable distribution of income, it might be necessary to abandon the private market system altogether, or at the very least, modify it to the degree that its foundations are undermined. Needless to say, bourgeois economics defines "ethical" and "equitable" without reference to this alternative.

Complicating matters, the normative theory of state expenditure assumes that everyone benefits equally from a given expenditure (e.g., the police). The assumption is made that there is no link between the distribution of income and the welfare impact of state expenditures; for example, that individuals who cannot afford to travel benefit from highway expenditures as much as those who can. In the private market, bourgeois economists often justify inequalities in income distribution on the basis of "preserving incentives." No economist would ever dare say in public that inequalities in the welfare impact of "public" expenditures are required to preserve incentives.

Next we turn to macroeconomic fiscal theory, again beginning with an exposition of the main lines of the theory. Macroeconomics, like economics generally, uses the postulate-deductive form of equilibrium theory which begins with a few simple axioms and combines them to form a group of concepts that are logically interrelated. These concepts provide the basic terms of the system and describe the primary general relations between them.

The purpose of macroeconomic, or income theory, is to analyze the determinants of aggregate or total spending on commodities. The elementary concept is the utility of objects for individuals; the general relation is the principle of maximization of utility for individuals and returns (profits) for firms. A million light years, however, separate individual utility and demand for commodities from aggregate demand for commodities, and in macroeconomic theorizing, individual utility is ordinarily lost sight of. This means that macroeconomics in no sense can be considered pure economic theory.

In the most simple macroeconomic model total income, or the value of total production (Y), is constituted by consumption spending (C), investment spending (I), and government spending (G), $(Y = C + I + G)$. The level of employment is determined by the level of income or production $(E = E(Y))$. The price level (P) is assumed to be unchanged up to the point of full employment. When full employment is reached, the price level is determined by the level of spending.

Macro-theory does not independently investigate the determinants of consumption, which is made to depend on income via the "marginal propensity to consume" (MPC). The simplest form of the consumption function is $C = a + bY$, where a is the volume of consumption when income is zero, and b is the propensity to consume, or the proportion of income consumed. Income itself, and hence employment and prices, are thus determined by investment spending and government spending.

There are almost as many theories of investment as there are investment theorists. The original Keynesian theory, a simple one, views investment as depending on the anticipated rate of profit (p), the money supply (M), and society's preference for holding assets in liquid (cash) form (LP). Government spending is determined by the political authorities and is not subject to economic laws.

The elementary functional relations of the system are: (1) The higher the MPC, the higher the level of income and employment; (2) The greater the stock of money, the lower the rate of interest, the higher the volume of investment, and the higher the level of income and employment; and (3) The weaker the preference for holding assets in the form of cash, the greater the demand for bonds, the higher the price of bonds, the lower the rate of interest, and the greater the level of investment, income, and employment.

The system is said to be in equilibrium when the volume of production at current prices equals consumption, government spending, and intended investment. Actual investment equals intended investment when inventories of commodities are no lower or greater today than capitalists expected them to be yesterday, i.e., when today's sales equal yesterday's production. In this event, the market is cleared; there is no excess demand or supply. The peculiar characteristic of the Keynesian model is that the system may be in equilibrium even though there may be a sizeable amount of unemployment (or, alternatively, inflation).

Thus to increase employment, income must be increased. Income may be increased directly by raising the propensity to consume (for example, by deflating the economy and increasing the real value of savings, and hence liberating savings for consumption), by raising investment (e.g., by subsidies to capitalists), and by government spending or tax reductions. Income may be increased indirectly by increasing the supply of money, lowering the rate of interest, and hence raising the level of investment.

It should be obvious from this discussion that macro-theory was formulated with an eye to macro-policy—that in no sense can macro-theory be considered pure theory, or value-free theory. The orientation of macro-theory is toward the *control* of income, employment, and prices via state economic policy. Thus macro-theory, fiscal theory (the analysis of the effects of government spending, taxation, and borrowing), and fiscal policy (applied fiscal theory) all boil down to fundamentally the same phenomenon—how to make capitalism a viable economic and social system by keeping unemployment and inflation within reasonable bounds.

It should also be obvious that macro-theory (like microeconomic) is not a *social* science. It does not analyze the relations between men, but rather the relations between abstractions such as total income, the price level, etc.

Macro-theory of the type discussed above (i.e., theory which places primary emphasis on demand) has been popular during two historical eras—during the late mercantilist period and today, the epoch of monopoly capitalism. In both periods the state plays a central role in the economy. During the era of laissez faire, income theory was banished by the classical and neoclassical economists. Brought to life by Keynes, today it dominates economic thought in the advanced capitalist countries.

The main point is that macro-theory is at one and the same time the science and ideology of the ruling class—or, more precisely, the dominant stratum of the ruling class, the corporate oligarchy. The corporate oligarchy has long ago accepted the inevitability and desirability of economic self-regulation—or what is euphemistically called government intervention in the economy. What is more, the corporate oligarchy is the only segment of the ruling class which is in a position to effectively *control* macro-fiscal policy. I do not think that this assertion requires elaborate proof. There is a growing historical literature which describes the sources and development of a class consciousness on the part of the corporate rich, and there is a sociological literature which describes the modes of control by the corporations of the quasi-private planning and policy organizations such as CED, and the process of ideology formation in which these organizations play a decisive role. Even if such a literature did not exist, it is easy to understand why fiscal policy *must* be formulated in the interests of the hundred or so dominant corporations, because the health of the economy depends almost exclusively on the health of these giants.

Income theory, then, is a *technical* science to the degree that it has practical value to the corporations. To put it another way, income theory is scientific insofar as it is useful to preserve and extend monopoly capitalism as a system and perpetuate class divisions and class rule. On this criterion, for example, neo-Keynesian theory is more scientific than Keynes' original doctrines. A fiscal policy for growth is more practical than one for economic stabilization because of its bias in favor of investment, and hence profits.

On the other hand, income theory is not a *critical* science because it constitutes itself on the given economic and legal foundations of capitalism. It fails to make the foundations of capitalism themselves a subject for analysis. At best, then, income theory offers only a description of the *mechanics of operation* of advanced capitalist economies. A critical science is not a science of mechanics, but of real causes, historical causes; the variables are not abstractions such as the interest rate, or supply of money, but rather they are *human* agents.

Thus over the past 30 years there has developed an elaborate analysis of the determinants of income, employment, and production—an analysis which has proven to have great practical value in helping the state underwrite business investments and business losses—or to use the long-current euphemism, in helping the government to stabilize the economy and encourage it to grow. What is more, its practical value to the corporations and business in general is greatly enhanced by the fact that business increasingly takes it for granted that income theory *is* an accurate description of the economy.

On the other hand, few would place much confidence in the explanations of the ultimate causes of fluctuation and growth which are integral to income theory. These explanations run in terms of individual psychological motivations and responses and abstract completely from the ever-changing, concrete socioeconomic setting which decisively conditions consumer and business behavior. The concepts of "propensities," "preferences," "anticipations and expectations" seem to Marxist economists to be very fragile foundations for such an elaborate structure as income theory. The alternative, and correct, path, in my view, is to submit consumption, investment, and government spending to a *structural* determination; that is, to deduce the implications for the volume of and changes in investment (or consumption) in the context of the *actual* behavior of large corporations operating in oligopolistic markets.

Perhaps an analogy will be useful at this stage. A good one is the relationship between medicine, on the one hand, and biochemistry, biophysics and other sciences which attempt to understand the body as a whole, on the other. To a surprising degree, there is frequently a great gulf separating medicine from the body sciences. The diagnosis and treatment of some diseases—a good example is mental illness—often remain unchanged when the body scientists advance their understanding of the causes of illness, for the simple reason that medicine remains an excellent description of the mechanics of the body. In fact, it is well known that in psychotherapy a priori statements about which technique will produce results with any given patient are very hard to come by. Often, the therapist is not even aware of why he has achieved results. One could make the same statement about some economic policymakers.

Income theory is neither right nor wrong—in the sense of being close to or distant from the real causes of economic change—because income theory does not pretend to investigate real causes. It is only more or less useful—more useful if the mechanics of operation of the economy are accurately specified, less useful if not. The main criterion of success is *results.*

Income theory can achieve good results even though its theoretical foundations may be weak. But it could get better results if it were scientifically based on real causes, as we will suggest below. The point which needs emphasis, however, is that it is impossible for an economic theory which exists to maintain capitalism and class rule to be based on real causes. The reason is that a causal science is a critical science, one which subjects the foundations of capitalism—as well as the transitory economic manifestations of these foundations—to analysis. Clearly, a theory which is designed to perpetuate the social and economic relations (and indirectly the taboos and superstitions) of capitalism will be of little value to anyone who wishes to question these relations and taboos and superstitions.

If the economic theory questioned its own assumptions, it would negate itself; and since income theory is first and foremost ruling-class theory, a critical theory would imply that the ruling class would have to question itself, its own right to rule, or negate itself. Let me illustrate with a simple example in the form of a hypothesis: suppose that inflation is caused by the groups or classes which benefit from inflation; suppose further that anti-inflation policy is in the hands of those who caused the inflation. The anti-inflation policy will leave some groups or classes worse off and some better off. Among those who will be better off, will be the group which was the prime mover behind the inflation, the original beneficiaries. Now suppose that the ruling class employs economists to study inflation— indeed, not only study inflation, but find acceptable ways to cause inflation. Clearly, a critical science of inflation would require that economists study not only their employers but themselves.

The economics profession adamantly refuses to do this—to consider itself a part of the experimental field. But it is obvious that economics as a technical science is a *social* phenomenon—and it may be true that only economists are in a position to comprehend their own social role. In fact, we believe it can be shown that the economist's tools have made it possible to have a little unemployment and a little inflation, an optimal situation for the corporations. For example, two famous economists, Paul Samuelson and Robert Solow, wrote an article entitled, "Our Menu of Policy Choices," in which "we" are given the "choice" of a little unemployment and a little inflation, or, alternatively, a little inflation and a little unemployment! Abolishing both unemployment and inflation is impossible given the fact (for bourgeois economists, the eternal fact) that employment depends on the growth of income, which in turn depends on investment, which in turn requires at least a slight profit inflation (that is, prices rising faster than money wages).

In short, income theory does not seek to remove the extremes of society—unemployment and inflation (and capital and labor, rich and poor, privileged and underprivileged, rulers and ruled)—but rather, to quote Marx, it attempts to "weaken their antagonisms and transform them into a harmonious whole," Marxists believe this to be impossible. And hence a critical bourgeois social science, including income theory, is for this reason impossible.

Let us now turn to the treatment which public finance affords the relationship between budgetary policy and economic growth. "Growth models in their present form," Peacock and Wiseman write, "cannot be treated as anything more than exercises in a technique of arrangement." The basic reason that income and growth theory is unrealistic is the failure to include a theory of state expenditures. Evsey Domar once noted that government expenditures can be dealt with in one of three ways: they can be assumed to be "exogenous" to the system, they can be merged with consumption expenditures, or they can be assumed "away altogether." The latter alternative is completely unsatisfactory, and to assume that government expenditures are determined by "outside" forces is tantamount to an admission that they are beyond the realm of comprehension. Merging all government spending with private consumption merely substitutes fiction for fact.

Paradoxically, government spending is increasingly placed in the middle of discussions of growth and stagnation. Most economists view the state as a kind of *deus ex machina* and assume that government spending not only can but should make up the difference between the actual volume of private expenditures and the level of spending which will keep unemployment down to a politically tolerable minimum. State expenditures in this way are incorporated into models of fluctuations and growth. However, the *actual* determinants of government spending are not considered; rather, what is considered is the volume of spending and taxation necessary to achieve certain goals given certain assumptions and characteristics of the given model.

The reason why economists do not know the actual determinants of government expenditure is not hard to find. There are no markets for most goods and services provided by the state, and hence it is not possible to lean on the doctrine of revealed preferences. Thus a theory of state expenditures requires an examination of the forces influencing and conditioning demand. But utility theory forbids any inquiry into these forces—putting aside statistical explanations such as the age-mix of the population, climatic conditions, and the like.

This line of thinking leads to the conclusion that before fiscal theory can lay claim to being a critical science, the laws which govern the determination of the volume and composition of state expenditures, and the relation between expenditures and taxes, must be uncovered. This means that fiscal theory must have a clear notion of the character of the state under monopoly capitalism—fiscal theory is then a branch of the theory of the state.

Space does not permit any but the briefest discussion of the elements which truly scientific fiscal theory must contain.

First of all, a clear distinction must be made between socially necessary costs and economic surplus—a distinction between the value of total output and the costs of producing that output. The concept of "necessary costs" is value-free in the sense that it has meaning independently of any given economic system. Necessary costs are outlays required to maintain the economy's productive capacity and labor force in their given state of productivity or efficiency. The difference between total output and necessary costs constitutes economic surplus. Further, a distinction must be made between what may be called discretionary uses of the surplus by the state, and nondiscretionary spending. Without these distinctions, it is not possible to evaluate the role of state expenditure in the determination of aggregate demand and economic growth.

To the degree that state expenditure constitutes necessary costs, state outlays merely substitute for private outlays; hence, do not have any independent effect on aggregate demand. The only difference is that taxpayers as a whole, rather than as a specific industry or branch of the economy, are charged with the costs. An example is education outlays required to maintain the labor force in its given state of productivity.

To the degree that state expenditures comprise economic surplus, and to the degree that the surplus consists of nondiscretionary spending (e.g., education outlays required to raise the skill level of a labor force in accordance with advancing technology), state outlays again substitute for private spending—and aggregate demand remains unchanged. In our view, nondiscretionary spending is made up of two main categories: first, a large part of collective consumption—expenditures on social amenities laid out more or less voluntarily by residents in a given community; second, what might be called complementary investments, a special form of private investment the costs of which are borne by the taxpayer, and without which private investment would be unprofitable. Water investments in agricultural districts would be a good example.

Additional demand, and hence economic surplus, *is* generated, first, by wasteful and destructive outlays (the main example being military spending) and, second, discretionary investments, or state investments made to encourage future private accumulation (e.g., industrial development parks). In this case, there is an increment to demand and surplus because private capital would otherwise not have made the expenditure. Here the rise in government spending will be financed largely out of taxes and thus at the expense of private consumption. The state will in this event create more surplus (or savings) than it absorbs.

Finally, transfer payments (e.g., debt interest and farm payments) generate more surplus than they absorb because they alter the distribution of personal income in the direction of greater inequality.

Whether or not fiscal policy can be a viable instrument for maintaining a respectable volume of demand depends on whether or not total state spending generates more surplus than it absorbs. If so, then the state budget must continuously increase for the economy to remain in the same place. If not, then state expenditures cannot be considered in any sense autonomous, and correspondingly, the state cannot be considered to be able to act independently of the specific interests of specific firms, industries, or other segments of the ruling class. Of course, the truth lies somewhere in between these extremes—exactly where we do not know. But often it is more scientific to admit to an area of ignorance than to confidently predict that capitalism can or cannot save itself by the utilization of budgetary policy.

PART 3

Economic Philosophies

Worldly Philosophies

SMITH, MILL, MARX, MARSHALL, AND KEYNES

Adam Smith is the intellectual father of what is now labelled classical economics. In the later works of Mill, Marshall, and Keynes we see not only the evolution of "western economics," but a concern for areas of inadequate performance. For example, Mill raised the problem of distribution; Keynes the problem of full employment. In addition, they disagreed as to whether the system was tending upward in a progressive spiral or toward a stationary state. The common ground among Mill, Marshall, and Keynes was the belief that these problems could be resolved within the capitalistic system. Some modifications may be necessary, but the system was basically sound. The works of Karl Marx stand as a direct challenge to the soundness of the capitalistic system. His distinction lies in a theoretical analysis which concluded that capitalism could not resolve its problems within its own system. A word of caution. These excerpts only hint at the richness of thought of our "founding fathers" and again we urge the student to dip into the originals.

Wealth of Nations, Adam Smith

The greatest improvement in the productive powers of labor, and the greater part of the skill, dexterity, and judgment with which it is anywhere directed, or applied, seem to have been the effects of the division of labor.

The effects of the division of labor, in the general business of society, will be more easily understood by considering in what manner it operates in some particular manufactures. It is commonly supposed to be carried furthest in some very trifling ones; not perhaps that it really is carried further in them than in others of more importance: but in those trifling manufactures which are destined to supply the small wants of but a small number of people, the whole number of workmen must necessarily be small; and those employed in every different branch of the work can often be collected into the same workhouse, and placed at once under the view of the spectator. In those great manufactures, on the contrary, which are destined to supply the great wants of the great body of the people, every different branch of the work employs so great a number of workmen that

From the books *The Wealth of Nations* by Adam Smith. Introduction by Professor Edwin R. A. Seligman. Vols. I and II. Everyman's Library Edition. Published by E. P. Dutton & Co., Inc., and reprinted with their permission.

it is impossible to collect them all into the same workhouse. We can seldom see more, at one time, than those employed in one single branch. Though in such manufactures, therefore, the work may really be divided into a much greater number of parts than in those of a more trifling nature, the division is not near so obvious, and has accordingly been much less observed.

To take an example, therefore, from a very trifling manufacture; but one in which the division of labor has been very often taken notice of, the trade of the pin-maker; a workman not educated to this business (which the division of labor has rendered a distinct trade), nor acquainted with the use of the machinery employed in it (to the invention of which the same division of labor has probably given occasion), could scarce, perhaps, with his utmost industry, make one pin in a day, and certainly could not make 20. But in the way in which this business is now carried on, not only the whole work is a peculiar trade, but it is divided into a number of branches, of which the greater part are likewise peculiar trades. One man draws out the wire, another straightens it, a third cuts it, a fourth points it, a fifth grinds it at the top for receiving the head; to make the head requires two or three distinct operations; to put it on is a peculiar business, to whiten the pins is another; it is even a trade by itself to put them into the paper; and the important business of making a pin is, in this manner, divided into about 18 distinct operations, which, in some manufactories, are all performed by distinct hands, though in others the same man will sometimes perform two or three of them. I have seen a small manufactory of this kind where ten men only were employed, and where some of them consequently performed two or three distinct operations. But though they were very poor, and therefore but indifferently accommodated with the necessary machinery, they could, when they exerted themselves, make among them about 12 pounds of pins in a day. There are in a pound upwards of 4,000 pins of a middling size. Those ten persons, therefore, could make among them upwards of 48,000 pins in a day. Each person, therefore, making a tenth part of 48,000 pins, might be considered as making 4,800 pins in a day. But if they had all wrought separately and independently, and without any of them having been educated to this peculiar business, they certainly could not each of them have made 20, perhaps not one pin in a day; that is, certainly, not the 240th, perhaps not the 4,800th part of what they are at present capable of performing, in consequence of a proper division and combination of their different operations.

In every other art and manufacture, the effects of the division of labor are similar to what they are in this very trifling one; though, in many of them, the labor can neither be so much subdivided, nor reduced to so great a simplicity of operation. The division of labor, however, so far as it can be introduced, occasions, in every art, a proportionable increase of the

productive powers of labor. The separation of different trades and employments from one another seems to have taken place in consequence of this
advantage. This separation, too, is generally carried furthest in those countries which enjoy the highest degree of industry and improvement; what
is the work of one man in a rude state of society being generally that of
several in an improved one. In every improved society, the farmer is generally nothing but a farmer; the manufacturer, nothing but a manufacturer. The labor, too, which is necessary to produce any one complete
manufacture is almost always divided among a great number of hands.

This great increase of the quantity of work which, in consequence
of the division of labor, the same number of people are capable of performing, is owing to three different circumstances; first, to the increase of
dexterity in every particular workman; second, to the saving of the time
which is commonly lost in passing from one species of work to another;
and last, to the invention of a great number of machines which facilitate
and abridge labor, and enable one man to do the work of many.

This division of labor, from which so many advantages are derived,
is not originally the effect of any human wisdom, which foresees and intends that general opulence to which it gives occasion. It is the necessary
though very slow and gradual consequence of a certain propensity in
human nature which has in view no such extensive utility; the propensity
to truck, barter, and exchange one thing for another.

Whether this propensity be one of those original principles in human
nature of which no further account can be given; or whether, as seems
more probable, it be the necessary consequence of the faculties of reason
and speech, it belongs not to our present subject to inquire. It is common
to all men, and to be found in no other race of animals, which seem to
know neither this nor any other species of contracts. Two greyhounds, in
running down the same hare, have sometimes the appearance of acting
in some sort of concert. Each turns her towards his companion, or endeavors to intercept her when his companion turns her towards himself. This,
however, is not the effect of any contract, but of the accidental concur-
rence of their passions in the same object at that particular time. Nobody
ever saw a dog make a fair and deliberate exchange of one bone for another
with another dog. Nobody ever saw one animal by its gestures and natural
cries signify to another, this is mine, that yours; I am willing to give this
for that. When an animal wants to obtain something either of a man or of
another animal, it has no other means of persuasion but to gain the favor
of those whose service it requires. A puppy fawns upon its dam, and a
spaniel endeavors by a thousand attractions to engage the attention of its
master who is at dinner, when it wants to be fed by him. Man sometimes
uses the same arts with his brethren, and when he has no other means of
engaging them to act according to his inclinations, endeavors by every

servile and fawning attention to obtain their good will. He has not time, however, to do this upon every occasion. In civilized society he stands at all times in need of the cooperation and assistance of great multitudes, while his whole life is scarce sufficient to gain the friendship of a few persons. In almost every other race of animals each individual, when it is grown up to maturity, is entirely independent, and its natural state has occasion for the assistance of no other living creature. But man has almost constant occasion for the help of his brethren, and it is in vain for him to expect it from their benevolence only. He will be more likely to prevail if he can interest their self-love in his favor, and show them that it is for their own advantage to do for him what he requires of them. Whoever offers to another a bargain of any kind, proposes to do this. Give me that which I want, and you shall have this which you want, is the meaning of every such offer; and it is in this manner that we obtain from one another the far greater part of those good offices which we stand in need of. It is not from the benevolence of the butcher, the brewer, or the baker that we expect our dinner, but from their regard to their own interest. We address ourselves, not to their humanity but to their self-love, and never talk to them of our own necessities but of their advantages.

What are the common wages of labor, depends everywhere upon the contract usually made between those two parties, whose interests are by no means the same. The workmen desire to get as much, the masters to give as little as possible. The former are disposed to combine in order to raise, the latter in order to lower the wages of labor.

It is not, however, difficult to foresee which of the two parties must, upon all ordinary occasions, have the advantage in the dispute, and force the other into a compliance with their terms. The masters, being fewer in number, can combine much more easily; and the law, besides, authorizes, or at least does not prohibit their combinations, while it prohibits those of the workmen. We have no acts of parliament against combining to lower the price of work; but many against combining to raise it. In all such disputes the masters can hold out much longer. A landlord, a farmer, a master manufacturer, a merchant, though they did not employ a single workman, could generally live a year or two upon the stocks which they have already acquired. Many workmen could not subsist a week, few could subsist a month, and scarce any a year without employment. In the long run the workman may be as necessary to his master as his master is to him; but the necessity is not so immediate.

We rarely hear, it has been said, of the combinations of masters, though frequently of those of workmen. But whoever imagines, upon this account, that masters rarely combine, is as ignorant of the world as of the subject. Masters are always and everywhere in a sort of tacit, but constant and uniform combination, not to raise the wages of labor above their actual rate. To violate this combination is everywhere a most unpopular action, and a sort of reproach to a master among his neighbors and equals. We seldom, indeed, hear of this combination, because it is the usual, and one may say, the natural state of things, which nobody ever hears of. Masters, too, sometimes enter into particular combinations to sink the wages of labor even below this rate. These are always conducted with the utmost silence and secrecy, till the moment of execution, and when the workmen yield, as they sometimes do, without resistance, though severely felt by them, they are never heard of by other people. Every individual who employs his capital in the support of domestic industry, necessarily endeavors so to direct that industry that its produce may be of the greatest possible value.

The produce of industry is what it adds to the subject or materials upon which it is employed. In proportion as the value of this produce is great or small, so will likewise be the profits of the employer. But it is only for the sake of profit that any man employs a capital in the support of industry; and he will always, therefore, endeavor to employ it in the support of that industry of which the produce is likely to be of the greatest value, or to exchange for the greatest quantity either of money or of other goods.

But the annual revenue of every society is always precisely equal to the exchangeable value of the whole annual produce of its industry or rather is precisely the same thing with that exchangeable value. As every individual, therefore, endeavors as much as he can both to employ his capital in the support of domestic industry . . . every individual necessarily labors to render the annual revenue of the society as great as he can. He generally, indeed neither intends to promote the public interest, nor knows how much he is promoting it . . . he intends only his own gain, and he is in this, as in many other cases, led by an invisible hand to promote an end which was no part of his intention.

Theses on Feuerbach and Das Kapital, Karl Marx

The philosophers have only interpreted the world, in various ways; the point, however, is to change it.

Historical Tendency of Capitalist Accumulation. What does the primitive accumulation of capital, i.e., its historical genesis, resolve itself into? In so far as it is not immediate transformation of slaves and serfs into wage laborers, and therefore a mere change of form, it only means the expropriation of the immediate producers, i.e., the dissolution of

From *Selected Works of Karl Marx and Frederick Engles*, pp. 30, 235–7. Reprinted by permission of International Publisher's Co., Inc. Copyright © 1968.

private property based on the labor of its owner. Private property, as the antithesis to social, collective property, exists only where the means of labor and the external conditions of labor belong to private individuals. But according as these private individuals are laborers or not laborers, private property has a different character. The numberless shades that it at first sight presents, correspond to the intermediate stages lying between these two extremes. The private property of the laborer in his means of production is the foundation of petty industry, whether agricultural, manufacturing, or both; petty industry, again, is an essential condition for the development of social production and of the free individuality of the laborer himself. Of course, this petty mode of production exists also under slavery, serfdom, and other states of dependence. But it flourishes, it lets loose its whole energy, it attains its adequate classical form, only where the laborer is the private owner of his own means of labor set in action by himself; the peasant of the land which he cultivates, the artisan of the tool which he handles as a virtuoso.

This mode of production presupposes parceling of the soil, and scattering of the other means of production. As it excludes the concentration of these means of production, so also it excludes cooperation, division of labor within each separate process of production, the control over, and the productive application of, the forces of nature by society, and the free development of the social productive powers. It is compatible only with a system of production, and a society, moving within narrow and more or less primitive bounds. To perpetuate it would be, as Pecqueur rightly says, "to decree universal mediocrity." At a certain stage of development, it brings forth the material agencies for its own dissolution. From that moment, new forces and new passions spring up in the bosom of society; but the old social organization fetters them and keeps them down. It must be annihilated; it is annihilated. Its annihilation, the transformation of the individualized and scattered means of production into socially concentrated ones, of the pygmy property of the many into the huge property of the few, the expropriation of the great mass of the people from the soil, from the means of subsistence, and from the means of labor, this fearful and painful expropriation of the mass of the people forms the prelude to the history of capital. It comprises a series of forcible methods, of which we have passed in review only those that have been epoch-making as methods of the primitive accumulation of capital. The expropriation of the immediate producers was accomplished with merciless vandalism, and under the stimulus of passions the most infamous, the most sordid, the pettiest, the most meanly odious. Self-earned private property, that is based, so to say, on the fusing together of the isolated, independent laboring individual with the conditions of his labor, is supplanted by capitalistic private property, which rests on exploitation of the nominally free labor of others, i.e., on wage-labor.

As soon as this process of transformation has sufficiently decomposed the old society from top to bottom, as soon as the laborers are turned into proletarians, their means of labor into capital, as soon as the capitalist mode of production stands on its own feet, then the further socialization of labor and further transformation of the land and other means of production into socially exploited and, therefore, common means of production, as well as the further expropriation of private proprietors, takes a new form. That which is now to be expropriated is no longer the laborer working for himself, but the capitalist exploiting many laborers.- This expropriation is accomplished by the action of the immanent laws of capitalistic production itself, by the centralization of capital. One capitalist always kills many. Hand in hand with this centralization, or this expropriation of many capitalists by few, develop, on an ever-extending scale, the cooperative form of the labor process, the conscious technical application of science, the methodical cultivation of the soil, the transformation of the instruments of labor into instruments of labor only usable in common, the economizing of all means of production by their use as the means of production of combined, socialized labor, the entanglement of all peoples in the net of the world market, and with this, the international character of the capitalistic regime. Along with the constantly diminishing number of the magnates of capital, who usurp and monopolize all advantages of this process of transformation, grows the mass of misery, oppression, slavery, degradation, exploitation; but with this too grows the revolt of the working class, a class always increasing in numbers, and disciplined, united, organized by the very mechanism of the process of capitalist production itself. The monopoly of capital becomes a fetter upon the mode of production, which has sprung up and flourished along with, and under, it. Centralization of the means of production and socialization of labor at last reach a point where they become incompatible with their capitalist integument. This integument is burst asunder. The knell of capitalist private property sounds. The expropriators are expropriated.

The capitalist mode of appropriation, the result of the capitalist mode of production, produces capitalist private property. This is the first negation of individual private property, as founded on the labor of the proprietor. But capitalist production begets, with the inexorability of a law of nature, its own negation. It is the negation of negation. This does not reestablish private property for the producer, but gives him individual property based on the acquisitions of the capitalist era, i.e., on cooperation and the possession in common of the land and of the means of production.

The transformation of scattered private property, arising from individual labor, into capitalist private property is, naturally, a process incomparably more protracted, violent, and difficult, than the transformation of capitalistic private property, already practically resting on socialized production, into socialized property. In the former case, we had the expropriation of the mass of the people by a few usurpers; in the latter, we have the expropriation of a few usurpers by the mass of the people.

Principles of Political Economy, J. S. Mill

It must always have been seen, more or less distinctly, by political economists, that the increase of wealth is not boundless: that at the end of what they term the progressive state lies the stationary state, that all progress in wealth is but a postponement of this, and that each step in advance is an approach to it. We have now been led to recognize that this ultimate goal is at all times near enough to be fully in view; that we are always on the verge of it, and that if we have not reached it long ago, it is because the goal itself flies before us. The richest and most prosperous countries would very soon attain the stationary state, if no further improvements were made in the productive arts, and if there were a suspension of the overflow of capital from those countries into the uncultivated or ill-cultivated regions of the earth.

This impossibility of ultimately avoiding the stationary state—this irresistible necessity that the stream of human industry should finally spread itself out into an apparently stagnant sea—must have been, to the political economists of the last two generations, an unpleasing and discouraging prospect; for the tone and tendency of their speculations goes completely to identify all that is economically desirable with the progressive state, and with that alone. With Mr. [James Ramsay] McCulloch, for example, prosperity does not mean a large production and a good distribution of wealth, but a rapid increase of it; his test of prosperity is high profits; and as the tendency of that very increase of wealth, which he calls prosperity, is towards low profits, economical progress, according to him, must tend to the extinction of prosperity. Adam Smith always assumes that the condition of the mass of the people, though it may not be positively distressed, must be pinched and stinted in a stationary condition of wealth, and can only be satisfactory in a progressive state. The doctrine that, to however distant a time incessant struggling may put off our doom, the progress of society must "end in shallows and in miseries," far from being, as many people still believe, a wicked invention of Mr. Malthus, was either expressly or tacitly affirmed by his most distinguished predecessors, and can only be successfully combated on his principles. Before attention had been directed to the principle of population as the active force in determining the remuneration of labor, the increase of mankind was virtually treated as a constant quantity: it was, at all events, assumed that in the natural and normal state of human affairs population must

From "Principles of Political Economy," Vol. 2 (New York: D. Appleton & Co., 1889), pp. 334–39.

constantly increase, from which it followed that a constant increase of
the means of support was essential to the physical comfort of the mass
of mankind. The publication of Mr. Malthus's *Essay* is the era from which
better views of this subject must be dated; and notwithstanding the
acknowledged errors of his first edition, few writers have done more
than himself, in the subsequent editions, to promote these juster and more
hopeful anticipations.

Even in a progressive state of capital, in old countries, a conscientious
or prudential restraint on population is indispensable, to prevent the
increase of numbers from outstripping the increase of capital, and the
condition of the classes who are at the bottom of society from being
deteriorated. Where there is not, in the people, or in some very large
proportion of them, a resolute resistance to this deterioration—a determination to preserve an established standard of comfort—the condition
of the poorest class sinks, even in a progressive state, to the lowest point
which they will consent to endure. The same determination would be
equally effectual to keep up their condition in the stationary state, and
would be quite as likely to exist. Indeed, even now, the countries in
which the greatest prudence is manifested in the regulating of population,
are often those in which capital increases least rapidly. Where there is an
indefinite prospect of employment for increased numbers, there is apt
to appear less necessity for prudential restraint. If it were evident that a
new hand could not obtain employment but by displacing, or succeeding
to, one already employed, the combined influences of prudence and public
opinion might in some measure be relied on for restricting the coming
generation within the numbers necessary for replacing the present.

I cannot, therefore, regard the stationary state of capital and wealth
with the unaffected aversion so generally manifested towards it by political
economists of the old school. I am inclined to believe that it would be,
on the whole, a very considerable improvement on our present condition.
I confess I am not charmed with the ideal of life held out by those who
think that the normal state of human beings is that of struggling to get
on; that the trampling, crushing, elbowing, and treading on each other's
heels, which form the existing type of social life, are the most desirable
lot of human kind, or anything but the disagreeable symptoms of one
of the phases of industrial progress. The northern and middle states of
America are a specimen of this stage of civilization in very favorable
circumstances; having, apparently, got rid of all social injustices and
inequalities that affect persons of Caucasian race and of the male sex,
while the proportion of population to capital and land is such as to ensure
abundance to every able-bodied member of the community who does not
forfeit it by misconduct. They have the six points of Chartism, and they
have no poverty: and all that these advantages seem to have yet done
for them (notwithstanding some incipient signs of a better tendency) is

that the life of the whole of one sex is devoted to dollar-hunting, and of the other to breeding dollar-hunters. This is not a kind of social perfection which philanthropists to come will feel any very eager desire to assist in realizing. Most fitting, indeed, is it, that while riches are power, and to grow as rich as possible the universal object of ambition, the path to its attainment should be open to all, without favor or partiality. But the best state for human nature is that in which, while no one is poor, no one desires to be richer, nor has any reason to fear being thrust back, by the efforts of others to push themselves forward.

That the energies of mankind should be kept in employment by the struggle for riches, as they were formerly by the struggle of war, until the better minds succeed in educating the others into better things, is undoubtedly more desirable than that they should rust and stagnate. While minds are coarse they require coarse stimuli, and let them have them. In the meantime, those who do not accept the present very early stage of human improvement as its ultimate type, may be excused for being comparatively indifferent to the kind of economical progress which excites the congratulations of ordinary politicians; the mere increase of production and accumulation. For the safety of national independence it is essential that a country should not fall much behind its neighbors in these things. But in themselves they are of little importance, so long as either the increase of population or anything else prevents the mass of the people from reaping any part of the benefit of them. I know not why it should be matter of congratulation that persons who are already richer than anyone needs to be, should have doubled their means of consuming things which give little or no pleasure except as representative of wealth; or that numbers of individuals should pass over, every year, from the middle classes into a richer class, or from the class of the occupied rich to that of the unoccupied. It is only in the backward countries of the world that increased production is still an important object: in those most advanced, what is economically needed is a better distribution, of which one indispensable means is a stricter restraint on population. Leveling institutions, either of a just or of an unjust kind, cannot alone accomplish it; they may lower the heights of society, but they cannot, of themselves, permanently raise the depths.

On the other hand, we may suppose this better distribution of property attained, by the joint effect of the prudence and frugality of individuals, and of a system of legislation favoring equality of fortunes, so far as is consistent with the just claim of the individual to the fruits, whether great or small, of his or her own industry. We may suppose, for instance, a limitation of the sum which any one person may acquire by gift or inheritance, to the amount sufficient to constitute a moderate independence. Under this twofold influence, society would exhibit these leading features: a well-paid and affluent body of laborers; no enormous fortunes, except what were earned and accumulated during a single life-time; but a much larger body of persons than at present, not only exempt from the coarser toils, but with sufficient leisure, both physical and mental, from mechanical details, to cultivate freely the graces of life, and afford examples of them to the classes less favorably circumstanced for their growth. This condition of society, so greatly preferable to the present, is not only perfectly compatible with the stationary state, but, it would seem, more naturally allied with the state than with any other.

Principles of Economics, Alfred Marshall

Economics is a study of men as they live and move and think in the ordinary business of life. But it concerns itself chiefly with those motives which affect, most powerfully and most steadily, man's conduct in the business part of his life. Everyone who is worth anything carries his higher nature with him into business; and, there as elsewhere, he is influenced by his personal affections, by his conceptions of duty and his reverence for high ideals.

The advantage which economics has over other branches of social science appears then to arise from the fact that its special field of work gives rather larger opportunities for exact methods than any other branch. It concerns itself chiefly with those desires, aspirations and other affections of human nature, the outward manifestations of which appear as incentives to action in such a form that the force or quantity of the incentives can be estimated and measured with some approach to accuracy; and which therefore are in some degree amenable to treatment by scientific machin-ery. An opening is made for the methods and the tests of science as soon as the force of a person's motives—not the motives themselves—can be approximately measured by the sum of money, which he will just give up in order to secure a desired satisfaction; or again by the sum which is just required to induce him to undergo a certain fatigue.

Economists study the actions of individuals, but study them in rela-tion to social rather than individual life; and therefore concern themselves but little with personal peculiarities of temper and character. They watch carefully the conduct of a whole class of people, sometimes the whole of a nation, sometimes only those living in a certain district, more often those engaged in some particular trade at some time and place: and by the aid of statistics, or in other ways then ascertain how much money on the average the members of the particular group, they are watching, are just willing to pay as the price of a certain thing which they desire, or how

From Alfred Marshall, *Principles of Economics,* pp. 14–15, 25–6, 33, 36–7. Reprinted by permission of St. Martin's Press, Inc., New York, The Macmillan Company of Canada, and The Macmillan Company of Houndmills Basingstoke Hampshire.

much must be offered to them to induce them to undergo a certain effort
or abstinence that they dislike. The measurement of motive thus obtained
is not indeed perfectly accurate; for if it were, economics would rank with
the most advanced of the physical science; and not, as it actually does,
with the least advanced.

The term "law" means then nothing more than a general proposition
or statement of tendencies, more or less certain, more or less definite. Many
such statements are made in every science. . . . Thus a law of social science,
or a Social Law, is a statement of social tendencies; that is, a statement
that a certain course of action may be expected under certain conditions
from the members of a social group.

Economic laws, or statements of economic tendencies, are those social
laws which relate to branches of conduct in which the strength of the
motives chiefly concerned can be measured by a money price.

It is sometimes said that the laws of economics are "hypothetical."
Of course, like every other science, it undertakes to study the effects which
will be produced by certain causes, not absolutely, but subject to the condition that other things are equal, and that the causes are able to work
out their effects undisturbed. Almost every scientific doctrine, when carefully and formally stated, will be found to contain some proviso to the
effect that other things are equal; the action of the causes in question is
supposed to be isolated, certain effects are attributed to them, but on
the hypothesis that no cause is permitted to enter except those distinctly
allowed for. It is true however that the condition that time must be
allowed for causes to produce their effects is a source of great difficulty
in economics. For meanwhile the material on which they work, and perhaps even the causes themselves, may have changed; and the tendencies
which are being described will not have sufficiently "long run" in which
to work themselves out fully.

Though economic analysis and general reasoning are of wide application, yet every age and every country has its own problems; and every
change in social conditions is likely to require a new development of
economic doctrines.

The General Theory of Employment, Interest, and Money, John Maynard Keynes

The outstanding faults of the economic society in which we live are
its failure to provide for full employment and its arbitrary and inequitable
distribution of wealth and incomes.

From *The General Theory of Employment, Interest, and Money*, by John Maynard
Keynes. Reprinted by permission of Harcourt, Brace,Jovanovich, Inc., 1965, pp. 372–4,
378.

Since the end of the 19th century significant progress towards the removal of very great disparities of wealth and income has been achieved through the instruments of direct taxation—income tax and surtax and death duties—especially in Great Britain. Many people would wish to see this process carried much further, but they are deterred by two considerations; partly by the fear of making skilful evasions too much worthwhile and also of diminishing unduly the motives towards risk-taking, but mainly, I think, by the belief that the growth of capital depends upon the strength of the motive towards individual saving and that for a large proportion of this growth we are dependent on the savings of the rich out of their superfluity.... We have seen that, up to the point where full employment prevails, the growth of capital depends not at all on a low propensity to consume but is, on the contrary, held back by it; and only in conditions of full employment is a low propensity to consume conducive to the growth of capital. Moreover, experience suggests that in existing conditions saving by institutions and through sinking funds is more than adequate, and that measures for the redistribution of incomes in a way likely to raise the propensity to consume may prove positively favorable to the growth of capital.

Thus our argument leads towards the conclusion that in contemporary conditions the growth of wealth, so far from being dependent on the abstinence of the rich, as is commonly supposed, is more likely to be impeded by it. One of the chief social justifications of great inequality of wealth is, therefore, removed. I am not saying that there are no other reasons, unaffected by our theory, capable of justifying some measure of inequality in some circumstances. But it does dispose of the most important of the reasons why hitherto we have thought it prudent to move carefully.

For my own part, I believe that there is social and psychological justification for significant inequalities of incomes and wealth, but not for such large disparities as exist today. There are valuable human activities which require the motive of money-making and the environment of private wealth-ownership for their full fruition. Moreover, dangerous human proclivities can be canalized into comparatively harmless channels by the existence of opportunities for money-making and private wealth, which, if they cannot be satisfied in this way, may find their outlet in cruelty, the reckless pursuit of personal power and authority, and other forms of self-aggrandizement. It is better that a man should tyrannize over his bank balance than over his fellow citizens; and whilst the former is sometimes denounced as being but a means to the latter, sometimes at least it is an alternative. But it is not necessary for the stimulation of these activities and the satisfaction of these proclivities that the game should be played for such high stakes as at present. Much lower stakes will serve the purpose equally well, as soon as the players are accustomed to them.

The task of transmuting human nature must not be confused with the task of managing it. Though in the ideal commonwealth men may have been taught or inspired or bred to take no interest in the stakes, it may still be wise and prudent statesmanship to allow the game to be played, subject to rules and limitations, so long as the average man, or even a significant section of the community, is in fact strongly addicted to the money-making passion.

The State will have to exercise a guiding influence on the propensity to consume partly through its scheme of taxation, partly by fixing the rate of interest, and partly, perhaps, in other ways. Furthermore, it seems unlikely that the influence of banking policy on the rate of interest will be sufficient by itself to determine an optimum rate of investment. I conceive, therefore, that a somewhat comprehensive socialization of investment will prove the only means of securing an approximation to full employment; though this need not exclude all manner of compromises and of devices by which public authority will cooperate with private initiative. But beyond this no obvious case is made out for a system of State Socialism which would embrace most of the economic life of the community. It is not the ownership of the instruments of production which it is important for the State to assume. If the State is able to determine the aggregate amount of resources devoted to augmenting the instruments and the basic rate of reward to those who own them, it will have accomplished all that is necessary.

Excerpts from
Capitalism and Freedom

MILTON FRIEDMAN

Here, in capsule form, are sections from the best-known statement of the "libertarian" view. The interested reader may want to compare this economic philosophy with its critique in the next essay.

In a much quoted passage in his inaugural address, President Kennedy said, "Ask not what your country can do for you—ask what you can do for your country." It is a striking sign of the temper of our times that the controversy about this passage centered on its origin and not on its content. Neither half of the statement expresses a relation between the citizen and his government that is worthy of the ideals of free men in a free society. The paternalistic "what your country can do for you" implies that government is the patron, the citizen the ward, a view that is at odds with the free man's belief in his own responsibility for his own destiny. The organismic, "what you can do for your country" implies that government is the master or the deity, the citizen, the servant or the votary. To the free man, the country is the collection of individuals who compose it, not something over and above them. He is proud of a common heritage and loyal to common traditions. But he regards government as a means, an instrumentality, neither a grantor of favors and gifts, nor a master or god to be blindly worshipped and served. He recognizes no national goal except as it is the consensus of the goals that the citizens severally serve. He recognizes no national purpose except as it is the consensus of the purposes for which the citizens severally strive.

The free man will ask neither what his country can do for him nor what he can do for his country. He will ask rather "What can I and my compatriots do through government" to help us discharge our individual

From *Capitalism and Freedom,* by Milton Friedman (Chicago: University of Chicago Press, 1962), pp. 1–21, 196–202. © 1962 by the University of Chicago. Reprinted by permission.

responsibilities, to achieve our several goals and purposes, and above all, to protect our freedom? And he will accompany this question with another: How can we keep the government we create from becoming a Frankenstein that will destroy the very freedom we establish it to protect? Freedom is a rare and delicate plant. Our minds tell us, and history confirms, that the great threat to freedom is the concentration of power. Government is necessary to preserve our freedom, it is an instrument through which we can exercise our freedom; yet by concentrating power in political hands, it is also a threat to freedom. Even though the men who wield this power initially be of good will and even though they be not corrupted by the power they exercise, the power will both attract and form men of a different stamp.

How can we benefit from the promise of government while avoiding the threat to freedom? Two broad principles embodied in our Constitution give an answer that has preserved our freedom so far, though they have been violated repeatedly in practice while proclaimed as precept.

First, the scope of government must be limited. Its major function must be to protect our freedom both from the enemies outside our gates and from our fellow-citizens: to preserve law and order, to enforce private contracts, to foster competitive markets. Beyond this major function, government may enable us at times to accomplish jointly what we would find it more difficult or expensive to accomplish severally. However, any such use of government is fraught with danger. We should not and cannot avoid using government in this way. But there should be a clear and large balance of advantages before we do. By relying primarily on voluntary cooperation and private enterprise, in both economic and other activities, we can insure that the private sector is a check on the powers of the governmental sector and an effective protection of freedom of speech, of religion, and of thought.

The second broad principle is that government power must be dispersed. If government is to exercise power, better in the county than in the state, better in the state than in Washington. If I do not like what my local community does, be it in sewage disposal, or zoning, or schools, I can move to another local community, and though few may take this step, the mere possibility acts as a check. If I do not like what my state does, I can move to another. If I do not like what Washington imposes, I have few alternatives in this world of jealous nations.

The very difficulty of avoiding the enactments of the federal government is of course the great attraction of centralization to many of its proponents. It will enable them more effectively, they believe, to legislate programs that—as they see it—are in the interest of the public, whether it be the transfer of income from the rich to the poor or from private to governmental purposes. They are in a sense right. But this coin has two sides. The power to do good is also the power to do harm; those who control the power today may not tomorrow; and, more important, what one man regards as good, another may regard as harm. The great tragedy of the drive to centralization, as of the drive to extend the scope of government in general, is that it is mostly led by men of good will who will be the first to rue its consequences.

The preservation of freedom is the protective reason for limiting and decentralizing governmental power. But there is also a constructive reason. The great advances of civilization, whether in architecture or painting, in science or literature, in industry or agriculture, have never come from centralized government. Columbus did not set out to seek a new route to China in response to a majority directive of a parliament, though he was partly financed by an absolute monarch. Newton and Leibnitz; Einstein and Bohr; Shakespeare, Milton, and Pasternak; Whitney, McCormick, Edison, and Ford; Jane Addams, Florence Nightingale, and Albert Schweitzer; no one of these opened new frontiers in human knowledge and understanding, in literature, in technical possibilities, or in the relief of human misery in response to governmental directives. Their achievements were the product of individual genius, of strongly held minority views, of a social climate permitting variety and diversity.

Government can never duplicate the variety and diversity of individual action. At any moment in time, by imposing uniform standards in housing, or nutrition, or clothing, government could undoubtedly improve the level of living of many individuals; by imposing uniform standards in schooling, road construction, or sanitation, central government could undoubtedly improve the level of performance in many local areas and perhaps even on the average of all communities. But in the process, government would replace progress by stagnation, it would substitute uniform mediocrity for the variety essential for that experimentation which can bring tomorrow's laggards above today's mean....

It is widely believed that politics and economics are separate and largely unconnected; that individual freedom is a political problem and material welfare an economic problem; and that any kind of political arrangements can be combined with any kind of economic arrangements. The chief contemporary manifestation of this idea is the advocacy of "democratic socialism" by many who condemn out of hand the restrictions on individual freedom imposed by "totalitarian socialism" in Russia, and who are persuaded that it is possible for a country to adopt the essential features of Russian economic arrangements and yet to ensure individual freedom through political arrangements. The thesis of this chapter is that such a view is a delusion, that there is an intimate connection between economics and politics, that only certain combinations of political and economic arrangements are possible and that in particular, a society which is socialist cannot also be democratic, in the sense of guaranteeing individual freedom.

Economic arrangements play a dual role in the promotion of a free society. On the one hand, freedom in economic arrangements is itself a component of freedom broadly understood, so economic freedom is an end in itself. In the second place, economic freedom is also an indispensable means toward the achievement of political freedom.

The first of these roles of economic freedom needs special emphasis because intellectuals in particular have a strong bias against regarding this aspect of freedom as important. They tend to express contempt for what they regard as material aspects of life, and to regard their own pursuit of allegedly higher values as on a different plane of significance and as deserving of special attention. For most citizens of the country, however, if not for the intellectual, the direct importance of economic freedom is at least comparable in significance to the indirect importance of economic freedom as a means to political freedom.

The citizen of Great Britain, who after World War II was not permitted to spend his vacation in the United States because of exchange control, was being deprived of an essential freedom no less than the citizen of the United States, who was denied the opportunity to spend his vacation in Russia because of his political views. The one was ostensibly an economic limitation on freedom and the other a politicial limitation, yet there is no essential difference between the two.

The citizen of the United States who is compelled by law to devote something like 10 percent of his income to the purchase of a particular kind of retirement contract, administered by the government, is being deprived of a corresponding part of his personal freedom. How strongly this deprivation may be felt and its closeness to the deprivation of religious freedom, which all would regard as "civil" or "political" rather than "economic," were dramatized by an episode involving a group of farmers of the Amish sect. On grounds of principle, this group regarded compulsory federal old-age programs as an infringement of their personal individual freedom and refused to pay taxes or accept benefits. As a result, some of their livestock were sold by auction in order to satisfy claims for social security levies. True, the number of citizens who regard compulsory old-age insurance as a deprivation of freedom may be few, but the believer in freedom has never counted noses.

A citizen of the United States who under the laws of various states is not free to follow the occupation of his own choosing unless he can get a license for it, is likewise being deprived of an essential part of his freedom. So is the man who would like to exchange some of his goods with, say, a Swiss for a watch but is prevented from doing so by a quota. So also is the Californian who was thrown into jail for selling Alka-Seltzer at a price below that set by the manufacturer under so-called fair trade laws. So also is the farmer who cannot grow the amount of wheat he wants. And so on. Clearly, economic freedom, in and of itself, is an extremely important part of total freedom.

Viewed as a means to the end of political freedom, economic arrangements are important because of their effect on the concentration or dispersion of power. The kind of economic organization that provides economic freedom directly, namely, competitive capitalism, also promotes political freedom because it separates economic power from political power and in this way enables the one to offset the other.

Historical evidence speaks with a single voice on the relation between political freedom and a free market. I know of no example in time or place of a society that has been marked by a large measure of political freedom, and that has not also used something comparable to a free market to organize the bulk of economic activity.

Because we live in a largely free society, we tend to forget how limited is the span of time and the part of the globe for which there has ever been anything like political freedom: the typical state of mankind is tyranny, servitude, and misery. The 19th century and early 20th century in the Western world stand out as striking exceptions to the general trend of historical development. Political freedom in this instance clearly came along with the free market and the development of capitalist institutions. So also did political freedom in the golden age of Greece and in the early days of the Roman era.

History suggests only that capitalism is a necessary condition for political freedom. Clearly it is not a sufficient condition. Fascist Italy and Fascist Spain, Germany at various times in the last 70 years, Japan before World Wars I and II, tzarist Russia in the decades before World War I— are all societies that cannot conceivably be described as politically free. Yet, in each, private enterprise was the dominant form of economic organization. It is therefore clearly possible to have economic arrangements that are fundamentally capitalist and political arrangements that are not free.

Even in those societies, the citizenry had a good deal more freedom than citizens of a modern totalitarian state like Russia or Nazi Germany, in which economic totalitarianism is combined with political totalitarianism. Even in Russia under the Tzars, it was possible for some citizens, under some circumstances, to change their jobs without getting permission from political authority, because capitalism and the existence of private property provided some check to the centralized power of the state.

The relation between political and economic freedom is complex and by no means unilateral. In the early 19th century, Bentham and the Philosophical Radicals were inclined to regard political freedom as a means to economic freedom. They believed that the masses were being hampered by the restrictions that were being imposed upon them, and that if political reform gave the bulk of the people the vote, they would do what was good for them, which was to vote for laissez faire. In retrospect, one cannot say that they were wrong. There was a large measure of political reform that was accompanied by economic reform in the direction of a great deal of laissez faire. An enormous increase in the well-being of the masses followed this change in economic arrangements.

The triumph of Benthamic liberalism in 19th-century England was followed by a reaction toward increasing intervention by government in economic affairs. This tendency to collectivism was greatly accelerated, both in England and elsewhere, by the two World Wars. Welfare rather than freedom became the dominant note in democratic countries. Recognizing the implicit threat to individualism, the intellectual descendants of the Philosophical Radicals—Dicey, Mises, Hayek, and Simons, to mention only a few—feared that a continued movement toward centralized control of economic activity would prove *The Road to Serfdom*, as Hayek entitled his penetrating analysis of the process. Their emphasis was on economic freedom as a means toward political freedom.

Events since the end of World War II display still a different relation between economic and political freedom. Collectivist economic planning has indeed interfered with individual freedom. At least in some countries, however, the result has not been the suppression of freedom, but the reversal of economic policy. England again provides the most striking example. The turning point was perhaps the "control of engagements" order which, despite great misgivings, the Labour party found it necessary to impose in order to carry out its economic policy. Fully enforced and carried through, the law would have involved centralized allocation of individuals to occupations. This conflicted so sharply with personal liberty that it was enforced in a negligible number of cases, and then repealed after the law had been in effect for only a short period. Its repeal ushered in a decided shift in economic policy, marked by reduced reliance on centralized "plans" and "programs," by the dismantling of many controls, and by increased emphasis on the private market. A similar shift in policy occurred in most other democratic countries.

The proximate explanation of these shifts in policy is the limited success of central planning or its outright failure to achieve stated objectives. However, this failure is itself to be attributed, at least in some measure, to the political implications of central planning and to an unwillingness to follow out its logic when doing so requires trampling rough-shod on treasured private rights. It may well be that the shift is only a temporary interruption in the collectivist trend of this century. Even so, it illustrates the close relation between political freedom and economic arrangements.

The basic problem of social organization is how to coordinate the

economic activities of large numbers of people. Even in relatively backward societies, extensive division of labor and specialization of function
is required to make effective use of available resources. In advanced
societies, the scale on which coordination is needed, to take full advantage
of the opportunities offered by modern science and technology, is enormously greater. Literally millions of people are involved in providing one
another with their daily bread, let alone with their yearly automobiles.
The challenge to the believer in liberty is to reconcile this widespread
interdependence with individual freedom.

Fundamentally, there are only two ways of coordinating the economic
activities of millions. One is central direction involving the use of coercion
—the technique of the army and of the modern totalitarian state. The other
is voluntary cooperation of individuals—the technique of the market place.

The possibility of coordination through voluntary cooperation rests
on the elementary—yet frequently denied—proposition that both parties to
an economic transaction benefit from it, *provided the transaction is bilater-
ally voluntary and informed.*

Exchange can therefore bring about coordination without coercion.
A working model of a society organized through voluntary exchange is a
free private enterprise exchange economy—what we have been calling
competitive capitalism.

In its simplest form, such a society consists of a number of independent households—a collection of Robinson Crusoes, as it were. Each household uses the resources it controls to produce goods and services that it
exchanges for goods and services produced by other households, on terms
mutually acceptable to the two parties to the bargain. It is thereby enabled
to satisfy its wants indirectly by producing goods and services for others,
rather than directly by producing goods for its own immediate use. The
incentive for adopting this indirect route is, of course, the increased product
made possible by division of labor and specialization of function. Since
the household always has the alternative of producing directly for itself,
it need not enter into any exchange unless it benefits from it. Hence, no
exchange will take place unless both parties do benefit from it. Cooperation is thereby achieved without coercion.

Specialization of function and division of labor would not go far if
the ultimate productive unit were the household. In a modern society, we
have gone much farther. We have introduced enterprises which are intermediaries between individuals in their capacities as suppliers of service
and as purchasers of goods. And similarly, specialization of function and
division of labor could not go very far if we had to continue to rely on the
barter of product for product. In consequence, money has been introduced
as a means of facilitating exchange, and of enabling the acts of purchase
and of sale to be separated into two parts.

Despite the important role of enterprises and of money in our actual economy, and despite the numerous and complex problems they raise, the central characteristic of the market technique of achieving coordination is fully displayed in the simple exchange economy that contains neither enterprises nor money. As in that simple model, so in the complex enterprise and money-exchange economy, cooperation is strictly individual and voluntary *provided*: (1) that enterprises are private, so that the ultimate contracting parties are individuals and (2) that individuals are effectively free to enter or not to enter into any particular exchange, so that every transaction is strictly voluntary.

It is far easier to state these provisos in general terms than to spell them out in detail, or to specify precisely the institutional arrangements most conducive to their maintenance. Indeed, much of technical economic literature is concerned with precisely these questions. The basic requisite is the maintenance of law and order to prevent physical coercion of one individual by another and to enforce contracts voluntarily entered into, thus giving substance to "private." Aside from this, perhaps the most difficult problems arise from monopoly—which inhibits effective freedom by denying individuals alternatives to the particular exchange—and from "neighborhood effects"—effects on third parties for which it is not feasible to charge or recompense them. . . .

So long as effective freedom of exchange is maintained, the central feature of the market organization of economic activity is that it prevents one person from interfering with another in respect of most of his activities. The consumer is protected from coercion by the seller because of the presence of other sellers with whom he can deal. The seller is protected from coercion by the consumer because of other consumers to whom he can sell. The employee is protected from coercion by the employer because of other employers for whom he can work, and so on. And the market does this impersonally and without centralized authority.

Indeed, a major source of objection to a free economy is precisely that it does this task so well. It gives people what they want instead of what a particular group thinks they ought to want. Underlying most arguments against the free market is a lack of belief in freedom itself.

The existence of a free market does not of course eliminate the need for government. On the contrary, government is essential both as a forum for determining the "rules of the game" and as an umpire to interpret and enforce the rules decided on. What the market does is to reduce greatly the range of issues that must be decided through political means, and thereby to minimize the extent to which government need participate directly in the game. The characteristic feature of action through political channels is that it tends to require or enforce substantial conformity. The great advantage of the market, on the other hand, is that it permits wide diversity. It is, in political terms, a system of proportional representation. Each man can vote, as it were, for the color of tie he wants and get it; he does not have to see what color the majority wants and then, if he is in the minority, submit.

It is this feature of the market that we refer to when we say that the market provides economic freedom. But this characteristic also has implications that go far beyond the narrowly economic. Political freedom means the absence of coercion of a man by his fellow men. The fundamental threat to freedom is power to coerce, be it in the hands of a monarch, a dictator, an oligarchy, or a momentary majority. The preservation of freedom requires the elimination of such concentration of power to the fullest possible extent and the dispersal and distribution of whatever power cannot be eliminated—a system of checks and balances. By removing the organization of economic activity from the control of political authority, the market eliminates this source of coercive power. It enables economic strength to be a check to political power rather than a reinforcement.

Economic power can be widely dispersed. There is no law of conservation which forces the growth of new centers of economic strength to be at the expense of existing centers. Political power, on the other hand, is more difficult to decentralize. There can be numerous small independent governments. But it is far more difficult to maintain numerous equipotent small centers of political power in a single large government than it is to have numerous centers of economic strength in a single large economy. There can be many millionaires in one large economy. But can there be more than one really outstanding leader, one person on whom the energies and enthusiasms of his countrymen are centered? If the central government gains power, it is likely to be at the expense of local governments. There seems to be something like a fixed total of political power to be distributed. Consequently, if economic power is joined to political power, concentration seems almost inevitable. On the other hand, if economic power is kept in separate hands from political power, it can serve as a check and a counter to political power.

The force of this abstract argument can perhaps best be demonstrated by example. Let us consider first, a hypothetical example that may help to bring out the principles involved, and then some actual examples from recent experience that illustrate the way in which the market works to preserve political freedom.

One feature of a free society is surely the freedom of individuals to advocate and propagandize openly for a radical change in the structure of the society—so long as the advocacy is restricted to persuasion and does not include force or other forms of coercion. It is a mark of the political freedom of a capitalist society that men can openly advocate and work for socialism. Equally, political freedom in a socialist society would require that men be free to advocate the introduction of capitalism. How could the freedom to advocate capitalism be preserved and protected in a socialist society?

In order for men to advocate anything, they must in the first place be able to earn a living. This already raises a problem in a socialist society, since all jobs are under the direct control of political authorities. It would take an act of self-denial whose difficulty is underlined by experience in the United States after World War II with the problem of "security" among federal employees, for a socialist government to permit its employees to advocate policies directly contrary to official doctrine.

But let us suppose this act of self-denial to be achieved. For advocacy of capitalism to mean anything, the proponents must be able to finance their cause—to hold public meetings, publish pamphlets, buy radio time, issue newspapers and magazines, and so on. How could they raise the funds? There might and probably would be men in the socialist society with large incomes, perhaps even large capital sums in the form of government bonds and the like, but these would of necessity be high public officials. It is possible to conceive of a minor socialist official retaining his job although openly advocating capitalism. It strains credulity to imagine the socalist top brass financing such "subversive" activities.

The only recourse for funds would be to raise small amounts from a large number of minor officials. But this is no real answer. To tap these sources, many people would already have to be persuaded, and our whole problem is how to initiate and finance a campaign to do so. Radical movements in capitalist societies have never been financed this way. They have typically been supported by a few wealthy individuals who have become persuaded—by a Frederick Vanderbilt Field, or an Anita McCormick Blaine, or a Corliss Lamont, or by a Friedrich Engels. This is a role of inequality of wealth in preserving political freedom that is seldom noted— the role of the patron.

In a capitalist society, it is only necessary to convince a few wealthy people to get funds to launch any idea, however strange, and there are many such persons, many independent foci of support. And, indeed, it is not even necessary to persuade people or financial institutions with available funds of the soundness of the ideas to be propagated. It is only necessary to persuade them that the propagation can be financially successful; that the newspaper or magizine or book or other venture will be profitable. The competitive publisher, for example, cannot afford to publish only writing with which he personally agrees; his touchstone must be the likelihood that the market will be large enough to yield a satisfactory return on his investment.

In this way, the market breaks the vicious circle and makes it possible ultimately to finance such ventures by small amounts from many people without first persuading them. There are no such possibilities in the socialist society; there is only the all-powerful state.

Let us stretch our imagination and suppose that a socialist government is aware of this problem and is composed of people anxious to preserve freedom. Could it provide the funds? Perhaps, but it is difficult to see how. It could establish a bureau for subsidizing subversive propaganda. But how could it choose whom to support? If it gave to all who asked, it would shortly find itself out of funds, for socialism cannot repeal the elementary economic law that a sufficiently high price will call forth a large supply. Make the advocacy of radical causes sufficiently remunerative, and the supply of advocates will be unlimited.

Moreover, freedom to advocate unpopular causes does not require that such advocacy be without cost. On the contrary, no society could be stable if advocacy of radical change were costless, much less subsidized. It is entirely appropriate that men make sacrifices to advocate causes in which they deeply believe. Indeed, it is important to preserve freedom only for people who are willing to practice self-denial, for otherwise freedom degenerates into license and irresponsibility. What is essential is that the cost of advocating unpopular causes be tolerable and not prohibitive.

But we are not yet through. In a free market society, it is enough to have the funds. The suppliers of paper are as willing to sell it to the *Daily Worker* as to the *Wall Street Journal*. In a socialist society, it would not be enough to have the funds. The hypothetical supporter of capitalism would have to persuade a government factory making paper to sell to him, the government printing press to print his pamphlets, a government post office to distribute them among the people, a government agency to rent him a hall in which to talk, and so on.

Perhaps there is some way in which one could overcome these difficulties and preserve freedom in a socialist society. One cannot say it is utterly impossible. What is clear, however, is that there are very real difficulties in establishing institutions that will effectively preserve the possibility of dissent. So far as I know, none of the people who have been in favor of socialism and also in favor of freedom have really faced up to this issue, or made even a respectable start at developing the institutional arrangements that would permit freedom under socialism. By constrast, it is clear how a free market capitalist society fosters freedom.

A striking practical example of these abstract principles is the experience of Winston Churchill. From 1933 to the outbreak of World War II, Churchill was not permitted to talk over the British radio, which was, of course, a government monopoly administered by the British Broadcasting Corporation. Here was a leading citizen of his country, a Member of Parliament, a former cabinet minister, a man who was desperately trying by every device possible to persuade his countrymen to take steps to ward off the menace of Hitler's Germany. He was not permitted to talk over the radio to the British people because the BBC was a government monopoly and his position was too "controversial."

Another striking example, reported in the January 26, 1959 issue of *Time*, has to do with the "Blacklist Fadeout." Says the *Time* story:

> The Oscar-awarding ritual is Hollywood's biggest pitch for dignity, but two years ago dignity suffered. When one Robert Rich was announced as top writer for the *The Brave One*, he never stepped forward. Robert Rich was a pseudonym, masking one of about 150 writers . . . blacklisted by the industry since 1947 as suspected Communists or fellow travelers. The case was particularly embarrassing because the Motion Picture Academy had barred any Communist or Fifth Amendment pleader from Oscar competition. Last week both the Communist rule and the mystery of Rich's identity were suddenly rescripted.
>
> Rich turned out to be Dalton (*Johnny Got His Gun*) Trumbo, one of the original "Hollywood Ten" writers who refused to testify at the 1947 hearings on Communism in the movie industry. Said producer Frank King, who had stoutly insisted that Robert Rich was "a young guy in Spain with a beard": "We have an obligation to our stockholders to buy the best script we can. Trumbo brought us *The Brave One* and we bought it". . . .
>
> In effect it was the formal end of the Hollywood black list. For barred writers, the informal end came long ago. At least 15 percent of current Hollywood films are reportedly written by blacklist members. Said Producer King, "There are more ghosts in Hollywood than in Forest Lawn. Every company in town has used the work of blacklisted people. We're just the first to confirm what everybody knows."

One may believe, as I do, that communism would destroy all of our freedoms, one may be opposed to it as firmly and as strongly as possible, and yet, at the same time, also believe that in a free society it is intolerable for a man to be prevented from making voluntary arrangements with others that are mutually attractive because be believes in or is trying to promote communism. His freedom includes his freedom to promote communism. Freedom also, of course, includes the freedom of others not to deal with him under those circumstances. The Hollywood blacklist was an unfree act that destroys freedom because it was a collusive arrangement that used coercive means to prevent voluntary exchanges. It didn't work precisely because the market made it costly for people to preserve the blacklist. The commercial emphasis, the fact that people who are running enterprises have an incentive to make as much money as they can, protected the freedom of the individuals who were blacklisted by providing them with an alternative form of employment, and by giving people an incentive to employ them.

If Hollywood and the movie industry had been government enterprises or if in England it had been a question of employment by the British Broadcasting Corporation it is difficult to believe that the "Hollywood Ten" or their equivalent would have found employment. Equally, it is difficult to believe that under those circumstances, strong proponents of individualism and private enterprise—or indeed strong proponents of any view other than the status quo—would be able to get employment.

Another example of the role of the market in preserving political freedom, was revealed in our experience with McCarthyism. Entirely aside from the substantive issues involved, and the merits of the charges made, what protection did individuals, and in particular government employees, have against irresponsible accusations and probings into matters that it went against their conscience to reveal? Their appeal to the Fifth Amendment would have been a hollow mockery without an alternative to government employment.

Their fundamental protection was the existence of a private market economy in which they could earn a living. Here again, the protection was not absolute. Many potential private employers were, rightly or wrongly, averse to hiring those pilloried. It may well be that there was far less justification for the costs imposed on many of the people involved than for the costs generally imposed on people who advocate unpopular causes. But the important point is that the costs were limited and not prohibitive, as they would have been if government employment had been the only possibility.

It is of interest to note that a disproportionately large fraction of people involved apparently went into the most competitive sectors of the economy—small business, trade, farming—where the market approaches most closely the ideal free market. No one who buys bread knows whether the wheat from which it is made was grown by a Communist or a Republican, by a constitutionalist or a Facist, or, for that matter, by a Negro or a white. This illustrates how an impersonal market separates economic activities from political views and protects men from being discriminated against in their economic activities for reasons that are irrevelant to their productivity—whether these reasons are associated with their views or their color.

As this example suggests, the groups in our society that have the most at stake in the preservation and strengthening of competitive capitalism are those minority groups which can most easily become the object of the distrust and enmity of the majority—the Negroes, the Jews, the foreign-born, to mention only the most obvious. Yet, paradoxically enough, the enemies of the free market—the Socialists and Communists—have been recruited in disproportionate measure from these groups. Instead of recognizing that the existence of the market has protected them from the attitudes of their fellow countrymen, they mistakenly attribute the residual discrimination to the market.

In the 1920s and the 1930s, intellectuals in the United States were overwhelmingly persuaded that capitalism was a defective system inhibiting economic well-being and thereby freedom, and that the hope for the future lay in a greater measure of deliberate control by political authorities over economic affairs. The conversion of the intellectuals was not achieved by the example of any actual collectivist society, though it undoubtedly was much hastened by the establishment of a communist society in Russia and the glowing hopes placed in it. The conversion of the intellectuals was achieved by a comparison between the existing state of affairs, with all its injustices and defects, and a hypothetical state of affairs as it might be. The actual was compared with the ideal.

The attitudes of that time are still with us. There is still a tendency to regard any existing government intervention as desirable, to attribute all evils to the market, and to evaluate new proposals for government control in their ideal form, as they might work if run by able, disinterested men, free from the pressure of special interest groups. The proponents of limited government and free enterprise are still on the defensive.

Yet, conditions have changed. We now have several decades of experience with governmental intervention. It is no longer necessary to compare the market as it actually operates and government intervention as it ideally might operate. We can compare the actual with the actual. Which if any of the great "reforms" of past decades has achieved its objectives? Have the good intentions of the proponents of these reforms been realized?

Regulation of the railroads to protect the consumer quickly became an instrument whereby the railroads could protect themselves from the competition of newly emerging rivals—at the expense, of course, of the consumer.

An income tax initially enacted at low rates and later seized upon as a means to redistribute income in favor of the lower classes has become a facade, covering loopholes and special provisions that render rates that are highly graduated on paper largely ineffective. A flat rate of 23.5 percent on presently taxable income would yield as much revenue as the present rates graduated from 20 to 91 percent. An income tax intended to reduce inequality and promote the diffusion of wealth has in practice fostered reinvestment of corporate earnings, thereby favoring the growth of large corporations, inhibiting the operation of the capital market, and discouraging the establishment of new enterprises.

Monetary reforms, intended to promote stability in economic activity and prices, exacerbated inflation during and after World War I and fostered a higher degree of instability thereafter than had ever been experienced before. The monetary authorities they established bear primary responsibility for converting a serious economic contraction into the catastrophe of the Great Depression from 1929 to 1933. A system established largely to prevent bank panics produced the most severe banking panic in American history.

An agricultural program intended to help impecunious farmers and to remove what were alleged to be basic dislocations in the organization of agriculture has become a national scandal that has wasted public funds, distorted the use of resources, riveted increasingly heavy and detailed controls on farmers, interfered seriously with United States foreign policy, and withal has done little to help the impecunious farmer.

A housing program intended to improve the housing conditions of the poor, to reduce juvenile delinquency, and to contribute to the removal of urban slums, has worsened the housing conditions of the poor, contributed to juvenile delinquency, and spread urban blight.

In the 1930s, "labor" was synonymous with "labor union" to the intellectual community; faith in the purity and virtue of labor unions was on a par with faith in home and motherhood. Extensive legislation was enacted to favor labor unions and to foster "fair" labor relation. Labor unions waxed in strength. By the 1950s, "labor union" was almost a dirty word; it was no longer synonymous with "labor," no longer automatically to be taken for granted as on the side of the angels.

Social security measures were enacted to make receipt of assistance a matter of right, to eliminate the need for direct relief and assistance. Millions now receive social security benefits. Yet the relief rolls grow and the sums spent on direct assistance mount.

The list can easily be lengthened: the silver purchase program of the 1930s, public power projects, foreign aid programs of the postwar years, F.C.C., urban redevelopment programs, the stockpiling program—these and many more have had effects very different and generally quite opposite from those intended.

There have been some exceptions. The expressways crisscrossing the country, magnificent dams spanning great rivers, orbiting satellites are all tributes to the capacity of government to command great resources. The school system, with all its defects and problems, with all the possibility of improvement through bringing into more effective play the forces of the market, has widened the opportunities available to American youth and contributed to the extension of freedom. It is a testament to the public-spirited efforts of the many tens of thousands who have served on local school boards and to the willingness of the public to bear heavy taxes for what they regarded as a public purpose. The Sherman antitrust laws, with all their problems of detailed administration, have by their very existence fostered competition. Public health measures have contributed to the reduction of infectious disease. Assistance measures have relieved suffering and distress. Local authorities have often provided facilities essential to the life of communities. Law and order have been maintained, though in many a large city the performance of even this elementary function of government has been far from satisfactory. As a citizen of Chicago, I speak feelingly.

If a balance be struck, there can be little doubt that the record is dismal. The greater part of the new ventures undertaken by government in the past few decades have failed to achieve their objectives. The United States has continued to progress; its citizens have become better fed, better clothed, better housed, and better transported; class and social distinctions have narrowed; minority groups have become less disadvantaged; popular culture has advanced by leaps and bounds. All this has been the product of the initiative and drive of individuals cooperating through the free market. Government measures have hampered not helped this development. We have been able to afford and surmount these measures only because of the extraordinary fecundity of the market. The invisible hand has been more potent for progress than the visible hand for retrogression.

Is it an accident that so many of the governmental reforms of recent decades have gone awry, that the bright hopes have turned to ashes? Is it simply because the programs are faulty in detail?

I believe the answer is clearly in the negative. The central defect of these measures is that they seek through government to force people to act against their own immediate interests in order to promote a supposedly general interest. They seek to resolve what is supposedly a conflict of interest, or a difference in view about interests, not by establishing a framework that will eliminate the conflict, or by persuading people to have different interests, but by forcing people to act against their own interest. They substitute the values of outsiders for the values of participants; either some telling others what is good for them, or the government taking from some to benefit others. These measures are therefore countered by one of the strongest and most creative forces known to man—the attempt by millions of individuals to promote their own interests, to live their lives by their own values. This is the major reason why the measures have so often had the opposite of the effects intended. It is also one of the major strengths of a free society and explains why governmental regulation does not strangle it.

The interests of which I speak are not simply narrow self-regarding interests. On the contrary, they include the whole range of values that men hold dear and for which they are willing to spend their fortunes and sacrifice their lives. The Germans who lost their lives opposing Adolf Hitler were pursuing their interests as they saw them. So also are the men and women who devote great effort and time to charitable, educational, and religious activities. Naturally, such interests are the major ones for few men. It is the virtue of a free society that it nonetheless permits these interests full scope and does not subordinate them to the narrow materialistic interests that dominate the bulk of mankind. That is why capitalist societies are less materialistic than collectivist societies.

Why is it, in light of the record, that the burden of proof still seems to rest on those of us who oppose new government programs and who seek to reduce the already unduly large role of government? Let Dicey answer: "The beneficial effect of State intervention, especially in the form of legislation, is direct, immediate, and, so to speak, visible, whilst its evil effects are gradual and indirect, and lie out of sight.... Nor ... do most people keep in mind that State inspectors may be incompetent, careless, or even occasionally corrupt...; few are those who realize the undeniable truth that State help kills self-help. Hence the majority of mankind must almost of necessity look with undue favor upon governmental intervention. This natural bias can be counteracted only by the existence, in a given society,... of a presumption or prejudice in favor of individual liberty, that is, of laissez faire. The mere decline, therefore, of faith in self-help— and that such a decline has taken place is certain—is of itself sufficient to account for the growth of legislation tending towards socialism."

The preservation and expansion of freedom are today threatened from two directions. The one threat is obvious and clear. It is the external threat coming from the evil men in the Kremlin who promise to bury us. The other threat is far more subtle. It is the internal threat coming from men of good intentions and good will who wish to reform us. Impatient with the slowness of persuasion and example to achieve the great social changes they envision, they are anxious to use the power of the state to achieve their ends and confident of their own ability to do so. Yet if they gained the power, they would fail to achieve their immediate aims and, in addition, would produce a collective state from which they would recoil in horror and of which they would be among the first victims. Concentrated power is not rendered harmless by the good intentions of those who create it.

The two threats unfortunately reinforce one another. Even if we avoid a nuclear holocaust, the threat from the Kremlin requires us to devote a sizable fraction of our resources to our military defense. The importance of government as a buyer of so much of our output, and the sole buyer of the output of many firms and industries, already concentrates a dangerous amount of economic power in the hands of the political authorities, changes the environment in which business operates and the criteria relevant for business success, and in these and other ways endangers a free market. This danger we cannot avoid. But we needlesly intensify it by continuing the present widespread governmental intervention in areas unrelated to the military defense of the nation and by undertaking ever new governmental programs—from medical care for the aged to lunar exploration.

As Adam Smith once said, "There is much ruin in a nation." Our basic structure of values and the interwoven network of free institutions will withstand much. I believe that we shall be able to preserve and extend freedom despite the size of the military programs and despite the economic powers already concentrated in Washington. But we shall be able to do so only if we awake to the threat that we face, only if we persuade our fellow men that free institutions offer a surer, if perhaps at times a slower, route to the ends they seek than the coercive power of the state. The glimmerings of change that are already apparent in the intellectual climate are a hopeful augury.

Elegant Tombstones:
A Note on Friedman's Freedom

C. B. MACPHERSON

Although it is not in itself a statement of economic "philosophy," Macpherson's reply to Friedman is germane to the problem of using economics to achieve an historical perspective.

Academic political scientists who want their students to think about the problem of liberty in the modern state are properly anxious to have them confront at first-hand various contemporary theoretical positions on the relation between freedom and capitalism. The range of positions is wide: at one extreme freedom is held to be incompatible with capitalism; at the other freedom is held to be impossible except in a capitalist society; in between, all sorts of necessary or possible relations are asserted. Different concepts of freedom are involved in some of these positions, similar concepts in others; and different models of capitalism (and of socialism) are sometimes being used. It is clearly important to sort them out. But there is some difficulty in finding adequate theoretical expositions of the second extreme position, which might be called the pure market theory of liberalism. These are very few of them. Probably the most effective, and the one most often cast in the role, is Milton Friedman's *Capitalism and Freedom* which is now apt to be treated by political scientists as the classic defense of free-market liberalism. As such it deserves more notice from the political theorists' standpoint than it got on publication, when its technical arguments about the possibility of returning to laissez faire attracted most attention. Whether or not *Capitalism and Freedom* is now properly treated as the classic defense of the pure market theory of liberalism, it is at least a classic example of the difficulty of moving from the level

From *Canadian Journal of Political Science* (March, 1968), pp. 95–106. Reprinted by permission of the Canadian Political Science Association, Kingston, Ontario, and the author.

of controversy about laissez faire to the level of fundamental concepts of freedom and the market.

This note deals with (1) an error which vitiates Friedman's demonstration that competitive capitalism coordinates men's economic activities without coercion; (2) the inadequacy of his arguments that capitalism is a necessary condition of political freedom and that socialism is inconsistent with political freedom; and (3) the fallacy of his case for the ethical adequacy of the capitalist principle of distribution.

Professor Friedman's demonstration that the capitalist market economy can coordinate economic activities without coercion rests on an elementary conceptual error. His argument runs as follows. He shows first that in a simple market model, where each individual or household controls resources enabling it to produce goods and services either directly for itself or for exchange, there will be production for exchange because of the increased product made possible by specialization. But "since the household always has the alternative of producing directly for itself, it need not enter into any exchange unless it benefits from it. Hence no exchange will take place unless both parties do benefit from it. Cooperation is thereby achieved without coercion" (p. 13). So far, so good. It is indeed clear that in this simple exchange model, assuming rational maximizing behavior by all hands, every exchange will benefit both parties, and hence that no coercion is involved in the decision to produce for exchange or in any act of exchange.

Professor Friedman then moves on to our actual complex economy, or rather to his own curious model of it:

> As in [the] simple model, so in the complex enterprise and money-exchange economy, cooperation is strictly individual and voluntary *provided*: (*a*) that enterprises are private, so that the ultimate contracting parties are individuals and (*b*) that individuals are effectively free to enter or not to enter into any particular exchange, so that every transaction is strictly voluntary (p. 14).

One cannot take exception to proviso (*a*): it is clearly required in the model to produce a cooperation that is "strictly individual." One might, of course, suggest that a model containing this stipulation is far from corresponding to our actual complex economy, since in the latter the ultimate contracting parties who have the most effect on the market are not individuals but corporations, and moreover, corporations which in one way or another manage to opt out of the fully competitive market. This criticism, however, would not be accepted by all economists as self-evident: some would say that the question who has most effect on the market is still an open question (or is a wrongly-posed question). More investigation and analysis of this aspect of the economy would be valuable. But political scientists need not await its results before passing judgment on Friedman's position, nor should they be tempted to concentrate their attention on proviso (*a*). If they do so they are apt to miss the fault in proviso (*b*), which is more fundamental, and of a different kind. It is not a question of the correspondence of the model to the actual: it is a matter of the inadequacy of the proviso to produce the model.

Proviso (*b*) is "that individuals are effectively free to enter or not to enter into any particular exchange," and it is held that with this proviso "every transaction is strictly voluntary." A moment's thought will show that this is not so. The proviso that is required to make every transaction strictly voluntary is not freedom not to enter into any *particular* exchange, but freedom not to enter into any exchange *at all*. This, and only this, was the proviso that proved the simple model to be voluntary and non-coercive; and nothing less than this would prove the complex model to be voluntary and noncoercive. But Professor Friedman is clearly claiming that freedom not to enter into any *particular* exchange is enough: "The consumer is protected from coercion by the seller because of the presence of other sellers with whom he can deal. . . . The employee is protected from coercion by the employer because of other employers for whom he can work . . ." (pp. 14–15).

One almost despairs of logic, and of the use of models. It is easy to see what Professor Friedman has done, but it is less easy to excuse it. He has moved from the simple economy of exchange between independent producers, to the capitalist economy, without mentioning the most important thing that distinguishes them. He mentions money instead of barter, and "enterprises which are intermediaries between individuals in their capacities as suppliers of services and as purchasers of goods" (pp. 13–14), as if money and merchants were what distinguished a capitalist economy from an economy of independent producers. What distinguishes the capitalist economy from the simple exchange economy is the separation of labor and capital, that is, the existence of a labor force without its own sufficient capital and therefore without a choice as to whether to put its labor in the market or not. Professor Friedman would agree that where there is no choice there is coercion. His attempted demonstration that capitalism coordinates without coercion therefore fails.

Since all his specific arguments against the welfare and regulatory state depend on his case that the market economy is not coercive, the reader may spare himself the pains (or, if an economist, the pleasure) of attending to the careful and persuasive reasoning by which he seeks to establish the minimum to which coercion could be reduced by reducing or discarding each of the main regulatory and welfare activities of the state. None of this takes into account the coercion involved in the separation of capital from labor, or the possible mitigation of this coercion by the regulatory and welfare state. Yet it is because this coercion can in principle be reduced by the regulatory and welfare state, and thereby the amount of effective individual liberty be increased, that liberals have been justified in pressing, in the name of liberty, for infringements on the pure operation of competitive capitalism.

While the bulk of *Capitalism and Freedom* is concerned with the regulatory and welfare state, Friedman's deepest concern is with socialism. He undertakes to demonstrate that socialism is inconsistent with political freedom. He argues this in two ways: (1) that competitive capitalism, which is of course negated by socialism, is a necessary (although not a sufficient) condition of political freedom; (2) that a socialist society is so constructed that it cannot guarantee political freedom. Let us look at the two arguments in turn.

The argument that competitive capitalism is necessary to political freedom is itself conducted on two levels, neither of which shows a necessary relation.

(a) The first, on which Friedman properly does not place very much weight, is a historical correlation. No society that has had a large measure of political freedom "has not also used something comparable to a free market to organize the bulk of economic activity" (p. 9). Professor Friedman rightly emphasizes "how limited is the span of time and the part of the globe for which there has ever been anything like political freedom" (p. 9); he believes that the exceptions to the general rule of "tyranny, servitude and misery" are so few that the relation between them and certain economic arrangements can easily be spotted. "The 19th century and early 20th century in the Western world stand out as striking exceptions to the general trend of historical development. Political freedom in this instance clearly came along with the free market and the development of capitalist institutions" (pp. 9–10). Thus, for Professor Friedman, "history suggests . . . that capitalism is a necessary condition for political freedom" (p. 10).

The broad historical correlation is fairly clear, though in cutting off the period of substantial political freedom in the West at the "early 20th century" Friedman seems to be slipping into thinking of economic freedom and begging the question of the relation of political freedom to economic freedom. But granting the correlation between the emergence of capitalism and the emergence of political freedom, what it may suggest to the student of history is the converse of what it suggests to Professor Friedman: i.e., it may suggest that political freedom was a necessary condition for the development of capitalism. Capitalist institutions could not be fully established until political freedom (ensured by a competitive party system with effective civil liberties) had been won by those who wanted capitalism to have a clear run: a liberal state (political freedom) was needed to permit and facilitate a capitalist market society.

If this is the direction in which the causal relation runs, what follows (assuming the same relation to continue to hold) is that freedom, or rather specific kinds and degrees of freedom, will be or not be maintained according as those who have a stake in the maintenance of capitalism think them useful or necessary. In fact, there has been a complication in this relation. The liberal state which had, by the mid-19th century in England, established the political freedoms needed to facilitate capitalism, was not democratic: that is, it had not extended political freedom to the bulk of the people. When, later, it did so, it began to abridge market freedom. The more extensive the political freedom, the less extensive the economic freedom became. At any rate, the historical correlation scarcely suggests that capitalism is a necessary condition for political freedom.

(b) Passing from historical correlation, which "by itself can never be convincing," Professor Friedman looks for "logical links between economic and political freedom" (pp. 11–12). The link he finds is that "the kind of economic organization that provides economic freedom directly, namely, competitive capitalism, also promotes political freedom because it separates economic power from political power and in this way enables the one to offset the other" (p. 9). The point is developed a few pages later. The greater the concentration of coercive power in the same hands, the greater the threat to political freedom (defined as "the absence of coercion of a man by his fellow men"). The market removes the organization of economic activity from the control of the political authority. It thus reduces the concentration of power and "enables economic strength to be a check to political power rather than a reinforcement" (p. 15).

Granted the validity of these generalizations, they tell us only that the market *enables* economic power to offset rather than reinforce political power. They do not show any necessity or inherent probability that the market *leads* to the offsetting of political power by economic power. We may doubt that there is any such inherent probability. What can be shown is an inherent probability in the other direction, i.e., that the market leads to political power being used not to offset but to reinforce economic power. For the more completely the market takes over the organization of economic activity, that is, the more nearly the society approximates Friedman's ideal of a competitive capitalist market society, where the state establishes and enforces the individual right of appropriation and the rules of the market but does not interfere in the operation of the market, the more completely is political power being used to reinforce economic power.

Professor Friedman does not see this as any threat to political freedom because he does not see that the capitalist market necessarily gives coercive power to those who succeed in amassing capital. He knows that the coercion whose absence he equates with political freedom is not just the physical coercion of police and prisons, but extends to many forms of economic coercion, e.g., the power some men may have over others' terms of employment. He sees the coercion possible (he thinks probable) in a socialist society where the political authority can enforce certain terms of employment. He does not see the coercion in a capitalist society where the holders of capital can enforce certain terms of employment. He does not see this because of his error about freedom not to enter into any particular exchange being enough to prove the uncoercive nature of entering into exchange at all.

The placing of economic coercive power and political coercive power in the hands of different sets of people, as in the fully competitive capitalist economy does not lead to the first checking the second but to the second reinforcing the first. It is only in the welfare-state variety of capitalism, which Friedman would like to have dismantled, that there is a certain amount of checking of economic power by political power.

The logical link between competitive capitalism and political freedom has not been established.

Professor Friedman argues also that a socialist society is so constructed that it cannot guarantee political freedom. He takes as the test of political freedom the freedom of individuals to propagandize openly for a radical change in the structure of society: in a socialist society the test is freedom to advocate the introduction of capitalism. He might have seemed to be on more realistic ground had he taken the test to be freedom to advocate different policies within the framework of socialism, e.g., a faster or slower rate of socialization, of industrialization, etc.: it is on these matters that the record of actual socialist states has been conspicuously unfree. However, since the denial of freedom of such advocacy has generally been on the ground that such courses would lead to or encourage the reintroduction of capitalism, such advocacy may all be subsumed under his test.

We may grant at once that in the present socialist states (by which is meant those dominated by communist parties) such freedom is not only not guaranteed but is actively denied. Professor Friedman does not ask us to grant this, since he is talking not about particular socialist states but about any possible socialist state, about the socialist state as such; nevertheless the actual ones are not far from his mind, and we shall have to refer to them again. His case that a socialist state as such cannot guarantee political freedom depends on what he puts in his model of the socialist state. He uses in fact two models. In one, the government is the sole employer and the sole source from which necessary instruments of effective political advocacy (paper, use of printing presses, halls) can be had. In the other, the second stipulation is dropped.

It is obvious that in either model a government which wished to prevent political advocacy could use its economic monopoly position to do so. But what Professor Friedman is trying to establish is something different, namely, that its economic monopoly position would render any socialist government, whatever its intentions, incapable of guaranteeing this political freedom. It may be granted that in the first model this would be so. It would be virtually impossible, for a government which desired to guarantee freedom of political advocacy, to provide paper, presses, halls, etc., to all comers in the quantities they thought necessary.

But in the second model this would not apply. The second model appears when Professor Friedman is urging a further argument, namely, that a government which desired to guarantee free political advocacy could not effectively make it possible because, in the absence of capitalism and hence of many and widely dispersed private fortunes, there would be no sufficient source of private funds with which to finance propaganda activities, and the government itself could not feasibly provide such funds. Here there is assumed to be a market in paper, presses, and halls: the trouble is merely shortage of funds which advocates can use in these markets.

This second argument need not detain us, resting as it does on the unhistorical assumption that radical minority movements are necessarily unable to operate without millionaire angels or comparably few sources of large funds. Nor, since the second argument assumes that paper, presses and halls can be purchased or hired, need we challenge the assumption put in the first model, that these means of advocacy are unobtainable in the socialist state except by asking the government for them.

We have still to consider the effect of the other stipulation, which is made in both models: that the government is the sole employer. Accepting this as a proper stipulation for a socialist model, the question to be answered is: does the monopoly of employment itself render the government incapable (or even less capable than it otherwise would be) of safeguarding political freedom? Friedman expects us to answer yes, but the answer is surely no. A socialist government which wished to guarantee political freedom would not be prevented from doing so by its having a monopoly of employment. Nor need it even be tempted to curtail political freedom by virtue of that monopoly. A government monopoly of employment can only mean (as Friedman allows) that the government and all its agencies are, together, the only employers. A socialist government can, by devolution of the management of industries, provide effective alternative employment opportunities. True, a government which wished to curtail or deny the freedom of radical political advocacy could use its monopoly of employment to do so. But such a government has so many other ways of doing it that the presence or absence of this way is not decisive.

It is not the absence of a fully competitive labor market that may disable a socialist government from guaranteeing political freedom; it is the absence of a firm will to do so. Where there's a will there's a way, and for all that Friedman has argued to the contrary, the way need have nothing to do with a fully competitive labor market. The real problem of political freedom in socialism has to do with the will, not the way. The real problem is whether a socialist state could ever have the will to guarantee political freedom. This depends on factors Friedman does not consider, and until they have been assessed, questions about means have an air of unreality, as has his complaint that Western socialists have not faced up to the question of means. We shall return to both of these matters after looking briefly at the factors which are likely to affect such a will to political freedom.

On the question of the will, we cannot say (nor indeed does Professor Friedman suggest) that a will to guarantee political freedom is impossible, or even improbable, in a socialist state. True, if one were to judge by existing socialist states controlled by communist parties, the improbability would be high. (We are speaking here of day-to-day political freedom, which is the question Friedman has set, and not with the will to achieve some higher level of freedom in an ultimately transformed society.) But if we are to consider, as Professor Friedman is doing, socialist states that might emerge in the West, we should notice the differences between the forces in the existing ones and those inherent in possible future Western ones.

There are some notable differences. First, the existing socialist states were virtually all established in underdeveloped societies, in which the bulk of the people did not have the work habits and other cultural attributes needed by a modern industrial state. They have had to change an illiterate, largely unpolitical, peasant population into a literate, politicized, industrially oriented people. While doing this they have had to raise productivity to levels which would afford a decent human minimum, and even meet a rising level of material expectations. The pressures against political freedom that are set up by these factors are obvious. In the few instances, e.g., Czechoslovakia, where socialism did not start from such an underdeveloped base, it started under an external domination that produced equal though different pressures against political freedom. None of these pressures would be present in a socialist state which emerged independently in an already highly developed Western society.

Second, in the existing socialist states the effort to establish socialism has been made in the face of the hostility of the Western powers, whether manifested in their support of counter-revolution or in "encirclement" or "cold war." The ways in which this fact has compounded the pressures against political freedom due to the underdeveloped base are obvious.

Presumably the force of this hostility would be less in the case of future socialist takeovers in Western countries.

Third, the existing socialist states were all born in revolution or civil war, with the inevitable aftermath that "deviations" from the line established from time to time by the leadership (after however much or little consultation) tend to be treated as treason against the socialist revolution and the socialist state. We may at least entertain the possibility of a socialist takeover in an advanced Western nation without revolution or civil war (as Professor Friedman presumably does, else he would not be so concerned about the "creeping socialism" of the welfare state). A socialist state established without civil war would not be subject to this third kind of pressure against political freedom.

Thus of the three forces that have made the pressures against political freedom generally predominate in socialist states so far, the first will be absent, the second reduced or absent, and the third possibly absent, in a future Western socialist state that emerged without external domination.

When these projections are borne in mind, Professor Friedman's complaint about Western socialists appears somewhat impertinent. He complains that "none of the people who have been in favor of socialism and also in favor of freedom have really faced up to this issue [of means], or made even a respectable start at developing the institutional arrangements that would permit freedom under socialism" (p. 19). Perhaps the reason is that they think it more important, in the interests of freedom, to examine and even try to influence the circumstances in which socialism might arrive, than to begin planning institutional arrangements. Western socialists who believe in political freedom are, or should be, more concerned with seeking ways to minimize the cold war (so as to minimize the chances that the second of the projected forces against political freedom will be present in the socialist transformation they hope to achieve in their country), and seeking ways to minimize the likelihood of civil war (so as to minimize the third of the forces against political freedom), than with developing "institutional arrangements that would permit freedom under socialism."

But although, in a socialist state, the existence of a predominant will for political freedom may be more important than institutional arrangements, the latter should not be neglected. For even where there is, on the whole, a will to guarantee political freedom, there are likely always to be some pressures against it, so that it is desirable to have institutions which will make infringements difficult rather than easy. What institutional arrangements, beyond the obvious ones of constitutional guarantees of civil liberties and a legal system able to enforce them, are required? Let us accept Professor Friedman's statement of additional minimum institutional requirements. Advocates of radical change opposed to the government's policies must be able to obtain the indispensable means of advocacy—paper, presses, halls, etc. And they must be able to propagandize without endangering their means of livelihood.

As we have already seen, there is no difficulty inherent in socialism in meeting the first of these requirements, once it is granted (as Professor Friedman's second model grants) that the absence of a complete capitalist market economy does not entail the absence of markets in paper, presses, and halls.

The second requirement seems more difficult to meet. If the government (including all its agencies) is the sole employer, the standing danger that the monopoly of employment would be used to inhibit or prevent certain uses of political freedom is obvious. The difficulty is not entirely met by pointing out that a socialist state can have any amount of devolution of industry or management, so that there can be any number of employers, or by stipulating as an institutional arrangement that this devolution be practiced. For it is evident that if there is a ubiquitous single or dominant political party operating in all industries and all plants (and all trade unions), it can make this multiplicity of employment opportunities wholly ineffective, if or in so far as it wishes to do so. The problem is not the absence of a labor market but the possible presence of another institution, a ubiquitous party which puts other things ahead of political freedom.

The stipulation that would be required to safeguard political freedom from the dangers of employment monopoly is not merely that there be devolution of management, and hence employment alternatives (which could be considered an institutional arrangement), but also that there be no ubiquitous party or that, if there is, such a party should consistently put a very high value on political freedom (which stipulation can scarcely be set out as an institutional arrangement). We are back at the question of will rather than way, and of the circumstantial forces which are going to shape that will, for the presence or absence of such a party is clearly going to depend largely on the circumstances in which a socialist state is established.

There is, however, one factor (which might be institutionalized) which may, in any socialist state established in the West, reduce even the possibility of such intimidation through employment monopoly. This is the decreasing necessity, in highly developed societies whose economic systems are undergoing still further and rapid technological development, of relating income to employment. One need not be as sanguine as some exponents of the guaranteed income to think it possible, even probable, that before any advanced Western nation chooses socialism it will have seen the logic of using its affluence and averting difficulties both political and economic by introducing a guaranteed minimum annual income to everyone regardless of employment. In this event, the technical problem

that worries Professor Friedman—how to ensure that a threat to employment and hence to livelihood could not be used to deny political freedom—
would no longer be a problem. A threat to employment would no longer
be a threat to livelihood. It would indeed be a cost, but as Professor Friedman says, "what is essential is that the cost of advocating unpopular causes
be tolerable and not prohibitive" (p. 18).

But even without such a separation of employment from income, the
technical problem of securing political freedom from being denied by the
withholding of employment can be met by such devolution of management as would constitute a set of alternative employments *provided* that
this is not offset by a ubiquitous party hostile to political freedom. If there
is such a party, no institutional arrangements for safeguarding political
freedom are reliable; if there is not, the institutional arrangements do not
seem to be difficult.

We noticed that Professor Friedman, in arguing that freedom would
be increased if most of the regulatory and welfare activities of contemporary Western states were abandoned, did not take into account the
coercion involved in the separation of capital from labor or the possible
mitigation of this coercion by the regulatory and welfare state. But in
Chapter 10, on the distribution of income, he does deal with a closely
related problem. Here he sets out the ethical case for distribution according to product, as compared with "another [principle] that seems ethically
appealing, namely, equality of treatment" (p. 162). Distribution according
to product he describes, accurately enough, as the principle "To each
according to what he and the instruments he owns produces" (pp. 161–
162): to be strictly accurate this should read "resources" or "capital and
land" instead of "instruments," but the sense is clear. This is offered as
"the ethical principle that would directly justify the distribution of income
in a free market society" (p. 161). We can agree that this is the only principle that can be offered to justify it. We may also observe that this principle is not only different from the principle "to each according to his
work," but is also inconsistent with it (except on the fanciful assumption
that ownership of resources is always directly proportional to work). Professor Friedman does not seem to see this. His case for the ethical principle
of payment according to product is that it is unthinkingly accepted as a
basic value-judgment by almost everybody in our society; and his demonstration of this is that the severest internal critics of capitalism, i.e. the
Marxists, have implicitly accepted it.

Of course they have not. There is a double confusion here, even if
we accept Friedman's paraphrase of Marx. Marx did not argue quite, as
Friedman puts it (p. 167), "that labor was exploited . . . because labor produced the whole of the product but got only part of it"—the argument was
rather that labor is exploited because labor produces the whole of the value

that is added in any process of production but gets only part of it—but Friedman's paraphrase is close enough for his purpose. Certainly the implication of Marx's position is that labor (though not necessarily each individual laborer) is entitled to the whole of the value it creates. But in the first place, this is, at most, the principle "to each according to his work," not "to each according to what he and the instruments he owns produces" or "to each according to his product." In the second place, Marx accepted "to each according to his work" only as a transitionally valid principle, to be replaced by the ultimately desirable principle "to each according to his need." Professor Friedman, unaccountably, only refers to this latter principle as "Ruskinian" (p. 167).

Having so far misread Marx, Professor Friedman gives him a final fling.

> Of course, the Marxist argument is invalid on other grounds as well . . . [most] striking, there is an unstated change in the meaning of "labor" in passing from the premise to the conclusion. Marx recognized the role of capital in producing the product but regarded capital as embodied labor. Hence, written out in full, the premises of the Marxist syllogism would run: "Present and past labor produce the whole of the product." The logical conclusion is presumably "Past labor is exploited," and the inference for action is that past labor should get more of the product, though it is by no means clear how, unless it be in elegant tombstones [pp. 167–168].

This nonsense is unworthy of Professor Friedman's talents. The Marxist premises are: Present labor, and the accumulation of surplus value created by past labor and extracted from the past laborers, produce the whole value of the product. Present labor gets only a part of that part of the value which it creates, and gets no part of that part of the value which is transferred to the product from the accumulated surplus value created by past labor. The logical conclusion is presumably that present labor is exploited and past labor was exploited, and the inference for action is that a system which requires constant exploitation should be abandoned.

Ignorance of Marxism is no sin in an economist, though cleverness in scoring off a travesty of it may be thought a scholarly lapse. What is more disturbing is that Professor Friedman seems to be satisfied that this treatment of the ethical justification of different principles of distribution is sufficient. Given his own first postulate, perhaps it is. For in asserting at the beginning of the book that freedom of the individual, or perhaps of the family, is the liberal's "ultimate goal in judging social arrangements," he has said in effect that the liberal is not required seriously to weigh the ethical claims of equality (or any other principle of distribution), let alone the claims of any principle of individual human development such as was given first place by liberals like Mill and Green, against the claims of free-dom (which to Friedman of course means market freedom). The humanist liberal in the tradition of Mill and Green will quite properly reject Fried-man's postulate. The logical liberal will reject his fallacious proof that the freedom of the capitalist market is individual economic freedom, his un-demonstrated case that political freedom requires capitalism, and his falla-cious defense of the ethical adequacy of capitalism. The logical humanist liberal will regret that the postulate and the fallacies make *Capitalism and Freedom* not a defense but an elegant tombstone of liberalism.

The Problems and Prospects
of Collective Capitalism

GARDINER C. MEANS

Here it is asserted that the evolution of private capitalism into "collective capitalism" has created a new set of problems with which traditional economic theory is not adequate to cope.

Thirty-six years ago, our system of private capitalism was in a state of collapse. A quarter of the labor force was unemployed, the economy was operating at less than two-thirds of its capacity, business enterprises were failing on all sides, farms were being foreclosed on a mass scale, and money, the medium of exchange which is at the heart of capitalism, was being wiped out by the closing of banks until the whole banking system ceased to operate. The collapse of the capitalist system predicted by Karl Marx seemed to be taking place before our eyes.

Then came a revolution. It was not the Marxian revolution in which labor seizes the instruments of production, but a more basic and less obvious revolution which rejected the principles and policies of private capitalism and made a start toward developing a new set of principles and policies applicable to a new type of capitalism.

This revolution rejected the principle that under capitalism automatic forces would tend to maintain full employment and that any significant departure from a prosperous condition is only temporary. It rejected the principle that automatic forces would tend to bring to each individual an income in proportion to his contribution to production, and that unemployment is the product of an individual's own laziness or moral lack. It rejected the principle that automatic forces of supply and demand would tend to maintain a fair balance between farm and industrial prices. At the London Conference of 1933 this revolution rejected the principle that

From *Journal of Economic Issues* (March, 1969), pp. 18–31. Reprinted by permission of the publisher.

automatic forces would correct any persistent unbalance in international payments.

These rejected principles were a fundamental part of the warp and woof of private capitalism. For more than one hundred years, these principles had been accepted as valid and had provided the basis for national policies.

Why this sudden wholesale rejection? The easy answer is to say that the policies based on these principles were not working. But why were the policies of private capitalism which had worked reasonably well for over a century failing to work? The principles on which they were based had been developed and refined by a host of able economists. Their logic had been epitomized by Léon Walras in his beautiful system of equations. Their validity for the economy of private capitalism was well established.

The answer is to be found in two great institutional changes which had taken place that destroyed the validity of the classical assumptions. One was a change in the characteristics of the predominant form of enterprise, and the other was a change in the characteristics of the predominant form of market.

For most of the 19th century, the predominant type of enterprise was the small private enterprise. Such enterprise was the basic concept of classical economic theory, and the economic system was analyzed as a system of small private enterprises interrelated through markets in which no individual enterprise had significant market power. Monopoly was recognized as an aberration to be broken up or regulated while prices in the competitive markets were presumed to adjust freely and flexibly to equate supply and demand. Thus, the policies of private capitalism were based on the twin assumptions of small private enterprises and flexible market prices. It was these policies that had failed 36 years ago.

By the 1930s, these assumptions had ceased to apply. The United States had become one in which the big modern corporation played a predominant role, and the great bulk of commodities and services entering the market were exchanged at inflexible, administered prices.

Today we see in the foreground the big modern corporation. Obviously it is not a private enterprise. There is nothing private about a corporation with a hundred thousand stockholders, a hundred thousand workers, hundreds of thousands of customers and thousands of suppliers. Also obviously, such a corporation is not government. It is an institution standing midway between private enterprise and public government.

In a very real sense, the modern corporation is a great collective. Its management tends to be a self-perpetuating body in control of the enterprise and the enterprise itself consists of all those participating in it—some supplying capital, some supplying manpower, some supplying raw materials and some providing the market. The responsibilities of management can no longer lie solely with the stockholders. Within the wide limits set by the new type of competition, management has the power to affect the interests of all the participants in the enterprise and the responsibility to use this power to balance these interests. The long-run survival of the collective as an independent institution is likely to depend on management's maintaining an effective balance between these often conflicting interests which give the collective its life. The very legitimacy of the power wielded by management depends on its achieving such a balance.

Also in the foreground of our real economic world is what I have called "administrative competition." It, like collective enterprise, lies outside the principles and policies of private capitalism. Administrative competition is a form midway between classical competition under which no one has any market power and classical monopoly in which pricing power is unique. Whether we call this "competition among the few" or administrative competition or use such misleading terms as "monopolistic competition" or "imperfect competition," it is essentially a form of competition in which a price (or wage rate) is not set by the equating of supply and demand but by administrative action, and held constant for a period of time and through a series of transactions.

Under administrative competition, demand and costs influence price but do not determine it. Demand can change without producing a change in price. Costs can change without producing a change in price. And a change in price can be made with no initiating change in demand or costs. Actual price becomes in some degree a matter of the arbitrary use of pricing power within the limits, often broad, set by demand and costs. At the same time, demand and costs tend in part to be a product of how this arbitrary power is used.

By the time of the great depression, the institutional changes of the preceding 50 years had converted a system of private capitalism into a system predominantly made up of huge collectives and markets in which prices are determined by administrative decision. The great evolution from private capitalism has given us a new form of the free enterprise system which may be called *Collective Capitalism.* It is a form of capitalism lying entirely outside the conceptions of John Stuart Mill and Karl Marx, and, of course, outside the conceptions of Adam Smith. [This new] collective capitalism has created a new set of problems with which classical theory is not competent to cope.

The first of the set of problems, and I think the most important, is the way we think about our economic system. There is a great and understandable tendency to describe the present-day economy as a private enterprise system, though with some important modifications. This tendency appears both in the teaching of economics and in the theorizing about the system.

I believe the time has come to reverse our field and describe our system as a collective enterprise system which has some elements of both private enterprise and government enterprise.

When we follow the implications of this reversal, the beginning theory course will describe our present economy as one in which big collective enterprises play a major role with the remainder of production carried on, for the most part, by government on the one hand and by private enterprise on the other. Similarly, price and wage analysis would first focus on administrative competition and the indeterminacy of prices and wage rates. Then classical monopoly and classical competition would be considered as special cases.

This procedure would be in sharp contrast with much of present-day teaching. For example, Samuelson's *Economics* starts the section on price determination with four chapters primarily devoted to the determination of price by supply and demand, followed by a chapter on equilibrium of the firm devoted mostly to pricing by a monopolist, and a final weak chapter on "imperfect competition." Since the great bulk of commodity and service transactions take place at administered prices, this approach from classical competition to administrative competition clearly leaves a false impression.

We do not yet know as much about administrative competition as we do about classical competition. Points that need to be covered are the indeterminacy of prices, their insensitivity to changes in demand and in costs, and the possibility of arbitrary prices changes. We also need to cover the possibility that administrative competition may result in higher cost as well, or instead of, lower prices. And one can question whether the neat curves of marginal cost and marginal revenue have much relevance to practical pricing decisions where pricing is aimed at a target rate of return. What is of major importance is that administrative competition should be the central focus of teaching.

Likewise in theoretical analysis there is need to posit in place of the simplified classical model of an economy *solely* involving classical competition and perfectly flexible prices and wages, a simplified model in which all production is carried on by collectives and all prices are administered prices. The theoretical implications of such an economy could then be adjusted to apply to an economy which has some classical competition and some government production.

I do not believe that we can fully understand the practical problems of collective capitalism or develop the best policies for dealing with them until we have made this revolution in teaching and theory. But already some of the practical problems are apparent and we are moving toward solutions. I will consider here five of the major problems created by collective capitalism, indicate some of the steps we have already taken toward their solution, and point the direction in which a satisfactory solution seems to me likely to lie.

The first practical problem is, of course, that of maintaining full employment. Under the theory of private capitalism, there was a price-adjustment mechanism which would automatically tend to maintain that level of aggregate demand necessary to eliminate involuntary unemployment and assure reasonably full employment. If aggregate demand was deficient, a fall in the price-wage level would increase the real value of the outstanding stock of money, making it greater than the public would choose to hold at the lower level of prices. This redundancy of money would restore real aggregate demand.

Under collective capitalism, the price-wage structure does not have that degree of flexibility necessary to allow this classical mechanism to work. Instead of a general fall in price level, a deficiency in aggregate demand creates a fall in employment and incomes which more than offsets the stimulating effect of any increase in the real stock of money.

The need for positive government action to maintain aggregate demand was fully recognized in the Employment Act of 1946, and there has been general agreement that monetary and fiscal measures should provide the primary means. But the 20 years of experience still leaves us with neither the institutions nor the policies which allow a fine tuning of aggregate demand, or even a reasonable certainty that coarse tuning can be maintained.

It is my own opinion that monetary measures can be a powerful tool for maintaining the appropriate level of aggregate demand, but we have not yet learned how to use them effectively.

Clearly we need to know more about the actual effect of monetary and fiscal policy on aggregate demand, and also to revise our monetary and fiscal institutions so as to be able to adjust aggregate demand to the level called for by our productive capacity. When I first introduced the concept of administered prices, I pointed out their implications for monetary policy, and more recently I have suggested how to reorder our monetary institutions to make them more effective instruments for regulating the level of aggregate demand. Once we get away from the overemphasis on fiscal policy and the interest effect of money, I believe we will develop a set of monetary institutions and monetary policies which will allow the fine adjustment necessary for maintaining the appropriate level of aggregate demand.

A second major problem of collective capitalism is a new type of inflation unknown to private capitalism. The inflation of classical theory was a demand inflation with a general rise in prices and wage rates. The inflation represented too much money chasing too few goods, and at least for a single country, it could be prevented by the fine tuning of aggregate demand to give both full employment and stability in the price level.

The new type of inflation arises from the indeterminacy of administered prices and wage rates, and from the market power they involve. It is sometimes called "cost-push" inflation with the implication that it results from labor's use of its power to push wage rates up faster than productivity. This is a theoretical possibility. But so also is it a theoretical possibility that business price administrators raise prices arbitrarily, without any increase in units costs or in demand. This could be called a "profits-push" inflation. Because this new type of inflation could be either a cost-push or a profits-push inflation and because it could only come where prices or wages are administered, I have chosen to call it "administrative inflation."

A characteristic of demand inflation under the conditions of collective capitalism shows itself first in the prices subject to classical competition, but only with substantial lag for administered prices and wage rates. It is also characteristic that it can occur only when aggregate demand is in excess of that needed for full employment. This was true of the inflation which followed the removal of price controls after World War II and of the Korean War inflation. Both were clearly demand inflations.

In contrast, an administrative inflation shows itself first in a rise of administered prices with no rise or fall in classically competitive prices, and it can occur whether or not there is full employment. The 1953 to 1958 price rise was clearly of this character. In that period, the bulk of the 8 percent rise in the wholesale price index was in administered prices, while the indexes for such categories as textiles and farm products went down, a finding that was inadvertently confirmed in a statistical analysis developed by proponents of the Chicago school. This 1953 to 1958 inflation occurred in a period of slack demand, as is indicated by the average unemployment of over 5 percent and the large amount of idle industrial capacity. When the Federal Reserve Board sought to control this inflation on the assumption that it was a demand inflation, it created the depression of 1957 to 1958. Throughout the period a paradox to classical theory existed: simultaneous inflation and underemployment. The inflation was clearly not the result of excess demand.

It has been suggested that administrative inflation can be controlled by maintaining a substantial cushion of unemployed labor and capital. But the administrative inflation of the 1950s occurred with 5 percent of the labor force unemployed. Even if such a cushion could be successful, full employment and creeping inflation would seem to be a more economic alternative than to force more than a million and a half of extra unemployment on those least able to bear the burden. Undoubtedly a system of price and wage controls could prevent administrative inflation, but again, the remedy would seem to me worse than the disease. I do not believe we have yet given the guideline approach an adequate test. Once the problem is fully understood, I believe that guidelines worked out by the government with the assistance of the leaders of enterprise, labor and consumers could eliminate administrative inflation, or keep it to an acceptable minimum. If not, more drastic measures would be needed.

A third problem created by collective capitalism concerns the external balance of payments. Under private capitalism and the gold standard, flexible prices and wage rates were expected to adjust automatically so as to correct any fundamental imbalance in payments between countries.

With the inflexibility of prices and wages under collective capitalism, the old gold-flow mechanism simply could not work. If prices and wage rates were flexible, a fall in the stock of money in the gold-losing country could be expected to bring a reduction in aggregate demand with a corrective effect of a reduced internal price level. But where prices are insensitive to declining demand, the reduced aggregate demand would result in unemployment. The old gold mechanism could have corrected an imbalance in payments, but it would do this by creating a depression in one country and a boom in the other.

The institutions set up at Bretton Woods are effective in prolonging the period in which change or special measures can correct an imbalance in payments and special drawing rights can extend the period, but neither can correct a fundamental imbalance except by abrupt and painful changes in exchange rates. Of course, we would have an automatic mechanism if we dropped the objective of exchange stability and let exchange rates work themselves out in the market, but this would set up speculative movements and lose the very real values of short-run exchange stability.

I believe that this problem will ultimately be solved by an intermediate course which gives short-run stability in exchange rates and long-run, but gradual, flexibility. Most of the advantages of exchange stability could be obtained if exchange rates were kept within a known narrow bracket for six months or one year at a time. For example, if periodic small changes in the bracket were made in the light of current balances but announced, say, six months or a year in advance, such a forward peg could give short-run stability of rates, avoid speculative pressures for change and yet over a period of years, allow very considerable but gradual changes in exchange rates.

Just what form the intermediate mechanism may take I cannot foresee. But it seems to me clear that changes in internal levels of employment as a method of exchange adjustment will not be tolerated; and that neither freely floating exchange rates nor fixed exchange rates with occasional exchange crises provides a satisfactory basis for adjusting the balance of payments.

A fourth problem arising from collective capitalism has to do with the allocation of resources. According to the theory and principles of private capitalism, a country's resources would tend to be best used if each small producer sought to maximize his profits. Competition would keep prices in reasonable relation to costs and the unseen hand would guide individuals into the most economic use of the resources available to them.

But the large collective enterprise and administrative competition do not fit into this beautiful picture. The powers of corporate management are only crudely controlled by the unseen hand. To maximize profits is often to make less than the most effective use of resources. And mistakes in a single management that would be of negligible importance in a small enterprise can affect the lives of tens or even hundreds of thousands of individuals in a big collective.

The answer to this problem is not to break up collective enterprises into such small pieces that classical competition can prevail. The affluence of our society arises in large part from the high productivity of our big collectives. We do need our antitrust laws and agencies to prevent monopoly where administrative competition can prevail, but these agencies cannot enforce classical competition. Nor is it a satisfactory answer to regulate these collectives except where technology requires monopoly, as in the case of the public utilities, for regulation involves a degree of centralization which tends to be deadening to initiative.

There are, however, two lines of development which are wholly compatible with our free enterprise system and could be expected to make collective capitalism operate more effectively in using our resources.

The first is to forge a criteria of performance for the management of our big collectives. It is an appropriate function of the big collectives to make profits. But the objective of *maximizing* profits is no longer appropriate. In my book on *Pricing Power and the Public Interest,* I examined this problem and suggested certain lines of approach based on target pricing and incentives to performance. Whether these or some other lines of approach are finally adopted, the managements of the big collectives do need a clarification of what constitutes good performance and incentives to stimulate such performance.

The second line of development which I believe would make the policy decisions of both the managers of collective enterprises and government more effective has to do with economic planning. Economic planning of the Russian type would clearly be incompatible with our free enterprise system. But advisory planning can provide business and government with valuable background against which to make specific decisions.

This brings me to the question: What is the future of collective capitalism? On this I am an optimist. I do not see this country reverting to private capitalism. Nor do I see us following the path of Russia. The major problems of collective capitalism are not the product of internal contradictions in our system, but the product of contradictions between collective capitalism and the set of policies appropriate to private capitalism. We have already made important progress toward developing new policies. As we come to recognize more thoroughly the imperatives of collective capitalism, I believe we will solve the major problems which it has created. I do not suggest that we will produce a perfect system. Nor do I suggest that the improvement in the workings of collective capitalism can be brought about easily. Resistance to change and the pressures of immediate self-interest will stand in the way. But I believe that the general interest in a well-running economy will override these resistances.

Thus I envisage a system in which fine tuning of aggregate demand, principally through monetary policy, will maintain a high level of employment of both men and machines; in which administrative inflation will be under practical control through advisory planning, wage-price guidelines and perhaps specific controls for strategic commodities; in which an external balance of payments will be maintained through exchange rates which are relatively fixed for short periods of time, but gradually change to correct fundamental imbalances; in which business decisions (as well as those of government) on the allocation of resources will be brought into closer relation to the public interest through advisory planning and clarification of what constitutes economic performance; and a complete system of government measures to support incomes of the disadvantaged at an acceptable minimum level, while above this level inequities are kept to a minimum through better operation of the economy and through the continued use of taxation.

I would expect such an economy to yield a steadily rising level of incomes, greater leisure and the funds to enjoy it, and the resources to help in the development of less developed countries. Whether the affluent life can also be a good life will be a real problem, but not one I will deal with here.

Our Obsolete Market Mentality

KARL POLANYI

Can the market system serve as a long-term vehicle for human progress?
The late Karl Polanyi delivers a thoughtful negative verdict.

The first century of the Machine Age is drawing to a close amid fear
and trepidation. Its fabulous material success was due to the willing,
indeed the enthusiastic, *subordination of man to the needs of the machine.*
[Laissez faire] capitalism was in effect man's initial response to the challenge of the Industrial Revolution. In order to allow scope to the use
of elaborate, powerful machinery, we transformed human economy into
a self-adjusting system of markets, and cast our thoughts and values in
the mold of this unique innovation.

Today, we begin to doubt the truth of some of these thoughts and
the validity of some of these values. Outside the United States, [laissez
faire] capitalism can hardly be said to exist any more. How to organize
human life in a machine society is a question that confronts us anew.
Behind the fading fabric of competitive capitalism there looms the portent
of an industrial civilization, with its paralyzing division of labor, standardi-
zation of life, supremacy of mechanism over organism, and organization
over spontaneity. Science itself is haunted by insanity. This is the abiding
concern.

No mere reversion to the ideals of a past century can show us the
way. We must brave the future, though this may involve us in an attempt
to shift the place of industry in society so that the extraneous fact of the
machine can be absorbed. The search for industrial democracy is not
merely the search for a solution to the problems of capitalism, as most

Reprinted from *Commentary*, by permission; copyright © 1947 by the American
Jewish Committee.

265

people imagine. It is a search for an answer to industry itself. Here lies the concrete problem of our civilization. Such a new dispensation requires an inner freedom for which we are but ill equipped. We find ourselves *stultified* by the legacy of a market-economy which bequeathed us over-simplified views of the function and role of the economic system in society. If the crisis is to be overcome, we must recapture a more realistic vision of the human world and shape our common purpose in the light of that recognition.

Industrialism is a precariously grafted scion upon man's age-long existence. The outcome of the experiment is still hanging in the balance. But man is not a simple being and can die in more than one way. The question of individual freedom, so passionately raised in our generation, is only one aspect of this anxious problem. In truth, it forms part of a much wider and deeper need—the need for a new response to the total challenge of the machine.

Our condition can be described in these terms: Industrial civilization may yet undo man. But since the venture of a progressively artificial environment cannot, will not, and indeed, should not, be voluntarily discarded, the task of adapting life *in such a surrounding* to the requirements of human existence must be resolved if man is to continue on earth. No one can foretell whether such an adjustment is possible, or whether man must perish in the attempt. Hence the dark undertone of concern.

Meanwhile, the first phase of the Machine Age has run its course. It involved an organization of society that derived its name from its central institution, *the market.* This system is on the downgrade. Yet our practical philosophy was overwhelmingly shaped by this spectacular episode. Novel notions about man and society became current and gained the status of axioms. Here they are.

As regards *man*, we were made to accept the heresy that his motives can be described as "material" and "ideal," and that the incentives on which everyday life is organized spring from the "material" motives. Both utilitarian liberalism and popular Marxism favored such views.

As regards *society*, the kindred doctrine was propounded that its institutions were "determined" by the economic system. This opinion was even more popular with Marxists than with liberals.

Under a market-economy both assertions were, of course, true. *But only under such an economy.* To overcome such doctrines, which constrict our minds and souls and greatly enhance the difficulty of the life-saving adjustment, may require no less than a reform of our consciousness.

[Laissez faire] economy, this primary reaction of man to the machine, was a violent break with the conditions that preceded it. A chain-reaction was started—what before was merely isolated markets was transmuted into a self-regulating *system* of markets. And with the new economy, a new society sprang into being. The crucial step was this: labor and land were made into commodities, that is, they were treated *as if* produced for sale. Of course, they were not actually commodities, since they were either not produced at all (as land) or, if so, not for sale (as labor). Yet no more thoroughly effective fiction was ever devised. By buying and selling labor and land freely, the mechanism of the market was made to apply to them. There was now supply of labor, and demand for it; there was supply of land, and demand for it. Accordingly, there was a market price for the use of labor power, called wages, and a market price for the use of land, called rent. Labor and land were provided with markets of their own, similar to the commodities proper that were produced with their help. The true scope of such a step can be gauged if we remember that labor is only another name for man, and land for nature. The commodity fiction handed over the fate of man and nature to the play of an automaton running in its own grooves and governed by its own laws.

Nothing similar had ever been witnessed before. Under the mercantile regime, though it deliberately pressed for the creation of markets, the converse principle still operated. Labor and land were not entrusted to the market; they formed part of the *organic structure* of society. Where land was marketable, only the determination of price was, as a rule, left to the parties; where labor was subject to contract, wages themselves were usually assessed by public authority. Land stood under the custom of manor, monastery, and township, under common-law limitations concerning rights of real property; labor was regulated by laws against beggary and vagrancy, statutes of laborers and artificers, poor laws, guild and municipal ordinances. In effect, all societies known to anthropologists and historians restricted markets to commodities in the proper sense of the term.

Market-economy thus created a new type of society. The economic or productive system was here entrusted to a self-acting device. An institutional mechanism controlled human beings in their everyday activities as well as the resources of nature. This instrument of material welfare was under the sole control of the incentives of hunger and gain—or, more precisely, fear of going without the necessities of life, and expectation of profit. So long as no propertyless person could satisfy his craving for food without first selling his labor in the market, and so long as no propertied person was prevented from buying in the cheapest market and selling in the dearest, the blind mill would turn out ever-increasing amounts of commodities for the benefit of the human race. Fear of starvation with the worker, lure of profit with the employer, would keep the vast establishment running.

In this way an "economic sphere" came into existence that was sharply delimited from other institutions in society. Since no human aggregation can survive without a functioning productive apparatus, its embodiment in a distinct and separate sphere had the effect of making the "rest" of society dependent upon that sphere. This autonomous zone, again, was regulated by a mechanism that controlled its functioning. *As a result, the market mechanism became determinative for the life of the body social.* No wonder that the emergent human aggregation was an "economic" society to a degree previously never even approximated. "Economic motives" reigned supreme in a world of their own, and the individual was made to act on them under pain of being trodden under foot by the juggernaut market. Such a forced conversion to a utilitarian outlook fatefully warped Western man's understanding of himself.

This new world of "economic motives" was based on a fallacy. Intrinsically, hunger and gain are no more "economic" than love or hate, pride or prejudice. No human motive is per se economic. There is no such thing as a *sui generis* economic experience in the sense in which man may have a religious, aesthetic, or sexual experience. These latter give rise to motives that broadly aim at evoking similar experiences. In regard to material production these terms lack self-evident meaning.

The evidence of facts, I feel, should at this point be adduced. *First,* there are the discoveries of primitive economics. Two names are outstanding: Bronislaw Malinowski and Richard Thurnwald. They and some other research workers revolutionized our conceptions in this field and, by so doing, founded a new discipline. The myth of the individualistic savage had been exploded long ago. Neither the crude egotism, nor the apocryphal propensity to barter, truck, and exchange, nor even the tendency to cater to one's self was in evidence. But equally discredited was the legend of the communistic psychology of the savage, his supposed lack of appreciation for his own personal interests. (Roughly, it appeared that man was very much the same all through the ages. Taking his institutions not in isolation, but in their interrelation, he was mostly found to be behaving in a manner broadly comprehensible to us.) What appeared as "communism" was the fact that the productive or economic system was usually arranged in such a fashion as not to threaten any individual with starvation. His place at the campfire, his share in the common resources, was secure to him, whatever part he happened to have played in hunt, pasture, tillage, or gardening.

Second, there is no difference between primitive and civilized society in this regard. Whether we turn to ancient city-state, despotic empire, feudalism, 13th-century urban life, 16th-century mercantile regime, 18th-century regulationism—invariably the economic system is found to be merged in the social. Incentives spring from a large variety of sources, such as custom and tradition, public duty and private commitment, religious observance and political allegiance, judicial obligation and administrative regulation as established by prince, municipality, or guild. Rank and status, compulsion of law and threat of punishment, public praise and private reputation, insure that the individual contributes his share to production. Fear of privation or love of profit need not be altogether absent. Markets occur in all kinds of societies, and the figure of the merchant is familiar to many types of civilization. But isolated markets do not link up into an economy. The motive of gain was specific to merchants, as was valor to the knight, piety to the priest, and pride to the craftsman. The notion of making the motive of gain universal never entered the heads of our ancestors. At no time prior to the second quarter of the 19th century were markets more than a subordinate feature in society.

Third, there was the startling abruptness of the change. A free market for labor was born in England only about a century ago. The ill-famed Poor Law Reform (1834) abolished the rough-and-ready provisions made for the paupers by patriarchal governments. The poorhouse was transformed from a refuge of the destitute into an abode of shame and mental torture to which even hunger and misery were preferable. Starvation or work was the alternative left to the poor. Thus was a competitive national market for labor created. Within a decade, the Bank Act (1844) established the principle of the gold standard; the making of money was removed from the hands of the government regardless of the effect upon the level of employment. Simultaneously, reform of land law mobilized the land, and repeal of the Corn Laws (1846) created a world pool of grain, thereby making the unprotected Continental peasant-farmer subject to the whims of the market. Thus were established the three tenets of economic liberalism, the principle of which market economy was organized: that labor should find its price on the market; that money should be supplied by a self-adjusting mechanism; that commodities should be free to flow from country to country irrespective of the consequences—in brief, a labor market, the gold standard, and free trade. A self-inflammatory process was induced, as a result of which the formerly harmless market pattern expanded into a sociological enormity.

These facts roughly outline the genealogy of an "economic" society. Under such conditions the human world must appear as determined by "economic" motives.

Under capitalism, every individual has to earn an income. If he is a worker, he has to sell his labor at current prices; if he is an owner, he has to make as high a profit as he can, for his standing with his fellows will depend upon the level of his income. Hunger and gain—even if vicariously—make them plow and sow, spin and weave, mine coal, and pilot planes. Consequently, members of such a society will *think of themselves* as governed by these twin motives. In actual fact, man was never as selfish as the theory demanded. Though the market mechanism brought his dependence upon material goods to the fore, "economic" motives never formed with him the sole incentive to work. In vain was he exhorted by economists and utilitarian moralists alike to discount in business all other motives than "material" ones. On closer investigation, he was still found to be acting on remarkably "mixed" motives, not excluding those of duty toward himself and others—and maybe, secretly, even enjoying work for its own sake.

However, we are not here concerned with actual, but with assumed motives, not with the psychology, but with the *ideology* of business. *Not on the former, but on the latter, are views of man's nature based.* For once society expects a definite behavior on the part of its members, and prevailing institutions become roughly capable of enforcing that behavior, opinions on human nature will tend to mirror the ideal whether it resembles actuality or not. Accordingly, hunger and gain were defined as economic motives, and man was supposed to be acting on them in everyday life, while his other motives appeared more ethereal and removed from humdrum existence. Honor and pride, civic obligation and moral duty, even self-respect and common decency, were now deemed irrelevant to production, and were significantly summed up in the word "ideal." Hence man was believed to consist of two components, one more akin to hunger and gain, the other to honor and power. The one was "material," the other "ideal"; the one "economic," the other "noneconomic"; the one "rational," the other "nonrational." The Utilitarians went so far as to identify the two sets of terms, thus endowing the economic side of man's character with the aura of rationality. He who would have refused to imagine that he was acting for gain alone was thus considered *not only immoral, but also mad.*

The market mechanism, moreover, created the delusion of economic determinism as a general law for all human society. Under a market-economy, of course, this law holds good. Indeed, the working of the economic system here not only "influences" the rest of society, but determines it—as in a triangle the sides not merely influence, but determine, the angles. In Maine's famous phrase, "contractus" replaced "status"; or, as Tönnies preferred to put it, "society" superseded "community"; or, in terms of the present article, *instead of the economic system being embedded in social relationships, these relationships were now embedded in the economic system.*

While social classes were directly, other institutions were indirectly determined by the market mechanism. State and government, marriage and the rearing of children, the organization of science and education, of religion and the arts, the choice of profession, the forms of habitation, the shape of settlements, the very aesthetics of private life—everything had to comply with the utilitarian pattern, or at least not interfere with the working of the market mechanism. But since very few human activities can be carried on in the void; even a saint needing his pillar, the indirect effect of the market system came very near to determining the whole of society. It was almost impossible to avoid the erroneous conclusion that as "economic" man was "real" man, so the economic system was "really" society.

Yet it would be truer to say that the basic human institutions abhor unmixed motives. Just as the provisioning of the individual and his family does not commonly rely on the motive of hunger, so the institution of the family is not based on the sexual motive. Sex, like hunger, is one of the most powerful of incentives when released from the control of other incentives. That is probably why the family in all its variety of forms is never allowed to center on the sexual instinct, with its intermittencies and vagaries, but on the combination of a number of effective motives that prevent sex from destroying an institution on which so much of man's happiness depends. Sex in itself will never produce anything better than a brothel, and even then it might have to draw on some incentives of the market mechanism. An economic system actually relying for its mainspring on hunger would be almost as perverse as a family system based on the bare urge of sex.

To attempt to apply economic determinism to all human societies is little short of fantastic. Nothing is more obvious to the student of social anthropology than the variety of institutions found to be compatible with practically identical instruments of production. Only since the market was permitted to grind the human fabric into the featureless uniformity of selenic erosion has man's institutional creativeness been in abeyance.

No protest of mine, I realize, will save me from being taken for an "idealist." For he who decries the importance of "material" motives must, it seems, be relying on the strength of "ideal" ones. Yet no worse misunderstanding is possible. Hunger and gain have nothing specifically "material" about them. Pride, honor, and power, on the other hand, are not necessarily "higher" motives than hunger and gain. Our animal dependence upon food has been bared and the naked fear of starvation permitted to run loose. Our humiliating enslavement to the "material," which all human culture is designed to mitigate, was deliberately made more rigorous. This is at the root of the "sickness of an acquisitive society" that Tawney warned of. And Robert Owen's genius was at its best when, a century before, he described the profit motive as "a principle entirely unfavorable to individual and public happiness."

I plead for the *restoration of that unity of motives* which should inform man in his everyday activity as a producer, for the reabsorption of the economic system in society, for the creative adaptation of our ways of life to an industrial environment.

On all these counts, laissez faire philosophy, with its corollary of a marketing society, falls to the ground. It is responsible for the splitting up of man's vital unity into "real" man, bent on material values, and his "ideal" better self. It is paralyzing our social imagination by more or less unconsciously fostering the prejudice of economic determinism. It has done its service in that phase of industrial civilization which is behind us. At the price of impoverishing the individual, it enriched society. Today, we are faced with the vital task of *restoring the fullness of life to the person, even though this may mean a technologically less efficient society.* In different countries in different ways, classical [laissez faire] liberalism is being discarded. On Right and Left and Middle, new avenues are being explored. British Social-Democrats, American New Dealers, and also European fascists and American anti-New Dealers of the various "managerialist" brands, reject the liberal [laissez faire] utopia. Nor should the present political mood of rejection of everything Russian blind us to the achievement the Russians in creative adjustment to some of the fundamental aspects of an industrial environment.

On general grounds, the Communist's expectation of the "withering away of the state" seems to me to combine elements of liberal utopianism with practical indifference to institutional freedoms. As regards the withering state, it is impossible to deny that industrial society is complex society, and no complex society can exist without organized power at the center. Yet, again, this fact is no excuse for the Communist's slurring over the question of concrete institutional freedoms. It is on this level of realism that the problem of individual freedom should be met. *No human society is possible in which power and compulsion are absent, nor is a world in which force has no function.* [Laissez faire] philosophy gave a false direction to our ideals in seeming to promise the fulfillment of such intrinsically utopian expectations.

The breakdown of market-economy imperils two kinds of freedom: some good, some bad.

That the freedom to exploit one's fellows, or the freedom to make inordinate gains without commensurable service to the community, the freedom to keep technological inventions from being used for the public benefit, or the freedom to profit from public calamities secretly engineered for private advantage, may disappear, together with the free market, is all to the good. But the market economy under which these freedoms throve also produced freedoms that we prize highly. Freedom of conscience, freedom of speech, freedom of meeting, freedom of association, freedom to choose one's job—we cherish them for their own sake. Yet to a large extent they were *by-products* of the same economy that was also responsible for the evil freedoms.

The existence of a separate economic sphere in society created, as it were, a gap between politics and economics, between government and industry, that was in the nature of a no man's land. As division of sovereignty between pope and emperor left medieval princes in a condition of freedom sometimes bordering on anarchy, so division of sovereignty between government and industry in the 19th century allowed even the poor man to enjoy freedoms that partly compensated for his wretched status. Current skepticism in regard to the future of freedom largely rests on this. There are those who argue, like Hayek, that since free institutions were a product of market-economy, they must give place to serfdom once that economy disappears. There are others, like Burnham, who assert the inevitability of some new form of serfdom called "managerialism."

Arguments like these merely prove to what extent economistic prejudice is still rampant. For such determinism, as we have seen, is only another name for the market mechanism. It is hardly logical to argue the effects of its absence on the strength of an economic necessity that derives from its presence. And it is certainly contrary to Anglo-Saxon experience. Neither the freezing of labor nor selective service abrogated the essential freedoms of the American people, as anybody can witness who spent the crucial years 1940 to 1943 in these States. Great Britain during the war introduced an all-round planned economy and did away with that separation of government and industry from which 19th-century freedom sprang, yet never were public liberties more securely entrenched than at the height of the emergency. In truth, we will have just as much freedom as we will desire to create and to safeguard. There is no *one* determinant in human society. Institutional guarantees of personal freedom are compatible with any economic system. In market society alone did the economic mechanism lay down the law.

What appears to our generation as the problem of capitalism is, in reality, the far greater problem of an industrial civilization. The economic [libertarian] is blind to this fact. In defending capitalism as an economic system, he ignores the challenge of the Machine Age. Yet the dangers that make the bravest quake today transcend economy. The idyllic concerns of trust-busting and Taylorization have been superseded by Hiroshima. Scientific barbarism is dogging our footsteps. The Germans were planning a contrivance to make the sun emanate death rays. We, in fact, produced a burst of death rays that blotted out the sun. Yet the Germans had an evil philosophy, and we had a humane philosophy. In this we should learn to see the symbol of our peril.

Among those in America who are aware of the dimensions of the problem, two tendencies are discernible: some believe in elites and aristocracies, in managerialism and the corporation. They feel that the whole of society should be more intimately adjusted to the economic system, which they would wish to maintain unchanged. This is the ideal of the Brave New World, where the individual is conditioned to support an order that has been designed for him by such as are wiser than he. Others, on the contrary, believe that in a truly democratic society, the problem of industry would resolve itself through the planned intervention of the producers and consumers themselves. Such conscious and responsible action is, indeed, one of the embodiments of freedom in a complex society. But, as the contents of this article suggest, such an endeavor cannot be successful unless it is disciplined by a total view of man and society very different from that which we inherited from market economy.

The Irrational System

PAUL BARAN AND PAUL SWEEZY

A radical view of the failure of capitalism, not only from an economic,
but from a moral point of view.

The paycheck is the key to whatever gratifications are allowed to
working people in this society; such self-respect, status, and recognition
by one's fellows as can be achieved depend primarily on the possession
of material objects. The worker's house, the model of his automobile, his
wife's clothes—all assume major significance as indexes of success or failure. And yet within the existing social framework these objects of consumption increasingly lose their capacity to satisfy. Forces similar to those
which destroy the worker's identification with his work lead to the erosion
of his self-identification as a consumer. With goods being sought for their
status bearing qualities, the drive to substitute the newer and more expensive for the older and cheaper ceases to be related to the serviceability
of the goods and becomes a means of climbing up a rung on the social
ladder.

In this way consumption becomes a sort of extension and continuation of the process of earning a livelihood. Just as the worker is always
under pressure to get ahead at the expense of his fellows at the shop or
office, so the consumer pursues the same goals at the expense of his neighbors after work. Neither worker nor consumer is ever really satisfied;
they are always on the lookout for a new job, always wanting to move
to a better neighborhood. Work and consumption thus share the same
ambiguity: while fulfilling the basic needs of survival, they increasingly
lose their inner content and meaning.

From "The Irrational System," by Paul Baran and Paul Sweezy, in *Monopoly Capital*,
Monthly Review Press, 1968, pp. 345–49, 351–53, 362–67. Reprinted by permission of
Monthly Review Press. Copyright © 1966 by Paul M. Sweezy.

Nor are matters any better when it comes to another aspect of the worker's nonwork life—the expenditure of leisure time. Leisure has traditionally been thought of as serving the purpose of "recreation," that is to say the revival and refocusing of mental and psychic energies from their compulsory commitment to work to genuinely interesting pursuits. Now, however, the function of leisure undergoes a change. As Erich Fromm has observed, leisure becomes a synonym of time spent in passivity, of idleness. It no longer signifies doing what a person *wants* to do, as distinct from doing, at work, what he *must* do; to an ever-increasing extent it means simply doing nothing. And the reason for doing nothing is partly that there is so little that is humanly interesting to do, but perhaps even more because the emptiness and purposelessness of life in capitalist society stifles the desire to do anything.

This propensity to do nothing has had a decisive part in determining the kinds of entertainment which are supplied to fill the leisure hours— in the evenings, on weekends and holidays, during vacations. The basic principle is that whatever is presented—reading matter, movies, radio and TV programs—must not make undue demands on the intellectual and emotional resources of the recipients; the purpose is to provide "fun," "relaxation," a "good time"—in short, passively absorbable amusement. Even the form and organization of the material is affected. The show is continuous, the movie theater can be entered at any time; the book can be read from front to back or from back to front; skipping a few installments of a serial does not matter; the TV can be switched from channel to channel without loss of coherence or comprehension.

Other forms of "killing time"—what a revealing expression!—are hardly more exacting. Being a sports fan does not involve participation in any activity or acquiring any skill. Events are provided for all seasons, and it is not even necessary to attend in person since giant corporations find it a profitable form of advertising to sponsor radio and TV broadcasts of games and matches. Elaborate statistical records are compiled and regularly published in specialized books and periodicals, enabling even fans who have never played a game in their lives to discuss the various teams and players with all the assurance of experts. Being interested at different times of the year in the sports appropriate to the season turns into something people have in common. Like the largely imaginary good and bad points of different makes and models of automobiles, the strengths and weaknesses of teams and players become topics of conversation which the inherent triviality of the theme transforms into mere chatter.

Perhaps nothing is more symptomatic of the part played by leisure in daily life than this degeneration of conversation into chatter. Like friendship, conversation presupposes the existence of some common purposes, interests, and activities. Friendship implies an emotional commit-

ment; conversation demands an intellectual effort. When these precon-
ditions do not exist—when people exist together but do not relate to one
another in any fundamental way—both friendship and conversation are
bound to atrophy. When people have nothing to say, "small talk" becomes
the order of the day. As the word friend fades and comes to designate
someone whom one happens to have met, it applies to a multitude of
acquaintances and to no one in particular. Social gatherings are motivated
less by a desire to be with other people than by fear of being alone. People's unrelatedness at these gatherings is often and characteristically dissolved in alcohol.

The satisfaction derived from this kind of conviviality is fleeting;
the hangover is inevitable. Although suffocating in his solitude, the individual does not overcome it, as David Riesman has observed, by becoming
a particle in a crowd. The misery of loneliness and the horror of together-
ness produce an attitude of ambivalence between involvement and withdrawal. Leaving one party with the thought that he might as well have
stayed at home, he goes to another thinking that he might as well be there.
Thus he is drawn into an uninterrupted whirl of socializing—on different
levels and scales of course, depending on class, status, and income—or
concluding, as Arthur Miller has put it, that if one has to be alone one
may as well stay by oneself, he turns into a recluse, spending hours on
end "working around the house," mowing the lawn, pottering in the back-
yard. Brooding and muttering to himself, he turns on the radio, listens to
a scrap of news or a singing commercial, switches over to the TV to see
the end of a Western, leaves both and looks absent-mindedly at the newspaper filled with accounts of crime and scandal—in short, shifts restlessly
from one way of doing nothing to another way of doing nothing, all the
while longing for and dreading the beginning of the work week when he
will start longing for and dreading the coming of the weekend.

In these conditions the sensation produced by leisure is closely related to that experienced at work—grinding, debilitating boredom. Only
it must be added that the boredom lived through in the hours and days
of free time can be even more oppressive than that endured during the
work week. In the case of work it appears to be natural, an aspect of
the grim necessity to earn one's bread in the sweat of one's brow. All of
human history has taught people to take it for granted that physical suffering and psychic distress are the price of survival. And as long as scarcity
dominated the human condition, this calculus, cruel as it undoubtedly
was in the light of the idleness and luxury enjoyed by the privileged few,
appeared cogent and convincing to the have-nots. For them every shortening of the work day, every reduction in the work week were precious
steps in the direction of freedom.

Today we must ask what remains of that cogency, of that progress toward freedom when the torture of work buys a longer span of nonwork which is itself robbed of all joy, which turns into an extension of work itself, into the emptiness, tedium, and torpor of modern leisure? What rationality is left in bearing the self-denial, the repression, the compulsion of work when what follows at the end of the working day and the working week is the barren desert of boredom that is free time in this society?

Repression has always marked the exploitation of man by man. Curbing the striving for freedom, subduing the aversion to toil and self-denial, destroying the sense of compassion and solidarity with fellow men, repression has forced man into molds making him fit to exploit and be exploited. As Freud put it, "it is impossible to ignore the extent to which civilization is built up on renunciation of instinctual gratifications, the degree to which the existence of civilization presupposes the non-gratification (suppression, repression, or something else?) of powerful instinctual urgencies."

For many centuries the forces of repression derived much of their formidable power from two sources which remained relatively invariant. One was the state of constricting scarcity which was—in the conditions of the time, rightly—considered to be an inescapable fact of nature. The incidence of burdens imposed by that scarcity was of course open to question and criticism: the injustices associated with it gave rise to almost continuous popular protest; convincing arguments could be and were advanced to show that in a different social order the dire effects of scarcity could be mitigated. But the existence of scarcity could not be denied. And the recognition of its existence necessarily implied the recognition of the inevitability of life-long labor and bare subsistence standards of living for the vast majority of mankind.

The other source of fuel for the engine of repression is closely related to the first: the people's unquestioning belief in the basic principles underlying the taboos and prohibitions, the rules and regulations governing the behavior of men in society. These principles, elaborated by society's cultural and religious apparatus, transmitted from one generation to the next, internalized and appearing as an immutable aspect of "human nature," coagulated into a conscience, a superego, ever watchful and sternly punishing violators of its precepts with bitter feelings of guilt. Society thus acquired what might be called a psychic police force effectively upholding spiritual "law and order."

What distinguishes our time from all earlier epochs is that by now in the advanced capitalist countries the mechanism of repression has accomplished its historical mission. The work discipline and self-denial which it imposed made possible the massive accumulation of capital and with it the building up of an enormously productive industrial apparatus. The development of automation and cybernation in the last two decades signals the end of the long, long era in which the inevitability of scarcity constituted the central fact of human existence. There can be no doubt that the continued acceptance of that inevitability under conditions such as prevail in the United States today is false consciousness par excellence. It now serves only to maintain and support an oppressive social order, and its sway over the minds of people reflects nothing but the anachronistic prevalence of an outlived ideology.

This state of affairs cannot be changed by wishing or incantation. Declarations that what the United States needs is a "spiritual revival" or a clarification of "national goals" are as symptomatic of the pathological condition they are directed against as of a profound inability to comprehend its nature and origins. When a writer as sensitive and observant as Paul Goodman truthfully states that "our society cannot have it both ways: to maintain a conformist and ignoble system *and* to have skilled and spirited men to man the system with," only to conclude that "if 10,000 people in all walks of life will stand up on their two feet and talk out and insist, we shall get our country back," one gets the full measure of the failure of even our best social critics to face up to the real character and dimensions of the crisis of our time.

For behind the emptiness, the degradation, and the suffering which poison human existence in this society lies the profound irrationality and moral bankruptcy of monopoly capitalism itself. No outraged protests, no reforms within the monopoly capitalist framework can arrest the decay of the whole. And as becomes clearer every day, this decay makes increasingly problematical the rationality of even the most spectacular advances in scientific knowledge and technical and organizational skills. Improvements in the means of mass communication merely hasten the degeneration of popular culture. The utmost perfection in the manufacture of weapons of destruction does not make their production rational. The irrationality of the end negates all improvements of the means. Rationality itself becomes irrational. We have reached a point where the only true rationality lies in action to overthrow what has become a hopelessly irrational system.

Will such action be forthcoming in sufficient volume and intensity to accomplish its purpose? The future of the United States and of monopoly capitalism obviously depends on the answer. So also, though more indirectly, does the future of mankind itself for a long time to come.

The answer of traditional Marxian orthodoxy—that the industrial proletariat must eventually rise in revolution against its capitalist oppressors—no longer carries conviction. Industrial workers are a diminishing minority of the American working class, and their organized cores in the basic industries have to a large extent been integrated into the system as consumers and ideologically conditioned members of the society. They are not, as the industrial workers were in Marx's day, the system's special victims, though they suffer from its elementality and irrationality along with all other classes and strata—more than some, less than others.

The system of course has its special victims. They are the unemployed and the unemployable, the migrant farm workers, the inhabitants of the big city ghettos, the school dropouts, the aged subsisting on meager pensions—in a word, the outsiders, those who because of their limited command over purchasing power are unable to avail themselves of the gratifications, such as they are, of consumption. But these groups, despite their impressive numbers, are too heterogeneous, too scattered and fragmented, to constitute a coherent force in society. And the oligarchy knows how, through doles and handouts, to keep them divided and to prevent their becoming a lumpen-proletariat of desperate starvelings.

If we confine attention to the inner dynamics of advanced monopoly capitalism, it is hard to avoid the conclusion that the prospect of effective revolutionary action to overthrow the system is slim. Viewed from this angle, the more likely course of development would seem to be a continuation of the present process of decay, with the contradiction between the compulsions of the system and the elementary needs of human nature becoming ever more insupportable. The logical outcome would be the spread of increasingly severe psychic disorders leading to the impairment and eventual breakdown of the system's ability to function even on its own terms.

But as we emphasized, advanced monopoly capitalism does not exist in isolation, and any speculation about its future which takes account only of its inner laws and tendencies is certain to be misleading. The United States dominates and exploits to one extent or another all the countries and territories of the so-called free world and correspondingly meets with varying degrees of resistance. The highest form of resistance is revolutionary war aimed at withdrawal from the world capitalist system and the initiation of social and economic reconstruction on a socialist basis. Such warfare has never been absent since the Second World War, and the revolutionary peoples have achieved a series of historic victories in Vietnam, China, Korea, Cuba, and Algeria. These victories, taken together with the increasingly obvious inability of the underdeveloped countries to solve their problems within the framework of the world capitalist system, have sown the seeds of revolution throughout the continents of Asia, Africa, and Latin America. Some of these seeds will sprout and ripen rapidly, others slowly, still others perhaps not until after a long period of germination. What seems in any case clear is that they are now implanted beyond any prospect of exterpation. It is no longer mere rhetoric to speak of the world revolution: the term describes what is already a reality and is certain to become increasingly the dominant characteristic of the historical epoch in which we live.

The implications of this fact for the future of monopoly capitalism are only beginning to become apparent. The ruling class of the United States understands, instinctively and through experience, that every advance of the world revolution is a defeat—economic, political, and moral—for itself. It is determined to resist such advances wherever they may threaten, by whatever means may be available; and it counts on its enormous superiority in the technology of warfare to bring it victory. But the truth is that in this struggle there can be no real victories for the counter-revolutionary side. Underlying the revolutionary upsurge are real economic, social, and demographic problems; and is the very nature of counter-revolution to prevent these problems from being rationally attacked, let alone solved. Counter-revolution may win, indeed already has won, many battles, but the war goes on and inexorably spreads to new peoples and new regions. And as it spreads so does the involvement of the United States.

No one can now foresee all the consequences for the United States of this increasing commitment to the cause of world counter-revolution, but equally no one can doubt that it will profoundly affect the inner as well as the outer course of events. In the long run its main impact may well be on the youth of the nation. The need for military manpower seems certain to rise sharply; it may soon be normal for young Americans to spend several years of their lives, if they are lucky enough to survive, fighting in the jungles and mountains of Asia, Africa, and Latin America. The psychic stress and physical suffering experienced by them and their families will add a new dimension to the agony inflicted by an anti-human social order. Will the effect be merely to hasten the process of decay already so far advanced? Will the shock perhaps awaken more and more people to the urgent need for basic change? Or will, as some believe, the increasingly evident hopelessness of its cause lead the American ruling class to the ultimate irrationality of unleashing nuclear holocaust?

That no one can now answer these questions means that all the options are not foreclosed, that action aimed at altering the course of events has a chance to succeed. There are even indications, especially in the Negro freedom movement in the South, in the uprisings of the urban ghettos, and in the academic community's mounting protest against the war in Vietnam, that significant segments of the American people are ready to join an active struggle against what is being cumulatively revealed as an intolerable social order. If this is so, who can set limits to the numbers who may join them in the future?

But even if the present protest movements should suffer defeat or prove abortive, that would be no reason to write off permanently the possibilty of a real revolutionary movement in the United States. As the world revolution spreads and as the socialist countries show by their example that it is possible to use man's mastery over the forces of nature to build a rational society satisfying the human needs of human beings, more and more Americans are bound to question the necessity of what they now take for granted. And once that happens on a mass scale, the most powerful supports of the present irrational system will crumble and the problem of creating anew will impose itself as a sheer necessity. This will not happen in five years or ten, perhaps not in the present century: few great historical dramas run their course in so short a time. But perhaps even fewer, once they are fairly started, change their nature or reverse their direction until all their potentialities have been revealed. The drama of our time is the world revolution; it can never come to an end until it has encompassed the whole world.

In the meantime, what we in the United States need is historical perspective, courage to face the facts, and faith in mankind and its future. Having these, we can recognize our moral obligation to devote ourselves to fighting against an evil and destructive system which maims, oppresses, and dishonors those who live under it, and which threatens devastation and death to millions of others around the globe.

The Limits of American Capitalism

ROBERT L. HEILBRONER

Is capitalism static or dynamic; changeless or in flux? Here is a view
that asserts that a deep-seated "revolution" is in process in our very
midst.

The definition of "capitalism" seemed of primary importance in
establishing the boundaries of change, and for this reason the slow left-
ward movement of the business ideology assumed a putative central role
in enlarging the perimeter of social action.

Assuming that the ideology of business would continue along its
gradual path of liberalization, how far did this mean that capitalism could
change? What limits, we asked, were inherent in the system, rather than
in any particularly ideology of the day?

The answer at which we have arrived is necessarily imprecise, but
it does not seem entirely indeterminate. In the dynamic process of social
change, the economic relationships that give rise to privilege are those
that fix the degree of social resistance, and these relationships give us a
general indication of what is possible and what is not.

It is not difficult to recapitulate this difference. What seems possible
is to bring about social change—in the distribution of wealth or in the
control over output or in the imaginative destination of society or its
relations with the noncapitalist world—that stops short of an intolerable
curtailment of those privileges that all elites within American capitalism—
and indeed, the general public as well—are eager to protect. What is impossible, within the time period in which we are interested, is to effect
changes that would involve the virtual destruction of the central institutions of the system itself. This means, for example, that the distribution

of wealth can be corrected at the bottom but not at the top. It means that the control over output can be improved very greatly, but that the essential commercial character of a market system is beyond alteration. It means that a considerable accommodation can be made with the noncapitalist world, but that the imagination of that world (or of the American mind) is not likely to be captured by the capitalist rhetoric. There are, in a word, deep-seated attributes to the quality of American life that constitute an impregnable inner keep of the system of American capitalism as we know it.

And yet, if we now recall our earlier concern with feudalism, we will recall that, despite the seeming impregnability of its institutions in the 13th century, by the 18th century somehow the system had nonetheless changed out of all recognition. Hence we must ask whether the inner keep of capitalism, although out of range of bombardment today, may not also be ultimately vulnerable to the kind of penetration that finally invested the feudal citadels of privilege.

The question asks us to reflect on how feudalism expired. The answer is not by revolution. However important for other reasons, the revolutions of the 18th and 19th centuries merely ripped off the tattered covers of feudalism to reveal new economic societies, already full-formed and operative, beneath them. Rather, feudalism gave way to capitalism as part of a subversive process of historic change in which a newly emerging attribute of daily life proved to be as irresistibly attractive to the privileged orders of feudalism as it was ultimately destructive of them.

This subversive influence was the gradual infiltration of commercial relationships and cash exchanges into the everyday round of feudal existence, each act of marketing binding men more fully into the cash nexus and weakening by that degree the traditional duties and relationships on which feudalism was based. Against this progressive monetization the old order struggled in vain, for the temptations and pleasures of the cash economy were greater than the erosion of privileges that went with it: "It is the costliness of clothes that is destroying the nobles of our German lands," wrote one chronicler, telling of a widow who sold a village to raise the price of a blue velvet gown to wear to a tournament.

Could there be an equivalent of that powerfully disintegrative and yet constitutive force in our day—a force sufficiently overwhelming to render impotent the citadel of capitalism and yet as irresistibly attractive to its masters as the earlier current of change was to feudalism? I think there is such a force, and that it already bulks very large within our world, where it is cumulatively and irreversibly altering the social system even more rapidly than did the process of monetization during the medieval era. This revolutionary power is the veritable explosion of organized knowledge and its applied counterpart, scientific technology, in modern times.

The extraordinary rate of expansion of this explosion is sufficiently familiar to require only a word of exposition. There is, for instance, the often-quoted but still astonishing statement that of all the scientists who have ever lived in all of history, half are alive today. There is the equally startling calculation that the volume of scientific publication during the past ten to fifteen years is as large as or larger than that of all previous ages. Such examples are no doubt more impressionistic than exact, but they serve accurately enough to convey the notion of the exponential growth of scientific inquiry in our day. As to the equally phenomenal growth of the powers of the technology, if that needs any demonstration, there is the contrast cited by Kenneth Boulding between the decades needed to reconstruct Germany after the Thirty Years' War or the centuries needed to recuperate from the physical destruction that accompanied the collapse of the Roman Empire and the scant 20 years in which the shattered and burned cities of modern Europe and Japan were rebuilt after the Second World War.

This explosion of science and scientifically based technology is often thought of as a product *of* capitalism, insofar as it arose within a capitalist milieu and in an age dominated by capitalism. Yet the association was far more one of coexistence than of causal interrelation. Science, as we know it, began well before capitalism existed and did not experience its full growth until well after capitalism was solidly entrenched. At best we can say that the secular air of bourgeois culture was compatible with, perhaps even conducive to, scientific investigation, but we can hardly credit the acceleration of scientific activities after the middle of the 19th century—the work of Darwin, Maxwell, Rutherford, Freud, Mendel, not to mention the great contemporary mathematicians—to the direct stimulus or patronage of capitalism itself.

Perhaps more surprising, even scientific technology exhibits but little debt to the existence of capitalism. The technology on which capitalism began its long course of growth in the 18th and early 19th centuries was mainly of a pragmatic, intuitive, prescientific kind. The Second Law of Thermodynamics was not formulated by Kelvin until 1851, and its immense practical significance was only slowly realized thereafter. The English textile, iron and steel, or chemical industries were founded and prospered with no "scientific" underpinnings at all. The same is true for the young railroad industry, for canal building, or road laying. Even as late as the mid-19th century, a proposal by the famous Siemens brothers of Berlin that cable be scientifically tested before being laid was dismissed by British engineers as "humbug."

There was, of course, a certain amount of systematic industrial experimentation in the mid-1800s, and a burst of important inventions, many of which depended on some application of scientific knowledge, in the second half of the century. Yet the deliberate employment of scientific investigation to create or refine the technology of production was considerably delayed in arriving. In this country the first private industrial laboratory was not built until 1900 by the General Electric Company, and organized research and development on a large scale did not really get under way until 1913.

Thus we find the flowering of science and the application of science to technology—the very hallmarks of the modern era—to be currents that arose *within* capitalism, but that do not owe their existence directly to capitalism. Rather, like the first manifestations of the market in the medieval era, science and its technology emerge as a great underground river whose tortuous course has finally reached the surface during the age of capitalism, but which springs from far distant sources. But that is not where the resemblance ends. As with the emergent market forces, the river of scientific change, having now surfaced, must cut its own channel through the existing social landscape—a channel that will, as in the case with the money orientation in medieval life, profoundly alter the nature of the existing terrain. Indeed, if we ask what force in our day might in time be strong enough to undercut the bastions of privilege and function of capitalism and to create its own institutions and social structures in their place, the answer must surely be the one force that dominates our age—the power of science and of scientific technology.

There is, I suspect, little to argue about as to the commanding presence of science in modern times. What is likely to be a good deal less readily accepted, however, is the contention that this force will cause drastic modifications in, or even the eventual supersession of, capitalism. For at first glance the new current of history seems to have imparted an immense momentum to capitalism by providing it with the very thing it most required—a virtually inexhaustible source of invention and innovation to ensure its economic growth. Merely to review in our minds the broad areas of investment and economic output that owe their existence entirely to the laboratory work of the past three decades—the nuclear and space establishments, electronics, the computerization of industry, the wonder drugs, the creation of new materials such as plastics—is to reveal the breadth of this new gulf stream of economic nourishment.

Yet, like the attractions of the cash market for the feudal lord, the near-term advantages of science and technology conceal long-term conflicts and incompatibilities between this new force of history and its host society. Just as the insertion of cash exchanges into the fine structure of feudalism ultimately made obsolete the functional mechanism of a manorial society, so the insinuation of science and technology into the interstices of business enterprise promises to outmode the fundamental working arrangements of capitalism.

At least one of these disruptive manifestations is already familiar to us. This is the tendency of technology to create social problems that require *nonmarket controls* to correct or forestall. In part these agencies of control are contained and concealed within the centers of production themselves, where they show up as the rising echelons of corporate administration and supervision that are needed to regulate the underlying traffic of production. In part the controls show up in the familiar bureaus of government that directly oversee the operation of the new technology—the bureaus that cope, with greater or lesser success, with the social repercussions of transportation, nuclear energy, drugs, air pollution, etc. In still a different aspect, the controls invade areas of social life rather than production, as in the astonishing network of government required solely to manage the automobile (an effort that requires the labor of one out of every ten persons employed by all state and local governments) or in the multiplying administrative requirements of the mega-city, itself so much a product of modern technology. Meanwhile, in the background of the social system the controls are manifest as the growing apparatus of regulation over wages and prices, and over the total flow of economic activity all ultimately traceable to the need to intervene more closely into an economy of increasing technological complexity.

Not that the disruptive effect of technology is itself a new phenomenon. The dislocations of the technology of the prescientific age—say the spinning jenny—were quite as great as those of the modern age, such as the computer. The difference is that in an earlier age the repair of technological disturbances was largely consigned to the adaptive powers of the individual, to the ameliorative efforts of small-scale local government, and to the annealing powers of the market itself. Today, however, these traditional agencies of social recovery can no longer cope effectively with the entrance of technology. The individual, now typically a member of a small urban family rather than of a large extended rural family, is much less capable of withstanding economic displacement without external assistance. The local community, faced with large-scale problems of unemployment or ecological maladjustment brought about by technical change, has no recourse but to turn to the financial help and expertise available only from larger government units. The market, which no longer "clears" when the marketers are enormous firms rather than atomistic business units, also discovers that the only antidote to grave economic disjunction is the countervailing influence or *force majeur* of central governing authority. In a word, technology in the modern era seems to be exerting a steady push from many levels and areas of the economy in the direction of a society of *organization*.

This well-known effect of technical progress is, however, only the most obvious, and perhaps not the most fundamental, way in which the scientific current works against the enveloping economic order. A deeper cutting edge of technology lies in another attribute of its impact on society—its capacity to render redundant the physical energies of man, at least as these energies are mainly harnessed in a market setting. That is, machines do man's work for him, thereby freeing him from the bonds of toil and, not less important in the context of our inquiry, from the hegemony of the market process.

We can see this disemployment effect most dramatically in the case of agriculture. A century ago farming, as the basic activity of society, absorbed the working energies of 60 to 70 percent of the population. Today, although no less essential to the provisioning of the human community, agriculture requires only the effort of some 8 percent of the population (working only two-thirds as long as its forebears in the 1860s) and even this small fraction will probably be further reduced to about 4 to 5 percent within a decade.

But equally startling is the labor-displacing effect of modern technology in that congeries of activities associated with the extraction of basic materials from nature and their fabrication, assembly, conversion, or transport to point of sale. If we look back to 1900 we find that about 38 of every 100 working Americans were then employed in mining, manufacturing, the generation of power, transport, or construction. Since then science and technology have given us a stupendous array of new products, each requiring large amounts of human effort—the automobile and truck, the whole range of consumer durables, the communications industry, office machinery, new metals, fabrics, and materials of all kinds to name but a few. Yet at the end of that period the total requirements for labor in all the goods-centered industries had risen by only *two percentage points*, to 40 out of every 100 workers. As fast as demand grew for these myriad products, that fast did technology and science permit labor to be economized. During the era of the greatest increase in factory production ever known, virtually no increase in labor was needed—indeed, since the hours of work fell, there was actually a relatively *decreased* need for human effort in the output of goods.

The point is important enough to warrant another word of exposition. What technology has done over a 50-year span is to enable relatively fewer workers in the "goods sector" to supply the needs of a richer population. As the table below shows, this is due to a deep penetration of technology into mining, construction, transportation, and utilities. In manufacturing proper there was a 12 percent increase in labor needs in terms of relative *numbers* of men, although in terms of *hours*, there was a reduction of labor requirements here, too. By way of contrast, there has been an increase in the proportion of workers required to provide services —retail and wholesale trade, finance, government, domestic service, etc.

This secular shift takes on new significance in the light of the technology of automation. We do not yet know whether the new devices that count, sort, remember, check, and respond to stimuli will intensify the labor displacement process in those industries where technology has already long been at work. But there is reason to believe that technology has begun to invade what has heretofore been a sanctuary of relatively unmechanized work—the vast numbers of jobs in the office, administrative, and service occupations. In 1900 less than one-fourth of the total working population was employed in these nonfarm, nonfactory kinds of work—as lawyers, teachers, government officials, stenographers, book-keepers, clerks, servants. By 1960 more than half the labor force was in these jobs. And now, into this varied group of occupations, technology is starting to penetrate in the form of machines as complex as those that can read and sort checks or as relatively simple as those that dispense coffee and sandwiches.

Table 1. Workers Per 1,000 Population, United States

	1900	1965
Mining	10	3
Manufacturing	82	92
Construction	22	16
Transportation and utilities	27	21
All "goods sector" (above)	141	132
All service sector	93	178

Source: For 1900, *Historical Statistics of the United States* Bureau of the Census, Washington, 1960, Series D 57–71; for 1965, *Economic Indicators*.

This is not to maintain that no new areas of employment exist to take the place of those occupied by machinery. Certainly there remain very large and still untapped possibilities for work in the repair and reconstruction of the cities; the provision of education, public safety, and conveyance; in the improvement of health and recreation facilities; in the counseling of the young and the care of the aged; in the beautification of the environment. Provided only that demand can be marshaled for these activities, there will surely be no dearth of job prospects for the coming generation.

But that is precisely the point. The incursion of technology has pushed the frontiers of work from the farm to the factory, then from the factory to the store and the office, and now from store and office into a spectrum of jobs whose common denominator is that they require *public action and public funds* for their initiation and support. The employment-upsetting characteristics of technology thus act to speed capitalism along the general path of planning and control down which it is simultaneously impelled by the direct environment-upsetting impact of technological change.

If we look further ahead, the necessity for planning is apt to become still more pressing. Given the trajectory of present scientific capabilities, the day of a "fully automated" society is by no means a fantasy, although its realization may well require another century, or possibly more. But in the long evolutionary perspective in which we are now interested, one can surely look to the time when all or nearly all of the paid labor of our present society outside the categories of professional or managerial work (and a good deal within those echelons) could be accomplished by machinery with but little human supervision. That is to say, we can, without too much difficulty, imagine a time when as small a proportion of the labor force as now suffices to overprovide us with food will serve to turn out the manufactured staples, the houses, the transportation, the retail services, even the governmental supervision that will be required.

What the leisured—not to use the word "unemployed"—fraction of the population will then do with itself is an interesting and important question. If it is not to starve, it must be given the chance to share in society's output. Should there exist sufficient modes of activity resistive to mechanization, this may be accomplished through the market mechanism: instead of taking in one another's wash, we will buy one another's paintings. But even in this best outcome, the underlying processes of production, now enormously mechanized and intricately interconnected, would almost certainly require some form of coordination other than the play of market forces. And then, of course, if the leisured population does not find adequate opportunities for unmechanizable employments, it will simply have to be *given* a right to share in society's output—an even more basic infringement on the hegemony of the market.

Thus, in a manner not entirely dissimilar from the way in which the steady monetization of feudal life weakened the relevance and effectiveness of manorial ties, the incorporation of technology into the working mechanism of the capitalist system also renders less relevant and effective the market ties on which that system is ultimately founded. Partly because of the social disturbances it creates in an urban industrial environment, partly because of the progressive compression of the need for human effort in the provisioning of society, the steady entrance of technology into capitalism forces new social structures of control and supervision to rise within and over the marketplace.

But the erosion of the market goes deeper yet. For the introduction of technology has one last effect whose ultimate implications for the metamorphosis of capitalism are perhaps greatest of all. This is the effect of technology in steadily raising the average level of well-being, thereby gradually bringing to an end the condition of material need as an effective stimulus for human behavior.

This is by all odds the most generally hailed attribute of science and technology, for everyone recognizes that the end to want would represent the passage over an historic watershed. But it must be equally clear that such a passage will also represent a basic revision of the existential situation that has hitherto provided the main impetus for work. As the level of average enjoyments increases, as needs diminish and wants become of such relative unimportance that they can be easily foregone, the traditional stimuli of capitalism begin to lose their force. Occupations now become valued for their intrinsic pleasures rather than for their extrinsic rewards. The very decision to work or not becomes a matter of personal preference rather than of economic necessity. More telling, the drive for profit—the nuclear core of capitalist energy—becomes blunted as the purchasable distinctions of wealth decline. In a society of the imaginable wealth implicit in another hundred years of technical progress, who will wish to be the rich man's servant at any price? In such a society the services that have always been the prerogative of the rich will have to be performed by machine or dispensed with altogether—a state of affairs already visible in many areas if we compare the life of the wealthy today with that of the past.

All this is no doubt a gain in human dignity, as the bowers and scrapers, the waiters and flunkeys—not to mention the performers of menial tasks everywhere—escape from work hitherto performed only under the lash of necessity. But that is not an end to it. As a result of this inestimable gain in personal freedom, a fundamental assurance for social viability also vanishes, for the market stimuli that bring about social provisioning are no longer met with obedient responses. One has but to imagine employees in an industry of central importance going on strike, not with the slim backing of unemployment insurance and a small union supplement, as today, but with liquid assets sufficient to maintain them, if need be, for a year or more, to envisage the potential for social disorder inherent in the attainment of a genuinely widespread and substantial affluence.

Yet it is precisely such an affluence that is within clear sight provided that the impetus of science and technology continues to propel the economy for another century. In this impasse there is but one possible solution. *Some authority other than the market must be entrusted with the allocation of men to the essential posts of society should they lack for applicants.*

We have concerned ourselves so far only with the curious two-edged effect of science and technology on the functional aspects of capitalism, both sustaining and hurrying along its growth, and by that very fact pressing it into a more organized social form. Now we must pay heed to a second and perhaps even more critical effect. This is the conquest of the capitalist imagination by science and scientific technology.

I think it is fair to say that capitalism as an *idea* has never garnered much enthusiasm. The acquisitive behavior on which it is perforce based has suffered all through history from the moral ambivalence in which it has been held; all efforts to raise money-making to the level of a positive virtue have failed. The self-interest of the butcher and the baker to whom Adam Smith appealed in lieu of their benevolence may serve as powerful sources of social energy, but not as powerful avatars of social imagination.

By way of contrast, I think it is also fair to say that science and its technical application *is* the burning idea of the 20th century, comparable in its impact on men's minds to the flush of the democratic enthusiasm of the late 18th century or to the political commitment won by communism in the early 20th. The altruism of science, its "purity," the awesome vistas it opens, and the venerable path it has followed, have won from all groups, and especially from the young, exactly that passionate interest and conviction that is so egregiously lacking to capitalism as a way of life.

And it is not only within capitalism that the charismatic powers of science reveal their extraordinary appeal. Within the citadel of economic commitment itself, inside Russia, we hear that science, and science alone, has the capacity to penetrate and to overrule the orthodoxies of Marxist philosophy. A. J. Ayer, after lecturing at the Faculty of Philosophy in Moscow University in 1962 reports: "The prestige of science is so great that it is now becoming a question of (the philosophers) having to adapt their philosophical principles to current scientific theory than the other way round."

It is not alone that science carries a near-religious ethos of conviction and even sacrifice. In Russia as well as in America the new elites arising within the framework of the old society—and as a social order focused on economics, contemporary communism is, like capitalism, an "old" society—owe their ascendancy and their allegiance in large part of science. The scientific cadres proper, the social scientists, the government administrative personnel, even the military, all look to science not merely as the vehicle of their expertise but as the magnetic north of their compass of values. These new elites, as we have indicated, have not as yet divorced their social goals from those of the society to which they are still glad to pay allegiance, and no more than the 13th-century merchants huddled under the walls of a castle do they see themselves as the potential architects and lords of a society built around their own functions. But, as with the merchants, we can expect that such notions will in time emerge and assert their primacy over the aims of the existing order.

What sorts of notions are these apt to be?

One general direction of thought will surely be the primacy of scientific discovery as a central purpose of society, a *raison d'être* for its existence, perhaps even a vehicle for its religious impulses. To partake in the adventure of the scientific mission or its technological realization should accordingly become as dominating a motivation for the future as the wish to participate in economic adventure is at present, and no doubt the distribution of social resources and of privileges will reflect this basic orientation toward scientific exploration and application.

Not less characteristic will be an emphasis on rational solutions to social problems that are today not yet subject to human direction. Not alone economic affairs (which should become of secondary importance), but the numbers and location of the population, its genetic quality, the manner of social domestication of children, the choice of life-work—even the very duration of life itself—are all apt to become subjects for scientific investigation and control. Indeed, the key word of the new society is apt to be *control*.

It is tempting but idle to venture beyond these few suggestions. What manner of life, what institutions, what ideologies may serve the purposes of a society dedicated to the accumulation of scientific knowledge and power we cannot foretell; the variations may well be as great as those observable in societies dedicated to the accumulation of material wealth. Nor does there seem to be much point in attempting to foresee by what precise strategems the elites and ideas of the future may finally assert their claims. Who, for instance, could have foreseen that the long evolution into capitalism would require not merely the diffusion of market relations but the indispensable way station of mercantilism, the "mixed economy" of the 18th century? Or who could have predicted that the nobility of England, traditionally one of the haughtiest in Europe, would learn to protect its social privileges by intermarrying with the despised mercantile families, so that English feudalism could melt imperceptibly into a capitalist aristocracy, whereas in France the nobility would widen the social distance from the bourgeoisie until, as de Tocqueville says, "the two classes were not merely rivals, they were foes"?

Such twists of the historic route warn us that historic projection is rarely, if ever, a matter of simple extrapolation from the present and recent past. Neither routes nor time-tables are laid out in history with an eye to regularity or a concern for Euclidean simplicities. Should there arise radical parties in America, broadly based and aimed at a rational reorganization of economic affairs, the pace of transition would be quicker. Should there not—the perhaps pessimistic premise on which this analysis is based, for I do not believe that such parties are a likely phenomenon if capitalism achieves the degree of change that is within its compass—change will still occur, but more slowly. Veblen was too impatient for his engineers to take over; Schumpeter more realistic when he advised the intelligentsia to be prepared to wait in the wings for possibly a century, a "short run" in affairs of this kind, he said.

So, too, the examples of the past discourage us from attempting to prophesy the manner of demise of the social order to be superseded. The new institutions of social and economic control will appear only slowly and sporadically amid the older forms, and will lack for some time an articulate conception of a purposively constituted and consciously directed social system. The old ideas of the proper primacy of economic aims will linger together with newer ideas of the priority of scientific interests. And no doubt the privileges of the older order will endure side by side with those of the new, just as titles of nobility exist to this very day, some assimilated to the realities of capitalism, some adorning doormen or taxi drivers. It is conceivable that violence may attend the displacement of power and responsibility from one elite to another, but more probably the transfer will be imperceptible; managed as in the case of the English aristocracy, by the sons of the old elite entering the professions of the new.

All these are the merest speculations, difficult to avoid entirely, not to be taken too literally. What is certain is only one thing. It is the profound incompatibility between the new idea of the active use of science within society and the idea of capitalism as a social system.

The conflict does not lie on the surface, in any clash between the immediate needs of science and those of capitalism. It lies in the ideas that ultimately inform both worlds. The world of science, as it is applied by society, is committed to the idea of man as a being who shapes his collective destiny; the world of capitalism to an idea of man as one who permits his common social destination to take care of itself. The essential idea of a society built on scientific engineering is to impose human will on the social universe; that of capitalism to allow the social universe to unfold as if it were beyond human interference.

Before the activist philosophy of science as a social instrument, this inherent social passivity of capitalism becomes archaic and eventually intolerable. The "self-regulating" economy that is its highest social achievement stands condemned by its absence of a directing intelligence, and each small step taken to correct its deficiencies only advertises the inhibitions placed on the potential exercise of purposeful thought and action by its remaining barriers of ideology and privilege. In the end capitalism is weighed in the scale of science and found wanting, not alone as a system but as a philosophy.

That an ascendant science, impatient to substitute reason for blind obedience, inquiry for ideology, represents a great step forward for mankind I do not doubt. Yet it seems necessary to end on a cautionary note. Just as the prescient medievalist might have foreseen in capitalism the possibilities for the deformation of human life as well as for its immense improvement, so the approaching world of scientific predominance has its darker as well as its more luminous side. Needless to say, there lurks a dangerous collectivist tinge in the prospect of controls designed for the enlargement of man but inherently capable of his confinement as well. But beyond that there is, in the vista of a scientific quest grimly pursued for its own sake, a chilling reminder of a world where economic gains are relentlessly pursued for their own sake. Science is a majestic driving force from which to draw social energy and inspiration, but its very impersonality, its "value-free" criteria, may make its tutelary elites as remote and unconcerned as the principles in whose name they govern.

Against these cold and depersonalizing possibilities of a scientifically organized world, humanity will have to struggle in the future, as it has had to contend against not dissimilar excesses of economic involvement in this painful—but also liberating—stage of human development. Thus if the dawn of an age of science opens larger possibilities for mankind than it has enjoyed heretofore, it does not yet promise a society whose overriding aim will be the cultivation and enrichment of all human beings, in all their diversity, complexity, and profundity. That is the struggle for the very distant future, which must be begun, nonetheless, today.

Socialist Economy

ERNEST MANDEL

A long-term view of the economic possibilities of socialism.

The socialization of the major means of production and exchange brings into existence a new mode of production, no longer based on *private appropriation of the social surplus product.* During the period of transition from capitalism to socialism, however, socialization of the means of production is still linked with *private appropriation of the necessary product in the form of wages,* of exchange, of selling of labor-power for a money wage. Furthermore, part of the social surplus product is still appropriated in the form of individual consumer privileges, and under a bureaucratically deformed regime of the transitional society these privileges may assume very considerable dimensions. Private interest thus remains the basic stimulant of individual economic effort. The economy continues to be a money economy.

From the economic standpoint, the contradiction between a mode of production based on collective ownership of the major means of production and collective appropriation of the social surplus product, on the one hand, and on the other, the private interest which continues to operate as chief driving-force of individual economic activity, is a constant source of friction and contradiction under planned economy. But even more important than this economic contradiction is the *social* contradiction that follows from it. "Labor," regarded as the full development of all the potentialities of each individual, and at the same time as conscious service by

From *Marxist Economic Theory, Vol. 2,* by Ernest Mandel, pp. 654–86. Reprinted by permission of Monthly Review Press. Copyright © 1962, 1968 by Ernest Mandel. Translation Copyright © The Merlin Press, London, 1968.

the individual to society, is a concept which in the long run is incompatible with the concept of "labor" as the way of "earning one's living," of ensuring one's means of subsistence, or appropriating, so far as possible, all the goods and services that enable an individual to satisfy his needs.

So long as the economy continues to be fundamentally a money economy, with the satisfaction of the bulk of people's needs depending on the number of currency tokens a person possesses, and so long as, under conditions of relative shortage, rationing by the purse governs distribution, the struggle of all against all to appropriate a bigger proportion of these currency tokens will inevitably persist. So long as the exercise of certain social functions makes it easier to appropriate comparatively scarce goods and services, it is inevitable that the phenomena of careerism, nepotism, corruption, servility towards "superiors" and an autocratic attitude to "inferiors" will remain widespread. The absence of a genuine democracy of producers, consumers and citizens, of strict and untrammeled supervision by them of the activity of administrators and leaders, of the possibility of replacing the latter without coming up against a jointly organized resistance and without having to go beyond legal methods: all these gaps cannot but accentuate the corrupting influence of money in all spheres of social life. The continued existence of money and commodity economy in itself implies the survival of the phenomenon of universal "mercenariness" of life which their original appearance give rise to in primitive communities based upon the production of use-values. If, in the economy of the transitional period, access to comfort were institutionalized instead of remaining directly negotiable by means of money, the influence of this "mercenariness" would be indirect rather than direct—which does not mean that it would be any the less. The public discussions which have taken place in the U.S.S.R. about the abuses entailed by the stampede to get university places have told us a great deal on this point.

The authorities and the influential writers who continually declare, in the U.S.S.R. and elsewhere, that it is necessary first and foremost to "create a new outlook," that labor must first become "an individual necessity felt to be such by the individual," before material incentives can be abolished, and the transition made to distribution according to need, reveal a "voluntarist deviation" and reverse a relationship of cause and effect which is nevertheless quite obvious. It is necessary *first* to see the withering away of money economy through the production of an abundance of goods and services, before the psychological and cultural revolution can fully manifest itself, and a new socialist consciousness bloom in place of the egoistic mentality of the "old Adam." In the era of the transitional society, and *afortiori* in the U.S.S.R. or China, it is not "capitalist survivals" that give rise to a desire for individual enrichment, but *the everyday reality of distribution rationed by money.* To hope to create, under these conditions, a "communist consciousness" by means of a "struggle against the survivals from the capitalist past" is to undertake a real labor of Sisyphus.

Before the acquisitive outlook of individuals can disappear as the essential driving force of economic behavior, these individuals must have acquired experience that society has ceased to treat them as Cinderellas and become a generous and understanding mother, automatically satisfying all the basic needs of her children. This experience must have penetrated into the unconscious of individuals, there to encounter the echoes from the primitive-communist past which have never been completely buried by the effects of 7,000 years of exploitation of man by man. This experience must have produced a conscious awareness of the new situation, and, more than that, *new habits and customs,* for the psychological revolution to occur and for the "old Adam" to die and give place to the socialist or communist man of the future.

If Marxists consider that plenty is a necessary condition for the coming of a fully developed socialist society, it is in this sense and for this reason. The new way of life cannot be born otherwise than from the *integration* of a new mode of production and a new mode of distribution. It is not a matter of preaching socialist morality, but of creating the material social and psychological conditions for this morality to be applied by the great majority as a matter of course.

Since the beginning of the monopoly capitalist era and the rise of a powerful labor movement in the advanced industrial countries, individual wages are no longer the *only* way in which individual labor is paid for. Alongside them has appeared the *social dividend or social wage.* This means the totality of the payments which are made to the individual by society, regardless of what the former has or has not given in exchange, as an individual: free elementary (and, later, secondary) education; free school meals; free health services, free hospital care and even free prescriptions; free parks, museums and sports-grounds; free, or almost free, municipal services, such as public lighting; etc.

One must, of course, be clear about the meaning of the expression "free education" or "free health service." The freedom from payment applies only *to the individual; society,* must, of course, "pay" for these services, that is, devote part of its resources (of its total available labor-time) to the satisfaction of these needs. The "social wage" is thus the *socialization of the cost* of satisfying a certain number of needs for all citizens.

This "social wage" foreshadows, at least potentially, the mode of distribution of the future, that is, of an economy directed towards satisfying the needs of all individuals. An economy based on the satisfaction of needs differs from a commodity economy in so far as it satisfies these needs *a priori*, distributing goods and services *regardless of any exactly-measured counter-payment* (exchange) supplied by the individual.

Even in capitalist society, elementary education is free whether or not a child's parents pay their taxes, perform useful work for society, are "good citizens" or are hardened criminals.

But this "social wage" merely *foreshadows* the mode of distribution according to need; it does not offer a true image of it, even in societies which are in transition from capitalism to socialism (except, perhaps, where this transition takes place in the richest countries). It is only the commodity, money *form* of wages that has been given up; the *content*, poor and measured out with miserly care, is still the same.

Since we are still in an economy of semi-shortage, the social services are usually treated like poor relations. The way they are distributed is more akin to *rationing* than to *plenty*; sometimes it is even accompanied by an *obligation* (elementary education, vaccination, etc.). Excessively large classes; "mass-production" medical treatment ("doctoring on the cheap"); neglect of "nonpaying" clients in favor of "paying" ones—these features link the embryonic forms of the "social wage" which much more closely to the commodity society which has given rise to them than to the socialist society whose task will be to open the way to plenty. Only in a few special cases can the infinitely richer, freer and more varied content of the socialization of costs reveal itself; free libraries which offer practically *all* kinds of books which may be asked for (and here it is necessary that room in such libraries be not strictly rationed!); museums and parks, open free of charge, which enable all citizens to enjoy the pleasures formerly reserved to a few narrow strata of rich or highly educated people.

The prodigious development of the productive forces in the era of transition from capitalism to socialism makes it possible to set in motion two processes which radically alter the mode of distribution: on the one hand, the "social wage" must draw closer and closer to its "ideal" norm, that of plenty; on the other, more and more goods and services must pass out of the category of those distributed through exchange (purchase) and into that of goods and services distributed according to need.

The conditions governing this transformation of the mode of distribution are still linked to the requirements of a society based on semi-shortage. Before freeing itself from the heavy, age-old burden of economic calculation, society needs to calculate more exactly and precisely than ever before. The first goods and services to which the new norms of distribution can be applied are thus those

1. which are very homogeneous;
2. for which demand has become inelastic, in relation to a fall in prices and a rise in incomes;

3. which it is hard to use as products or services replacing those which are still distributed according to the norms of exchange of a commodity economy;

4. or the distribution of which in return for payment in money involves obvious injustices (actually reducing the national income), whereas free distribution would considerably enhance social welfare (providing a potential source of increase of the national income).

In short, society first socializes the costs of satisfying needs under conditions such that this socialization does not involve a considerable increase in these costs. When demand for a product has become inelastic, however much prices fall or incomes rise, the socialization of the costs of production of this product entails no extra charge for society as a whole. This is the position, for instance, with *salt* in every industrially advanced country, where consumption of it does not vary, in normal times, either with its price or with people's incomes.

The economic law which governs the withering-away of commodity economy can be formulated like this: as society gets richer, and as planned economy ensures a mighty expansion of the productive forces, it acquires the resources needed to socialize the costs of satisfying an increasing number of needs for all citizens. And as the standard of living of the citizens rises, the elasticity of demand for more and more goods and services declines to zero, or even becomes negative, in relation to price reductions and increases in income. In other words, for these two reasons, the advances of planned economy make it possible to transfer more and more goods and services into the category of those which can be distributed in accordance with needs.

A number of writers admit that such a *partial* transformation of the mode of distribution is feasible. But they do this, usually, only in order to deny at once that it could become universal in its application. Are there not constantly new needs arising, as fast as the "classical" needs are satisfied? Is it possible to bring *all* products, one after another, into the category of those which are distributed according to need, without at the same time giving rise to all-round wastage of society's resources, and thus seeing the reappearance of shortage in new spheres? Do not the products which satisfy even such basic needs as food, clothing and shelter vary *ad infinitum* in diversity and quality? Will not an attempt to do away with exchange and money in these spheres result in a dreary uniformity and lack of freedom?

Let us take first the question of the alleged variety of needs. Any moderately serious study of anthropology and history will show, on the contrary, how remarkably stable they are: food, clothing, shelter (and in certain climatic conditions, warmth), protection against wild animals and the inclemency of the seasons, the desire to decorate, the desire to exercise the body's muscles, the satisfaction of sexual needs, the maintenance of the species—there are half a dozen basic needs which do not seem to have changed since the beginning of *homo sapiens,* and which still account for the bulk of consumer expenditure.

To these we may add needs for hygiene and health-care (simple expressions of the instinct of self-preservation at a certain level of consciousness) and needs to enrich one's leisure (simple extensions of the needs to decorate, to exercise one's muscles, and to increase one's knowledge, which are as old as the human race), and we have almost exhausted the list of consumer expenses even in the richest countries of the world, on the basis of a small number of basic needs which are anthropological characteristics to a much greater extent than products of special historical conditions.

Since these needs have remained basically unchanged since the appearance of man on earth, and since even the richest classes of past ages have not extended their consumer expenditure beyond this remarkably short list of satisfactions, there is no reason to suppose that the coming of a socialist society, of abundance of products, and of individual and social consciousness at a much more mature level than ever before, will give rise to any revolutions in this sphere. Nowhere does the law of "diminishing returns" apply more than in regard to the intensity of needs. Thus the first objection is disposed of.

Let us now look at the apparently infinite variety of means to satisfy these few basic needs. There is, first, the problem of the *quantity* of the products required to meet these needs. On this point, history has already provided an answer, on the part of the possessing classes of our era. Between the stout country squire of the early 19th century stuffing himself with roast beef and swilling port wine, or the big bourgeois of the "Belle Epoque" with his 20-course dinners, on the one hand, and, on the other, the rich capitalist of today, slim, devoted to sport, and constantly watching his weight, the change is undeniable. With the increase in income, *the increasing consumption of food has given way to a more rational kind of consumption;* the criterion of health has superseded that of blind or showy self-indulgence. This change does not so much reflect and ethical progress as it reflects the demands of self-preservation, the self-interest of the individual himself.

The same applies where dress is concerned. True, in this sphere, especially among women, the amount of clothing "consumable" without damage to health and the possibilities of waste (clothes worn only once or twice) are much greater than in the sphere of food. Nevertheless, if the restraints of health do not apply here, those of *comfort* and *taste* soon come into play. Without the help of lackeys and servants it is not very comfortable to change one's clothes too often or even to possess too many. Indeed, though excesses in this sphere are constantly committed by the "new rich," several sociologists have observed that in the richest families of Britain and the United States a real reversal of this trend has occurred; clothes which are worn but comfortable, or simply clothes one likes, are preferred to clothes glowing with freshness or which are continually being replaced. Others even speak of a stylistic evolution in clothing, which they describe like this: "first, a steady trend toward uniformity, with the clothing worn by people of moderate income coming to approximate the appearance and materials of the clothing worn by people of high income; second, a decline in the number of frills, reflecting a movement in the direction of greater simplicity; third, and most recent, an 'accent on youth.'

The same situation exists in respect of housing and furnishing. When domestic servants and even housekeepers have vanished—and the new level of wages, together with social disapproval, will certainly make them vanish in the transitional society between capitalism and socialism!—there is a limit to the number of rooms one can *wish* to have (and can get) for one's accommodation, a limit dictated precisely by individual comfort. Already, today, except for a handful of millionaires, the luxury flat is preferred by most bourgeois to the 19th-century country house. Sweeping away the old-time rooms crowded with furniture and knick-knacks, the evolution of comfort and taste has dictated a mode of furnishing the sobriety and functional nature of which set a relatively narrow limit to quantitative accumulation. This tendency even goes so far as to impose a voluntary restriction on the number of gadgets.

There is no reason to suppose that these tendencies, which are already manifest in the last phase of capitalist society, *despite* a striking degree of social inequality and unlimited chances for waste on the part of the possessing classes, will be reversed in the era of transition from capitalism to socialism, or in socialist society itself. On the contrary, it is infinitely more probable that *rational consumption* will develop further, at the expense of consumption inspired by mere caprice, desire to show off, and lack of taste or sense of proportion, forms of consumption which, in capitalist society, are not so much "innate in the consumer" as dictated and conditioned by the general social climate and the efforts of advertisers.

It remains to consider the problem of the diversity and quality of products which, instead of their quantity, delay the coming of the times when demand for them becomes inelastic both to price changes and to income changes. The phenomena of diversity and quality are nowadays dictated by fashion, by the compartmentalizing of society, and by technical progress ("new products"). All these phenomena are, in the last analysis, *independent* of individual whims; even in capitalist society they are *social phenomena*, guided if not consciously determined by social forces.

Fashion is a typically social phenomenon, with the impetus coming from the side of the producers (the designers), not from that of the consumers. It is a few important *couturiers* in Paris who "make" fashion, not the "public." Already today, for the huge majority of consumers, the range of variety is remarkably *narrow,* and not at all limitless. At any given moment there are not an infinite number of styles "coexisting," but only a few. Even in the *haute couture* of our time, based on craft methods and the individual client, there are not "thousands" of different models; the number is more limited than is supposed. And alongside these specially-made models, intended for a few rich women, there is a small range of models which are mass-produced and intended for the masses. A socialist economy would probably be able to *expand* much more widely this range of varieties at present available, rather than have to restrict it, so as to be able to go over to distribution according to need. To do this it would rely on the law of large numbers, on the permanence of physical requirements, on the educative effect of "socialist advertising," on public opinion polls, on public competitions and other techniques which would make it possible really to proceed from the tastes and wishes of consumers in order to determine the variety of goods produced. For this reason we cannot go along with Oskar Lange and H. D. Dickinson when they propose to retain commodity economy in a socialist economy so far as all high-quality products are concerned.

As for new products, their mass production and their "launching" on the market, that is, their large-scale distribution among consumers, is already determined by the firms which produce them and not by the whims of the consumers. It is thus well and truly "planned"—but planned by a handful of capitalist firms, in accordance with criteria of private profit alone, and not in accordance with the objective and rational needs of the community and of the individuals composing it. How indeed can one talk of the consumer's "urgent need" for products which he does not know exist, "urgent needs" which do not reveal themselves until, as though by chance, the producer launches his new product on to the market?

A socialist society would of course not hand over this planning to the "masters" of production and of promotion. It would avoid duplication of work and obvious waste. But it would take into account much more fully than is done today the real wishes of consumers, through the use of all available techniques of sampling opinion, direct questioning and meetings of citizens. It would extend the range of choice much further than today. And as in the sphere of consumer durables the measurement of needs is much easier and more precise, and waste can be easily checked, it is also much easier to determine the quantity of products needed to be accumulated in store in order to produce inelasticity of demand in relation to prices and incomes.

A certain margin of uncertainty may, of course, continue to exist. It will long, if not always, remain possible that there will be a conflict between the socialization of certain household tasks and their carrying out on an individual basis with the help of improved mechanical means. The washing-machine and the dish-washing-machine will go on being sought for, even when a very extensive and convenient network of restaurants and laundries has put high-quality services, free, at the disposal of all citizens. A socialist society will never *dictate* to its members the obligatory use of communal services by refusing to make available to them the means of securing these same services on an individual basis. Because such a society will aim to satisfy *all* the rational needs of man, it will respect the need for periodical isolation and solitude, which is the dialectical and permanent corollary of man's social nature. Similarly, while the individual motor-car is obviously irrational as a means of transport in towns, it remains by far the most flexible means of transport for leisure trips over a short or medium distance, and even when travel by air, rail and bus are free, men will go on wanting a private motor-car in order to follow their own itineraries, stopping where trains and buses do not stop, or merely in order to be alone. A socialist society will respect these wishes and, far from condemning them as "petty-bourgeois survivals" will endeavor to meet these needs, the rational nature of which will be obvious to anyone of good faith.

There is thus no substantial obstacle to the progressive universalization of the new mode of distribution, according to need, without any counterpart in the form of an exactly measured amount of labor being required. On the contrary, present-day evolution, though distorted by all the consequences of a social setting dominated by money, exploitation, inequality and the desire to "succeed" at the expense of one's neighbor, already clearly shows the main lines of the future evolution of consumption. Consumption on a basis of plenty and freedom, far from developing without any limit towards irrational caprice and waste, will increasingly assume the form of *rational consumption*. The requirements of *physical health and mental and nervous equilibrium* will more and more take precedence over the other motives of human behavior. They will logically be the chief concerns of men whose basic needs have been met. Arrival at this conclusion requires no "idealization" of man. As we see from the example of food-consumption by the capitalists of today, this corresponds to the very nature of the vertical animal, to his most obvious physical interests.

While the "social wage" affects only a very small part of total consumption, its profound psychological and social implications remain limited or even quite hidden. The social climate of capitalism corrupts everything it touches, even those buds of the future society which are slowly opening within it.

But when the "social wage" extends to the bulk of individual consumption its economic, social and psychological implications are sharply manifest. Until then, economic growth, the rise in the standard of living, always implied an *extension of money and commodity economy*, in the era of transition from capitalism to socialism as in earlier periods. Now, however, they imply, on the contrary, a more and more marked *shrinkage* of measured exchanges and of the use of money.

This happens in the first place, for obvious economic reasons. If an increasing proportion of needs are satisfied without expenditure of money by the consumers, this expenditure must relate to an increasingly restricted sphere of economic life. And if *increasing* money income is spent on acquiring a steadily *decreasing* number of commodities and services, then useless tensions are caused. There would have to be either a frantic increase in prices in this sector, or else the artificial stimulation of a continual emergence of "new" products, and the appearance of "new needs," or else the soaking-up of an increasing proportion of this money income by means of taxation. The circulation of money would appear as more and more futile and pointless. In practice, the producers would receive ever-higher "wages," an increasing proportion of which would, however, be kept back at source, the remainder being spent on more and more casual and minor requirements. Money would thus in any case be excluded from the essential economic circuits, concerned with meeting basic and ordinary needs, and driven into the periphery of economic life (conspicuous consumption, gambling, forms of expenditure which socialist society would increasingly subject to more disapproval and penal taxation).

The most logical solution would be to *reduce*, and not increase, the amount of individual money wages and salaries, to reduce the circulation of money, in proportion as the new mode of distribution according to need spread and became general. "Individual wages" would become increasingly a small supplementary bonus to ensure the distribution of the last "scarce" goods and services, the last vestiges of "status" inherited from the age of social inequality. It would increasingly lose its function of preserving the consumer's freedom of choice, from the moment when plenty embraced an increasing range of goods and services. "Choice" will be restricted to spending one's time in shifting from one point of distribution to another, dividing one's time between one form of consumption and another, instead of substituting one form of expenditure for another. Commodity economy, money economy, the economy of semi-shortage, will have begun to wither away.

It is not only the logic of the new mode of production that will bring about this withering away of commodity production. *Automation* entails the same logical necessity in the sphere of production. The production of an abundance of goods and services is in fact accompanied by the more and more rapid elimination of all living, direct, human labor from the production process, and even from the distribution process (automatic power stations; goods trains driven by remote control; self-service distribution centers; automatic vending machines; mechanized and automatized offices, etc.). But the elimination of living human labor from production means the elimination of wages from the cost of production! The latter is increasingly reduced to the "costs" of operations between enterprises (purchase of raw materials and depreciation of fixed plant). Once these enterprises have been socialized, this involves much less transfers of real money than simply accounting in monetary units.

As services will continue nonautomatized for a longer period than goods, money economy will retreat more and more into the spheres of exchange of services for services, purchase of services by consumers, and purchase of services by the public sector. But in proportion as the principal services become automatized in their turn (e.g., public services, automatic machines for providing drinks and standardized articles of current use, laundries, etc.), money economy will become restricted more and more to "personal services" only, the most important of which (medicine and education) will, however, be the first to undergo a radical abolition of money relations for reasons of social priority. In the end, automation will leave to money economy only the periphery of social life: domestic servants and valets, gambling, prostitution, etc. But in a socialist society which ensures a very high standard of living and security to all its citizens, and an all-round revaluation of "labor," which will increasingly become intellectual labor, creative labor, who will want to undertake such forms of work? Socialist automation thus brings commodity economy to the brink of absurdity and will cause it to wither away.

This withering-away, begun in the sphere of distribution, will spread gradually into the sphere of production. Already in the era of transition from capitalism to socialism, socialization of the major means of production and planning imply a more and more general substitution of money of account for fiduciary money in the circulation of means of production.

So far we have considered only the economic consequences of the new mode of production, the withering-away of commodity economy and of money to which it will lead. We must now consider the social and psychological results, that is, the complete upheaval in relations between men, between individuals and society, as these have developed out of thousands of years of social experience derived from antagonism between classes of exploitation of man by man.

Free distribution of bread, milk and all other basic foodstuffs will bring about a psychological revolution without precedent in the history of mankind. Every human being will henceforth be ensured his subsistence and that of his children, merely by virtue of being a member of human society. For the first time since man's appearance on earth, *the insecurity and instability of material existence will vanish*, and along with it the *fear* and frustration that this insecurity causes in all individuals, including, indirectly, those who belong to the ruling classes.

It is this uncertainty about the morrow, this need to "assert oneself" in order to ensure one's survival in a frenzied struggle of all against all, that is at the basis of egoism and the desire for individual enrichment, ever since the beginning of capitalist society and even, to a certain extent, since the development of commodity economy. All the material and moral conditions for the withering away of egoism as a driving force in economic conduct will have vanished. True, individual ownership of consumer goods will doubtless expand to an unheard-of degree. But in face of the abundance of these goods, and the freedom of access to them, the *attachment* of men to ownership will likewise wither away. It is the adaptation of man to these new conditions of life that will create the basis for the "new man," socialist man, for whom human solidarity and cooperation will be as "natural" as is today the effort to succeed individually, at the expense of others. The brotherhood of man will cease to be a pious hope or a hypocritical slogan, to become a natural and everyday reality, upon which all social relations will increasingly be based.

Will an evolution along these lines be "contrary to human nature"? This is the argument invoked as a last resort against Marxism, against the prospect of a classless society. It is regularly put forward by those who do not know this human nature, who base themselves on crude prejudices or suspicions in order to identify morals and customs *derived from a certain socioeconomic context* with biological or anthropological characteristics alleged to be "unchangeable" in man. It is also invoked by those who endeavor to preserve at all costs a conception of man which is based on the idea of original sin and the impossibility of "redemption" on this earth.

But anthropology starts from the idea that that which is distinctive of man is precisely his *capacity for adaptation,* his capacity to create a second nature in the culture which forms the only framework in which he can live, as Professor A. Gehlen puts it.

These practically unlimited possibilities of adaptation and apprenticeship are the essential anthropological feature. Human "nature" is what precisely enables man continually to rise above what is merely biological, to continually surpass himself.

The tendency to competition, to the struggle of all against all, to the assertion of the individual by crushing other individuals, is not at all something innate in man; it is itself the product of an "acculturization," of an inheritance which is not biological but social, the product of particular social conditions. Competition is a tendency which is not "innate" but socially acquired. Similarly, cooperation and solidarity can be systematically acquired and transmitted as a social heritage, as soon as the social milieu has been radically changed in this direction.

More than that—a disposition to cooperation, to solidarity, to love of one's neighbor corresponds far better to specific biological needs and basic anthropological features than a tendency to competition, conflict or oppression of others.

The withering away of commodity and money economy is, however, only one of the factors bringing about the disappearance of social in-equality, classes and the state. The other factor is the considerable exten-sion and creative use of leisure.

The ruling class or stratum of society has always possessed the privi-lege of leisure. This is the section which, freed from the burden of having to work for its living, from the burden of physically exhausting labor, from mechanical work, has been able to devote itself more or less completely to the accumulation of knowledge and the management of the economy and of society. The extension of such leisure will make it possible for an increas-ing number of citizens to undertake and carry out these functions. This is the *technical* means to ensuring the progressive withering away of the state.

For nearly a century now the shortening of the working day has been a tremendous civilizing factor, as Karl Marx pointed out when the ten-hour day was introduced. It has provided the basis for everything worthwhile in present-day bourgeois democracy. Nevertheless, it is a contradictory phe-nomenon. The advantages gained by shortening the working day are largely offset by the lengthening of working life, the lengthening of the time spent in traveling to and from work, the intensification of physical effort (first for manual workers, then later, to an increasing extent, for office workers), and by the commercialization of leisure.

Furthermore, the big step forward essentially remains the change from the ten- or twelve-hour day to the eight-hour day. The latter became gen-eral in modern-type industry in the advanced capitalist countries around 1920. Since then, there has been only a relatively slight shortening in the manual worker's working day, the forty-hour week existing only in a few countries, where, moreover, it is accompanied by the five-day week, the week of 45, 44 or 42 hours spread over five days implying even a lengthen-ing of the working day.

We must take into account the considerably intensified pace of work since 1918, the nervous tension involved in operating equipment which is increasingly expensive and often dangerous, the often even greater tension experienced on the way to work, especially if the journey is made by mechanical transport, and also air pollution and insufficiently sound-proofed housing, if we are to draw up *a comprehensive balance-sheet of the physical, mental and nervous fatigue* suffered by the worker of today, as compared with that of the worker of 50 years ago. Much evidence from doctors confirms that this fatigue is greater than it was, in spite of free weekends and two or three weeks' annual holiday.

What follows from this is that a large part of "free time" is not "leisure time" at all but "time spent in getting rid of physical and nervous fatigue." The effect of holidays is largely neutralized because the worker takes his holiday when his organism is in such a state of fatigue that he is at first incapable of real, normal relaxation.

The commercialization of leisure is adapted to this condition of things. It starts from a recognition that after an ordinary working day the average contemporary proletarian is incapable of an intellectual or physical effort. But on the pretext of providing him with "relaxation" or "diversion," commercialized leisure causes either an atrophy of critical capacity or a morbid and lasting excitement which ends by degrading and disintegrating his personality to some degree. All the condemnations of "leisure civilization" nevertheless avoid the question: the ultimate cause of the degradation of leisure lies in the degradation of *work* and of *society.*

What is needed therefore, is a new and radical shortening of the time spent at work, in order to bring about the essential aim of socialism, which is that of the *self-management of producers and citizens.* Taking into account the present intensity of productive effort, the threshold at which the producer becomes materially capable of concerning himself currently, "habitually," with the management of the enterprise where he works, and with the state, is, apparently, *the half-day of work,* or a week of 20 or 24 hours, depending on whether working hours are fixed at five or at six hours a day. At the present rate of progress in productivity (an average of 5 percent per year in the highly-industrialized countries), within the framework of a rationally planned economy freed from all military or parasitic burdens, and consciously directly towards the priority purpose of saving human labor, this objective could be attained before the end of the 20th century. Even within the framework of capitalism, in the United States, the average length of the working week has fallen from 70 hours in 1850 and 60 in 1900 to 44 in 1940, 40 in 1950 and 37.5 in 1960, or a reduction of nearly 40 percent in half a century, nearly four hours per decade. On the basis of this same rate of decline the 24-hour week could be attained around 1990 to 2000 in a socialist society. The American economist George Soule comes to the same conclusion without leaving the framework of capitalist society—but without realizing all the contradictions implicit in such a forecast.

A more rapid reduction in the working day would undoubtedly be possible in a fully developed socialist society, but it would be held back by the raising of the school-leaving age (advancing from universal compulsory secondary education to universal compulsory higher education), and also by the lowering of the age of retirement. These changes would mean a more rational reduction in working hours *per human life* than a more rapid reduction in the working day—while productive life would continue to extend from 16 to 65.

A thoroughgoing reduction in the time spent at work would set the problem of leisure in an entirely different social context. Ultimately, of course, the "useful employment of leisure" is closely linked with the problem of *socializing the cost* of satisfying human needs, with the new mode of distribution. It is infinitely "cheaper" to satisfy the needs of 20 million workers with standardized television programs made up of mass-produced films, or newspapers published in millions of copies, than to satisfy them with high-quality theatrical performances, a wide variety of books or the means of *producing* culture instead of merely *consuming* it. It costs much less to make a film for a million spectators than to enable a million amateurs to make their own films. Galbraith attributes the increase in juvenile delinquency amid affluence to the inadequacy of public expenditure as compared with the excessive amount of private consumption of commercialized leisure. But with the raising of citizens' standards of living, and the general development of social wealth, the useful employment of leisure will become increasingly a transformation of the citizen from being a passive object to being a conscious creative participant in a variety of cultural activities (sport, art, science, literature, technique, education, exploration, etc.). At the same time, participation in the management of the economy and the leadership of social life, which today involves only a tiny fraction of the leisure of the workers as a whole (except in the case of the active members of the workers' organizations), will become more and more important as a way of using "free time." It also will tend to become active and creative rather than passive, as at present ("attendance at meetings" through a feeling of duty, of obligation to others, because one must, or out of personal interest which is often of a very dubious kind).

It is often objected that the workers "do not want to manage their enterprises." Usually, this refers either to attempts at "joint management" within a capitalist economy or to certain "marginal" experiments in the Eastern countries, that is, in both cases, to enterprises whose real fate is felt by the workers concerned to be settled elsewhere, and in socioeconomic context in which exhaustion and alienation on the part of the labor-force have not been reduced. If the worker declines to lose his precious hours of rest attending meetings on which *nothing decisive for his own fate* depends, that should not surprise us. It has been enough, however, in Yugoslavia, for the experience of self-management of enterprises to give the workers concerned the feeling that their activity in the sphere of management has a real and positive, effective influence on their standard of life, for an increasing proportion of the working masses to participate actively in the work of the workers' councils. The latter now control nearly a third of the financial resources of the enterprises.

Automation makes a big contribution to this process. It logically implies a tendency towards the elimination of the laborer, or even the skilled worker, from the production process. It tends to increase the labor-force employed before and after actual production (research and investigation work, administration and distribution), but to the extent that it takes place in a socialized, or already socialist, economy, *it does away with unskilled manual labor, reproducing only more and more highly skilled and "intellectual" labor.* It thus appears as the great force working to abolish the difference between manual work and mental work, leaving only the latter in existence.

The industrialization of agriculture, which has already gone very far in the United States and which is spreading in Western Europe, will be the last tendency of economic evolution connected with the withering-away of classes and of the state. It will cut down to a minimum the number of "countryfolk" engaged in "farm and field" work, and those who remain will be transformed more and more into agronomists, geotechnicians, and engineers in charge of automatic or semi-automatic agricultural machinery. The break-up of the big cities into homogeneous "new towns," each one self-sufficient, will do away with even the outward signs of the difference between "town" and "country" and create integrated areas embracing greenery, cultivation, housing, recreation and social life, and zones of industrial production.

Radical reduction in the size of these areas will make it possible to abolish to an ever-increasing extent those *delegations of power* which continue to predominate in the first phases of the withering away of classes and the state. They will replace self-management by citizens on a rota basis, in ad hoc social organizations, by self-management of *free communes of producers and consumers*, in which everybody will take it in turn to carry out administrative work, in which the difference between "directors" and "directed" will be abolished, and a federation of which will eventually cover the whole world.

Is this a Utopia? What is essential is to see that these possibilities are all contained in an advance of productivity made the most of by an economic system based partly on the socialization of the means of production and the creation of plenty in goods and services, and partly on the replacement of commodity economy by a mode of distribution which eliminates money and the desire for personal enrichment from the life of mankind.

Will the productive forces go on increasing indefinitely in a socialist society? It will be for the citizens of socialist society alone to answer this question, that is, it will really be a matter of free choice for them, and not of any "economic necessity." Under capitalism, and even in the transition period from capitalism to socialism, the idea of exercising "preference" as between the "marginal utility of net investment" and the "marginal utility of increased leisure" is basically absurd. Current consumption by producers, even when it is increasing, always falls short of felt needs; the length of the working day, even when it is being cut down, continues to be limited only by the state of physical and nervous fatigue beyond which output falls precipitously.

As against this, in a socialist society which ensures plenty in goods and services to its citizens, the possibility of a genuine choice between increased wealth and increased leisure will be given for the first time. This will be a real choice, in the sense that it will no longer depend on an economic need to meet pressing needs. The only economic demands which still exist will be that of renewing the stock of machinery (gross investment, depreciation) and that of ensuring an increase in the social product corresponding to the increase in population. As, however, it is to be hoped that socialist mankind will plan its population increase just as it will plan the economy, freedom of choice for the citizens will remain unimpaired.

In any case, economic growth is not an end in itself. The aim is to satisfy the needs of society, of the consumers, within the framework of optimum rational development of all human potentialities. Just as the *optimum* of consumption does not at all imply unlimited increase, the satisfaction of human needs does not in itself imply a continuous and unlimited expansion of the productive forces. When society possesses a stock of automatic machinery which is adequate to cover all current needs, including a reserve of multi-purpose machine-tools sufficient to cope with any emergency, it is probable that "economic growth" will be slowed down or even halted for a time. A man who is completely free from all material and economic worries will have been born; political economy will have had its day, because economic calculation will be finished. The question of "profitability" or of "economy of labor-time" will have vanished as a criterion of wealth, and will be replaced by the mere criterion of leisure and its best use, as Marx foresaw in a prophecy of genius:

> The theft of other people's labor, which is the basis of present-day wealth, is a wretched basis when compared with this new basis of wealth created by large-scale industry itself. As soon as labor in its direct form ceases to be the principal source of wealth, labor-time ceases, and must cease to be the measure of wealth, and therefore exchange-value must cease to be the measure of use-value. The surplus labor of the masses ceases to be the condition for the development of general wealth, just as the leisure of a minority ceases to be the condition for the development of the general capacities of the human mind. Thus there collapses production based on exchange-value, and the immediate process of material production loses its sordid and contradictory form. The free development of individuals, not the shortening of necessary labor-time in order to create surplus labor [becomes the aim of production]; it is thus now a matter of reducing to the minimum the necessary labor of all society, so as to make possible the artistic, scientific, etc. education of individuals through the leisure and resources thus created ...
>
> ... If the working masses themselves appropriate their surplus labor

—and if the disposable time thereby ceases to have a contradictory existence—necessary labor time will be limited by the needs of the social individual, and the development of society's productive forces will, on the other hand, increase so rapidly that the leisure of all will increase despite the fact that production will be directed towards increasing the wealth of all. For real wealth is the developed productive power of all the individuals. Thus it will no longer be labor-time that will be the standard of wealth, but leisure."[1]

Or, more precisely: the criterion of wealth will become men's free, rational, creative use of free time, directed towards their own development as complete and harmonious personalities.

But will this creative human activity, integrating theory and practice, leaving all mechanical and routine work to machines, passing from research to production and from the painter's studio to the site where a new town is being built amid the words—will it still be "labor"? This basic category of Maxist sociology and economics must in its turn be subjected to a critical analysis.

Labor is the fundamental characteristic of man. It is through labor that the human race appropriates its necessary means of life; it is labor which is at once the primary reason for, the product of and the cement of social relationships. Man does not become a social being in the anthropological sense of the word, does not acquire his normal physiological equipment, without a phase of "active socialization" which extends from his birth until puberty, if not until his physical and intellectual maturity.

But when the *need* to work in order to produce the means of life has gone, because machines by themselves carry out this work, what remains of labor as man's fundamental characteristic? Anthropology defines the concept of labor. What is, in fact, characteristic of man is *praxis*, action: "Man is a creature so constituted physically that he can survive only by acting."

Labor in the historical sense of the word, labor as it has been practiced up to now by suffering and miserable mankind, condemned to earn their bread in the sweat of their brows, is only the most wretched, the most "inhuman," the most "animal" form of human *praxis*. Just as for Frederick Engels the entire history of class-divided humanity is only the prehistory of mankind, so labor in its traditional form is only the prehistoric form of *creative, all-sided human praxis, which no longer produces things but harmoniously developed human personalities.* After the withering away of the commodity, of value, money, classes, the state and the social division of labor, fully developed socialist society will bring about the *withering away of labor* in the traditional sense of the word.

[1]K. Marx, *Grundrisse . . .* , Vol. 1, pp. 593, 6.

The final purpose of socialism cannot be the humanization of labor, any more than it can be the improvement of wages or of the wage relationship; there are only transitional stages, expedients and palliatives. A modern factory will never constitute a "normal" or "human" setting for human life, no matter how much the working day is shortened or the place and its machinery are adapted to man's needs. The process of the humanization of man will not be completed until labor has withered away and given place to creative *praxis* which is solely directed to the creation of human beings of all-round development.

For a long time, *homo faber*, man as producer of the instruments of labor, has been put before us as the real creator of civilization and of human culture. Recently, writers have tried to show that science, and even philosophy itself, has emerged progressively from productive labor in the strict sense, constantly nourishing itself from practice. The Dutch historian Huizinga has, however, sharply opposed this tradition, with his contrary conception, of *homo ludens*, "man at play," as the real creator of culture.

Marxism, brilliantly confirmed by all present-day anthropology, and to a large extent even by Freudian psychology, enables us to integrate these two currents of thought, each of which reflects a fundamental aspect of human history. At the start, man was both *faber* and *ludens*. Scientific and artistic techniques progressively separated off from production techniques; but, with their specialization, a social division of labor became indispensable for an initial phase of further progress. *Homo faber*, banished to outer darkness, has neither the resources nor the leisure for play, free creation, the spontaneous and disinterested exercise of his faculties, which is the specific aspect of human *praxis*. *Homo Ludens* has become, more and more, man of the privileged classes, that is, of the possessing classes and those dependent on them.

But thereby he has in turn suffered a special kind of alienation: his play becomes increasing *sad play*, and continues so even during the great centuries of social optimism (for instance, the 16th and 19th centuries). Freed from the constraint of routine work, reintegrated in the collective community, socialist man will once again become both *faber* and *ludens*, increasingly *ludens* and at the same time *faber*. Already today, attempts are being made to introduce more and more "play" into certain forms of work, and more and more "serious work" into play. The abolition of labor in the traditional sense of the word implies at the same time a new flowering of the chief productive force, the creative energy of man himself. Material disinterestedness is crowned by the creative spontaneity which brings together in the same eternal youth the playfulness of children, the enthusiasm of the artist, and the *eureka* of the scientist.

For the bourgeoisie, property means freedom. In an "atomized" society of commodity owners, this definition is broadly true; only a sufficient amount of property releases a man from the slavery of selling his labor-power to get the means of existence, from this condemnation to forced labor. This is why bourgeois philanthropists, no less than demagogues, ceaselessly call for the impossible "deproletarisation" of the proletariat through the "diffusion of property."

Vulgar Marxists have taken out of its context a famous phrase of Hegel's, quoted by Engels, according to which freedom is merely "the recognition of necessity." They interpret it in the sense that socialist man will be the subject to the same "iron economic laws" as capitalist man with the sole difference that, having become conscious of these laws, he will endeavor to "use them to his advantage."

This positivist variant of Marxism has nothing in common with the real humanist tradition of Marxist and Engels, with the boldness of their analysis and the profoundity of their vision of the future. Marx and Engels both repeated more than once that the realm of freedom begins *where necessity ends.* Even in a socialist society, factory work would continue to be a *sad necessity,* which was felt as such; it is in one's leisure hours that real freedom unfolds itself. The more that labor in the traditional sense of the word withers away, the more it is replaced by a creative *praxis* of all-round-developed and socially integrated personalities. The more man frees himself from his needs by satisfying them, the more does "the realm of necessity give place to the realm of freedom."

Human freedom is not a "freely accepted" constraint, nor is it a mass of instinctive and disorderly activities such as would degrade the individual. It is a self-realization of man which is an eternal becoming and an eternal surpassing, a continual enrichment of everything human, an all-round development of all facets of humanity. It is neither absolute rest nor "perfect happiness," but, after thousands of years of conflicts unworthy of man, the beginning of the real "human drama." It is a hymn sung to the glory of man by men aware of their limitations who draw from this awareness the courage to overcome them. To the man of today it seems impossible to be both doctor and architect, machine-builder and atom-smasher. But who can speak of limitations that man will *never* be able to break through, man who is stretching out his arms towards the stars, who is on the brink of producing life in test-tubes, and who tomorrow will embrace the entire family of mankind in a spirit of universal brotherhood?